STUDYING HORIYOSHI III

A Westerner's Journey Into the Japanese Tattoo

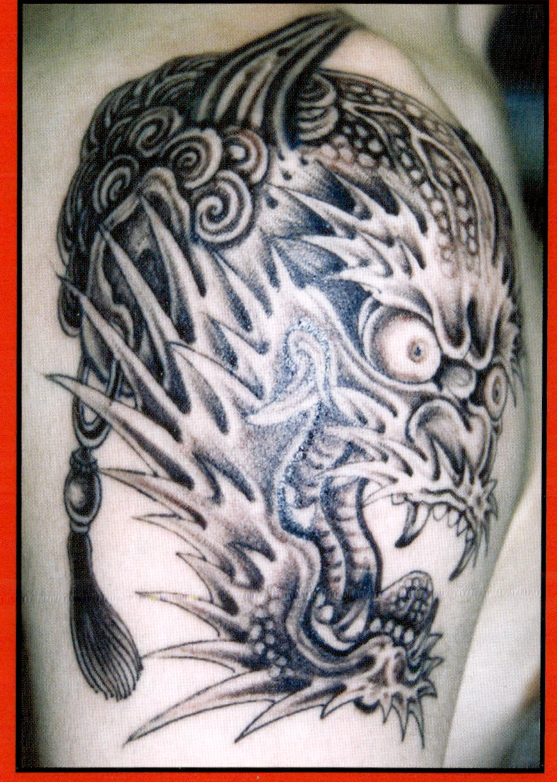

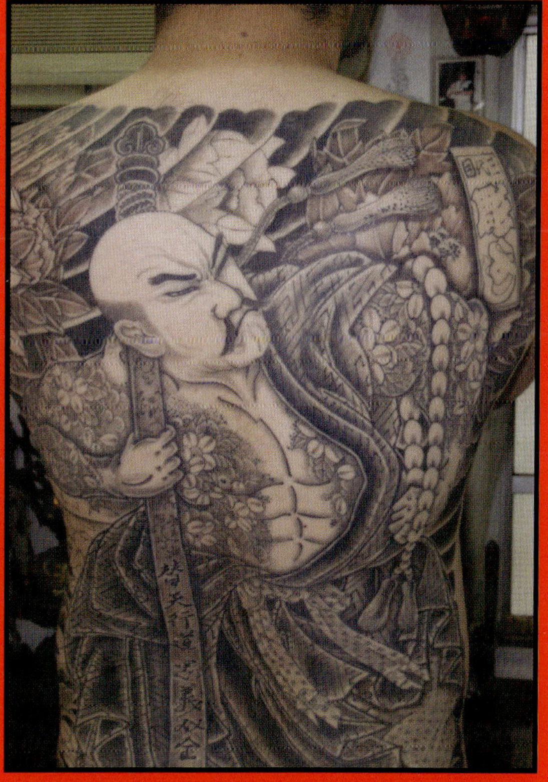

Jill "Horiyuki" Mandelbaum

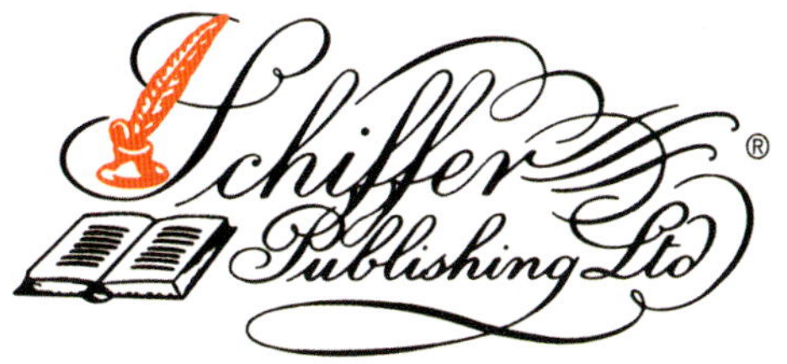

4880 Lower Valley Road, Atglen, Pennsylvania 19310

Dedication

In loving memory of my grandfather, Herbert Swirsky, who always encouraged me to pursue my passions- no matter now unconventional they were. He was a Navy man and always cheered on my first tattoos; the ones in my skin as well as the ones I did on other people. His love has been a constant source of motivation and confidence.

Library of Congress Control Number: 2007938901

Book Design by Colin Kenji Baker
Type set in Maiandra GD/Times New Roman

ISBN 978-0-7643-2968-5
Printed in China

Published by Schiffer Publishing Ltd.
4880 Lower Valley Road
Atglen, PA 19310
Phone: (610) 593-1777; Fax: (610) 593-2002
E-mail: Info@schifferbooks.com

For the largest selection of fine reference books on this and related subjects, please visit our web site at www.schifferbooks.com
We are always looking for people to write books on new and related subjects. If you have an idea for a book please contact us at the above address.

This book may be purchased from the publisher.
Include $3.95 for shipping.
Please try your bookstore first.
You may write for a free catalog.

In Europe, Schiffer books are distributed by
Bushwood Books
6 Marksbury Ave.
Kew Gardens
Surrey TW9 4JF England
Phone: 44 (0) 20 8392-8585; Fax: 44 (0) 20 8392-9876
E-mail: info@bushwoodbooks.co.uk
Free postage in the U.K., Europe; air mail at cost.

Table of Contents

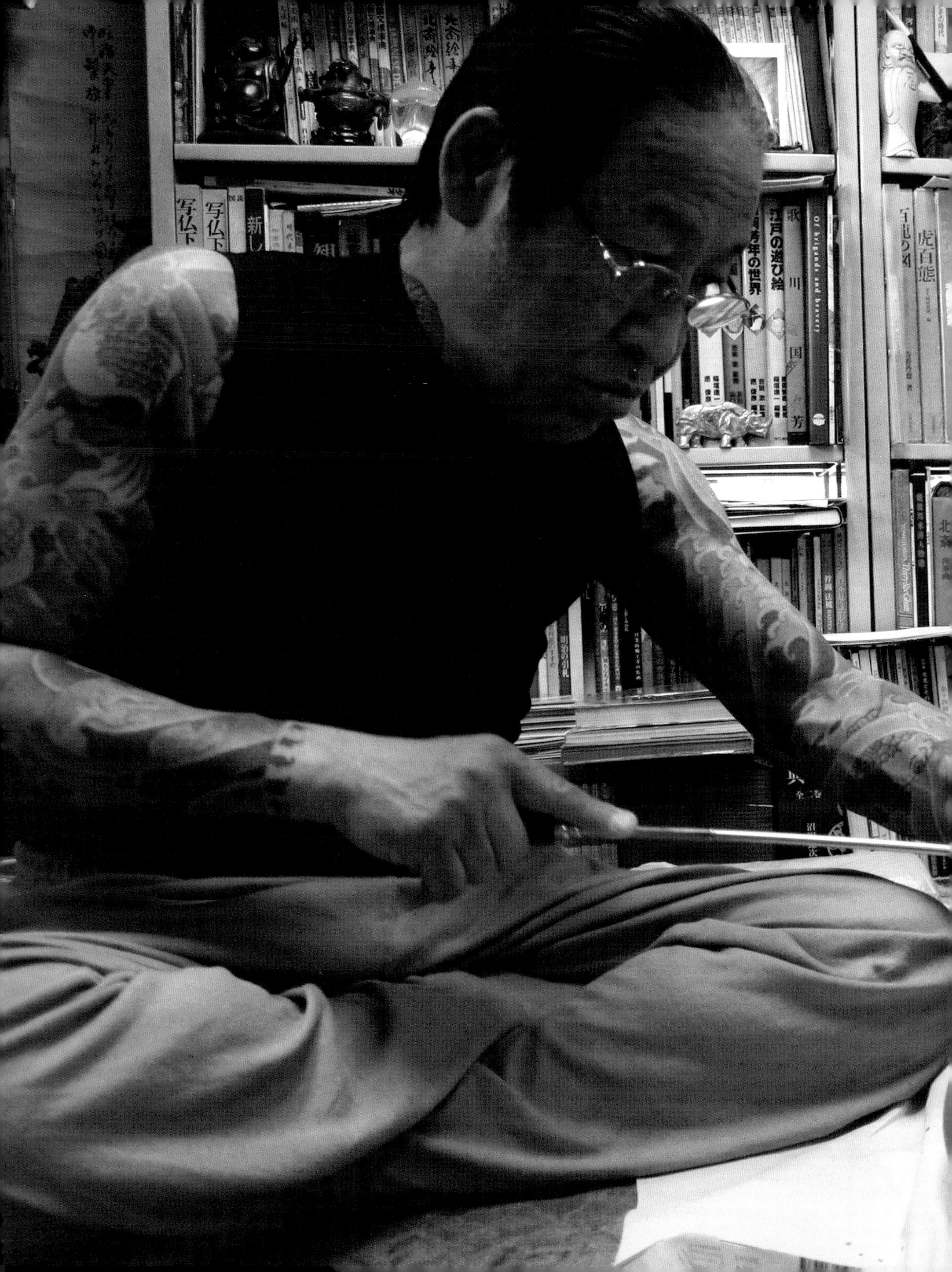
Of brigands and bravery
江戸の遊び絵
虎百態
北斎絵手本

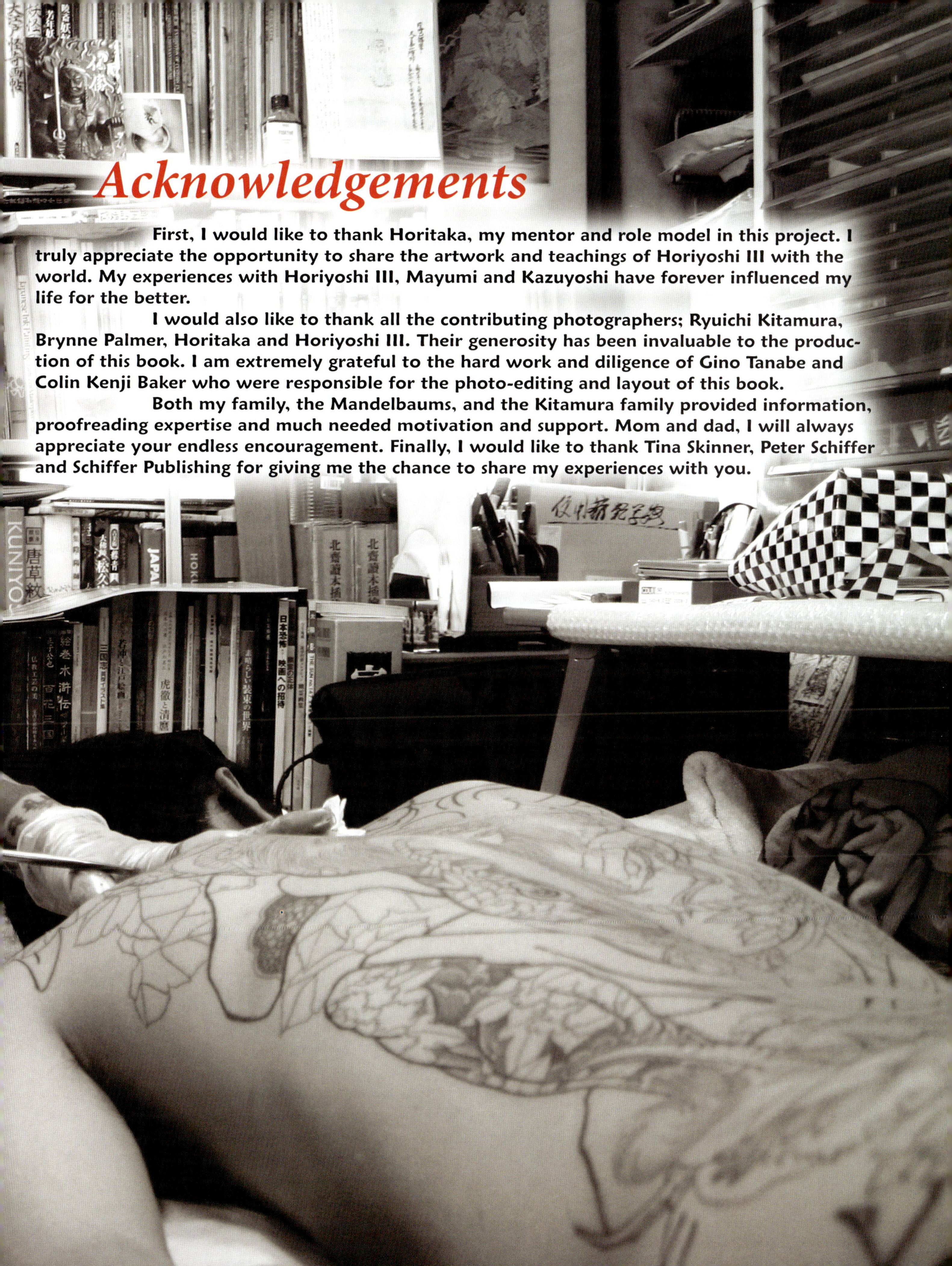

Acknowledgements

First, I would like to thank Horitaka, my mentor and role model in this project. I truly appreciate the opportunity to share the artwork and teachings of Horiyoshi III with the world. My experiences with Horiyoshi III, Mayumi and Kazuyoshi have forever influenced my life for the better.

I would also like to thank all the contributing photographers; Ryuichi Kitamura, Brynne Palmer, Horitaka and Horiyoshi III. Their generosity has been invaluable to the production of this book. I am extremely grateful to the hard work and diligence of Gino Tanabe and Colin Kenji Baker who were responsible for the photo-editing and layout of this book.

Both my family, the Mandelbaums, and the Kitamura family provided information, proofreading expertise and much needed motivation and support. Mom and dad, I will always appreciate your endless encouragement. Finally, I would like to thank Tina Skinner, Peter Schiffer and Schiffer Publishing for giving me the chance to share my experiences with you.

Love and Respect

I have often struggled to define the Japanese Tattoo and have spent the last decade as a humble student of this discipline. Visually, thematic elements and areas of coverage often serve as standards of authenticity. To others, the implementation of hand tools is a requirement. Historical accuracy as well as proper knowledge of mythology are often seen as necessary to execute the Japanese tattoo. And as with any cultural art, definitions and lore vary by era and artist. The Japanese tattoo becomes a nebulous concept, one that is not easily defined.

My definition is directly tied to the man who gave it to me. Since 1998 I have been a student of Yoshihito Nakano, working title; Horiyoshi III of Yokohama. He is the one who tattooed my back (by both machine and hand), gave me my title and taught me everything that I know about the Japanese tattoo. He has served as my principal inspiration, teacher, and is one I am proud to call my master.

To call a person one's master is not something to be taken lightly. And even this concept begs further definition. Horiyoshi III is obviously one who has achieved mastery of the tattoo arts; his craft is unparalleled with over thirty-five years as a full time tattooer. His technical skills are not limited to the needle either, virtuosity of brush and graphite is just as prolific. The knowledge he possesses of Japanese culture and history rivals that of any college professor. And he has lived the tattoo life of Japan for almost half a century, witnessing and participating in an era that will never be relived, only remembered.

However impressive this resume is, accomplishment alone does not define the mastery of Horiyoshi III to me. For me, it is love and respect. *Love and respect* for his craft, culture, master, family, students. It is his omnipresent motivator and the binding factor in all the aforementioned achievements. It is what has sustained him and kept his soul pure. *Love and respect* have kept him loyal to his craft; constantly innovating and striving to better his own work not just for his clients or ego, but for the betterment of the tattoo world as a whole. He has selflessly shared information, photographs and designs with the world. His loyalty is fervent; forever working to bring honor to his deceased master's name. He remembers a time when tattooing was despised and has devoted his life to the upliftment of the tattoo arts. His body, tattooed almost entirely by hand, has quite literally been given to the craft. Tattoos are far more than just pictures in skin to him, they are his life and his reason for living.

This is what I signed on for. This is the world I wanted to join. While the initial enticement was visual splendor and the rich culture of Japanese tattooing, what captivated me was the sense of honor and discipline, love and respect. I guess we all need something to believe in and Horiyoshi III was to become the head priest in my temple of tattooing. I have sworn my loyalty to him.

Five years ago, I received a phone call from then Jill Mandelbaum about working at my studio. Interested in further studying Japanese tattooing and encouraged by our mutual friend, Ed Hardy, Jill sought me out as the only American apprentice and liaison to the man she deemed to be the true essence of Japanese tattooing, Horiyoshi III. I was impressed by the *moxy* she had, cold calling a complete stranger and asking for a job, but I could not have predicted what would follow.

Last year, Jill Mandelbaum was titled Horiyuki by my own master, Horiyoshi III. She is the only Western woman to receive a title from my master and to my knowledge is the first Western woman to be titled by any Japanese master. Quite a surprise, a "Jew broad from Long Island" is not the most likely candidate for the naming. However, I think it all comes back to love and respect. While Jill may come from a different background than most Japanese tattooers, some things are universal. I have spent time with her family, I know her parents, the ones that instilled in her the core values that proved to be so crucial in her tattoo career as well as her life. They taught her discipline, the value of hard work and the importance of seeing things to fruition. They taught her respect for her elders and the importance of gratitude. Education and its importance were imparted to her. And maybe most importantly, they taught her loyalty and humility, for even though Jill is not technically an apprentice of Horiyoshi III, she treats him as her master and has never asked him for anything.

And thus, he thought it fitting to bestow a title on her. No one was more shocked than Horiyuki herself.

It has been a real pleasure watching Horiyuki grow and this book will mark a certain period of her life. It chronicles the study of the Horiyoshi III tradition of Japanese tattooing through a Western perspective. Mind you, this is not a book about Horiyuki, in fact, this book is a gesture on her part, an offering up to a man she can't even call her master. And thus an offering to tattooing itself.

Takahiro Kitamura
Horitaka
Summer 2007

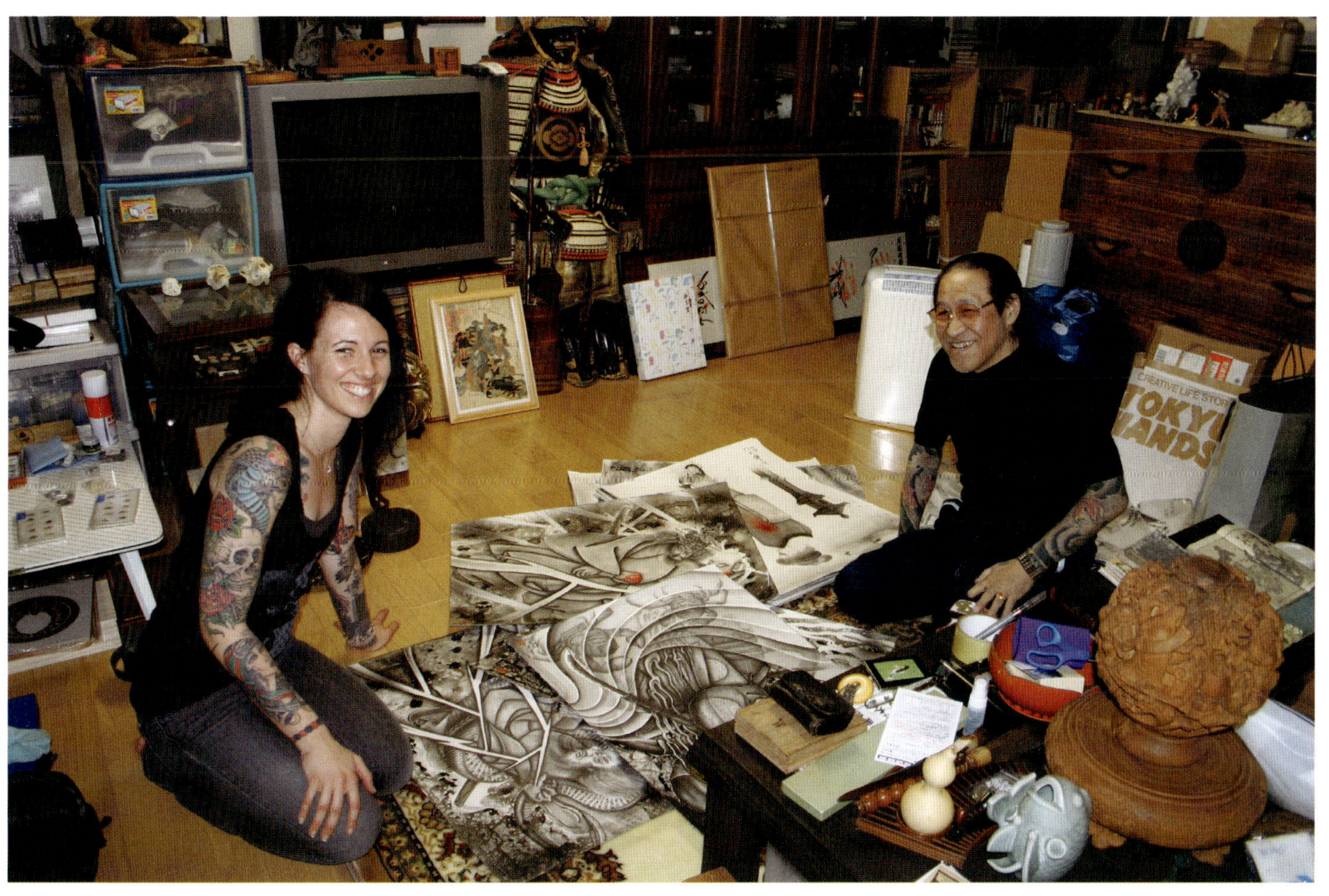

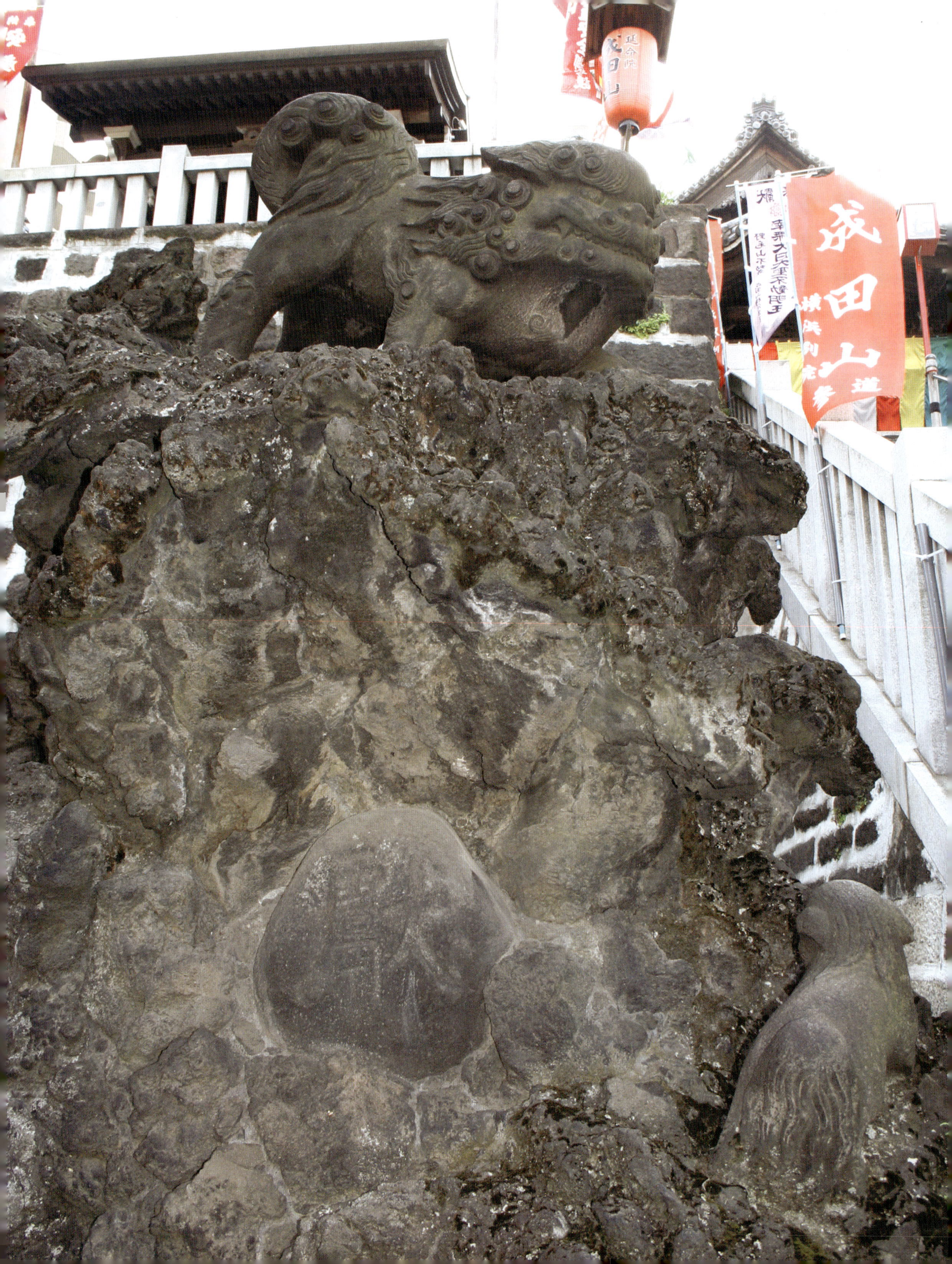
成田山
横浜別院
参道

Introduction

"The history of art is also the history of influences… A painting, like the artist, is part of a larger flow of ideas and culture." [1]

As I stood in front of The Studio, a large painting by Picasso displayed at the San Francisco Museum of Modern Art, all I could do was think of Horiyoshi III. The exhibit was about Picasso's influence on American art and I could not help but correlate this to the impact Horiyoshi III has had on American tattooing. The dialogue many twentieth century American painters shared with Picasso's work was the focus of the show. The SFMOMA described this exhibit as "offering unprecedented insight into the way Pablo Picasso's legacy aesthetically informed a country he never visited." Painters such as Max Weber and Jasper Johns spent endless hours in emulation so as to gain a better understanding of Picasso's work. This was how cubism was learned, through practice and imitation. These artists, along with many others, were relearning painting, unlearning their formal training in order to see a new vision under the tutelage of a teacher they would never meet. Transmission was through careful observation and the utilization of whatever text, image, or information was available.

At the beginning of the twentieth century, cubism was still very controversial. Picasso encouraged young artists to see things in a new manner, defying the very definition of rendering an object in paint. " Young painters should take up our researches in order to react clearly against us." [2] His work inspired many to test the limitations of art, encouraging many artists to search for and find their own personal voices. This eventually enabled many young artists to join the ranks, and arguably surpass, their European counterparts. Picasso has become a standard against which artists can measure their work and he has been elevated to the status of artistic legend as well as receiving household name recognition. Similarly in the West, the idea of the Japanese tattoo has become synonymous with the work of Horiyoshi III. He is the standard for tattooers in Japan as well as the rest of the world, and has defined contemporary notions of the Japanese tattoo.

Although never socially unacceptable per se, cubism has been misunderstood, criticized and has struggled to gain respect within the art world.

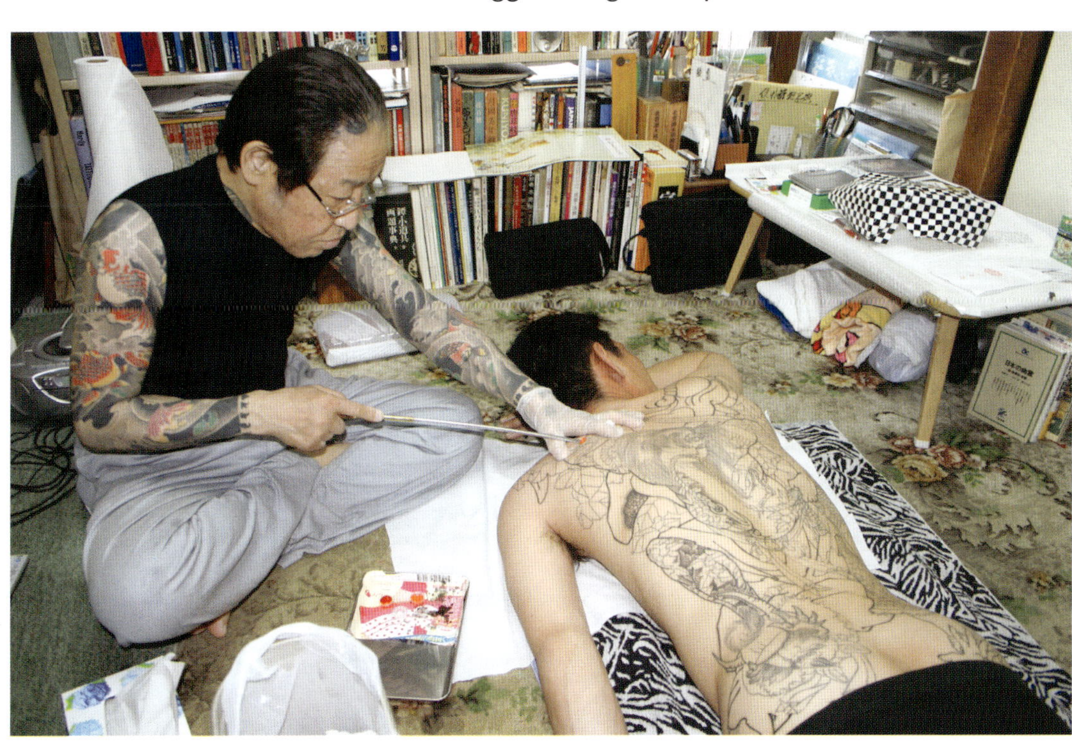

In both America and Japan there is a long history of social disdain for the practice of tattooing. There is still stigma attached to tattooing and limits are placed on the art form by its association with various sub cultures. It is my intent to present Japanese-style tattooing as a high art with Horiyoshi III as its vanguard. With each new project and book he publishes, he continues to dialogue with and challenge tattooers worldwide. The popularity of web sites, books and magazines relating to tattooing have had a comprehensive effect on the transportation of trends and styles throughout the tattoo community in a manner more rapid than ever before. Horiyoshi III has proudly contributed to this drift and has never hidden his work away from the public. He continues to compile a wealth of information in an attempt to educate the tattoo public and bring his expertise and ardent expression of Japanese culture to the masses. Today, these tomes give tattoo enthusiasts images with clear explanations and outline many facets of Japanese art and myth. His works have become indispensable reference tools to tattooers worldwide. His tattoo museum is a beacon of tattoo culture and continues his endeavor to share by displaying his personal tattoo collection. In short, all that he has, the knowledge, skill, and the artifacts of over a lifetime devoted to tattooing, is shared with all for the purpose of elevating the tattoo arts.

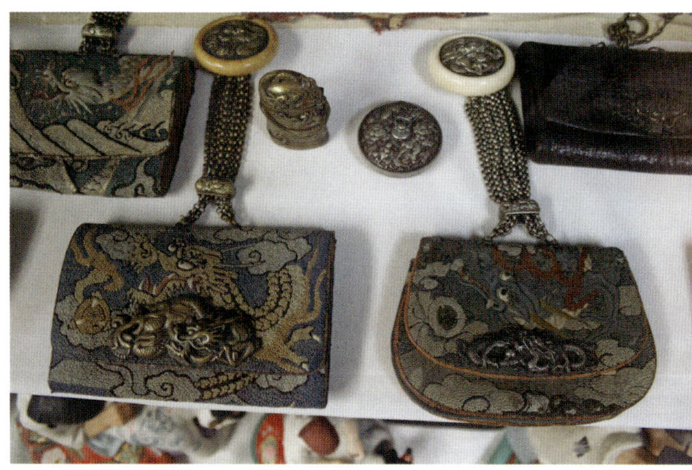

Dragon embroidery and hardware decorates antique wallets on display at the Yokohama Tattoo Museum. I noticed "tattoo designs" everywhere in Japan.

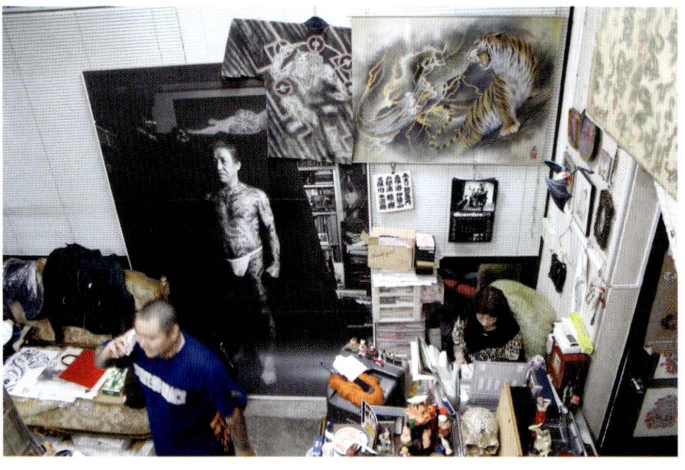

The Yokohama Tattoo Museum.

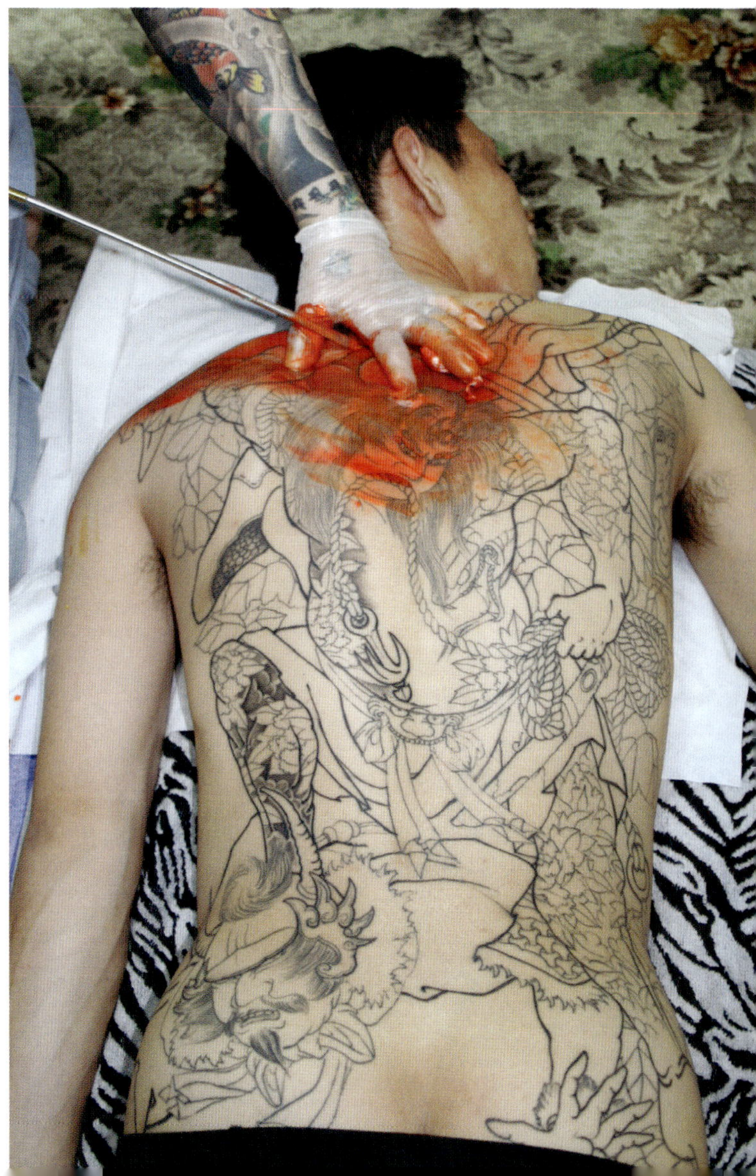

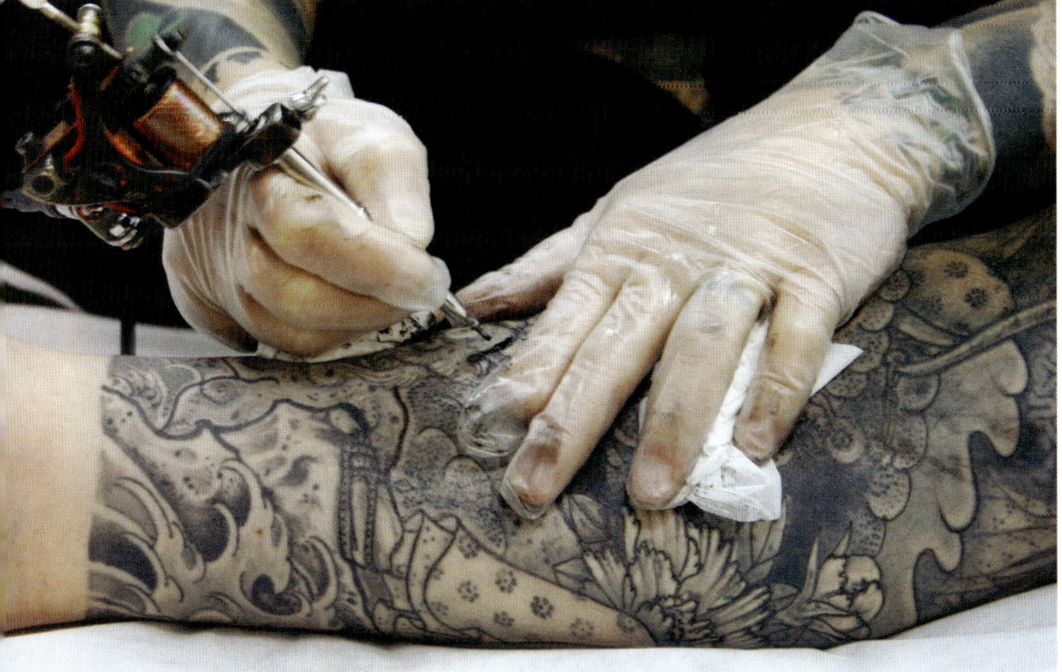

Below:
Horiyoshi III found inspiration for this depiction of Kumonryu in photographic stills of mixed martial arts fighters.

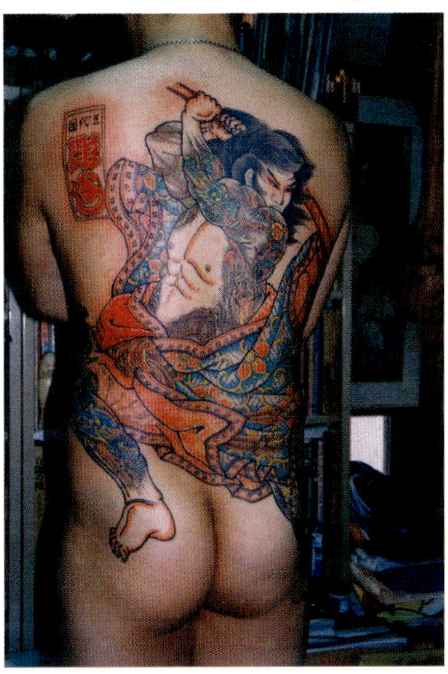

The tattoos that Horiyoshi III produces transmit all aspects of his learned technique and personal experience, echoing a range of taste that has evolved over decades of constant experimentation and an unvarying absorption of artistic influence. While rooted in Japanese art, the scope of his stimulus is seemingly endless. Horiyoshi III has never limited himself to conventional tattoo design or practice and has continually forged forward, from renovating the very design of hand tattoo equipment and needle configuration to constantly revising traditional tattoo design. What he has done is pave the way for tattoo artists of all disciplines. Japanese tattoos are another expression of the icons and religious beliefs of Japanese culture; or rather they are a part of the larger culture as a whole. This imagery is not autonomous to tattoo art; it merely reflects the Japanese perspective and aesthetic. Oftentimes, the genesis of conventional Japanese tattoo design can be traced to its origins in the art world of Asia, particularly in the use of Japanese prints in creating tattoo design. And while Horiyoshi III has most certainly paid homage to past masters in such a way, he has taken this formula and employed it, seeking muse elsewhere. A profound example of this type of application is his use of photos of Pride (Japanese mixed martial arts) fighters in place of appropriating poses from classic prints for warrior designs. Applying the same basic rules of composition to the new image, he devises a new design while evoking a style reminiscent of the great masters that he regards. The minute details in the work reflect his knowledge of era-appropriate costuming or armor. It should be noted that all artists, and most certainly Horiyoshi III's beloved Hokusai, drew from life at one time or another. Horiyoshi III has the abilities after years of experience to take a modern inspiration and give it that "Edo period" look. Among the other forms of art in his collection, he has a tremendous number of prints providing him with a vast fount of information to work from. There is no limit to his ingenuity and he collects relentlessly in order to better his art. These elements have come together to create his distinctive style, the Horiyoshi III tradition.

There are many different interpretations of the Japanese tattoo, often manifested as the teachings of different tattoo masters to their respective families. It is a duty of the apprentices to carry the artistic tradition of the master and hopefully gener-

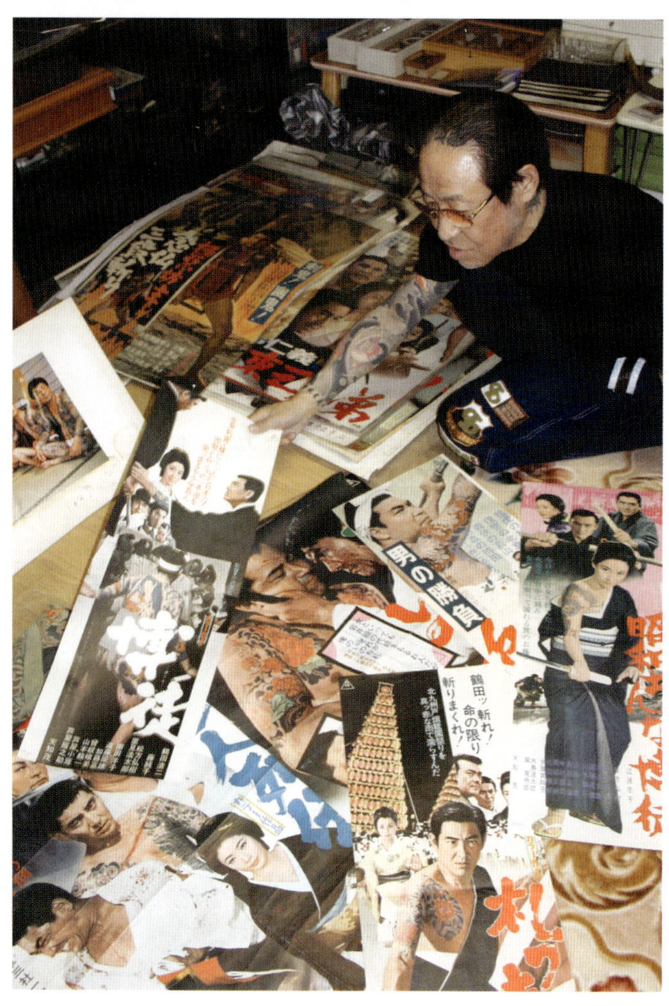

ate their own voice while reflecting the master's teachings in their own work. When I approached Horitaka about a job five years ago, I saw him as a carrier of this tradition. I was pursuing the Japanese style in my tattoo work and felt that I had grown stagnant in my previous situation. I was seeking other artists with similar passion. When I joined State of Grace, I did not anticipate what the future would hold for me in my pursuit of this visual style. Horitaka has been an inspiration and a constant source of encouragement for my tattoos and related projects. Even before I visited Japan for the first time, I was exposed to Horiyoshi III's teachings through Horitaka. Always removing himself, he has guided my work, avidly quoting the master and passing on his teachings through our drawing sessions. My understanding of Horiyoshi III's style and tattoo principles would not be possible without Horitaka's facilitation. He always humbles himself before his own master and has always put Horiyoshi III's thoughts and opinions before his own, deferring judgment in matters other than tattooing. He often receives advice from his master on business and personal issues as well. Horitaka takes his role as an apprentice very seriously and does not limit his responsibilities to his master solely to tattoo fabrication. Horiyoshi

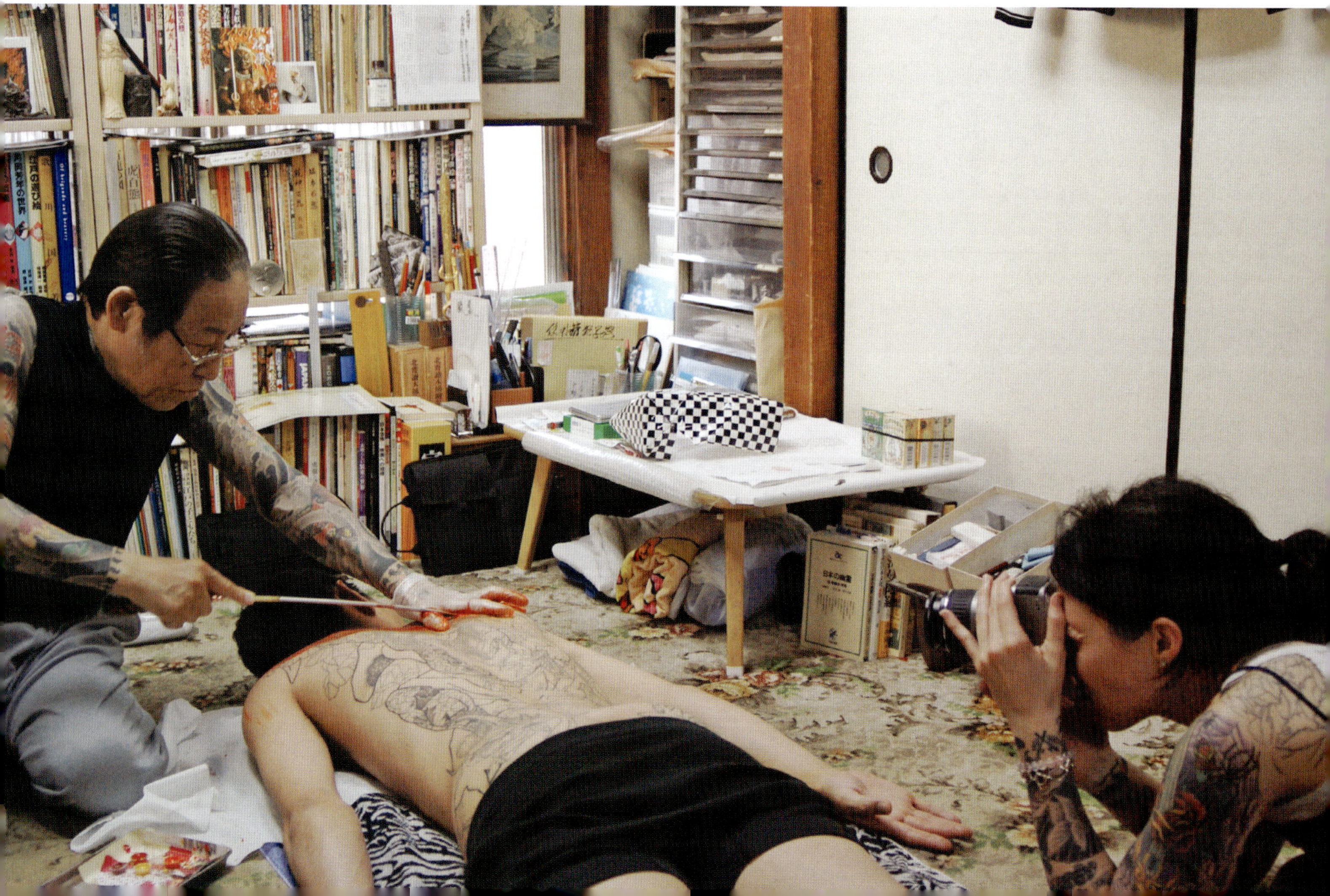

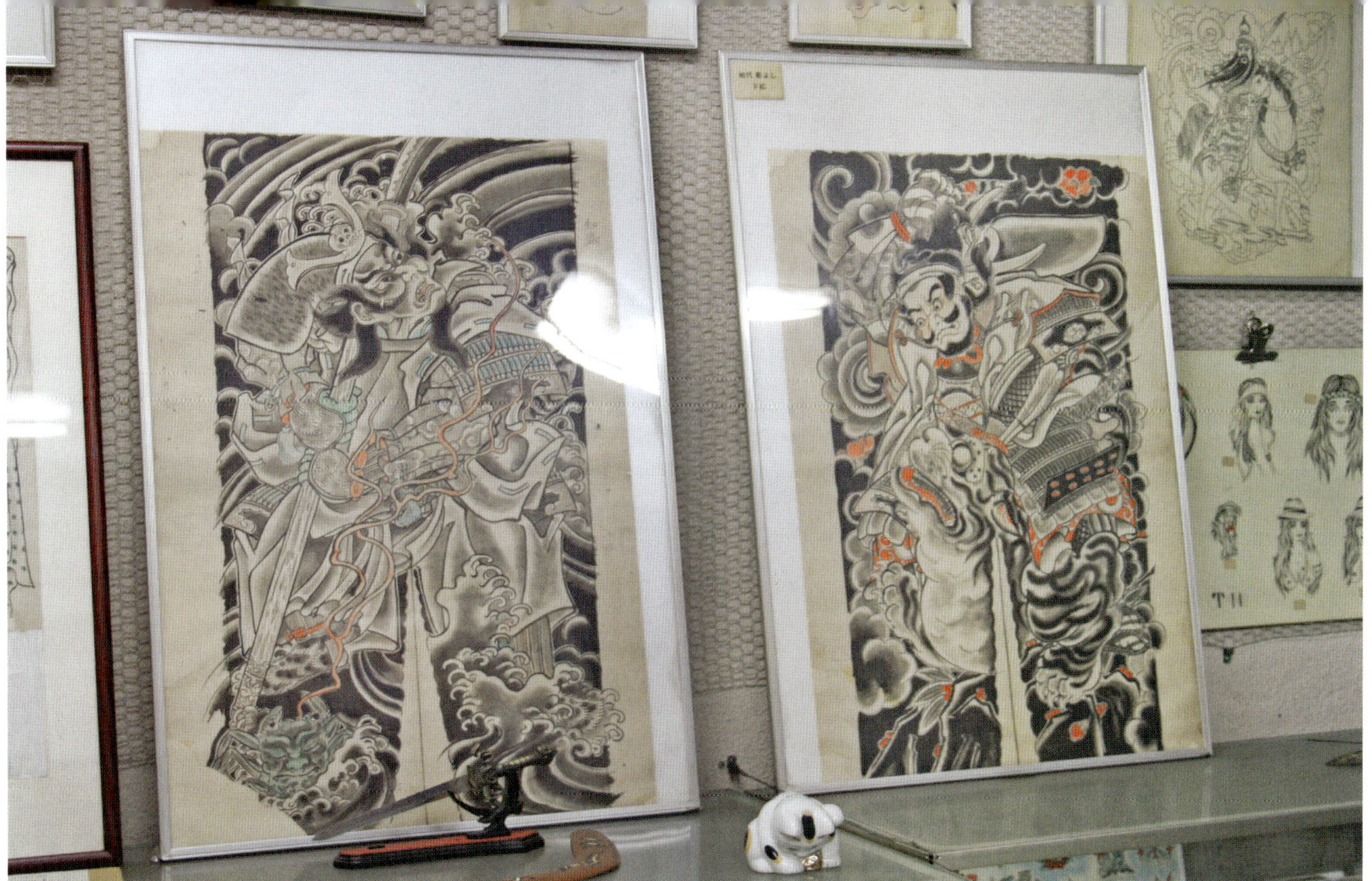

Shitae, preparatory drawings, used by Shodai Horiyoshi on display at the Yokohama Tattoo Museum.

III does not speak fluent English and depends on his apprentices to communicate his opinions and feelings with the Western world. Horitaka has taken the full-time job of being a spokesman for Horiyoshi III, acting as a translator, PR team, and mouthpiece. Horitaka is responsible for multiple books about Horiyoshi III, simultaneously giving our generation the chance to understand and enjoy the work of the great master during his lifetime, while promoting Japanese tattooing as a cultural endeavor with origins in Japanese art. It is my objective to show the same kind of respect to Horiyoshi III and Japanese culture that I have viewed in Horitaka's writings and actions. I want to do his master justice in my presentation of his wisdom and narratives.

Without Horitaka, my relationship with Horiyoshi III would not have been possible. He has brought me to Horiyoshi III under his own auspices and has acted as a liaison in facilitating our relationship. This started first in passing on the master's teachings, followed by introductions, tattoo appointments, and culminated in Horiyoshi III and his wife, Mayumi, bringing me into their home, letting me help at the studio and ultimately in the receiving of my title. These are relationships I value with all my heart. I try to follow in Horitaka's footsteps in my study of Japanese art and tattooing and by acting in a manner befitting a Japanese tattooer. In Japan it is the combination of talent and proper action that is respected in tattooing. Horitaka is an example of a tattooer who embodies both. His loyalty to his master is boundless and he has always professed that he will be an apprentice and student of Horiyoshi III until the day he dies. In May 2007, Horitaka and I went to Japan to visit Horiyoshi III and work on this book. Horiyoshi III recognizes Horitaka's commitment and during our trip granted him the high honor of the addition of *shodai* to his title. *Shodai* denotes the first of an independent lineage and marks the approval by the master for the apprentice to go out on his own, a graduation of sorts. Takahiro Kitamura[3] received the name Horitaka from his master in 1998 as an encouragement to pursue the Japanese style, and through his hard work and efforts has earned the right to have his own tattoo family and take on his own apprentices. Horitaka has always seen Horiyoshi III as a benchmark to model his own career after and always acknowledges his hard work and enormous level of output. With our shop and through his vast publications he is achieving his goals. I can only hope that this humble exploration of the Japanese tattoo can add to the celebration of the Horiyoshi III legacy.

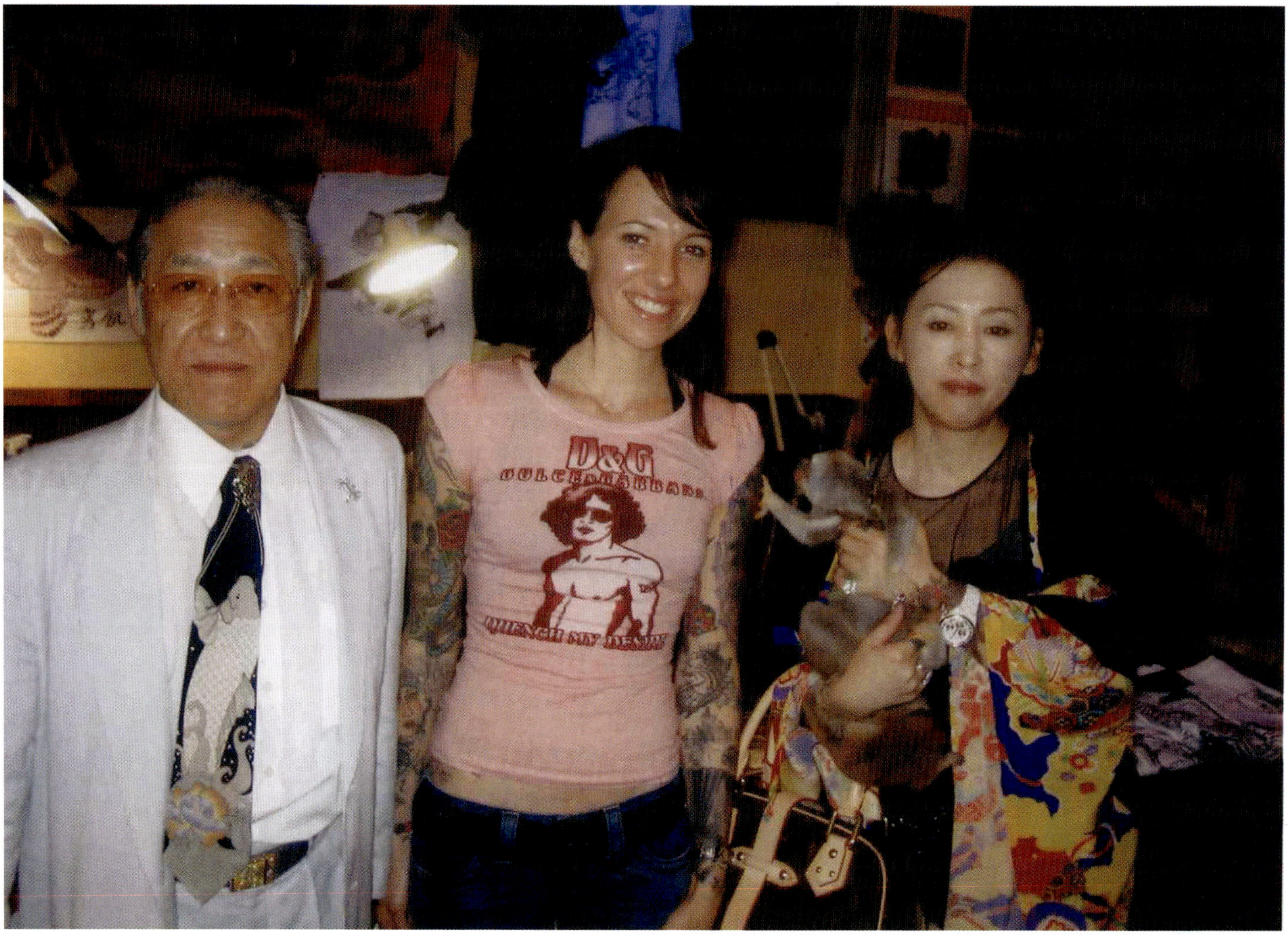

With Horiyoshi III and Mayumi, circa 2005.

[1]Weinberg, Adam D. Director's Foreword to *Picasso and American Art*, Michael FitzGerald. Whitney Museum of American Art, New York, In association with Yale University Press, New Haven and London, 2006,8.

[2]FitzGerald, Michael. *Picasso and American Art*, Michael FitzGerald. Whitney Museum of American Art, New York, In association with Yale University Press, New Haven and London, 2006,12.

[3]Unless otherwise specified all names in this book are in Western format, first name then last name.

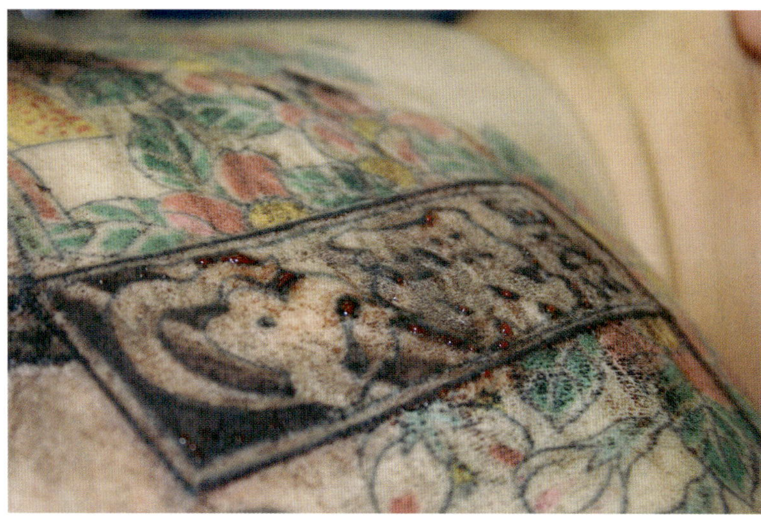

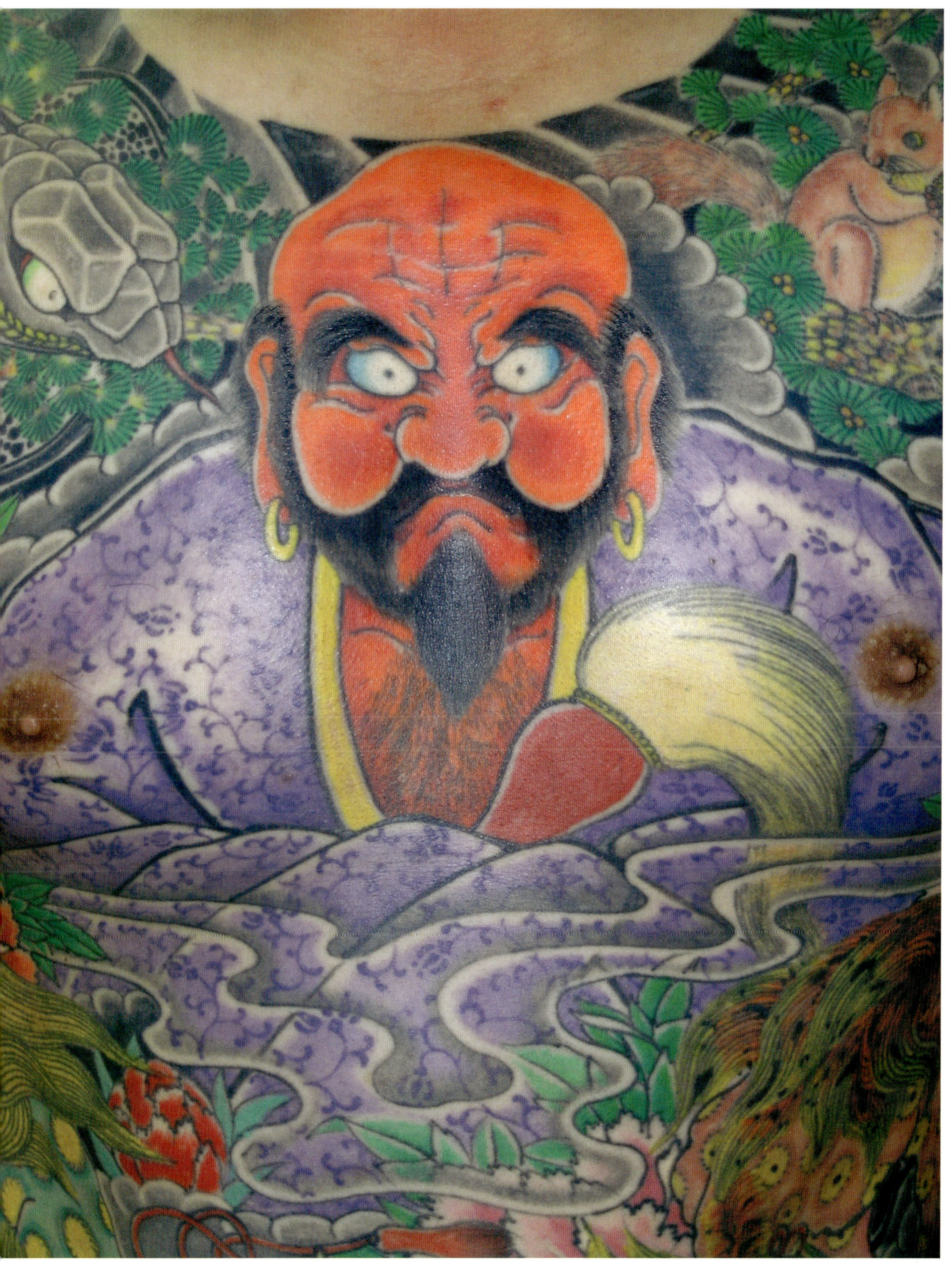

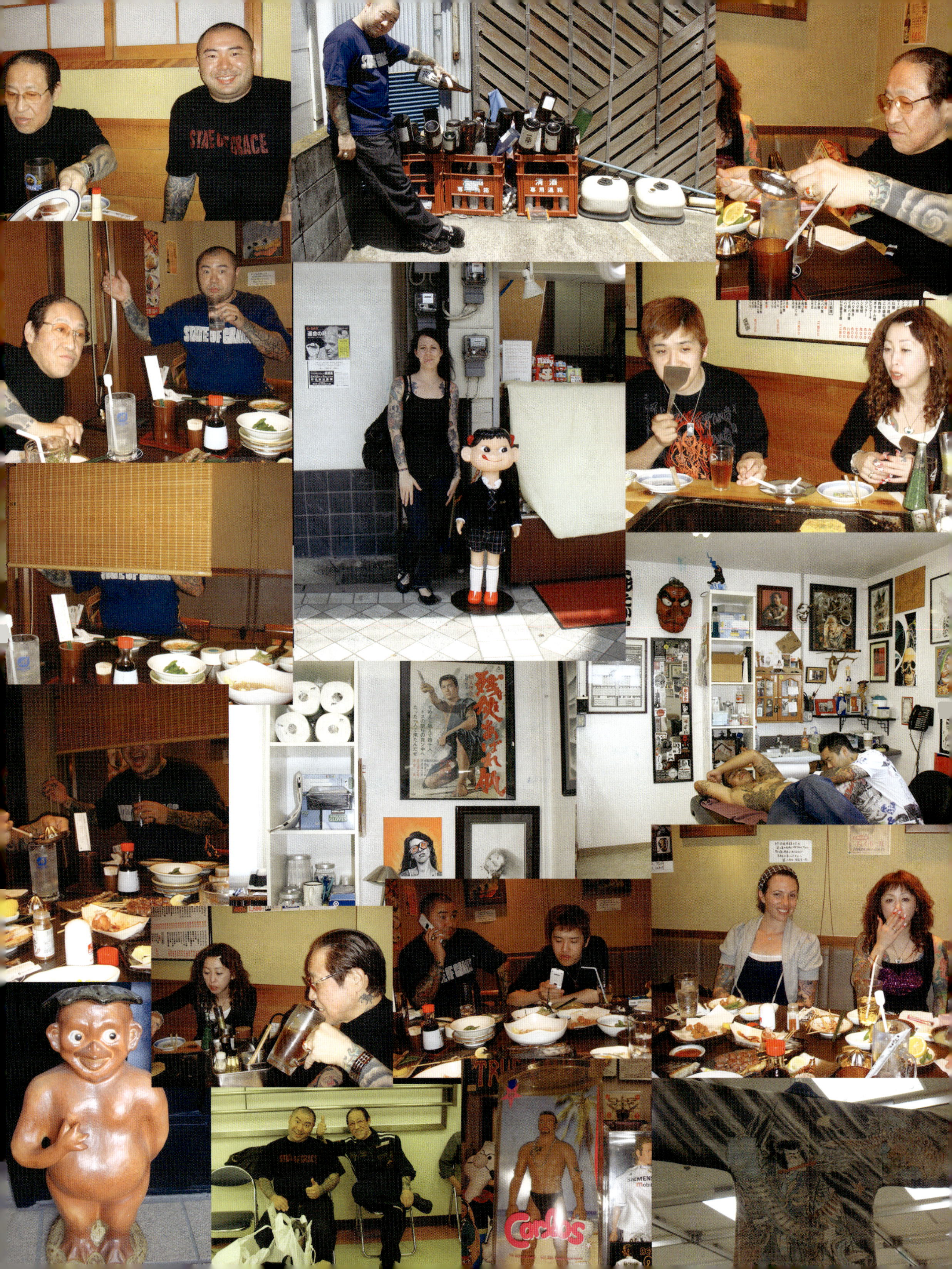
STATE OF GRACE
Carlos

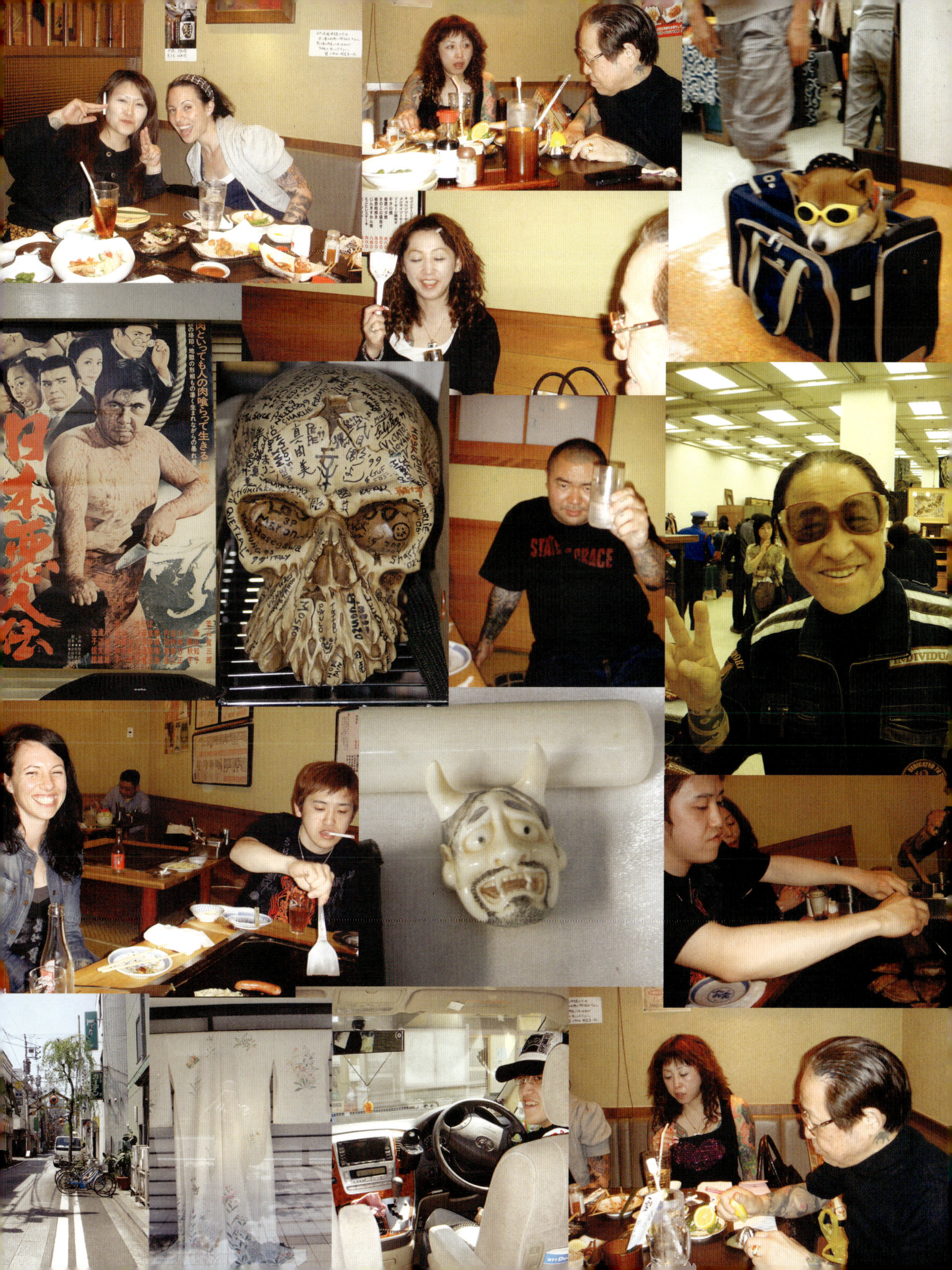

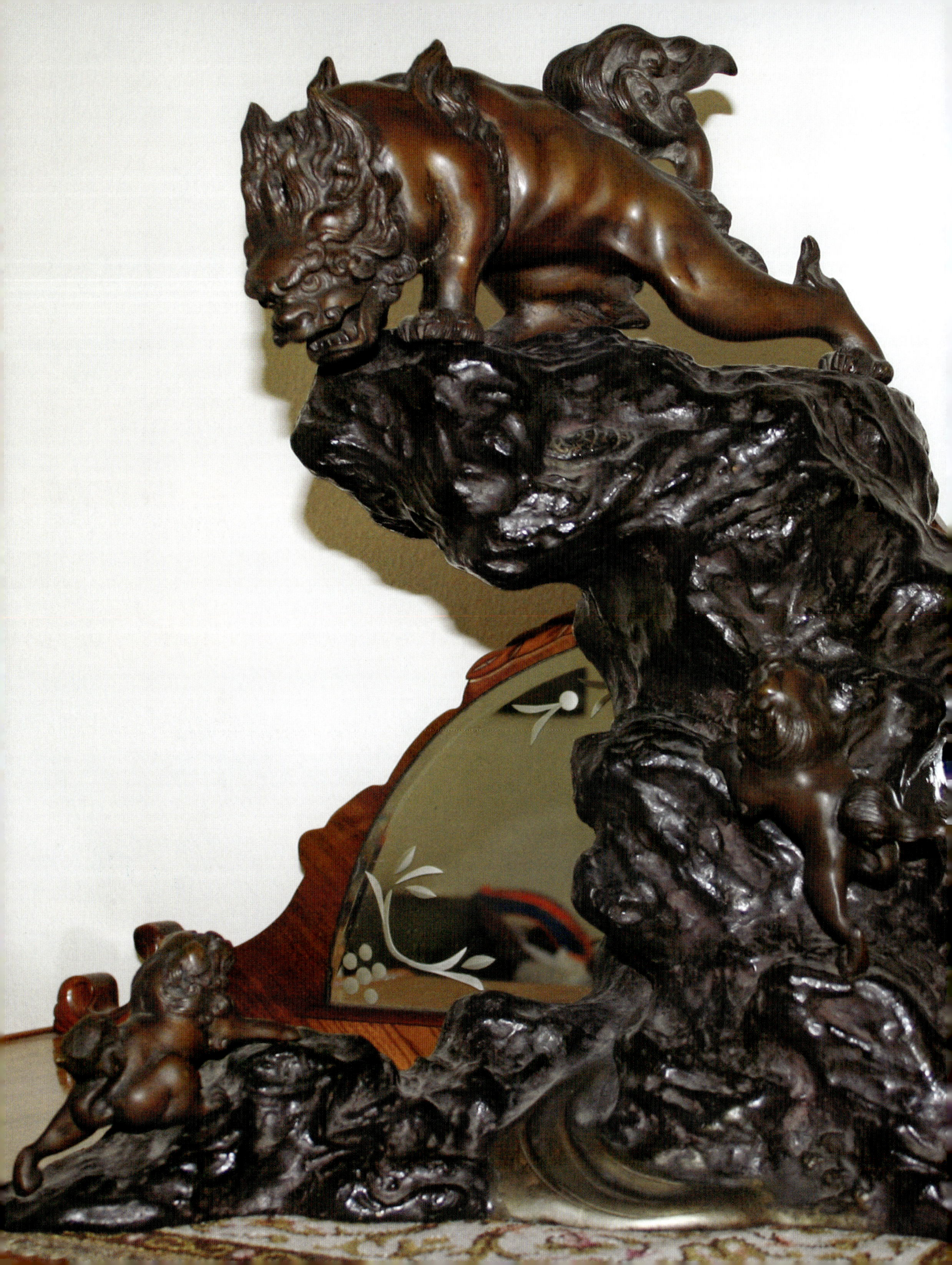

Chapter 1
Antique Fair

Another purpose of our visit to Japan was to visit Horiyoshi III and his family. When we were coordinating our travel plans, he mentioned that he would like us to be there on May third. This was the date of a semi-annual antique fair in Tokyo that Horiyoshi III has always attended. Horitaka realized that this was also my thirtieth birthday and made an effort to stall the trip, but Horiyoshi III paid no heed. "Cool we'll celebrate her birthday there!" Even the mention of a co-worker's family wedding fell on deaf ears; "you can find a gift at the fair." But, we needed no further encouragement to go to an antique fair with Horiyoshi III; we were ecstatic.

Horiyoshi III is an obsessive collector. Anyone who has seen his Yokohama Tattoo Museum has experienced his passion for collecting all that is tattoo related. In his home he has a special room, added on to his house no less, that is much like a humidor, preserving centuries of artifacts. Aside from being an avid Internet shopper, this self-taught historian of Japanese culture and fiery consumer loves the sport of bargaining at fairs.

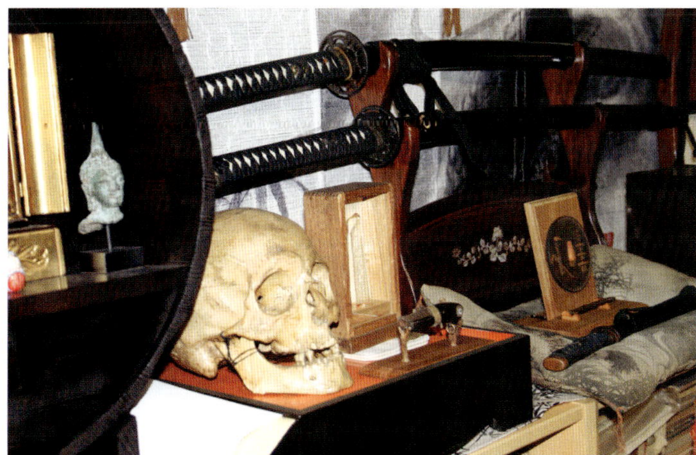

Horiyoshi III's antique room.

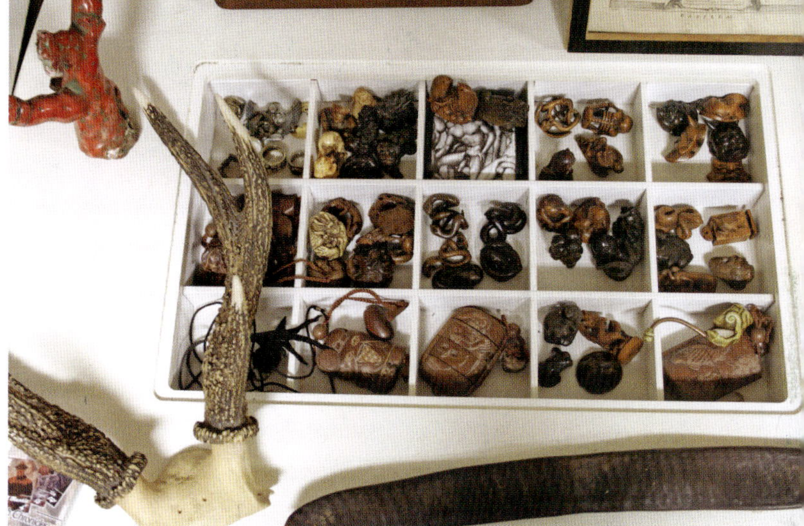

Netsuke, a toggle used to fasten a kimono sash. *Netsuke* are often decorated and/or carved from bone or wood.

Horitaka once shared an anecdote with me, recounting a moment with the master in Florence, Italy. He had watched him photograph a fountain where the water flowed out of a stone dog head. The master smiled and in simple English said "dog-face oni." We had discussed how he would and could find usable tattoo reference and inspiration everywhere. When I am in Japan I feel inundated with images, many of which appear in everyday life, that I equate with Japanese tattoos. This was especially true of the antique fair where I saw an abundance of objects that I recognized from looking at Japanese art; decorative, spiritual, new and old. We noted and named images of historical and mythological beings, as well as other animals common to tattooing, present before us in prints, statues, paintings and *netsuke*. We were opening ourselves up to absorb as much as we could. We bought what we could afford and took snapshots of as many items as we could.

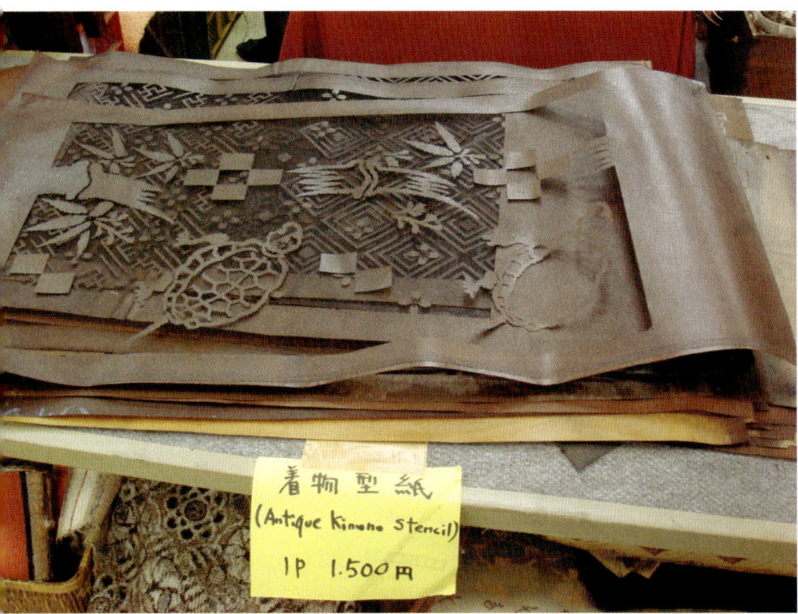

Stencils used to create the patterning for kimono.

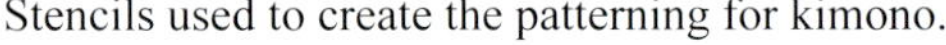

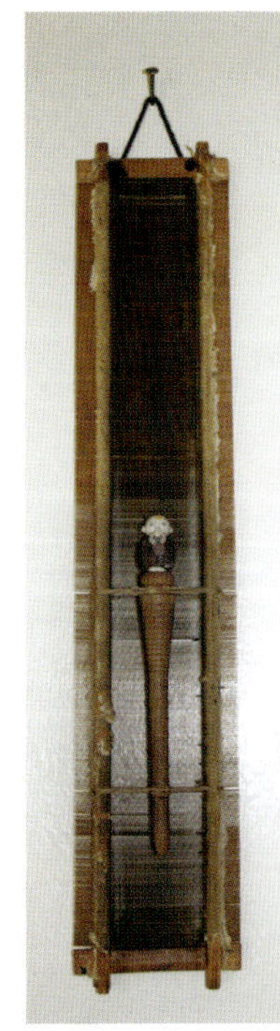

Walking through the aisles of the fair, our "tattoo filters" were on. By this I mean that we searched for tattoo inspiration and information everywhere we looked. This was our mid-term in Japanese art, where we tested our knowledge retention when faced with identifying images we had only seen in books. We saw every deity and folkloric character depicted somewhere, if on a print, painting, sculpture or pottery. We saw kimono; from fabric scraps, to obi sashes to full robes. We even saw stencils for creating the patterns on some kimono fabrics, some of which Horiyoshi III had purchased for use in future drawings.

The morning of the fair, Horiyoshi III had given us several gifts. He has always been extremely generous and most certainly assumes the role of benevolent master, but this is obviously not to fulfill some idealized role, rather an exhibition of his warm character. It is customary in Japan to exchange gifts with guests and early on I was coached on this. I always take time before my trips to pick out gifts for people I am visiting. One of the gifts I received from him was a very sweet looking -almost cute- wooden object mounted on bamboo. It turned out to be an ornate spindle used in the fabrication of kimono material. With these objects in mind, combined with the experience of combing through boxes of fabric and racks of robes, I thought of the many woodblock prints and Horiyoshi III drawings that I had seen. I felt newly connected to these images in a sensory or textural way that I hadn't previously experienced. For instance, in depictions of Suikoden warriors, oftentimes the moment captured is one of combat and boisterous movement. With a better understanding of kimono material and how these garments are worn, I can easily imagine the layers becoming airborne, flurrying as a sword or spear is wielded.

Unbeknownst to me, Horitaka had intended on buying my birthday gift at the antique fair. He later told me that he planned to wait for something to catch my eye, that he was sure something would jump out at us! We found it at a booth housing some furniture and a few choice statues. It was a bronze sculpture, about two feet high, of a *karajishi* (Chinese lion) and her two cubs. She stands on top of the mountain roar-

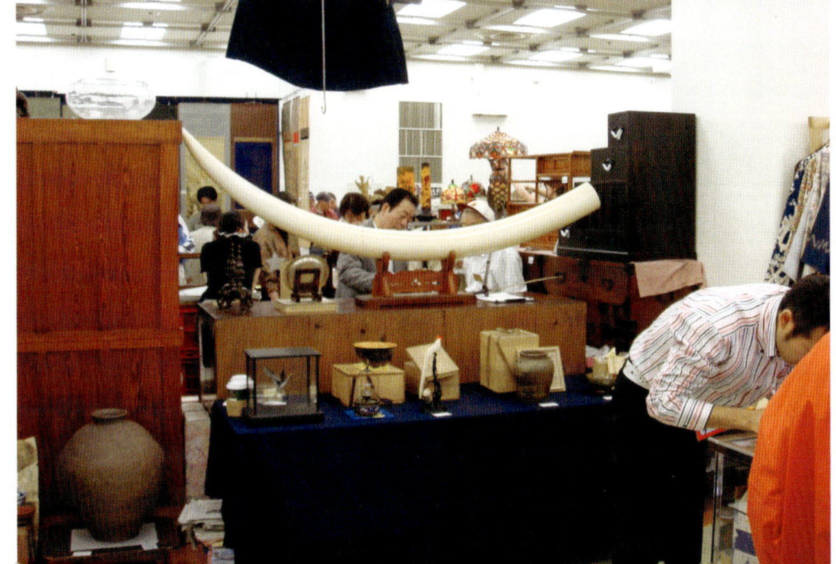

ing to her cubs below, as they make the treacherous ascent back to her. Later that evening as we shared the spoils of our day with Horiyoshi III and Mayumi, he explained to us the relevance of this story, which is often depicted in print and painting as well. He equated the mother *karajishi* with a teacher, as she pushes her young off the cliff and they must work to get back to her on their own. She stands at the top encouraging, but they must work to get to her. Pointing to one of the cubs he noted the confidence in the cub's stance, he was almost there, and this cub would succeed. The other cub, rearing back and separated from its mother by a stream of water shows hesitation in his stance. He would fail. It is interesting to hear this story from him, for as the teacher figure stands on top of the mountain looking down upon the students, he already knows their fate before they experience it for themselves. Far more than a case of tough love, it is a metaphor for learning through personal experience; encouragement and the understanding that one must carve one's own path. Horiyoshi III validated the purchase and said it would complete the presentation well to hang a scroll behind it with a *kanji* for "perseverance." "No picture, just writing hung on the wall behind it." Looking at the statue with him I felt like a *karajishi* cub. From his vantage point of years of experience, thousands of hours of practice, there he stood above me looking down. I hoped he didn't see any hesitation in my footing.

One of the many talents of Horiyoshi III is finding incredible objects at bargain prices so we were eager to see his purchases. The piece that Horiyoshi III was most interested in sharing with us was a woodblock print of a figure wearing a tattoo of the child warrior Oniwakamaru. I recognized the background pattern. It was a monochromatic blue plaid that Horiyoshi III called "Benkei Goushi" patterning. Horiyoshi III explained to us that this fabric was named for the warrior Musashibo Benkei. Earlier that day, at the fair, I had seen an antique coat bearing the same plaid. This correlation was first made in the *kabuki* theatre as this fabric became part of the costuming worn by actors portraying Musashibo Benkei. The significance of the plaid, in Horiyoshi III's print, connecting Oniwakamaru to Musashibo Benkei is that Oniwakamaru is the childhood name of Musashibo Benkei. This connection and wordplay both fascinates and entertains Horiyoshi III. The images in Japanese art that I have studied since my days at Cooper Union have always been two-dimensional. This anecdote gave me a tangible connection, through Horiyoshi III's eyes, to this interesting story. Sometimes the process of learning can be taken too seriously and Horiyoshi III's sense of humor gives us insight into that of the artists that created these pieces. Japanese art and culture is full of hidden meaning, double en tend res, frivolity; humor is an integral part of this outwardly stoic and reserved culture.

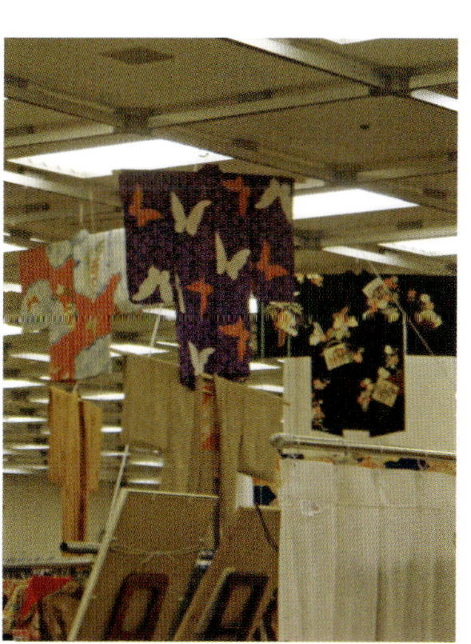

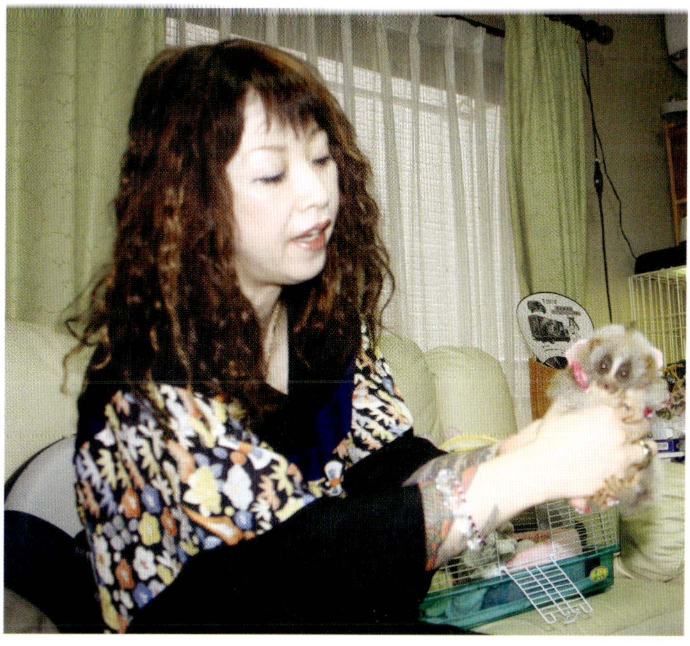

Back at the house, Mayumi showed us her purchases, which included a cloak and a top. These were modern pieces, constructed of recycled antique kimono fabric. She explained to me that the cloak was for summer, the fabric being very light and airy. The top was very stylish; ironically it reflected the current silhouette in women's wear known as "kimono sleeves." The Western adaptation of old Japanese clothing incorporates the dramatic wide sleeves of its namesake. The designer had sewn pieces of an all black textured fabric to another piece with graphic patterns. There was a stark contrast between the busy flowered pieces and the larger areas of fields of black. The patterned portions of the top were wide diagonal stripes, creating bold colorful shapes on the loose fitting blouse. My thoughts traversed between depictions of patterned textiles in the prints I have studied, such as in the many layers worn by women in winter prints, and the slight figure standing before me. This modern interpretation reinvents the identity of this antique fabric. I found myself connecting these observations together. There was a clear visual connection between the artistic renditions and the reinterpreted object.

As I collected far more objects than I could possibly fit into my luggage, I looked forward to displaying all of my new things in my home. I called my boyfriend and joked with him that we were redecorating upon my return. In addition to having an interesting living space, I wanted to be surrounded by inspirational images and objects. By submerging oneself in a visual element, one can assert influence over his/her own work; this can even occur subconsciously. Everyone's brain is conditioned in a style and as I studied art in Western institutions, I have spent as much time unlearning drawing styles as I have learning them. It can be difficult for Westerners to convey Japanese aesthetics for this reason. Being raised in Japan is an advantage to exploring the Japanese style in tattooing simply because Japanese tattoo iconography is generated by Japanese culture. In Western nations we associate dragons, koi, and cherry blossoms with tattoo designs. Images such as these are mundane in Japan, they may decorate anything from a shrine to a beer bottle. Even in much of Horiyoshi III's early and present work, he references famous art pieces by artists such as Hokusai, Kyosai, Kuniyoshi, Hogai as opposed to citing previous tattoo artists. Although it is believed that Kuniyoshi drew tattoo designs and was even tattooed himself, he is now in this day and age considered a mainstream fine artist and as such is recognized by art collectors and museums worldwide. And while his critical acclaim may have come later than deserved in his native land, his designs have influenced generations of tattooists and his prints have fetched high prices on the Western auction block.

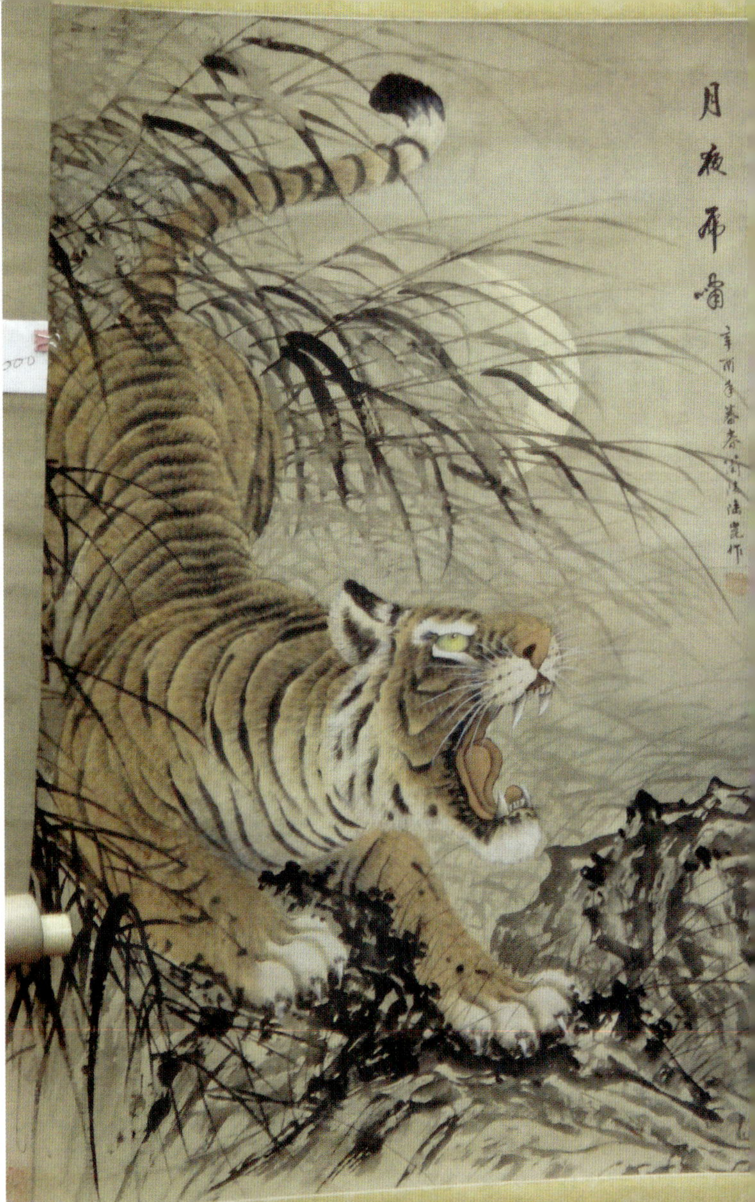

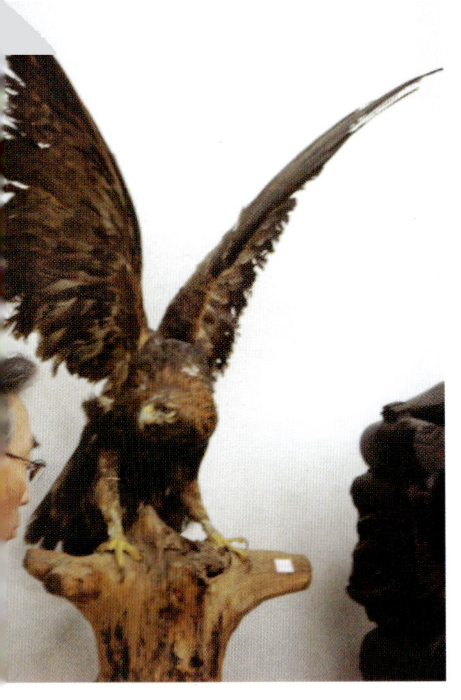

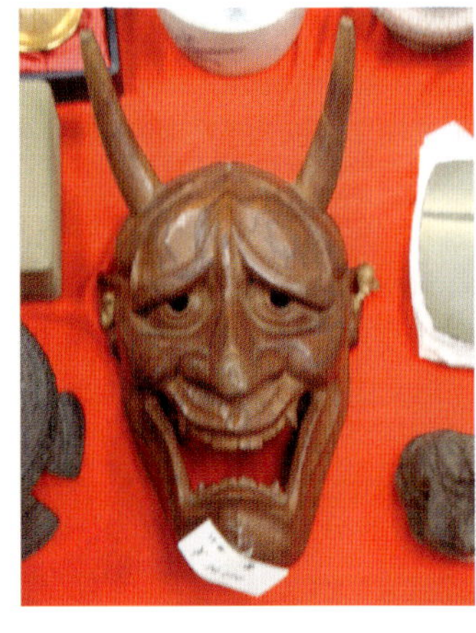

In contrast, many American tattoo designs such as roses, skulls, and snakes are associated with tattooing even when in a different context such as clothing. There is a marker that signifies "a tattoo"

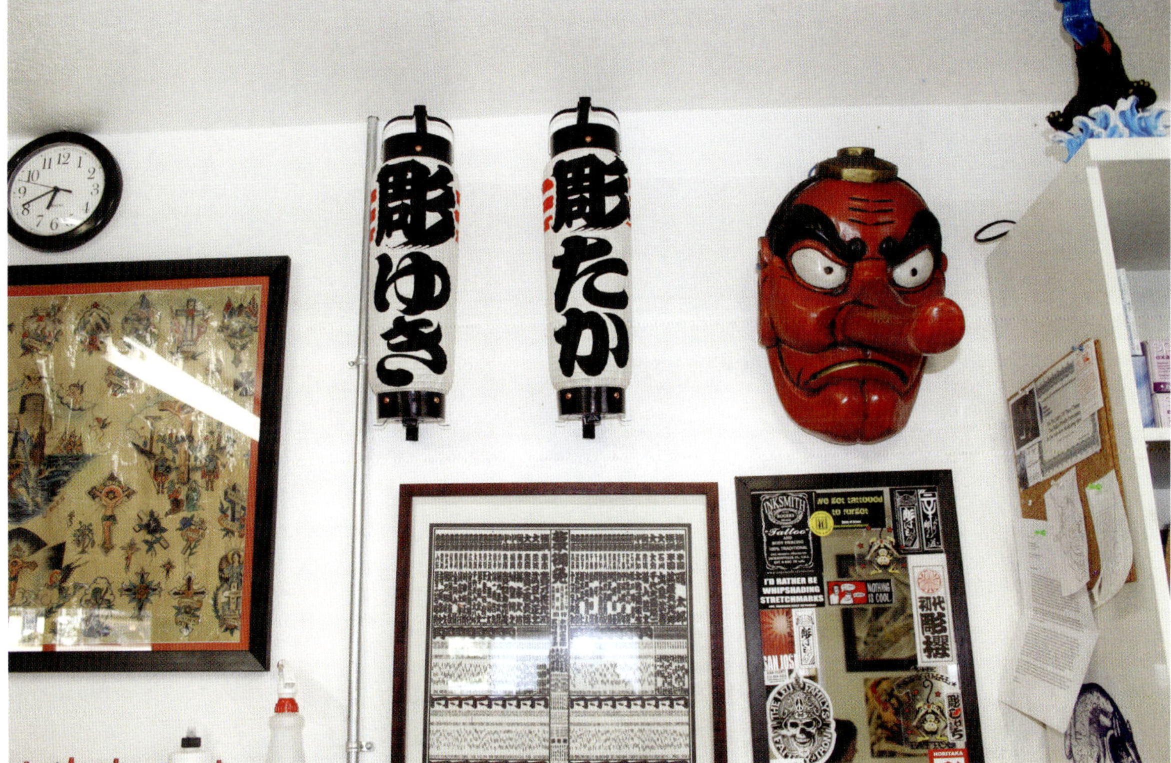

Right:
Japanese lanterns at State of Grace bearing the names Horiyuki (left) and Horitaka.

Below:
A woodblock print by Kuniyoshi of Suikoden warrior Hakujisso Hakusho attacking a village soldier.

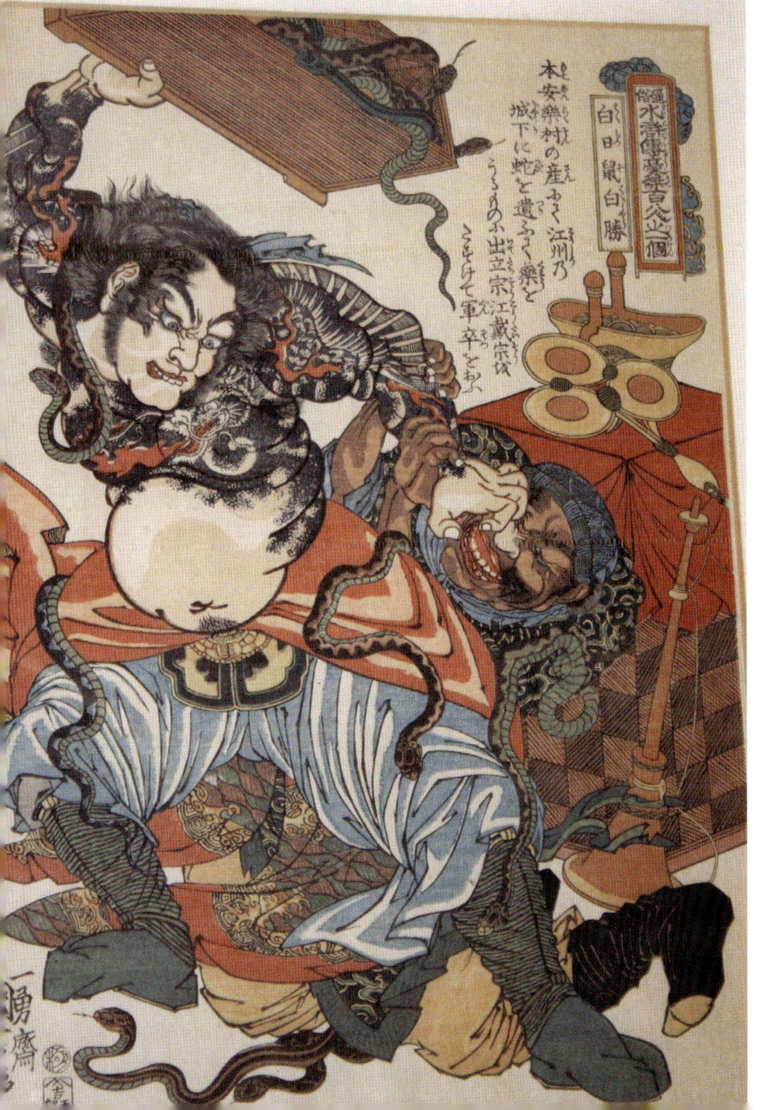

in such images. Maybe the difference is that American tattooing began as what Ed Hardy has termed a "folk art" while Japanese tattooing began as an extension of the popular arts of kabuki, kite making, and the woodblock print. This, of course, is not to imply superiority, but rather recognition of a different pool of artistic resource and reference. Icons of their culture surround the Japanese artists, living in Japan one's entire visual plane is taken over by the spectrum of Japanese icons and it is impossible to remain unaffected. There is evidence of this in their work and Westerners must be aware of this when subscribing to the Japanese style. When customers walk in to State of Grace, our shop in California, they equate the Japanese style tattoos being fashioned there with the many Japanese objects hanging on the walls; from Horiyoshi III paintings to the Japanese lanterns announcing the titled artists working there. Japanese tattoos are another expression of the icons and religious beliefs, adorning nearly every facet of their daily life. These images are not autonomous to tattooing, rather they express the taste and beliefs of a uniquely Japanese sensibility.

In order to properly convey a Japanese style it is important to submerge yourself in the culture by visiting Japan and continually looking at Japanese art. For example, Horitaka hopes that by encouraging his apprentice to decorate his house with Japanese art, through the constant exposure to

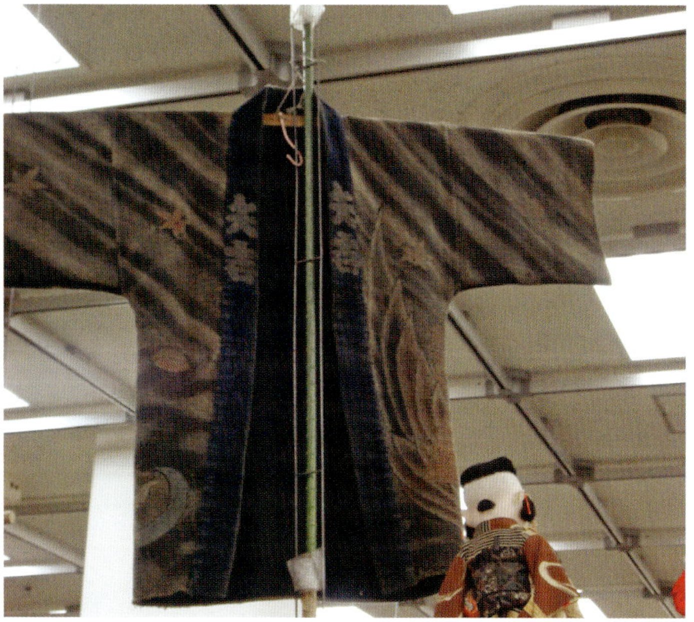

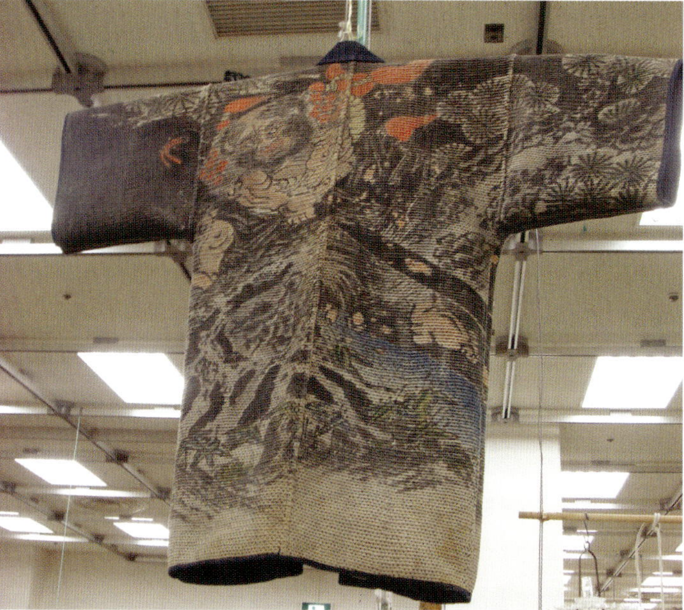

Hanten, traditional work coat, bearing the image of Suikoden hero Kaosho Rochishin. The image is based on a woodblock print by Kuniyoshi. Kaosho Rochishin, was also known as the "flower priest' because his body was covered in flower tattoos. Kaosho struggled with his devotion to Buddhism and made attempts to pursue a monastic life.

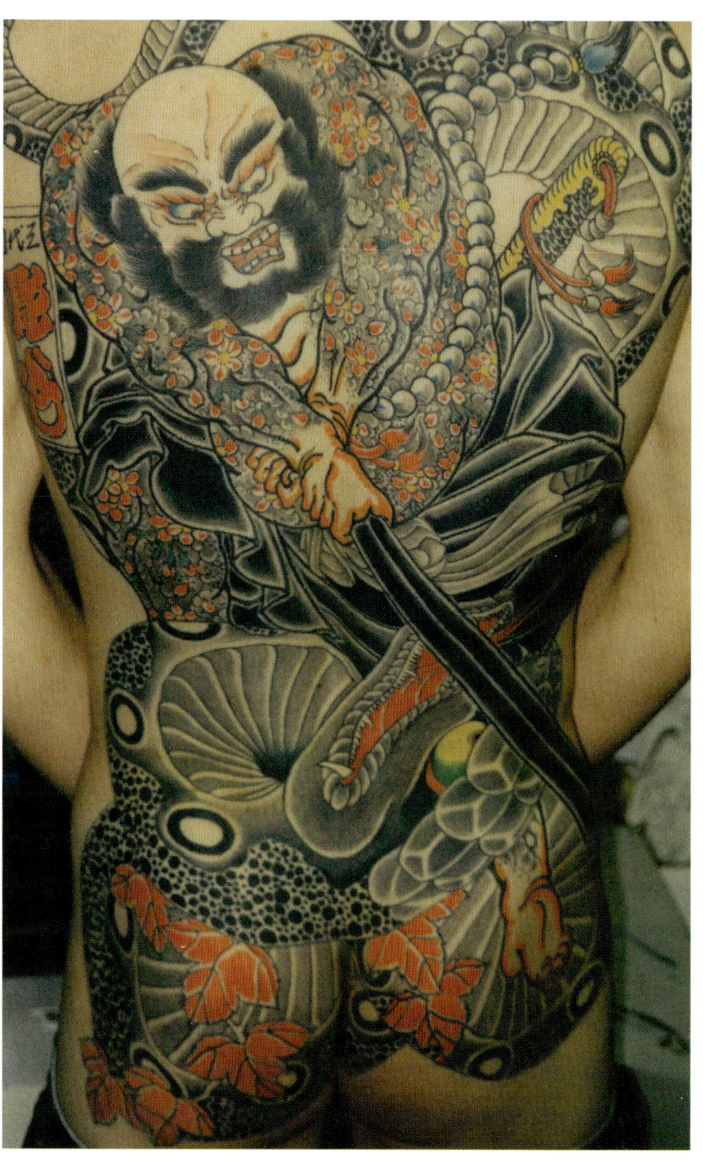

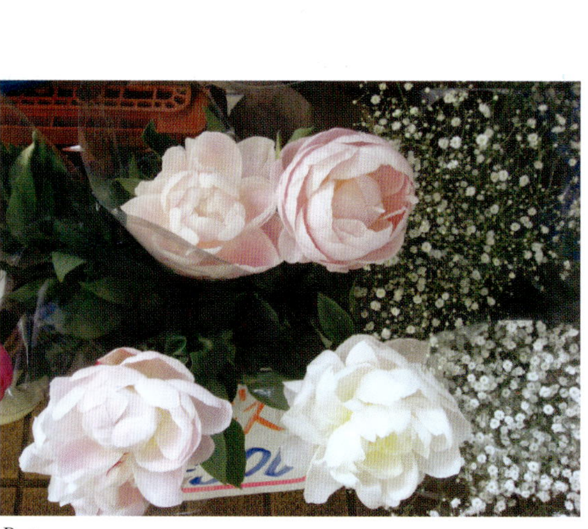

Botan, peony.

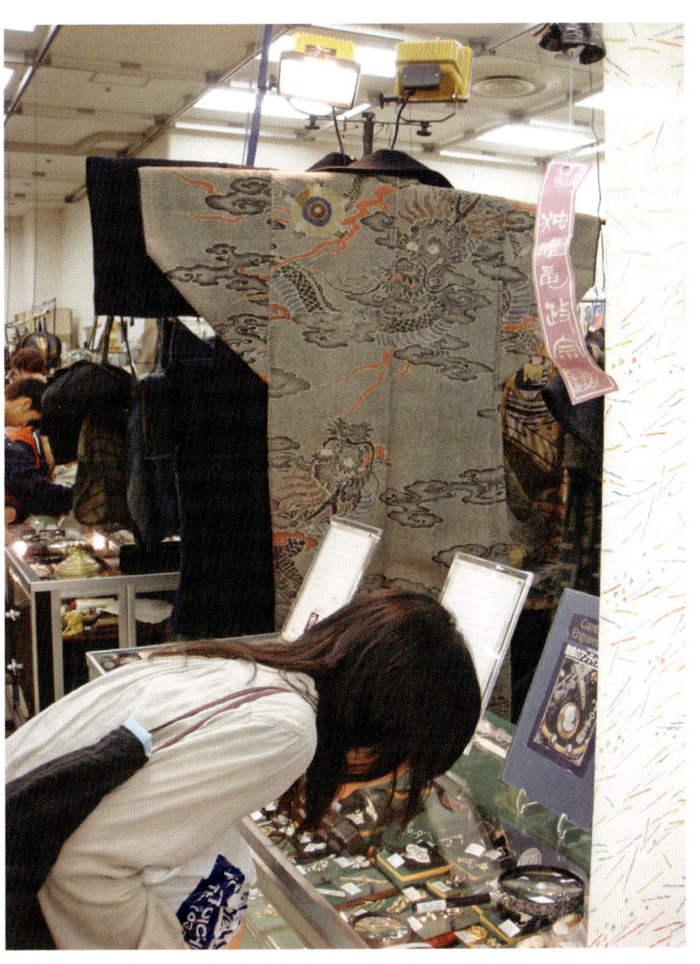

these images, he will more easily absorb the feelings evoked by them. By decorating his own house with Japanese art and images Horitaka believes the style will further penetrate and manipulate the apprentice's subconscious; in hopes of better conveying the Japanese aesthetic in his future tattoo work.

Horiyoshi III visits the fairs to collect relics of the past. Not surprisingly, his hobby of buying images and objects informs his opinions as a tattooer. He lives and breathes tattooing, it is his passion. I even noticed a small *netsuke* ghost hanging as a charm from his mobile phone. Such objects relate to tattooing but unlike in the West, such images explicate Japanese art as well as lend themselves to tattoo imagery. This elucidates our experiences at the fair, it is the reason we saw tattoo potential in nearly every object we encountered there.

Woodblock books in Horiyoshi III's study, note the use of a sword's *tsuba* as a paper weight.

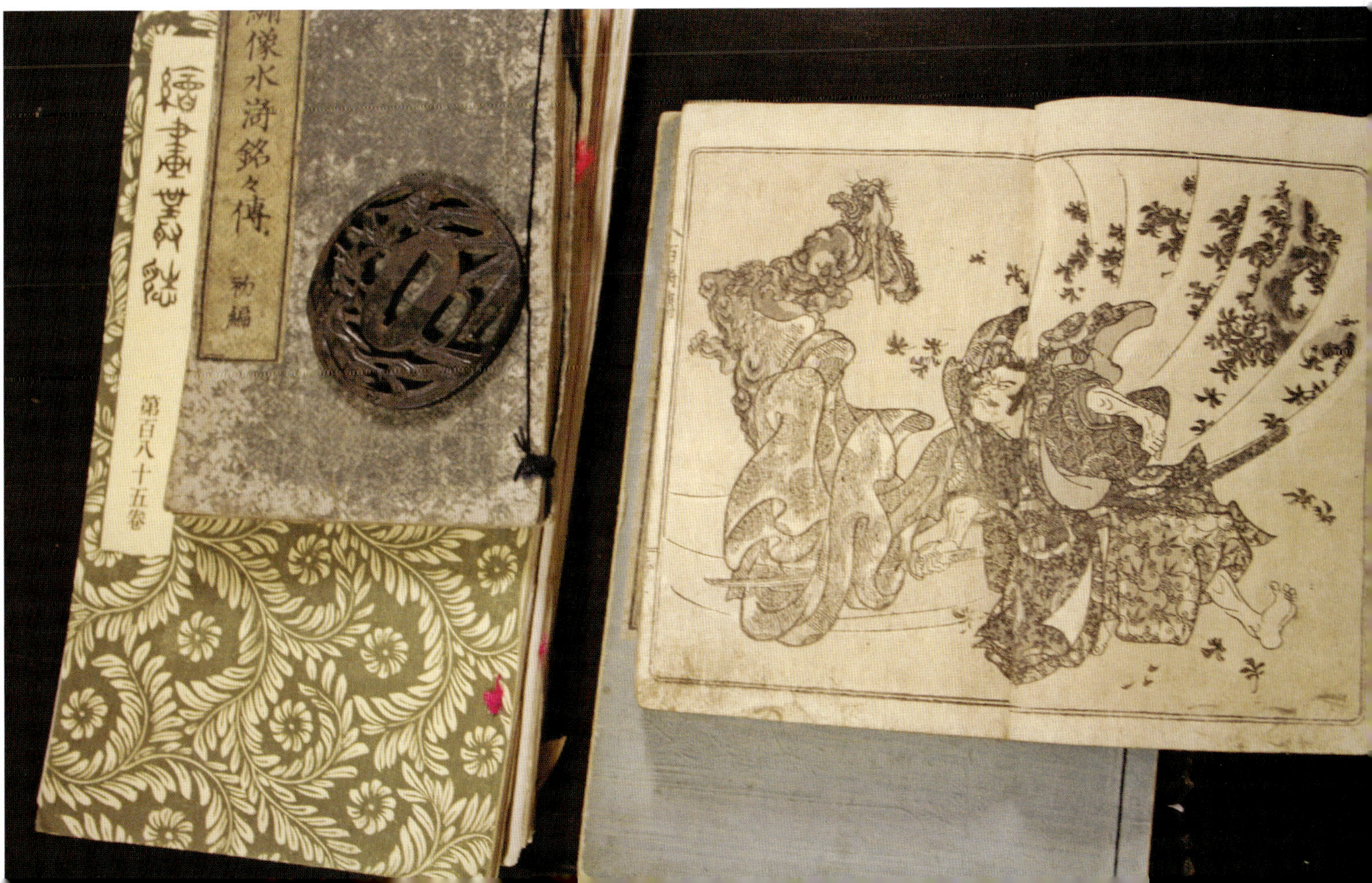

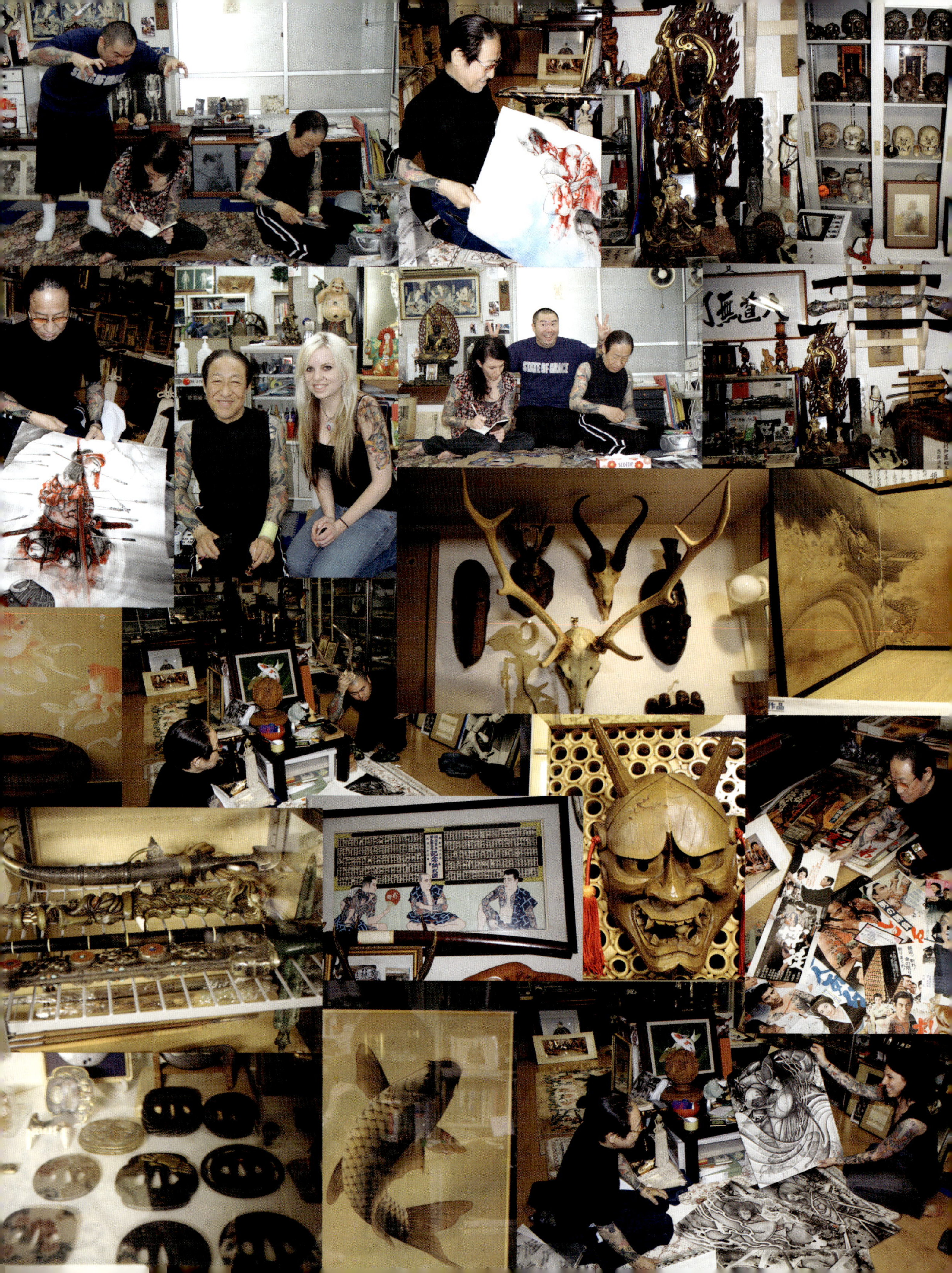
STATE OF GRACE

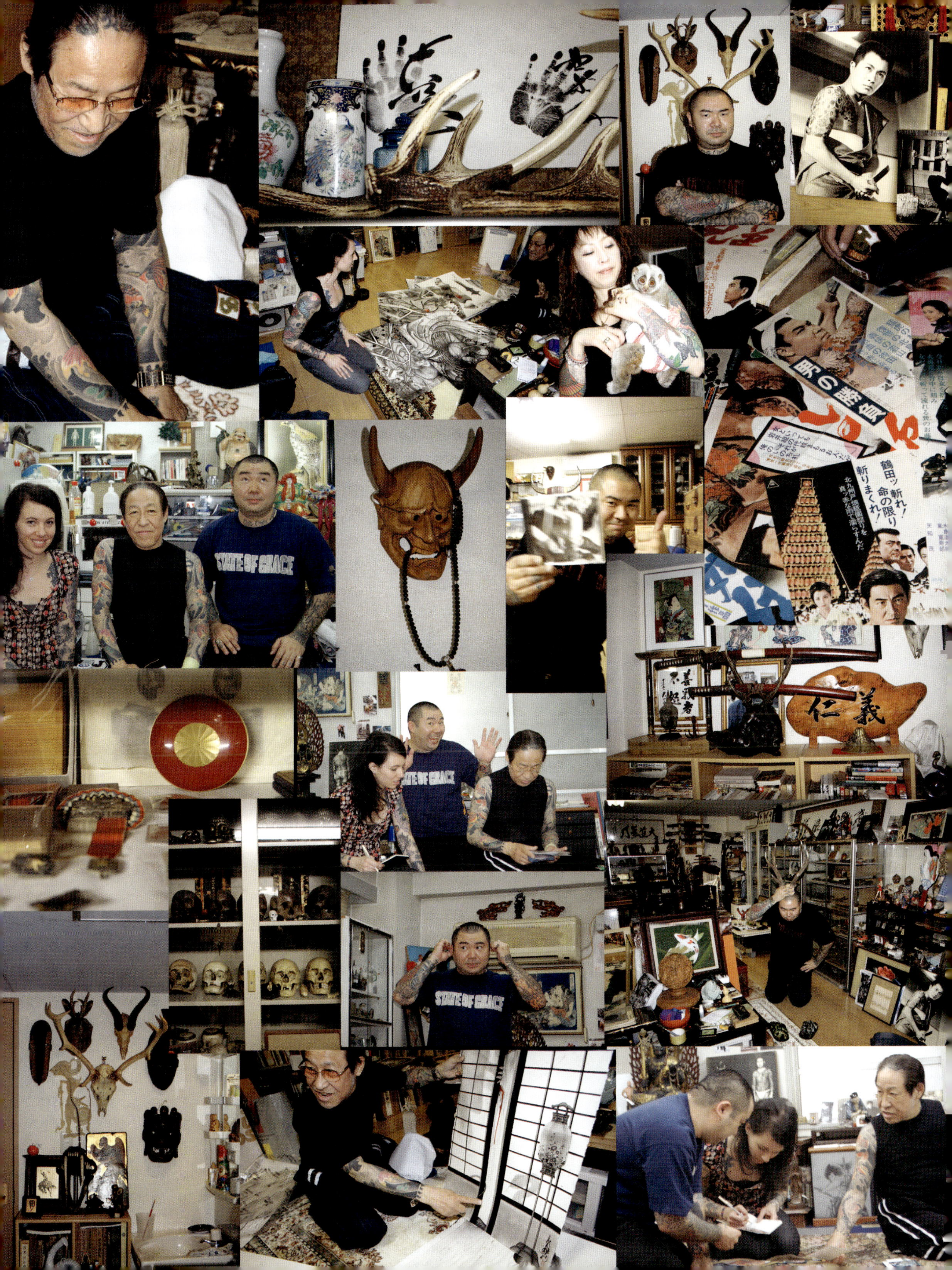
STATE OF GRACE
男の勝負
鶴田 斬れ！
命の限り
斬りまくれ！
仁 義

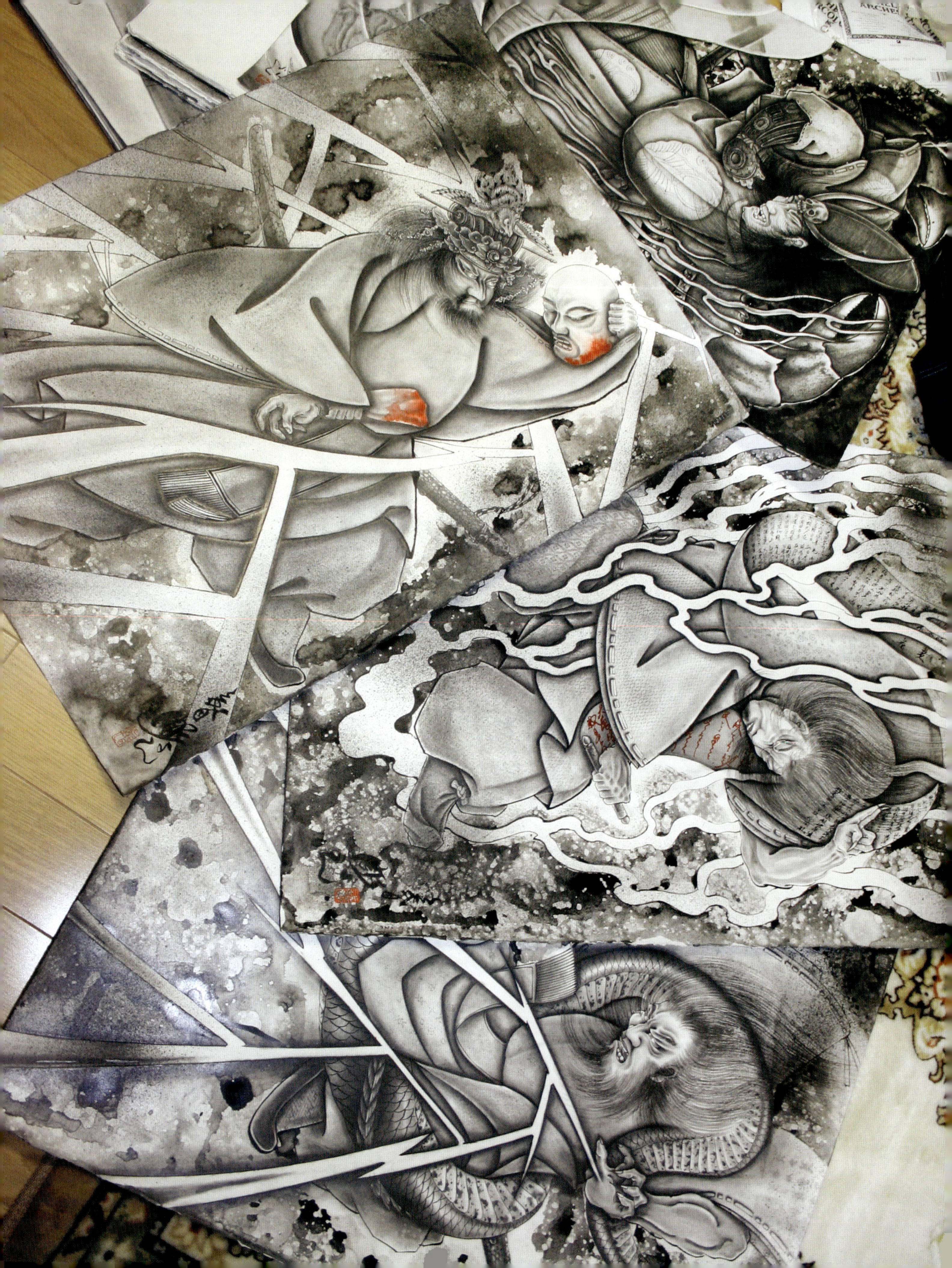

Chapter 2
Ghost Prints

There are few tattooers who are as prolific as Horiyoshi III. He is by no means slowing down: even past the age of sixty he continues to produce at an inexhaustible pace. His body of work is not limited to tattooing; he has produced countless drawings and paintings as well. To date, he has published three collections of drawings (*100 demons, 108 Heroes, The Namakubi*) with a total of over two hundred individual pieces. Though stylistically connected, each book is unique in its subject matter. Horiyoshi III is a self-taught artist who attributes his learning process to constant trial and error. As for the tools of his trade, he delights in finding art devices in the everyday items around him. Objects such as old toothbrushes and scraps of fabric find new life in the hands of this master. Horitaka attributes this attitude largely to Horiyoshi III's upbringing, frugality learned in the lean times of post-war Japan. Ever mindful of waste, Horiyoshi III also comes from a working class background. This is not to imply cheapness; Horiyoshi III is as generous financially as he is with his teaching, always indulging in the finer things in life. This generosity is lavished on his family and friends and I think may reflect the joy of upward mobility earned through hard work. He is the poor kid that made it. I have seen this behavior in my own father, a child of Holocaust survivors, who cannot stand the idea of wasted food yet proudly wears a gold Rolex. Horiyoshi III is a self made man who has not forgotten his roots even while appreciating his new lifestyle.

Horiyoshi III has developed a style of drawing based primarily on the layering of graphite and ink, or *sumi*. All of his books have been the exploration and refinement of experimental drawing techniques and this evolution is evident when viewing them chronologically. The notion of Horiyoshi III as a tattoo artist seems inconsequential; the term artist becomes more valid when examining his work in series. Each collection of work engages in dialogue with Japanese art and myth while simultaneously paying homage to, as well as placing Horiyoshi III in, a larger artistic tradition. He makes a conscious effort to align himself with the past masters of Japanese art while striving to create original bodies of work. This is especially true of his *108 Heroes of the Suikoden*, a Chinese tale that was illustrated

Tools of the trade. Horiyoshi III proudly displays some of his drawing implements, namely a shaving brush purchased at the *100 Yen* store.

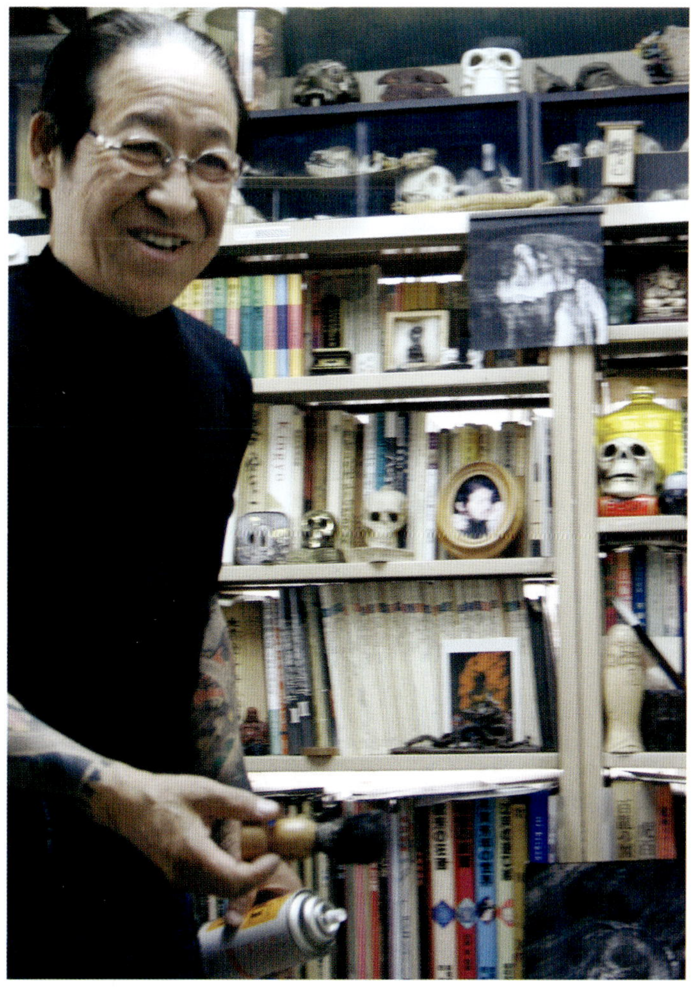

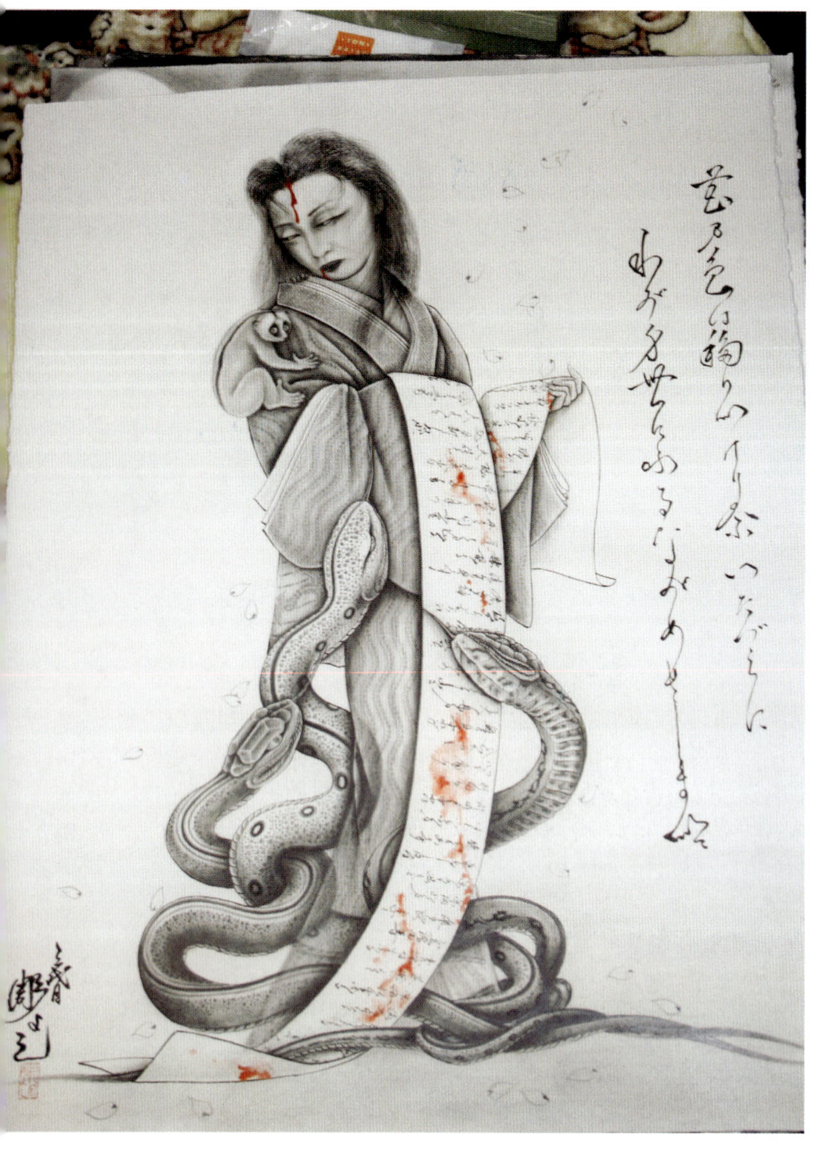

by almost every major print artist during the Edo and Meiji periods. This series holds monolithic significance to Japanese tattoo history and the prints made of the tattooed brigands almost two hundred years ago still serve as tattoo reference today. Horiyoshi III has added one hundred and eight new, and very tattooable, images to this library.

With his new series *36 Ghosts*, there will undoubtedly be comparisons to the celebrated prints published by Yoshitoshi between 1889 and 1892. This group of prints was inspired by the tradition of telling frightening stories by candlelight. Yoshitoshi's first successful body of work was a set of twenty-six images of such strange tales. This was to be followed by another group this time thirty-six "ghost" stories, which many scholars believe to be Yoshitoshi's last important series. I had the honor of seeing thirty-six ghost images by Horiyoshi III in person, life size, prior to publication.

While Horiyoshi III is most certainly aware of, and expectant of comparison to the important ghost series by Yoshitoshi, his decision to create a set of thirty-six prints came independently and for very different reasons. Japanese art is laden with double meanings and subtle nuance and numeric choices are rarely by accident. The *36 Ghosts* by Yoshitoshi happen to pay homage to an earlier work by thirty-six poets. Originally, Horiyoshi III had intended on drawing fifty ghosts but came upon a book from the early Genroku era (1688-1704), which changed his mind. The book showed a group of thirty-six Japanese Buddhist statues and was called *Sanjuroku Kin*. This title translates roughly as "36 birds," the discrepancy lying in that a *kin* in this case is a mythological bird not having a simple equivalent in Western culture. The title references a tale in Buddhist folklore in which a magical bird, *kin*, and its two attendants bothered a monk. The trio of visitors continued every hour for twelve hours and a total of thirty-six *kin*.

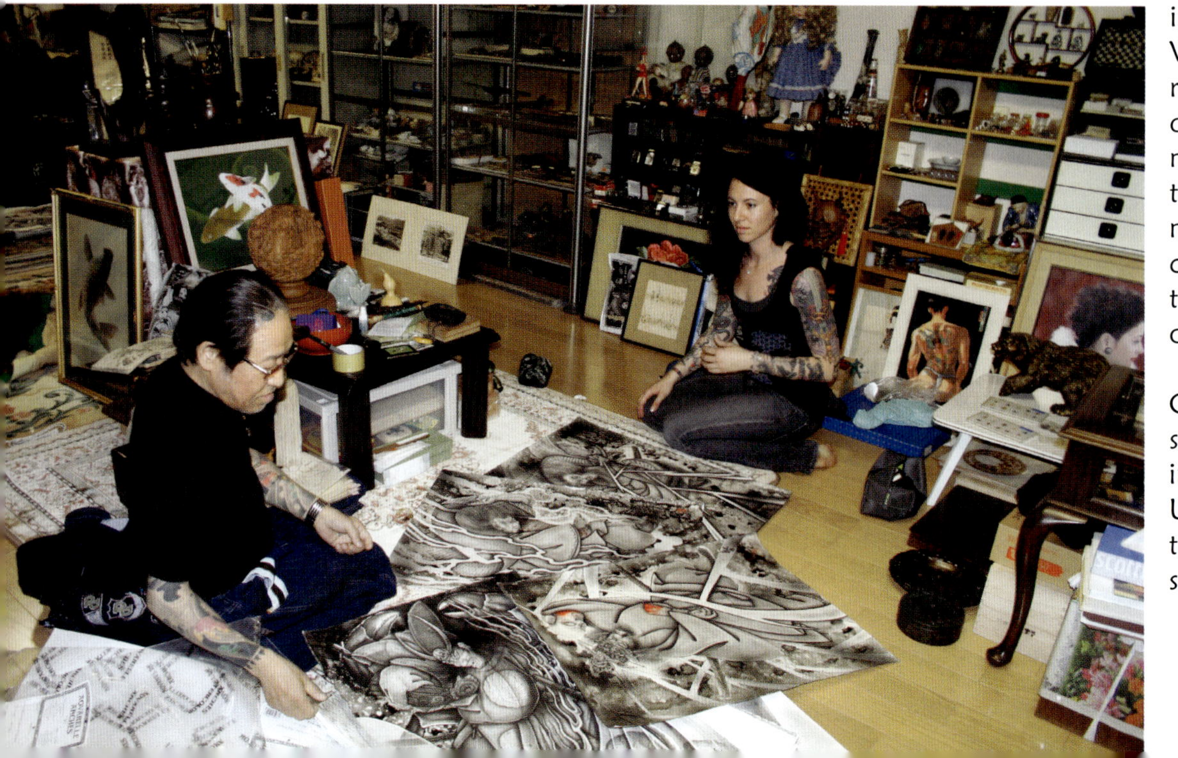

The *kanji*, or Chinese character, for *kin* struck Horiyoshi III as an inspiration for his series. Upon further investigation, he found an alternate symbol with the same pronunciation but resoundingly different definitions; blood sacrifice, shortcomings, and/or a rift between two people. This macabre twist on a word like *kin* seemed odd to him. It was a bit more than coincidental and at that moment, it seemed only proper given the subject matter of his series, to settle on the number thirty-six. The stark contrast in definition of the word *kin* is relative to the juxtaposition of a collection of thirty-six Buddhist statues and thirty-six ghost prints.

Another crucial difference between Yoshitoshi's series and the new *36 Ghosts* by Horiyoshi III is the subject matter. In Yoshitoshi's *36 Ghosts*, the translation is slightly misleading, as the collection is not entirely made up of ghosts. Rather, they are illustrations of tales of *youkai*, defined in English as hobgoblin. Ghosts are the dead in one form or another but a *youkai* can be defined as a person with exceptional power or ability or that has gone through some form of metamorphosis to become supernatural. For example, Yoshitoshi features Jigoku-dayu and Oniwakamaru in his series, neither of whom were ghosts. Jigoku-dayu was a privileged

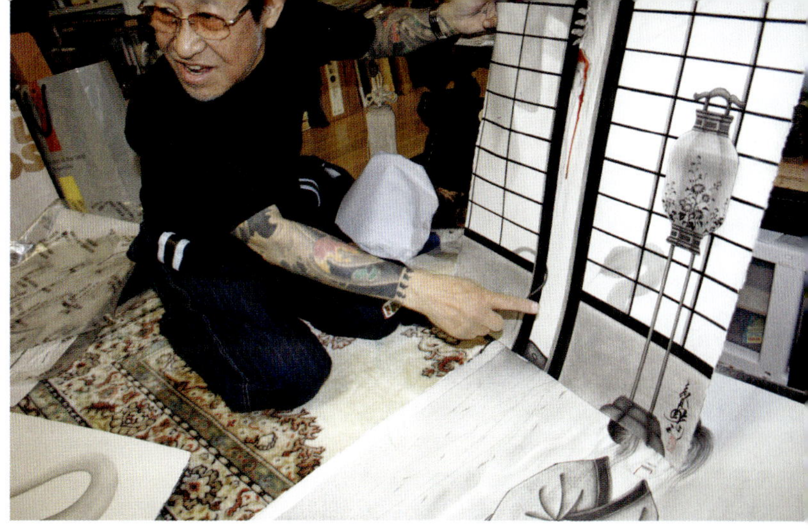

daughter of nobility forced into prostitution after the wartime death of her family. She painted images of hell on her robes and studied Buddhism to cope with the horrors of her existence. In Yoshitoshi's depiction of her, she is surrounded by dancing skeletons but is not herself a ghost. Another print shows Oniwakamaru battling a giant koi. Oniwakamaru eventually grows up to be a famous warrior and is most certainly not dead in the Yoshitoshi print. These are two examples of *youkai* prints, while sublime in their portrayal, have been mislabeled as ghosts. Horiyoshi III defines a ghost as a spirit that cannot rest peacefully. Every one of the thirty-six prints in Horiyoshi III's collection are true ghost stories, some popular legends and some of his own invention, and he is the first to illustrate a series such as this.

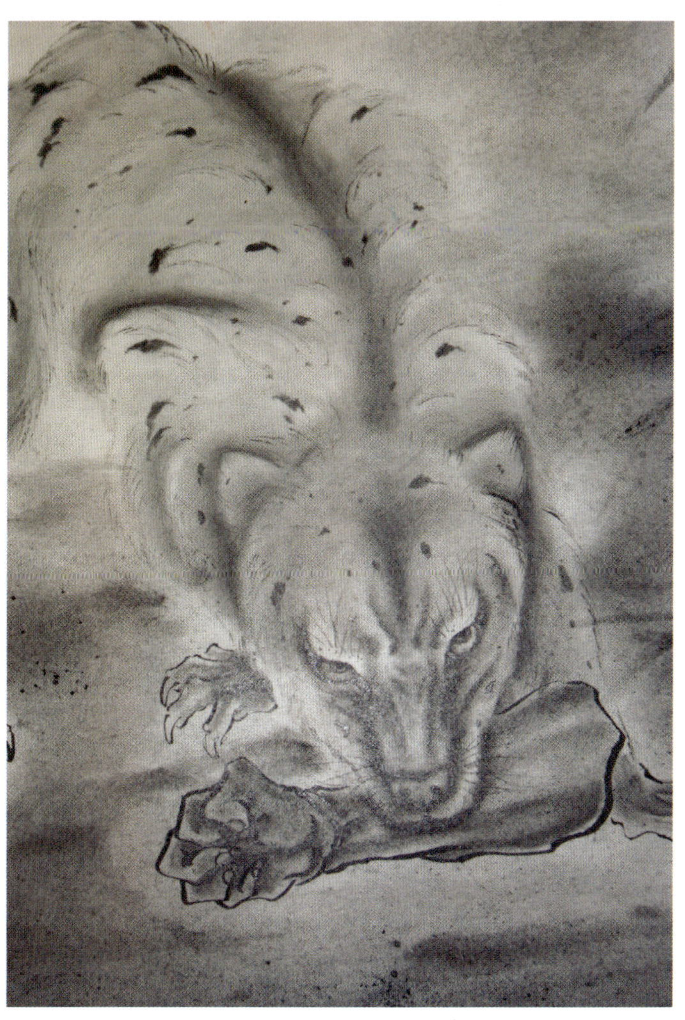

Thematically, many of the stories come from the theatre, *noh* and *kabuki*; others come from local legend and myth, while some are entirely from the imagination of the master himself. Japanese culture preaches the existence of a spirit in everyone. They believe good people go to heaven and that bad people go to hell. Ghosts are trapped in between, on earth. To become a ghost, there must be a malevolence or foul play that caused the person's death; they carry a grudge into the afterlife. Horiyoshi III defines a ghost as a spirit that cannot stay in the "other world" peacefully and is fated to wander in a past form, obsessed with revenge. He links this storytelling phenomenon to class war and inequities in the Japanese social structure. Ghosts give power to the powerless, they offer a

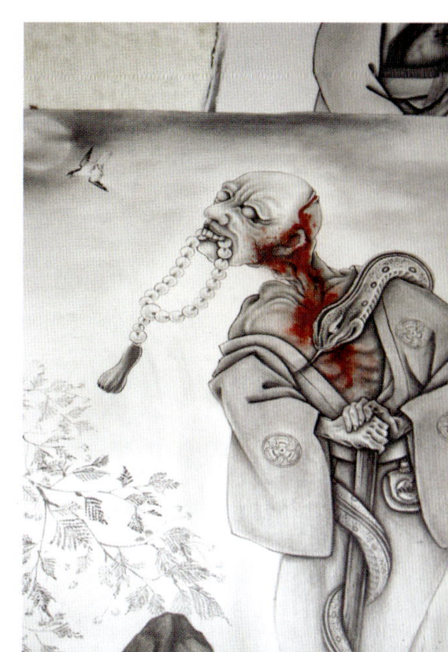

reversal of the power structure that is otherwise impossible. It is the only time the oppressed can have power and inflict revenge on a tormentor from a "higher" class. Ghost stories also warn against spiritual weakness and jealousy. In Horiyoshi III's words, "We are human, everybody has envy and desire… ghosts existence is a warning about envy and desire."

This is the political and historical context for this collection. There is also a visual experience that is universal without prior knowledge, the hand of the artist cultivated through years of practice and the evolution of his technique. Horiyoshi III draws from a spectrum of influence from comedy to the perverse. This is seen in the array of detail in the images. I noticed the presence of animals in many of the pieces. He credits Mayumi for this. In fact, as he spread the paintings out in front of us, we noted that over one third of the drawings included some form of animal life. He pointed out snakes, bats, crabs, cats, dogs, birds, dragons, and in the ghost portrait of Mayumi, she is shown with her unique pet, a slow lorry, clinging to her kimono. In addition to the vast array of fauna, there is attention paid to the plant kingdom in his images. This is not atypical to his work. Nature plays an important role in Japanese art and culture, and seasons are often denoted using the depiction of appropriately blooming flowers. The most common examples are cherry blossoms and peonies for spring, chrysanthemums and maple leaves for fall. We noticed irises in one of the drawings and learned that they too were a late spring flower. Little did we know at that time that we would soon see hundreds of them later that week in a shrine in Kyoto. Another detail that Horiyoshi III wanted us to note was the hour at which the images were placed. He pointed out a "*shoji* ghost" that he created, one casting a shadow outside a *shoji* screen door. The image captures a bright

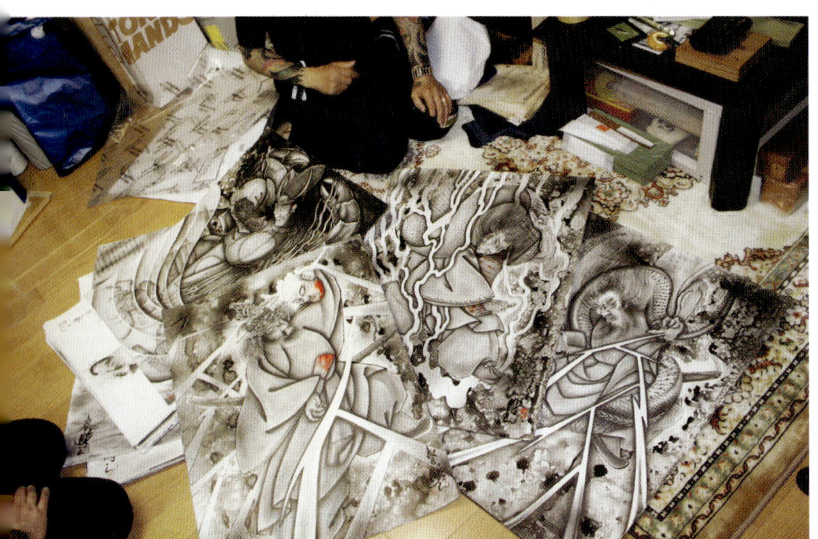

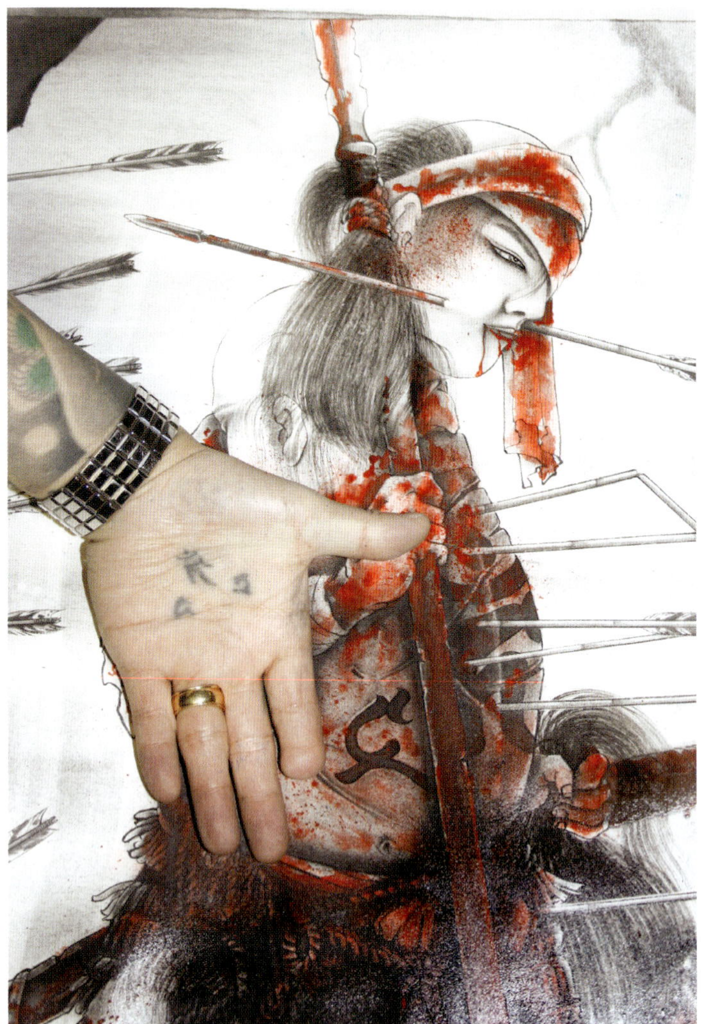

Horiyoshi III's left palm, tattooed with the *bonji* representing Fudōmyō-ō and attendants, Seitaka and Kongara. The warrior in the drawing bears these symbols on the frontispiece of his armor. This is one of Horiyoshi III's personal favorites and was especially proud of the warrior's "handsome" looks.

midday light that is called *hiru-sagari*. This lighting situation connotes the vantage point of the viewer from inside of the room. In another print dusk is used to enhance a depiction of a young arrow-pierced warrior's swan song. Horiyoshi III describes this as "strong light", the high contrast lighting used in this image is evocative, and tempers the image.

Horiyoshi III initially believed that ghost stories took place during the summer that it was a "ghost season." In the formative stages of his research, he was reading a Kabuki play about a female ghost named "Oiwa." Oiwa's husband was a samurai and he wanted to rid himself of her so he could be with another woman. He tried to contract out her death, but ultimately he killed her with poison. The poison caused her eye to swell up and her hair to fall out, leaving her condemned to roam the earth disfigured. In the end she comes back to

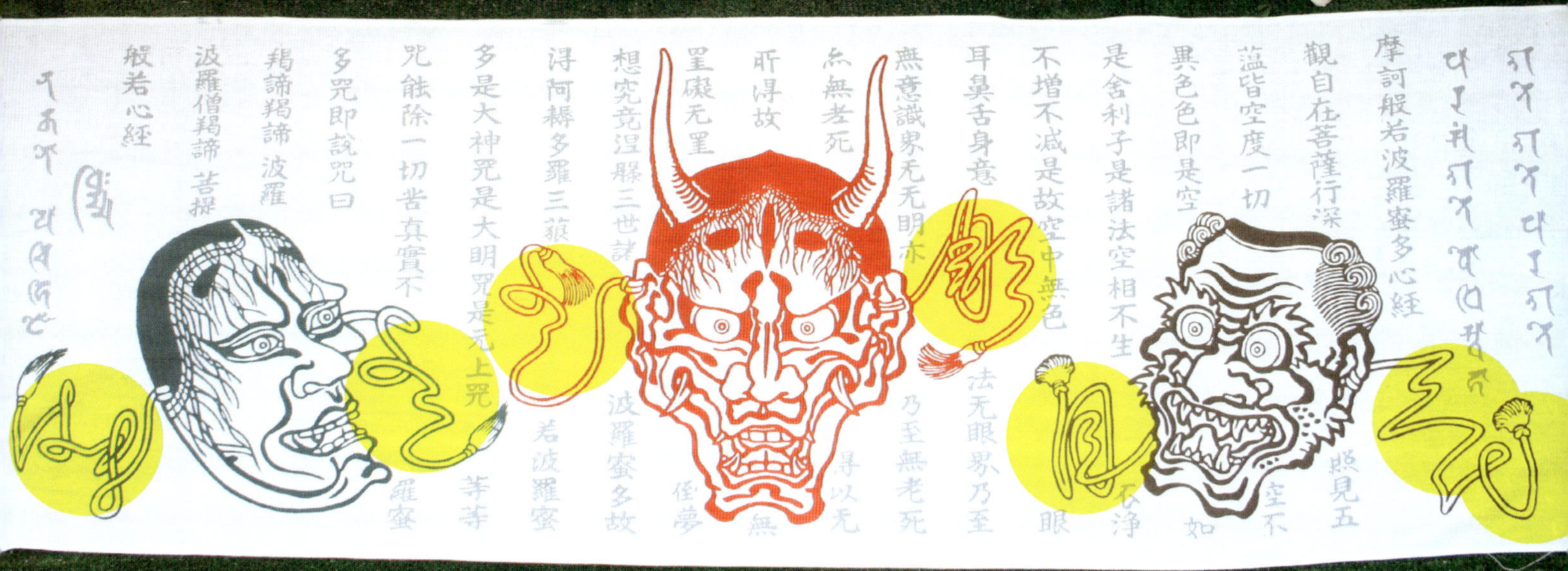

Above:
Tenugui by Horiyoshi III. The ropes of the mask spell out "San-dai-me, Hori-yo-shi, Yoko-hama" from right to left in *kanji* and *hiragana*.

Below:
Business card by Horiyoshi III with hidden text in the illustration. The highlighted *hiragana* spells out "*i-re-zu-mi*"- Japanese for tattoo.

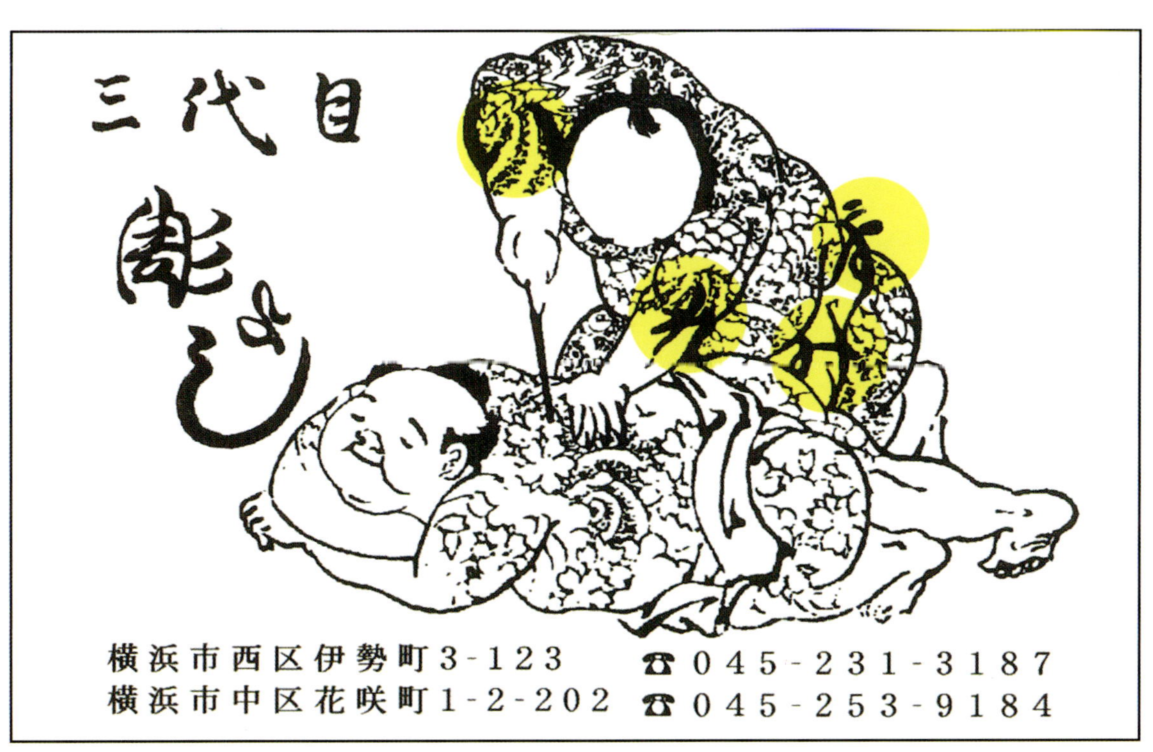

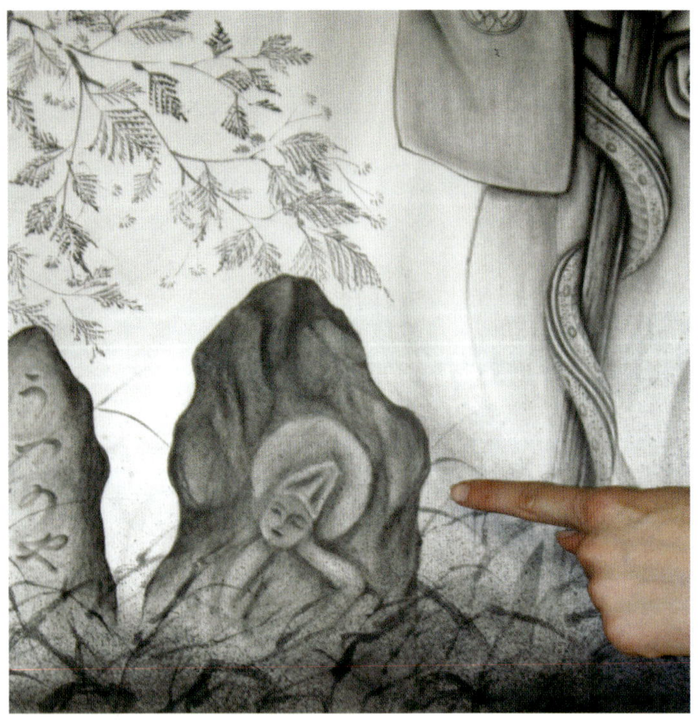

her husband as a ghost and kills him. The dramatic conclusion takes place in winter. This detail shifted Horiyoshi III's perspective and inspired him to expand the seasons depicted within the prints beyond summer.

Looking at the ghost prints with Horiyoshi III you can see his strong sense of humor. He loves hiding things within the drawings and delighted in pointing them out to us, male and female genitalia hidden in trees, kimono folds and rock formations. This is very common in Japanese print art: I have often seen hidden images in many Edo period prints. However, I think this goes beyond tradition. Horiyoshi III seems to be quite fond of the concept of hidden images and meanings. His old business card hides the word *irezumi*, "Yokohama" is written into his *tenugui*, and every piece of art he has given Horitaka for his convention graphics is laden with hidden messages. I later found many "magic eye" books in his studio, he is fascinated by the duality of these images. Subtle messages, meant to be overlooked by most are simply a trademark of Horiyoshi III's art. All of these minutiae build the whole, there are many layers both visually and conceptually in these works. His application of medium to paper is tedious, then layering as many details as he sees fit relative to the image. Horiyoshi III works off of feelings, or visual images he perceives, then evolves this by citing specific details such as objects, animals, or flowers.

Japanese culture is heavily laden with superstition. Numerology, as aforementioned, often plays a role in these notions. Horiyoshi III explained to me that the number four shares a phonetic association with the word for death. For this reason there are hotels in Japan that do not have fourth floors. This idea was brought to my attention when viewing an image of four Japanese masks. Masks are a common tattoo motif and I have always understood that Horiyoshi III instructs that masks be shown and tattooed in odd numbers. The choice of which masks belong together is also important as an entirely separate issue but the number is crucial, one, three, five, seven, nine. Here we saw Horiyoshi III in violation of his own rule, there were four. This was the fourth book in his series. He was deliberately calling to mind the concept of death. This unlucky hex, one that we were ever so mindful to avoid, was being confronted. This undoubtedly opened conversation on the subject and it was clear to me that a motivating factor behind this project was the master's confrontation of his own mortal-

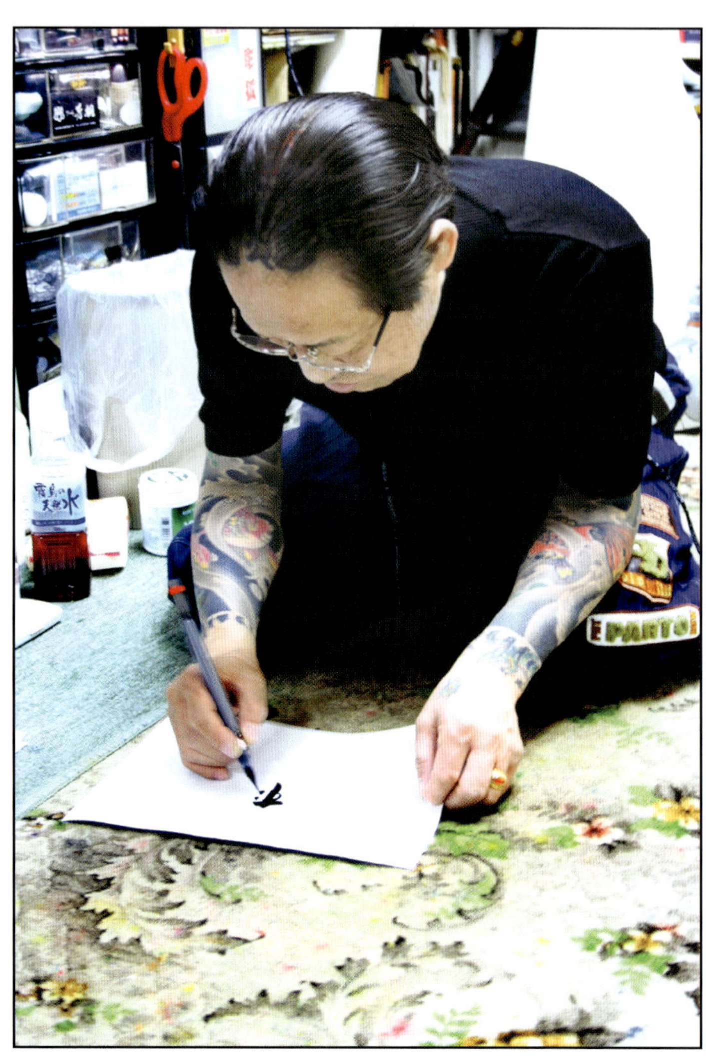

ity. Having the opportunity to see this whole piece with Horiyoshi III's disclosure felt like a glimpse into his psyche, or rather, a guided tour. He showed us the things that haunt him, if The *Namakubi* was a venture into his fascination with the macabre, then this delved much further. In one image, he pointed out his own tombstone. The name read Nakano and it contained a *bonji*, of his own creation, that symbolized *irezumi*, tattooing. I was to witness the inception of myth. There were many moments at which I was moved by his candor. Many people try to outrun death, deny it. He seemed to be exploring it as an artist. He has no qualms about his foray into the unmentionable, and beyond an almost spiritual, Buddhist acceptance, he seemed to almost take pleasure in it.

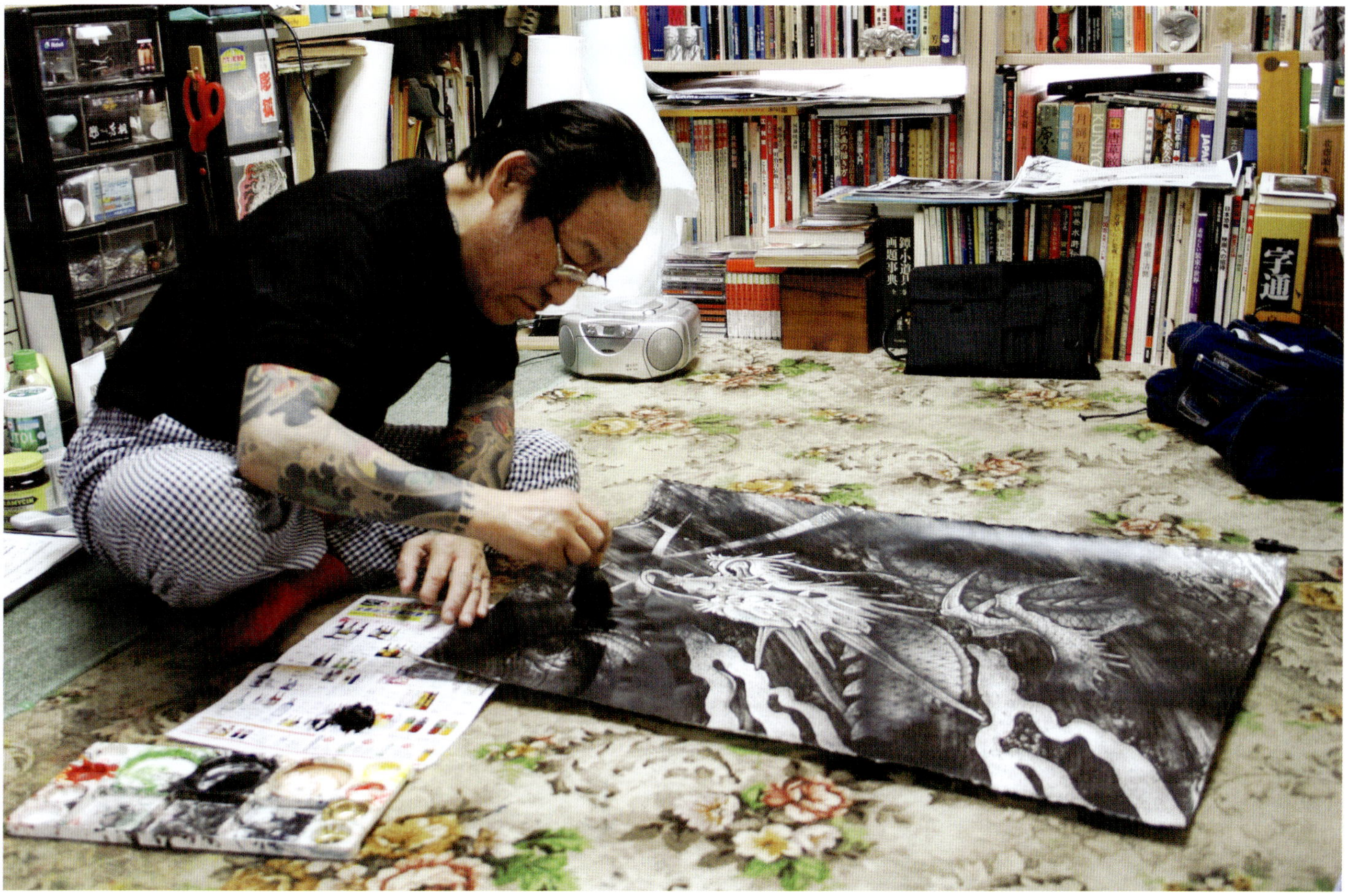

Many Western tattooers perpetuate tattoo designs by replicating the tattoo designs of the tattooists before them. Japanese tattooing is consistent with other forms of art that precede it, those created by the great masters of Japanese art. Rather than merely making new tattoo flash, Horiyoshi III has chosen to create drawings that simultaneously function as usable tattoo motif while following a larger artistic tradition and standard. For this reason,

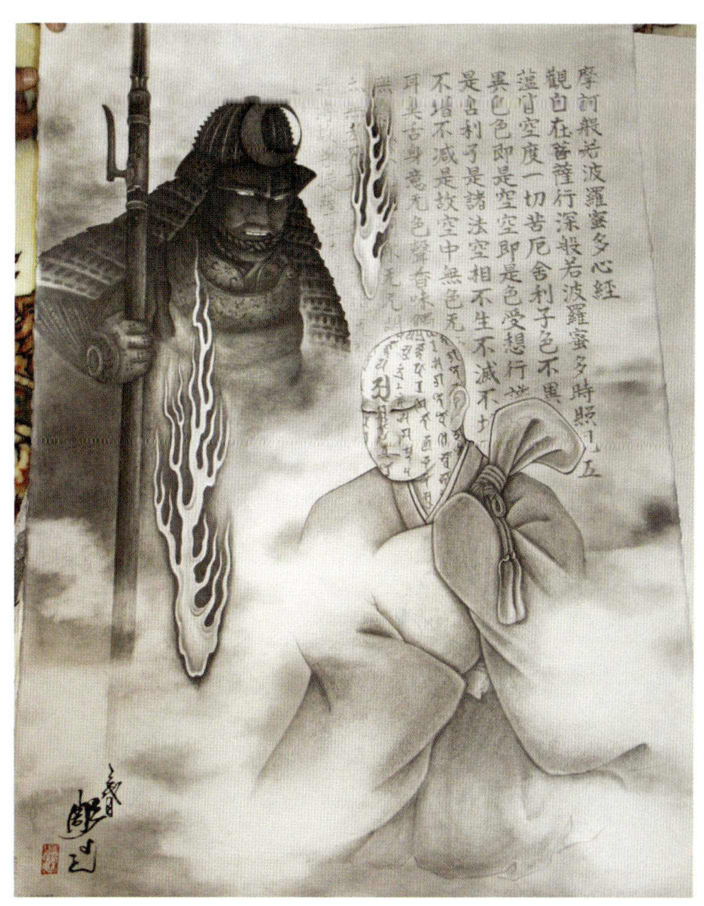

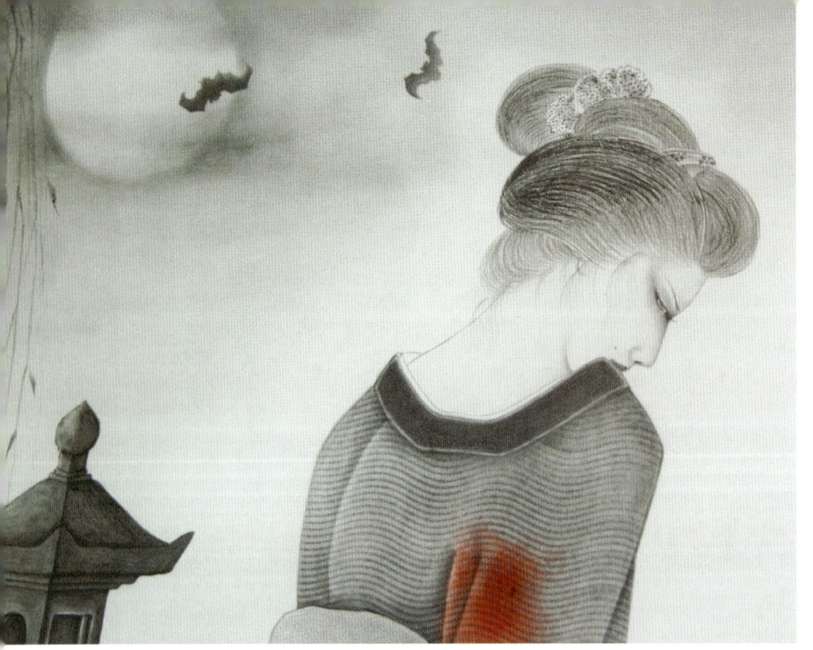

Horiyoshi III is challenged by the artists that inspire generations of tattoo artists, men like Kuniyoshi, Yoshitoshi, Kyosai and Hokusai. By creating works inspired by these great masters, he acknowledges their relevance to his craft while challenging his predecessors. The conception of such bodies of work is in effect rewriting tattoo history and updating the pool of reference material used by modern day tattooers. By making these stories and images more available, he is educating a generation and giving them a new visual reference for Japanese art and parable. His choice to publish English explanations in his work is deliberate, making his work accessible to the world at large. They can be used and enjoyed by all.

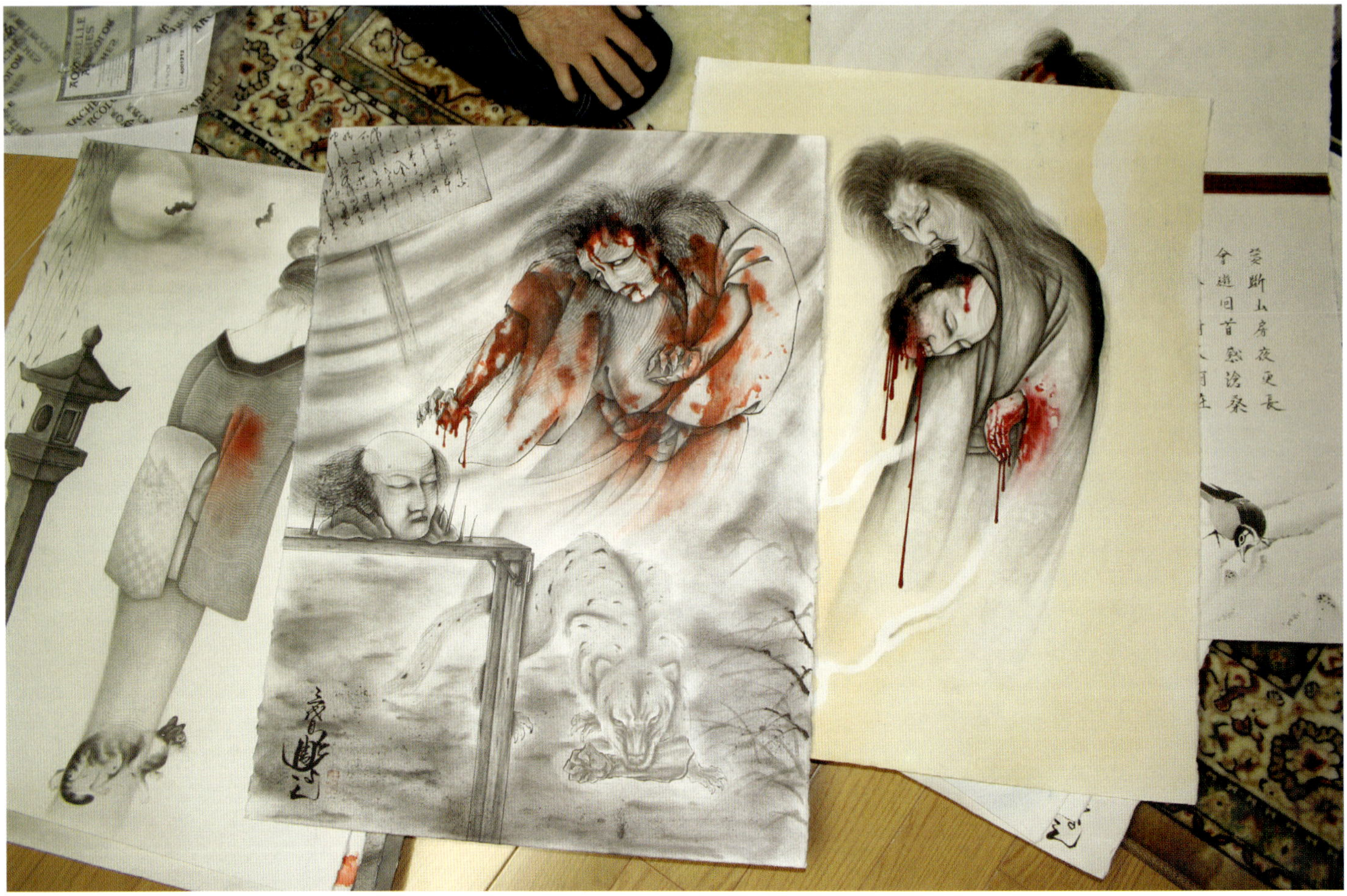

Both of these drawings depict a female ghost with a man's severed head. The one on the left is the last drawing he completed and the other one is the first of the series. Horiyoshi III felt that this comparison showed his artistic development during the project, most easily seen in the improved background and blood coloration. The redundant subject matter was purely coincidental and he only noticed this during his post project analysis.

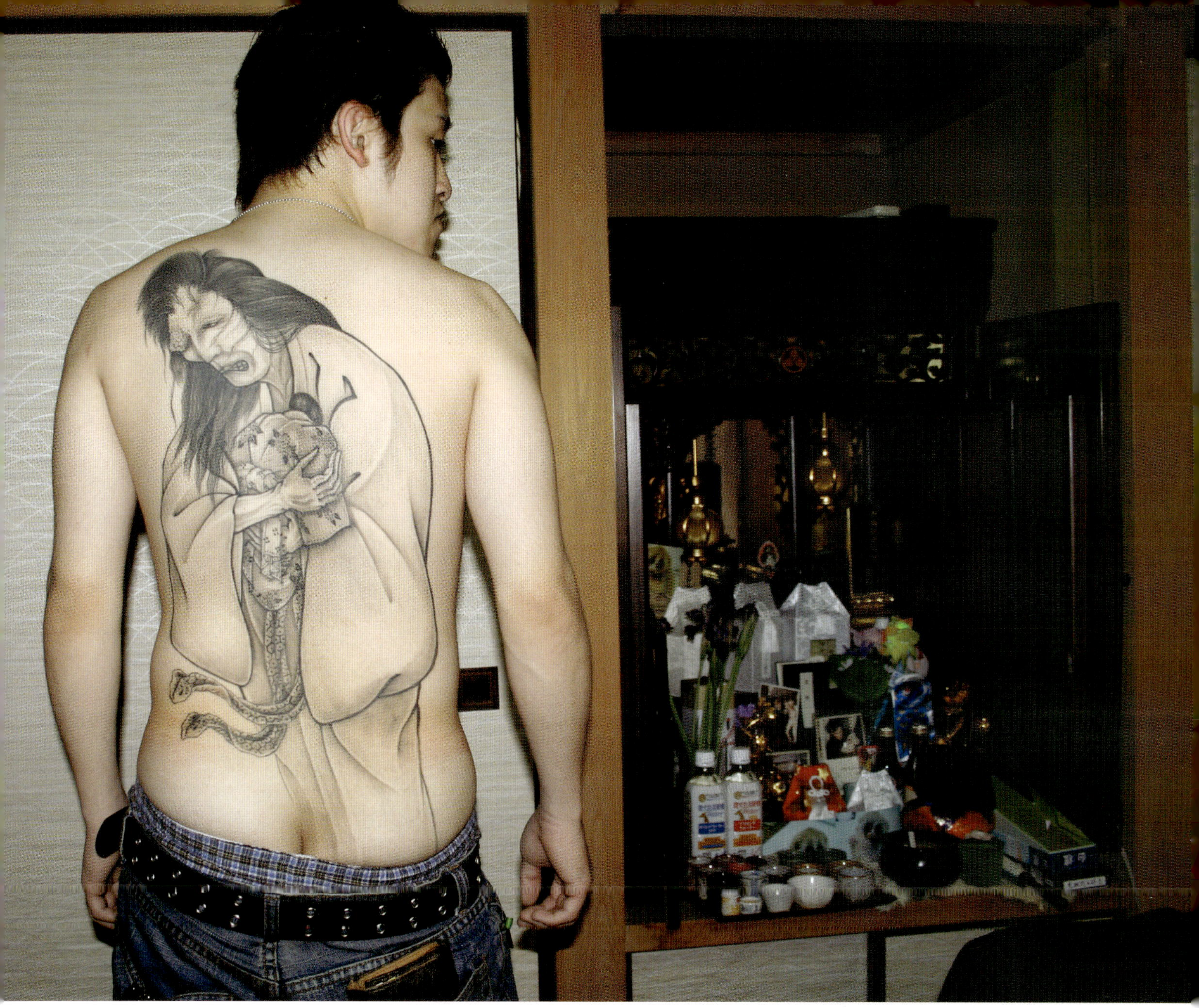

Horiyoshi III is in the process of tattooing his son with a bodysuit of ghosts with Oiwa as the central backpiece figure. When tattooing negative images such as a ghost or a severed head, it is Horiyoshi III's practice to counter the image with a good or pure symbol. He uses *bonji*- Japanese versions of Sanskrit representing Buddhist prayer and deities, to diffuse the negative energy and protect the wearer. There is similar attention to this "negative energy" in the Kabuki theatre tradition. Actors pray at temples before taking on certain roles, such as the cursed Oiwa character.

After the first tattoo session, Kazuyoshi's eye started to swell inexplicably. The same thing happened to Horiyoshi III and Mayumi started noticing bumps across her skin. She recounted to me that Horiyoshi III had not yet counterbalanced this image with a bonji, nor had Kazuyoshi made a visit to pray at the temple. They all felt that this was the reason for Kazuyoshi's swollen eye. Mayumi was perplexed that both her and her husband, even with the tattooed bonji they already wore, were also affected by the wrath of Oiwa. Kazuyoshi went and prayed to relieve his family's ailment. He understands the importance of visiting the temple in order to wear a bodysuit of ghosts and will be making yearly visits for the rest of his life. This is yet another example where spirituality, culture and tradition mix in the world of Japanese tattooing.

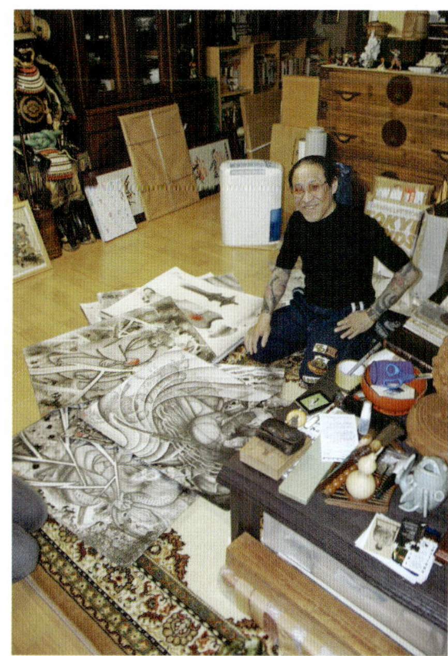

Gallery of Horiyoshi III Tattoos

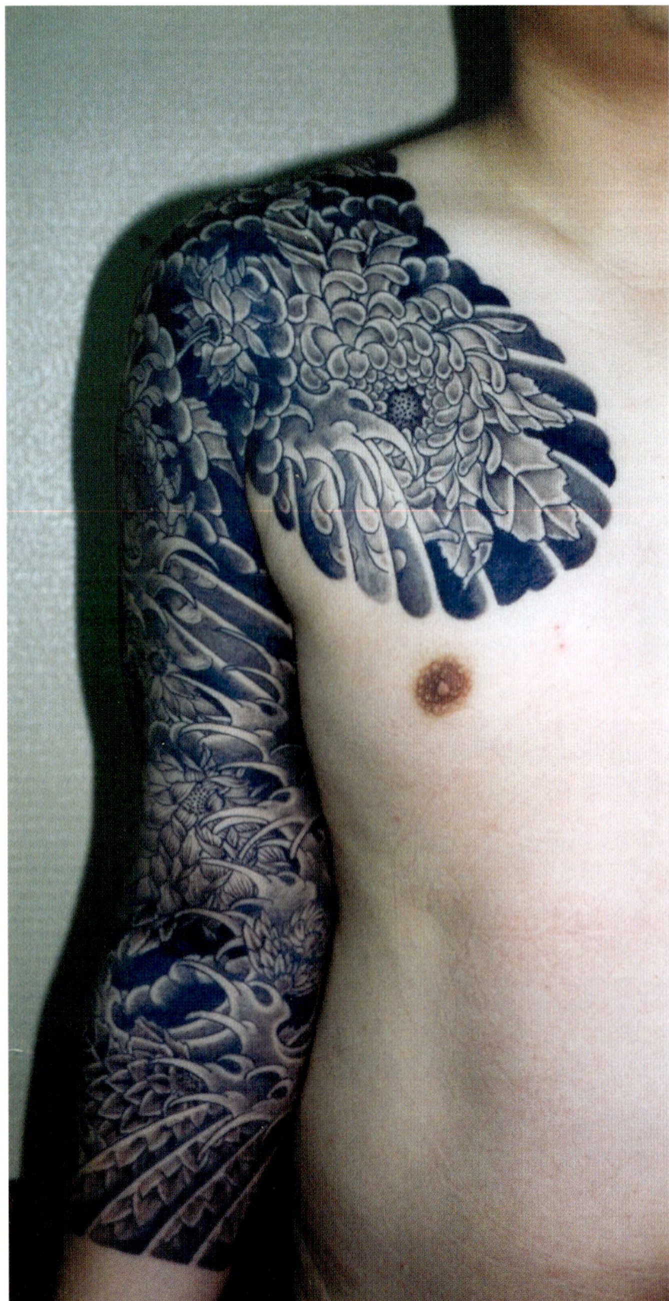

Kiku-sui. Chrysanthemum and water

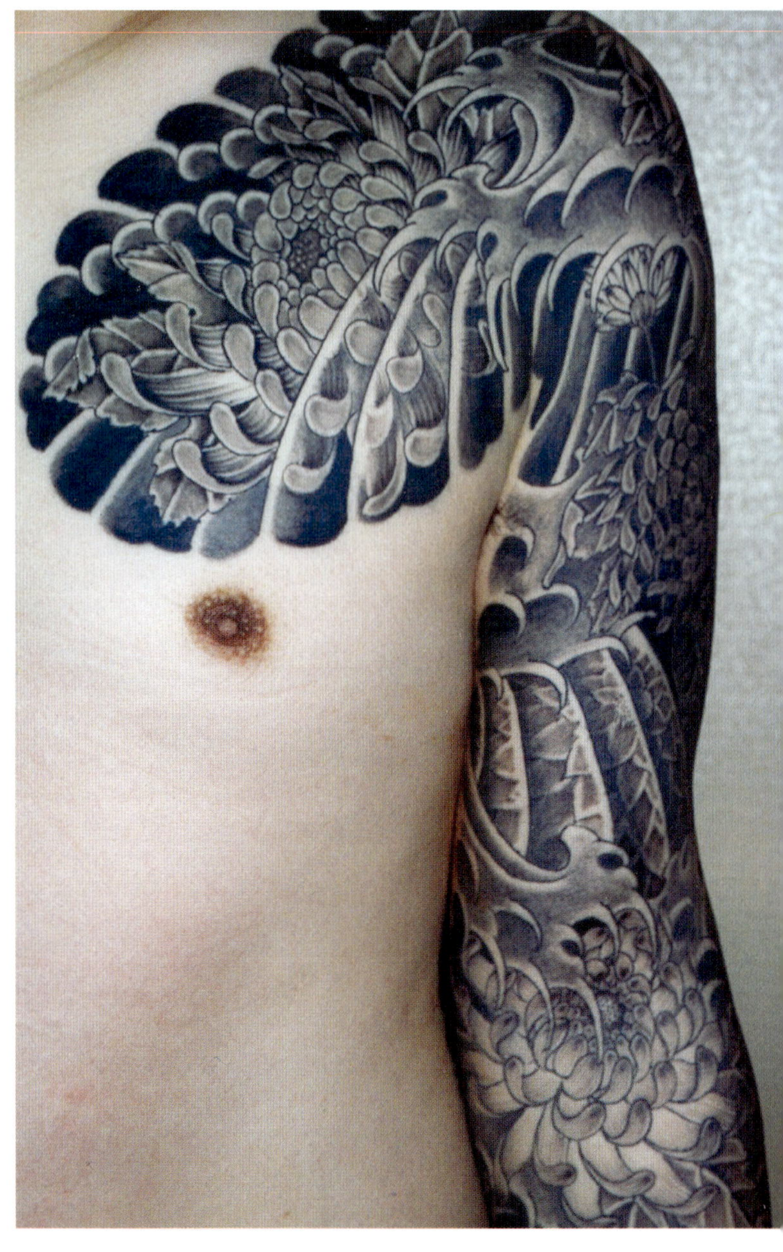

In a Chinese legend when koi fish spawn they are at their strongest and swim against the current. The strongest ones become dragons and fly out of the water. Not every koi fish becomes a dragon. In this pair of half-sleeves the koi on the right is making the transition to a dragon. This tale is believed to take place in the Yellow River and this is the purpose for the yellow color of the koi-dragon. The koi pictured below is not making it. This is apparent from his position, his stance is one of retreat. Another detail of this folk-tale illustrated in the tattoo is the fall season.

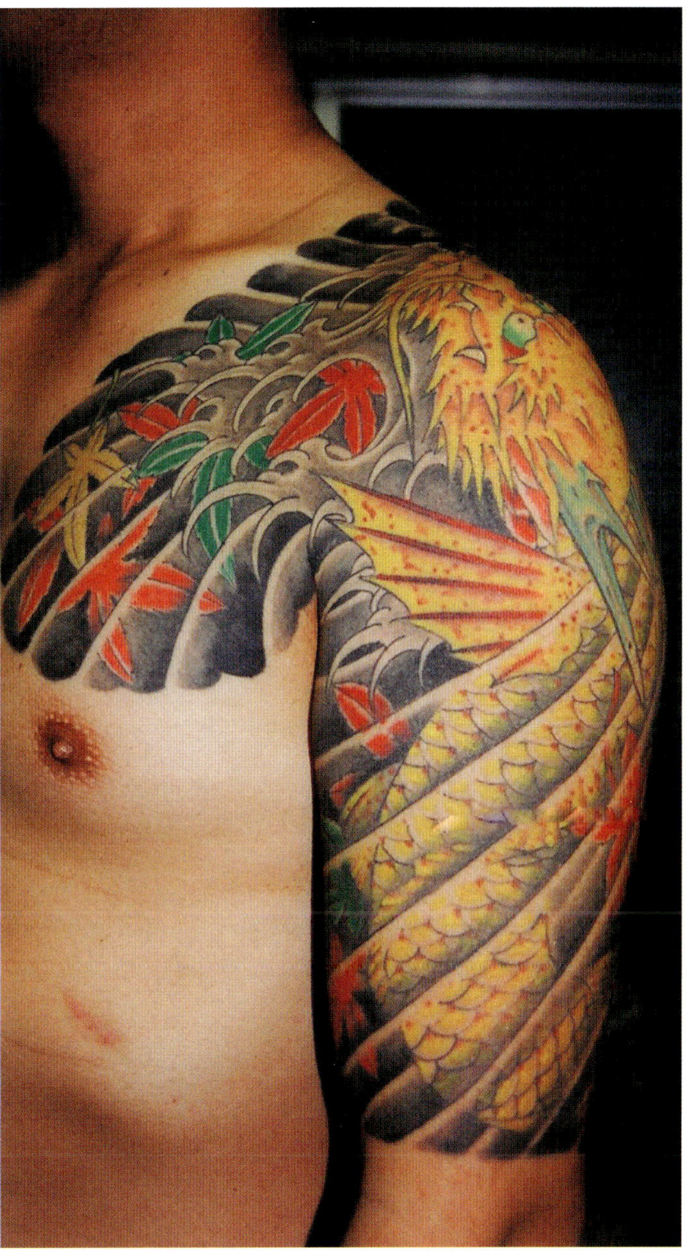

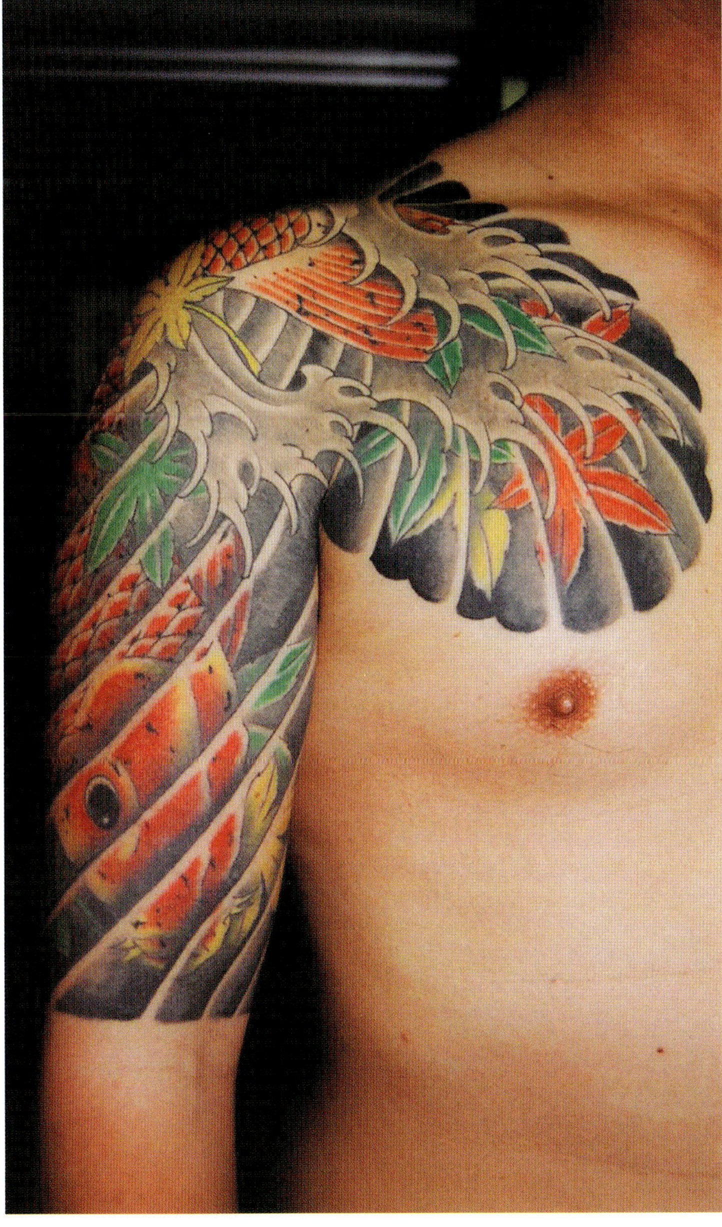

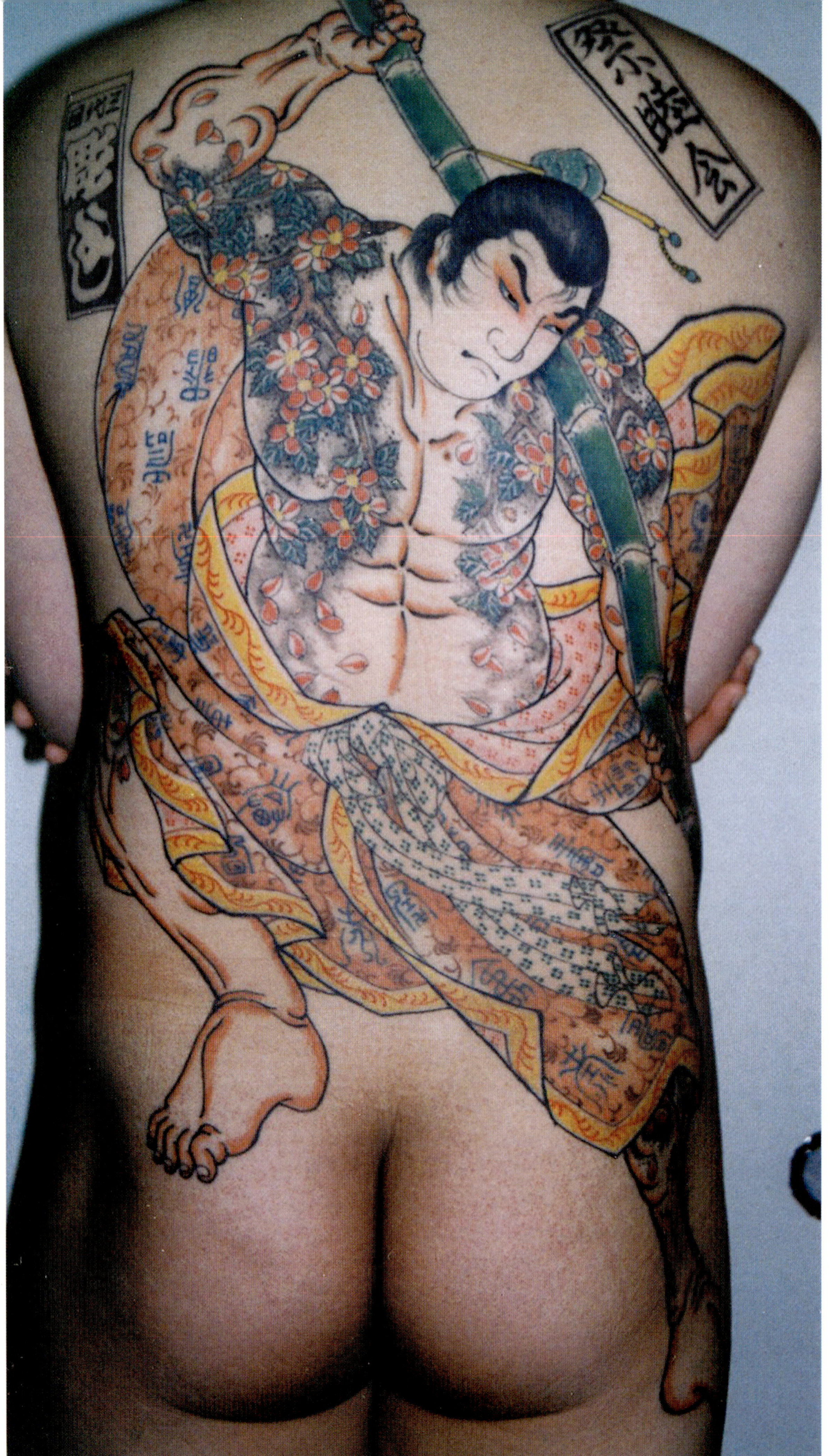

Left:
Ritsuchitaisai Genshouji. Suikoden hero, one of three brothers.

Opposite:
Ryu-ko. This depiction of a dragon and a tiger represents the "battle of heaven and earth."

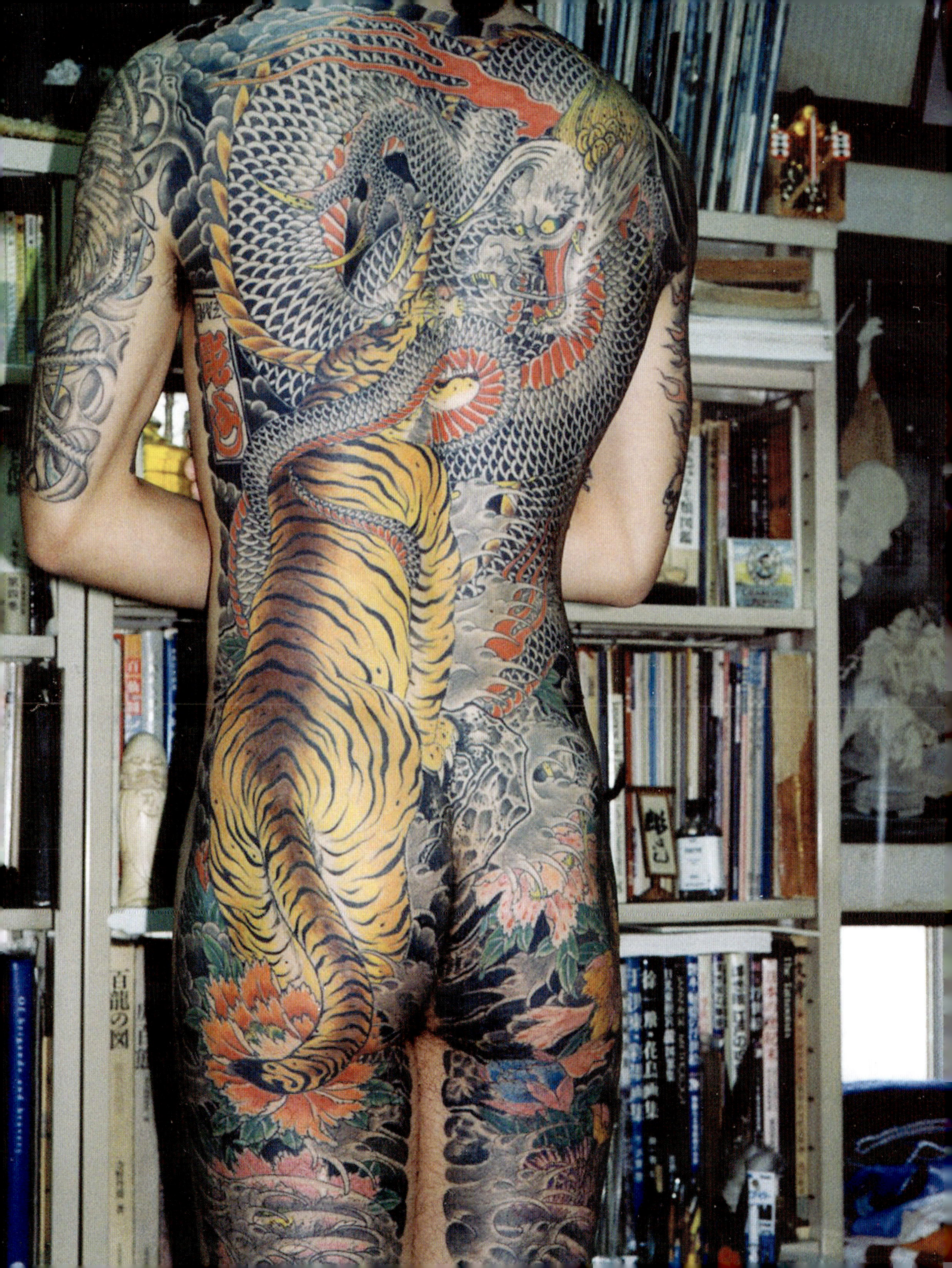
白龍の図

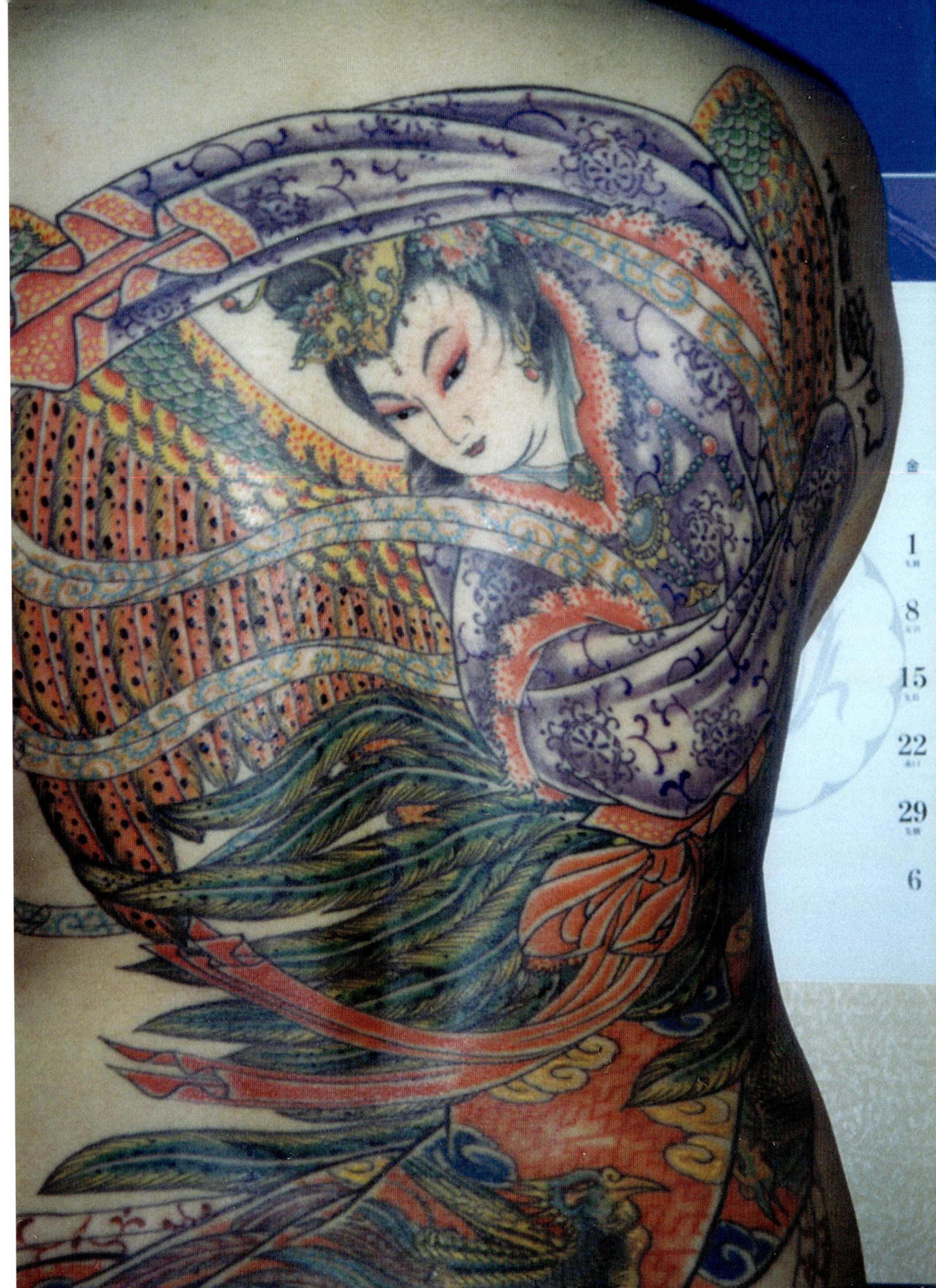

Opposite:
Tennyo. The beautiful winged maidens of Buddhist folklore, *tennyo* are similar to angels in Western mythology

Right:
Tennyo to ryu. Tennyo and dragon.

Horiyoshi III compared the two photos and stated: "The designs look the same but the women are different....[Points at each pair of eyes] There is a different placement of the signature, there are different patterns on the dress."

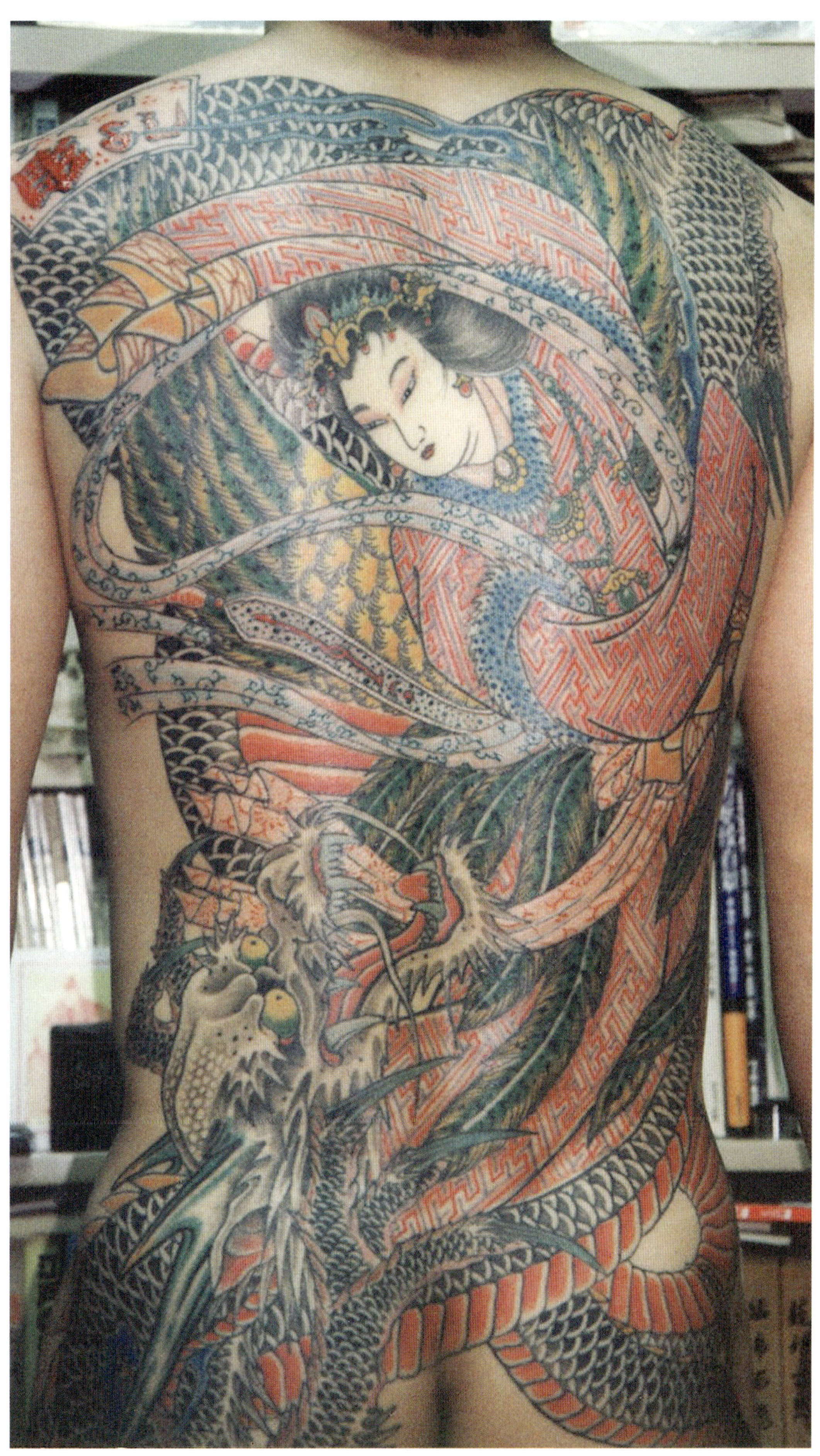

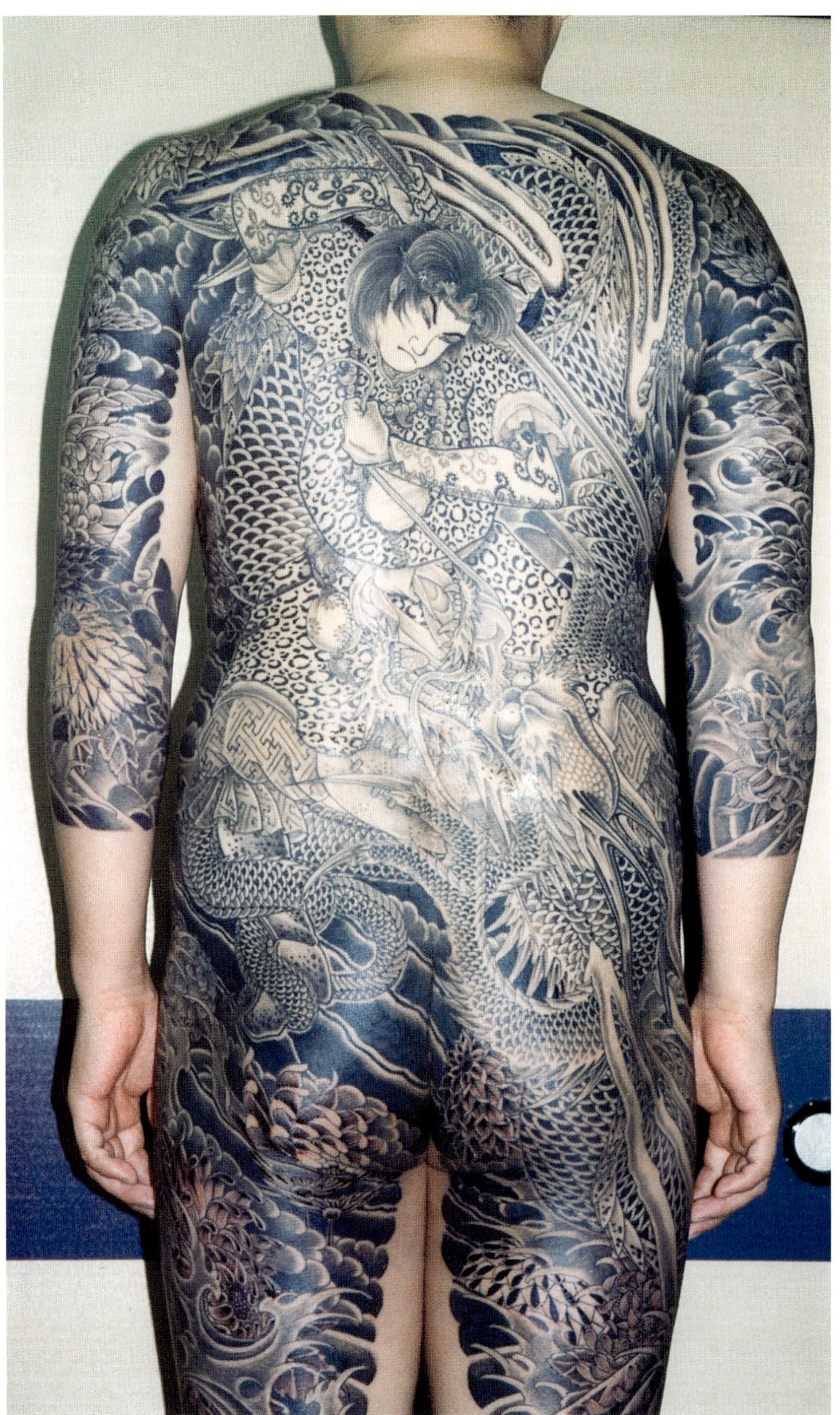

Left:
Susano-o no Mikoto. "In the story he fights and kills an eight-headed/eight-tailed snake. (Yamata no Orochi) In the tattoo I choose a dragon instead." Susano-o no Mikoto is the half-brother to the Shinto goddess Amaterasu Omikami. This *kami*, Shinto "divine-spirit", may symbolize tempestuous weather and is associated with natural disasters. A forefather to Japan's legacy of emperors, he is depicted in the tattoo with the three treasures of the empire he acquired during the battle with Yamata no Orochi. The famous sword, *kusunagi*, the jeweled necklace, *magatama*, and the sacred mirror, *yata no kagami*.

Opposite:
Ryu, dragon.

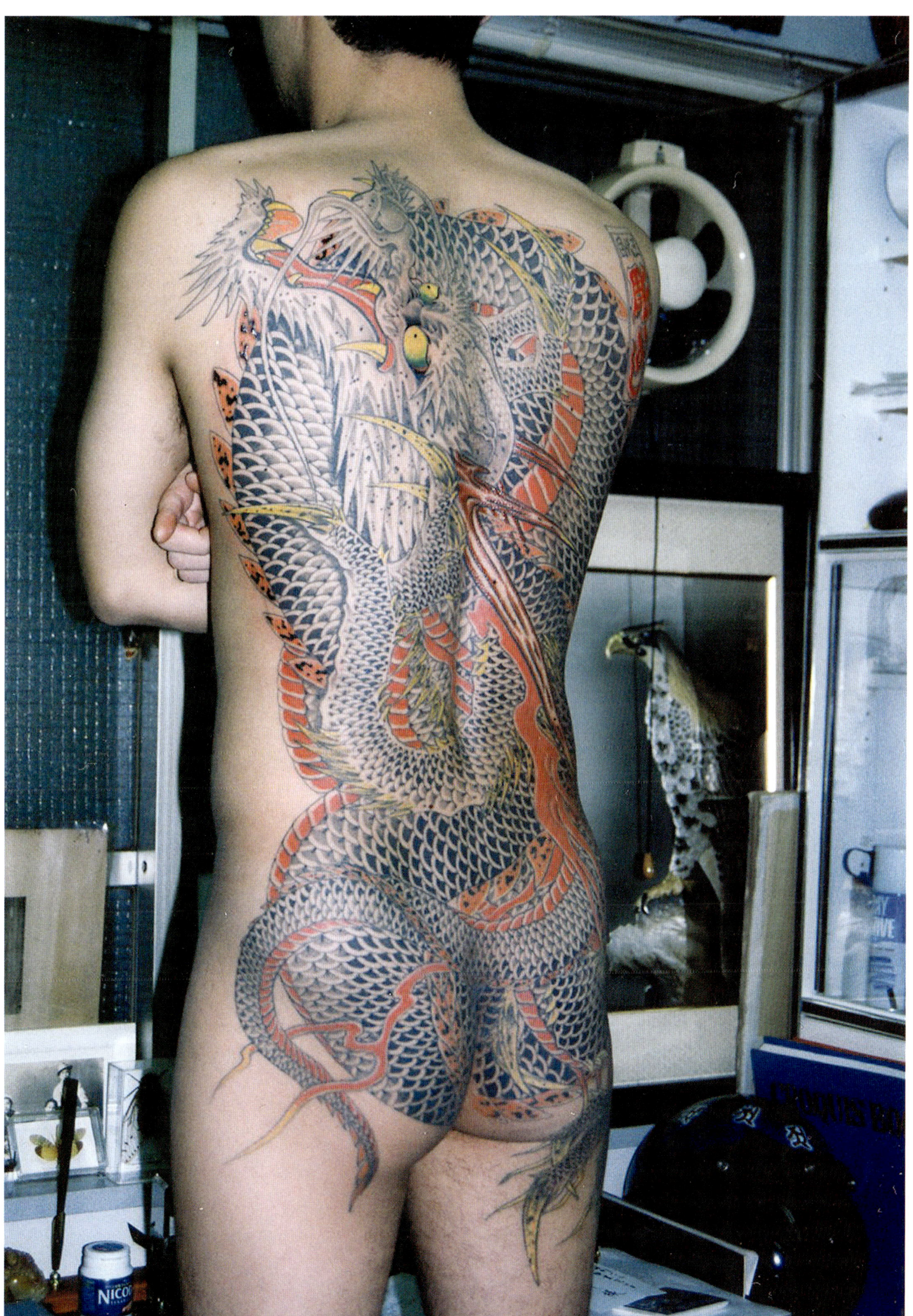

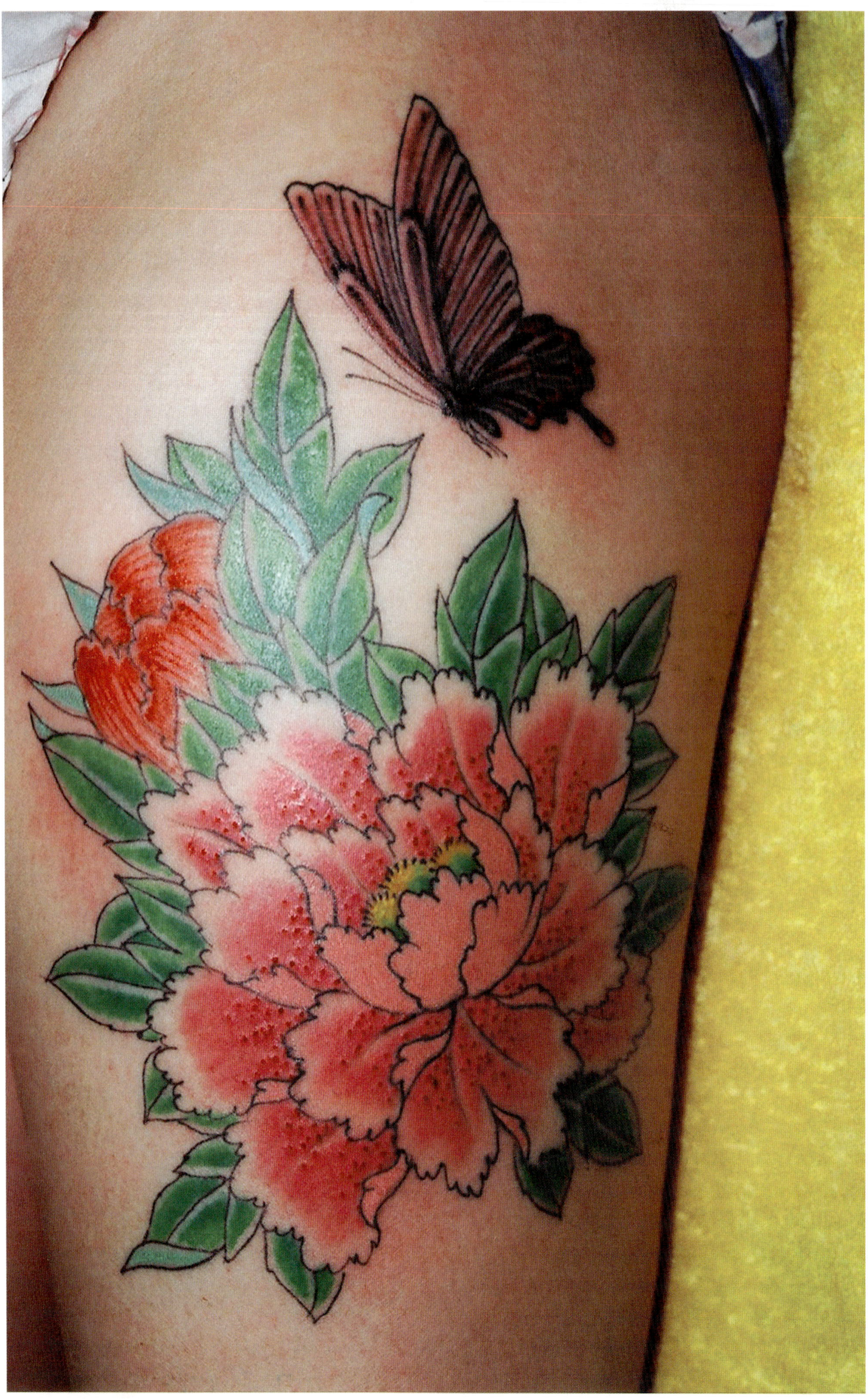

Left:
Botan to cho.
Peonies and butterfly. "New style."

Opposite:
Rain god.

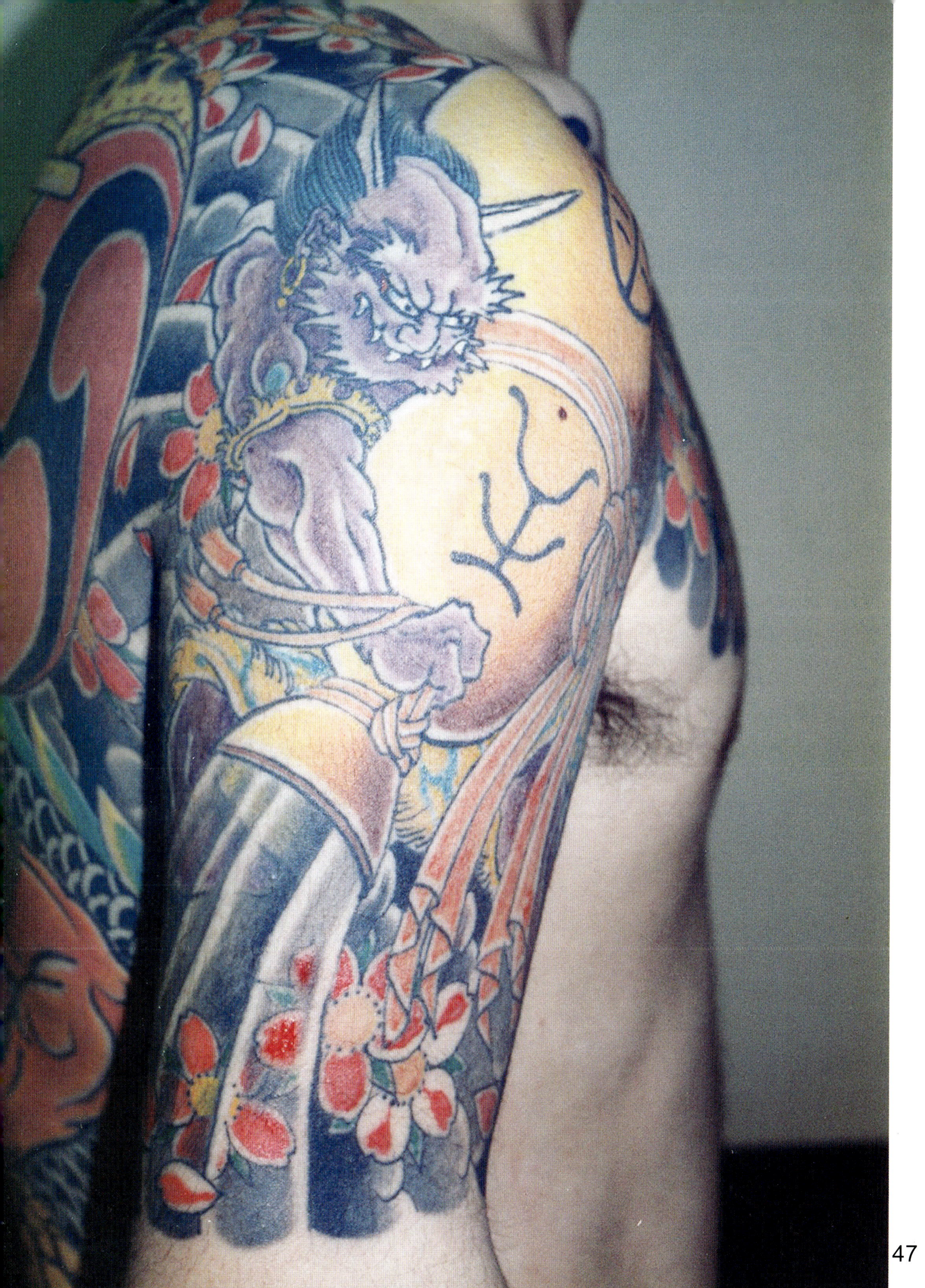

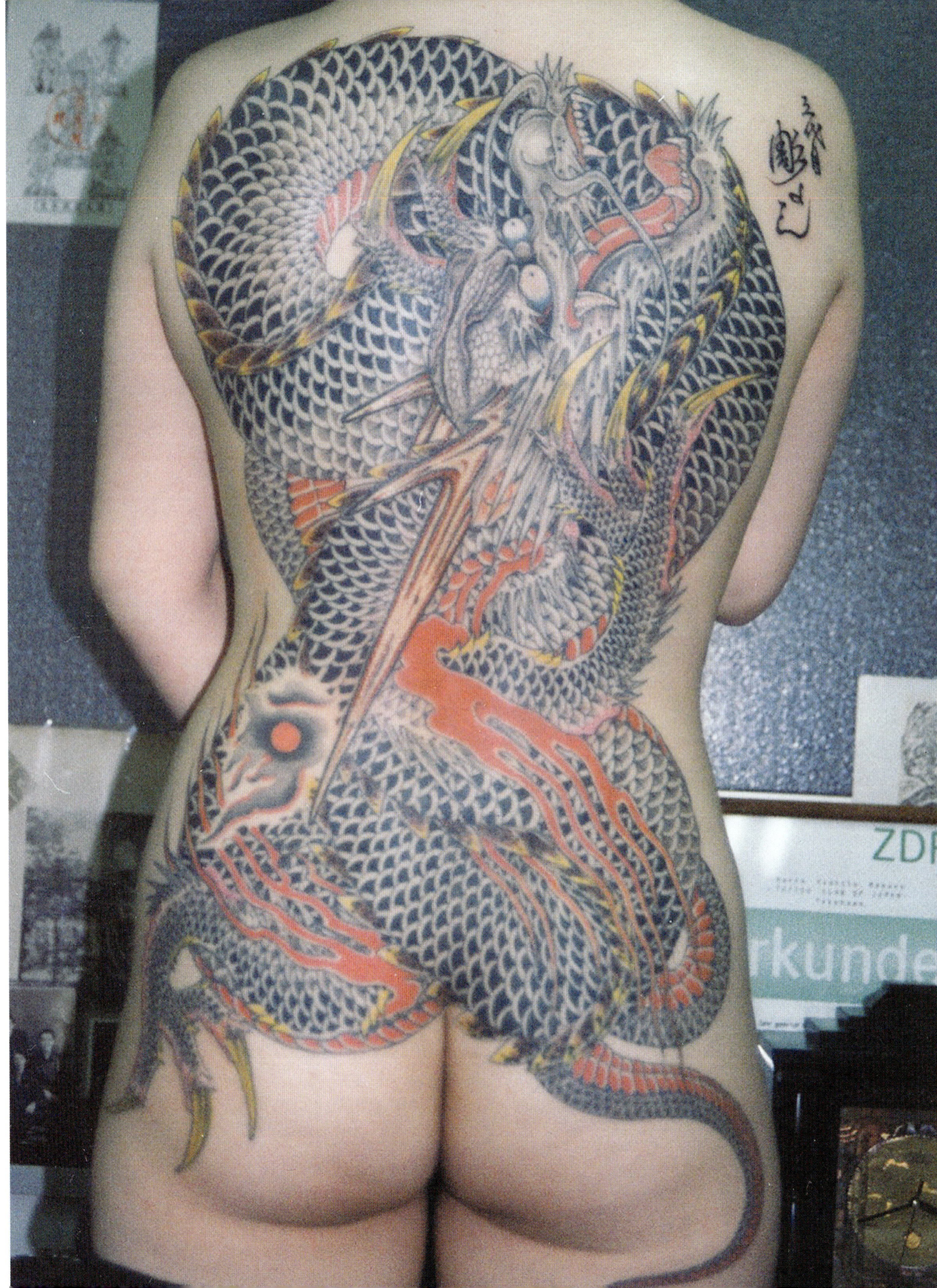
三代目
彫よし
ZDF
rkunde

To the left is a woman's backpiece of a dragon, to the right is a man's. Horiyoshi III pointed out the different fashion in which he signed his name to each piece. The loose calligraphy in the woman's backpiece appears feminine next to the bold "chop" used in the man's.

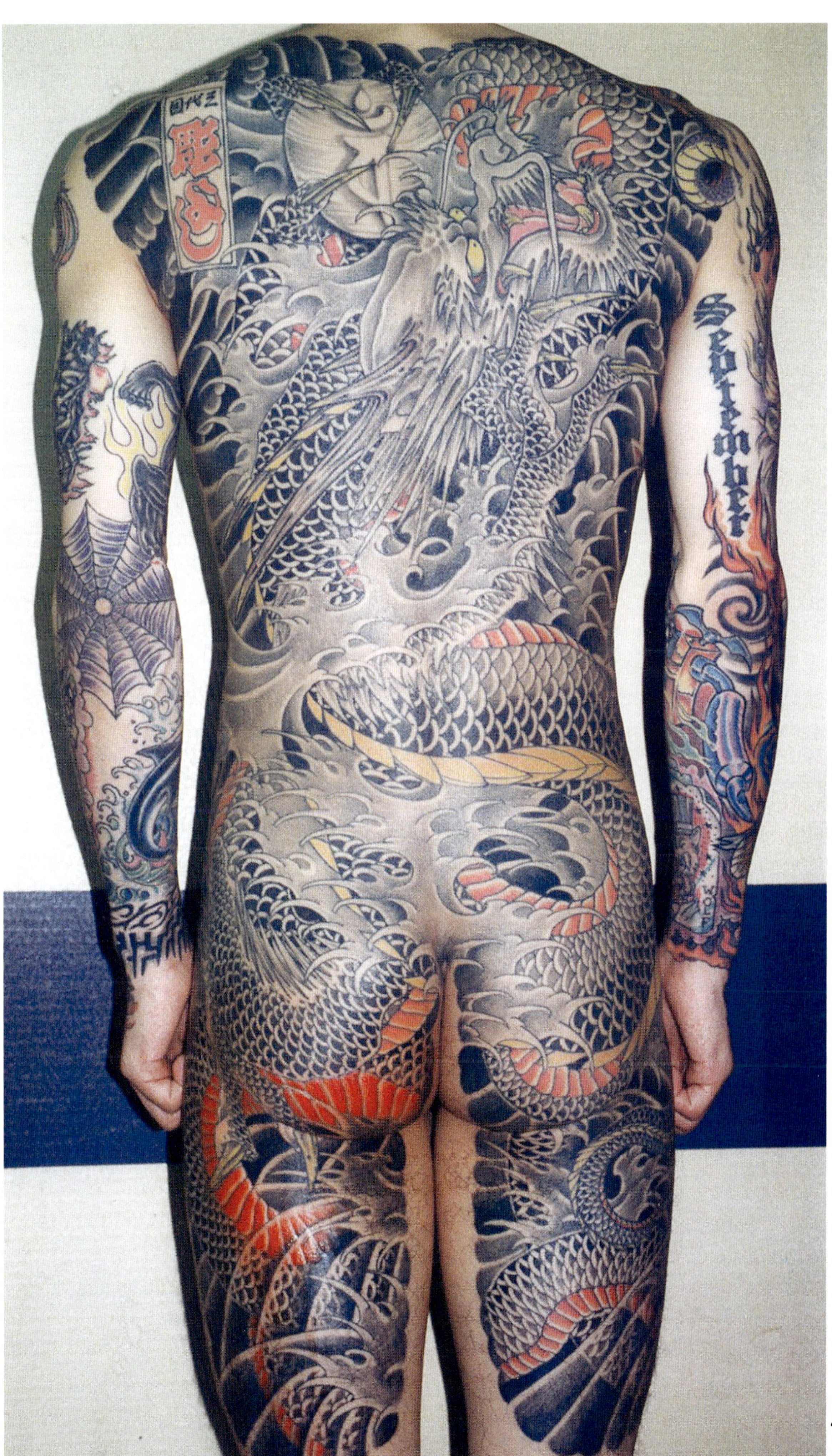

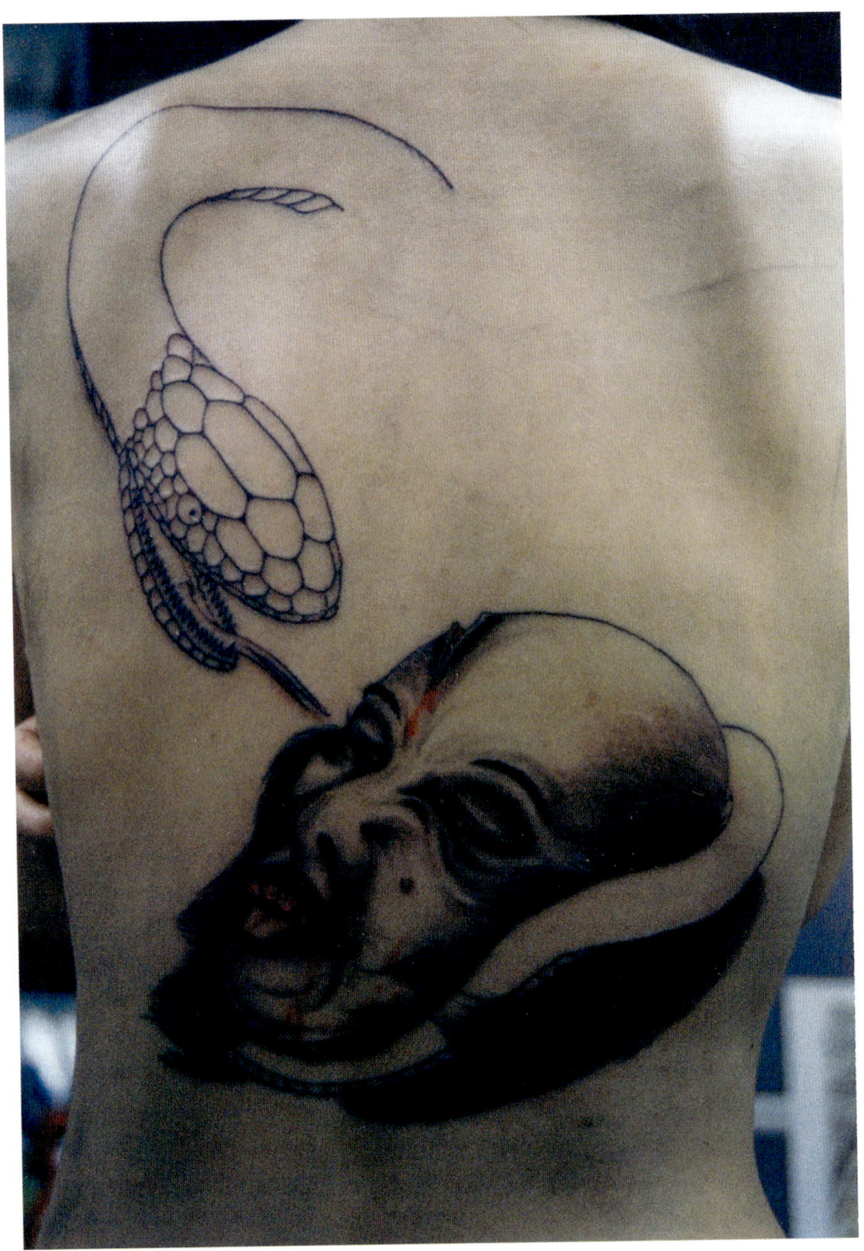

Left:
"In progress" photo of *namakubi to hebi*. Severed head and snake.

Opposite:
Ushiwakamaru, *karasu tengu to sakura*. This depicts the young warrior Ushiwakamaru learning swordsmanship from the crow *tengu*. They are using wooden swords because they are in practice.

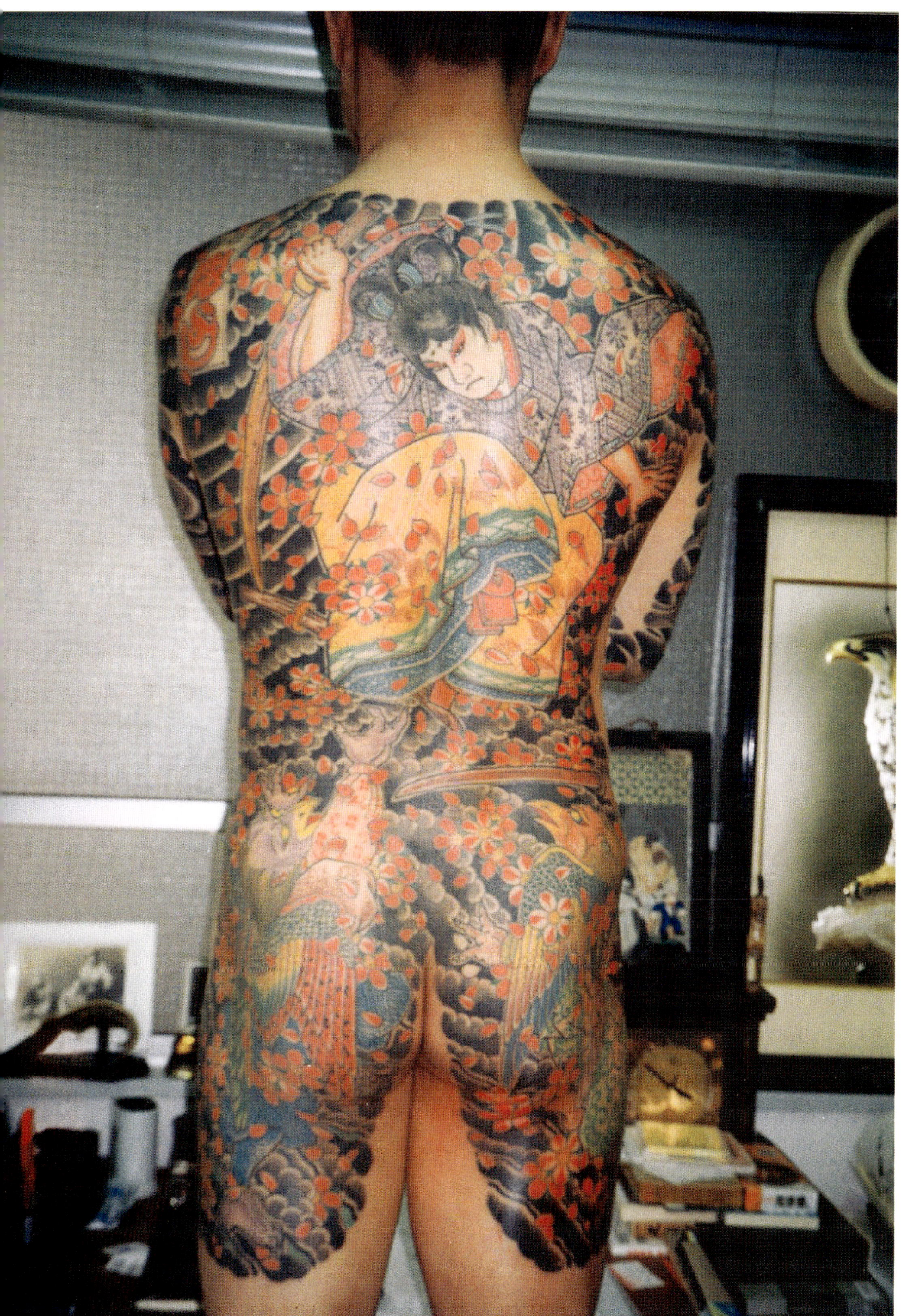

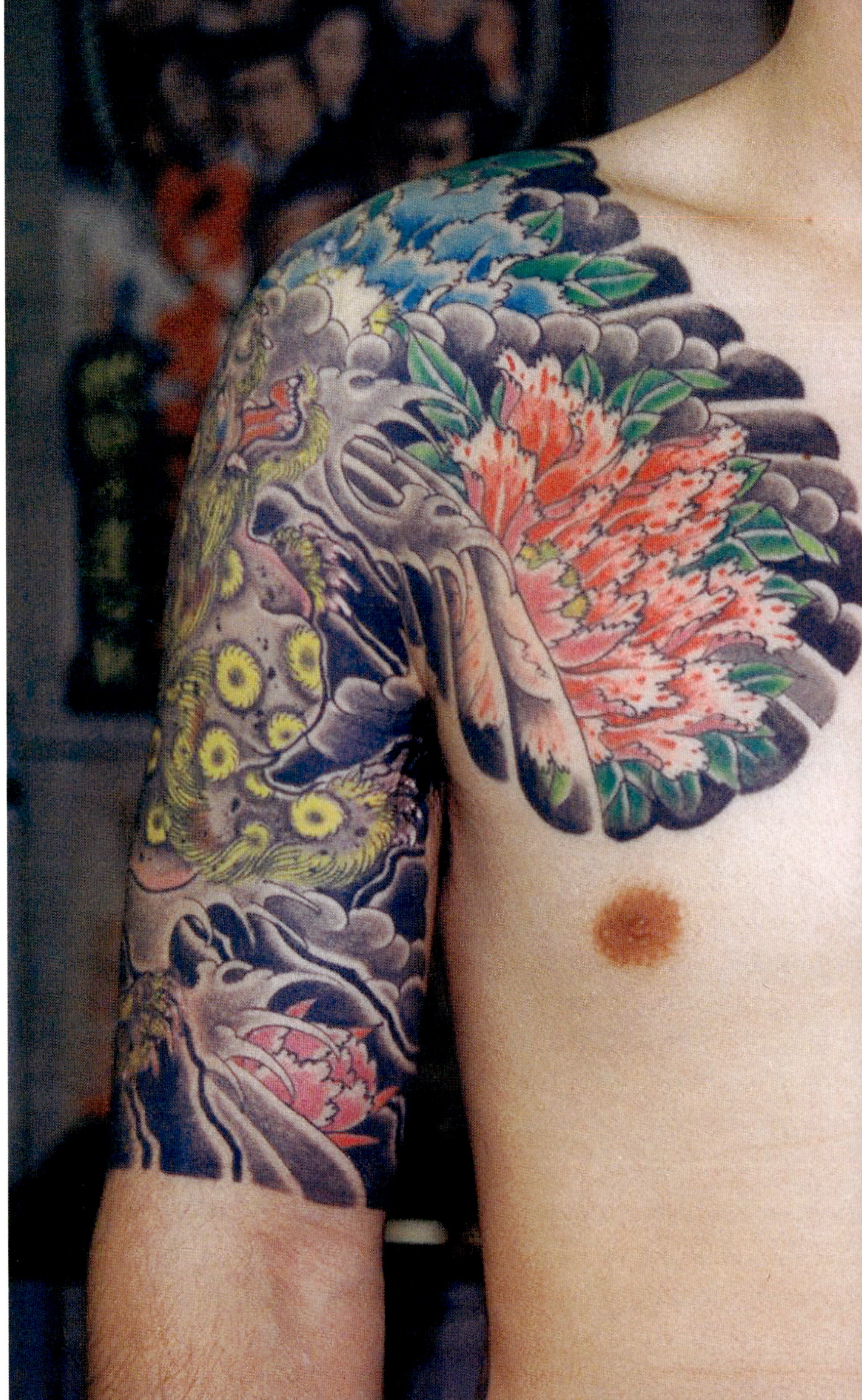

Karajishi to botan. The pairing of Chinese lion and peonies demonstrates the king of the beasts with the king of the plants.

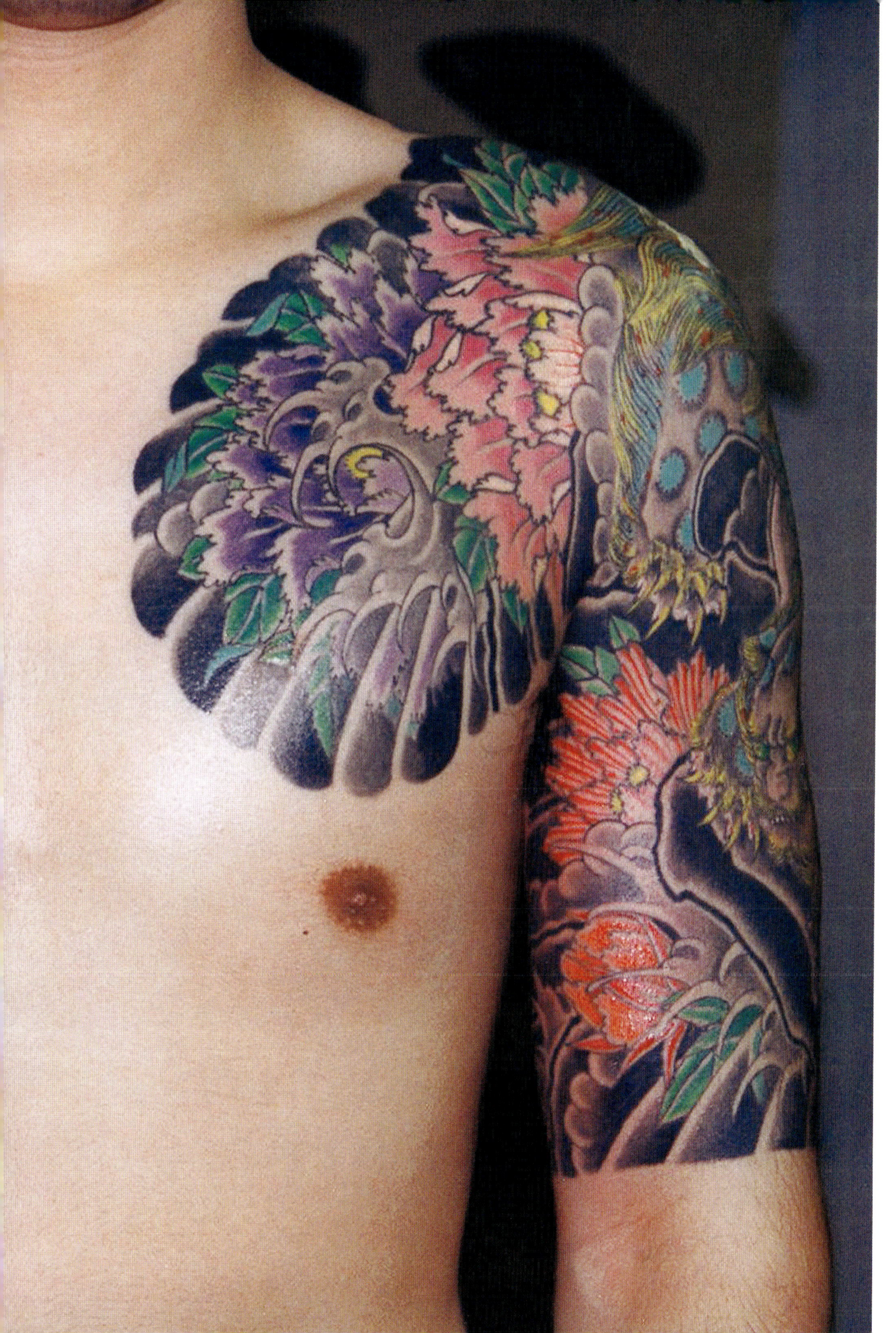

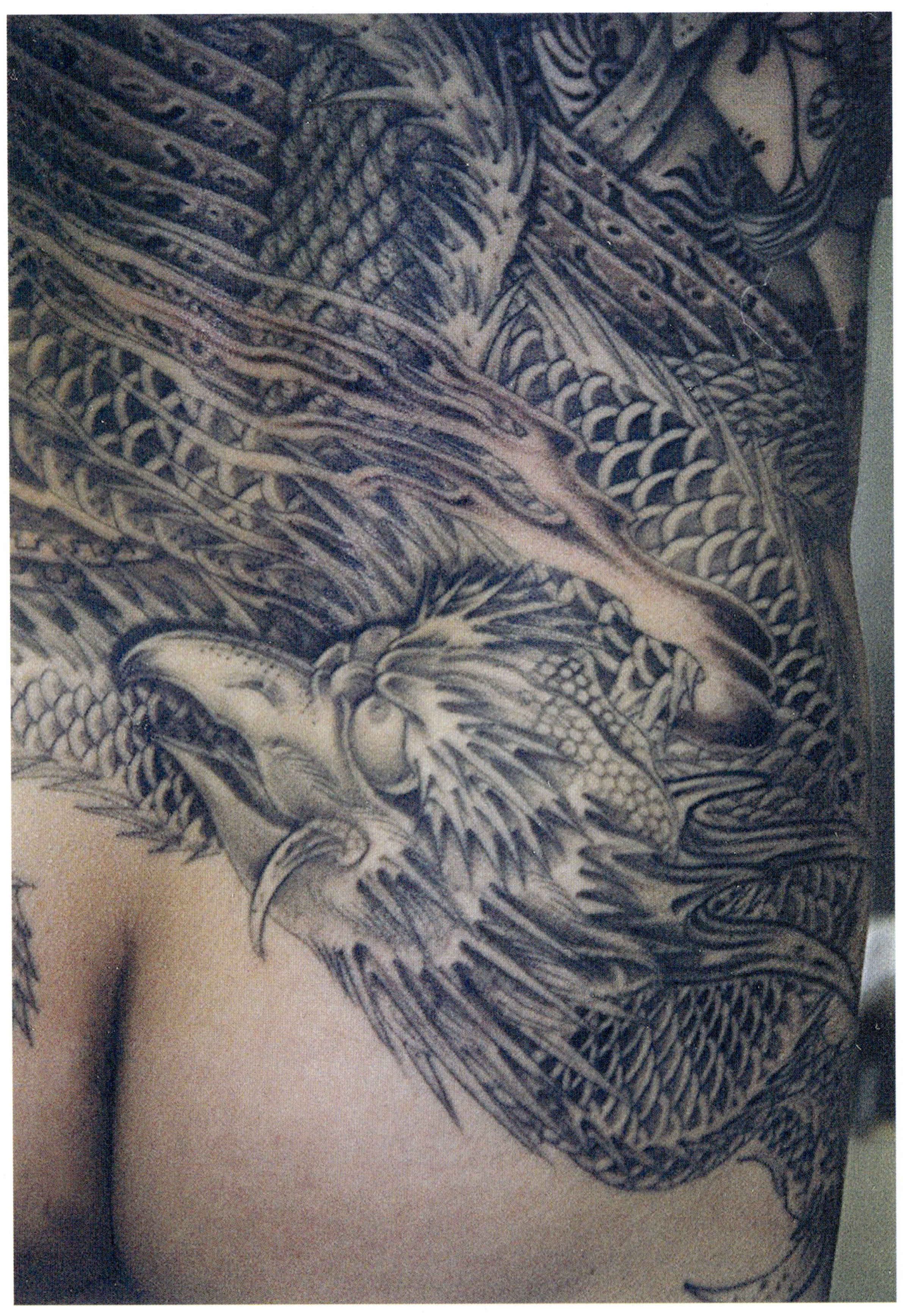

Left:
Garuda influenced *rai-ju*.

Opposite:
Namakubi.

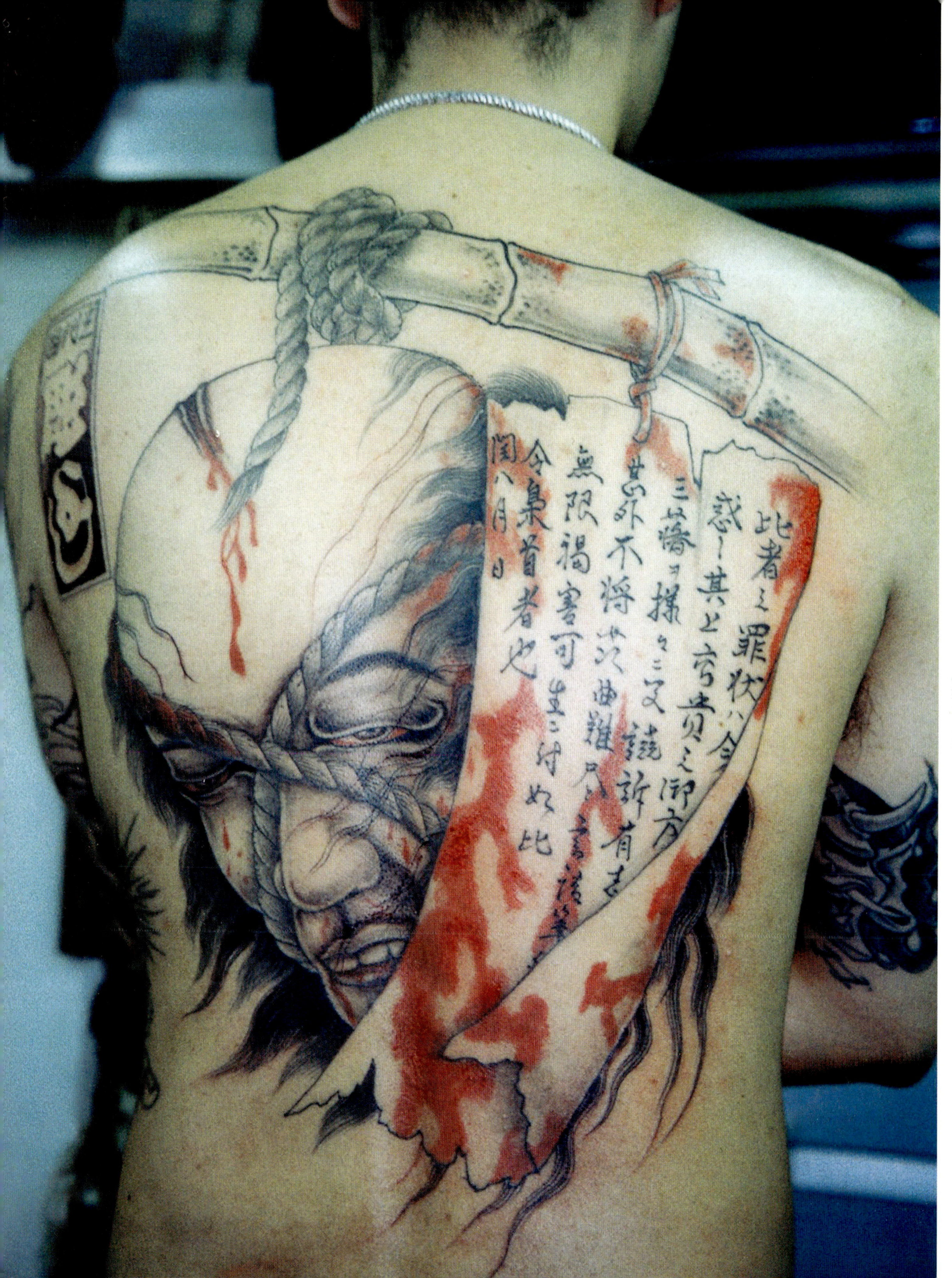

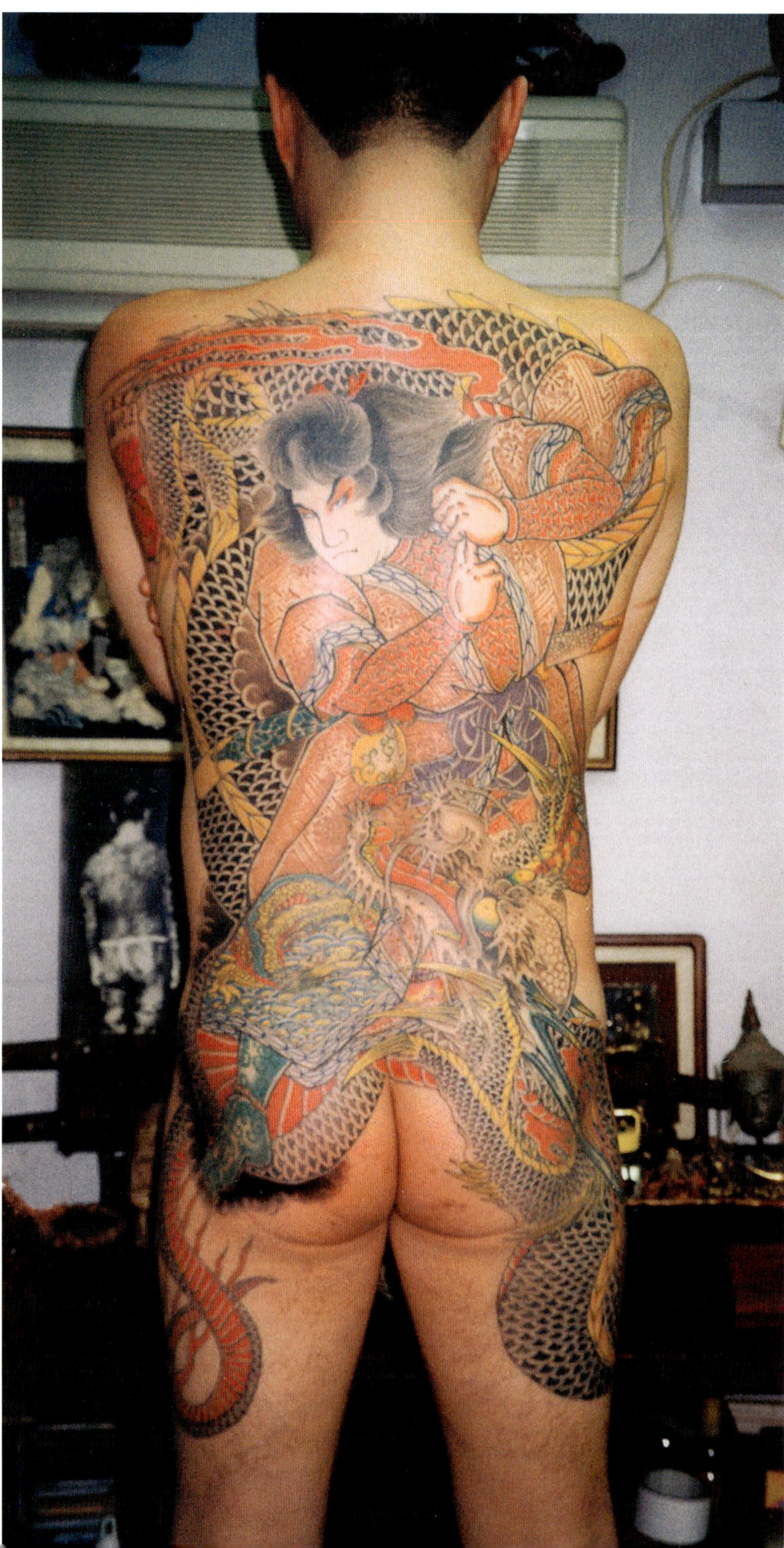

Left:
The thief turned hero, Unryukurou, is a character capable of harnessing the power of a dragon. He is a mountain-dwelling monk; he makes ritual hand gestures to evoke power.

Opposite:
Unryukurou carrying a talismanic sword wrapped in fabric.

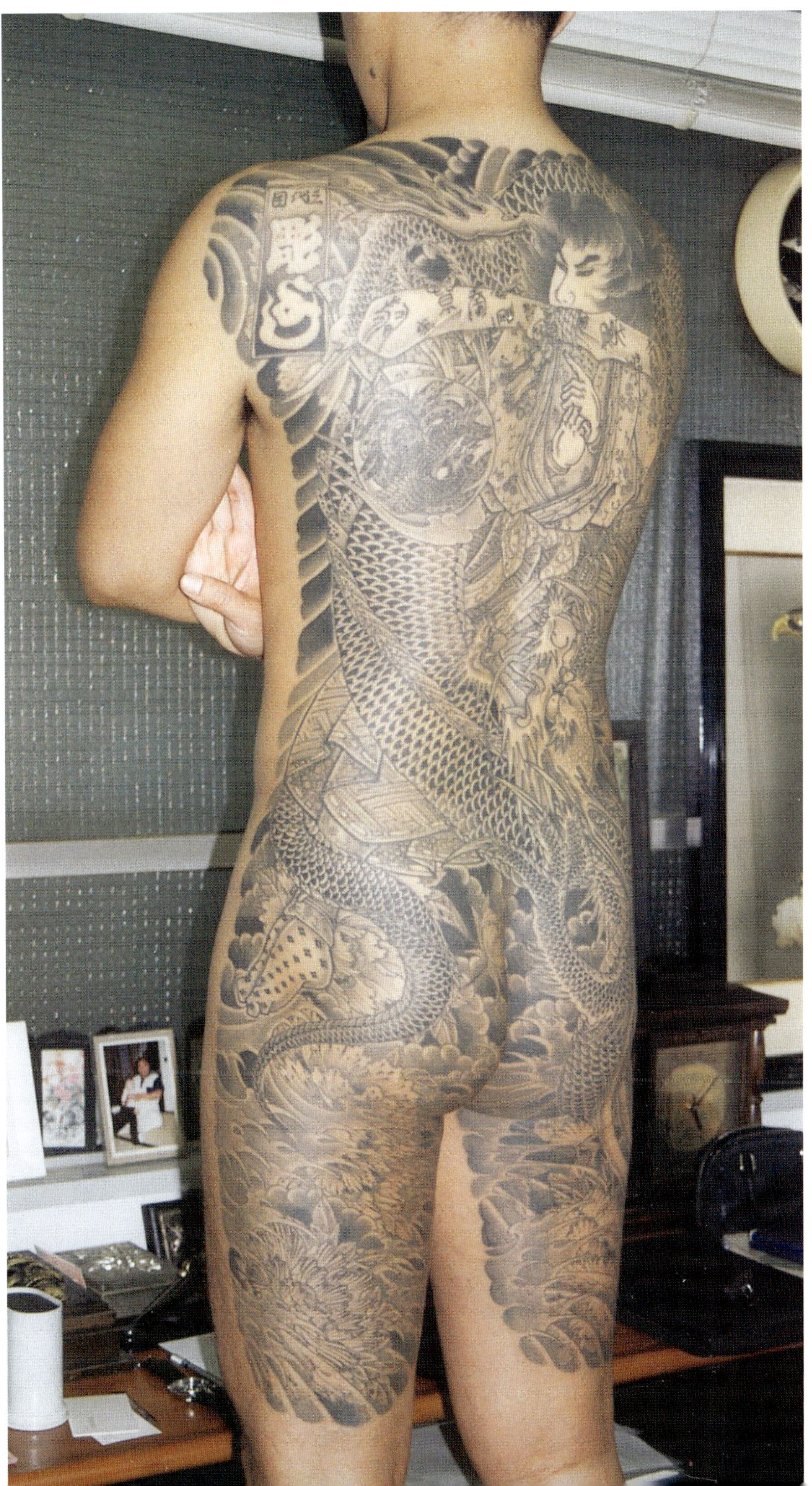

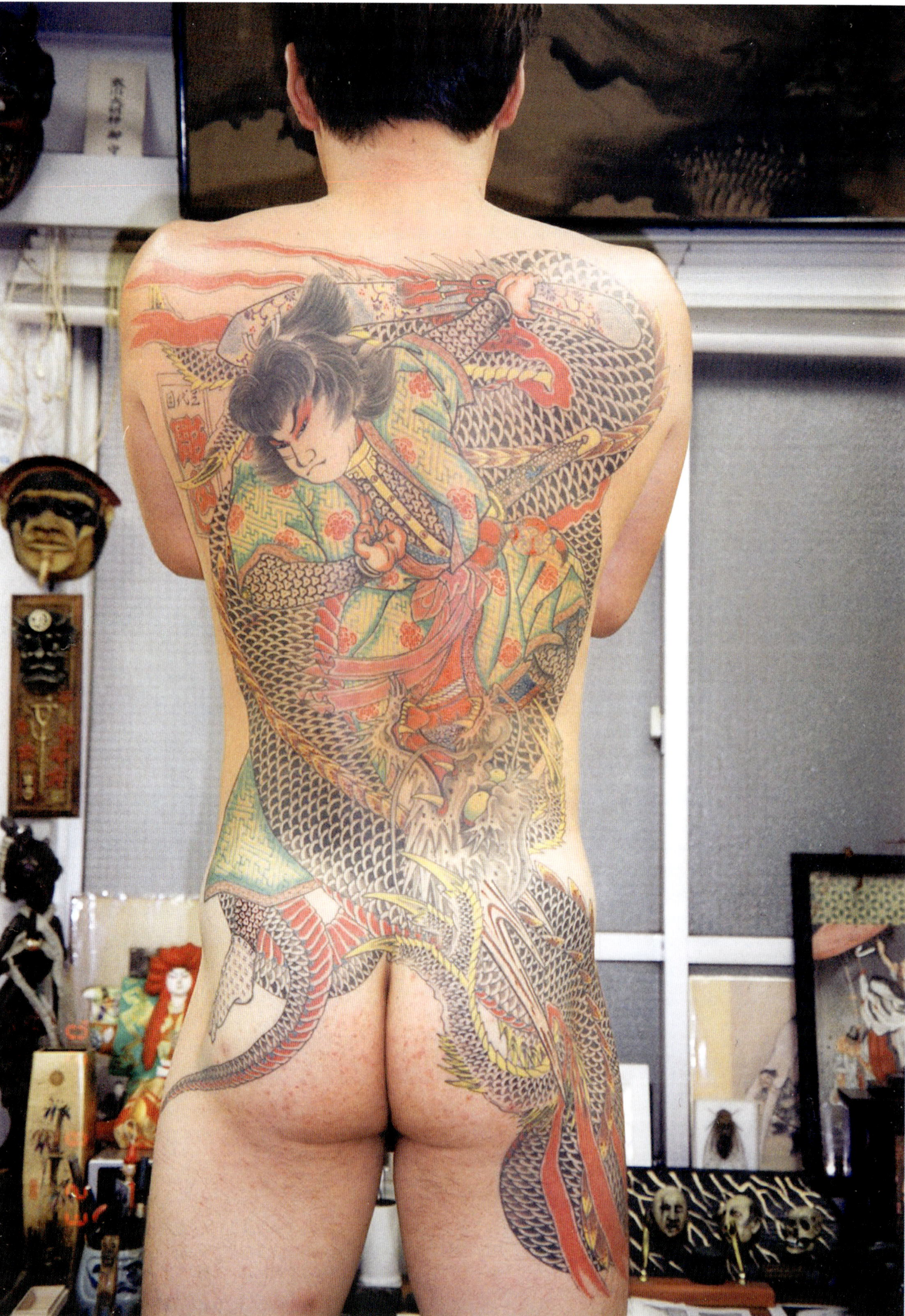

Left:
Unryukurou.

Opposite:
Namakubi, severed head; *hebi*, snake; *sakura*, cherry blossoms.

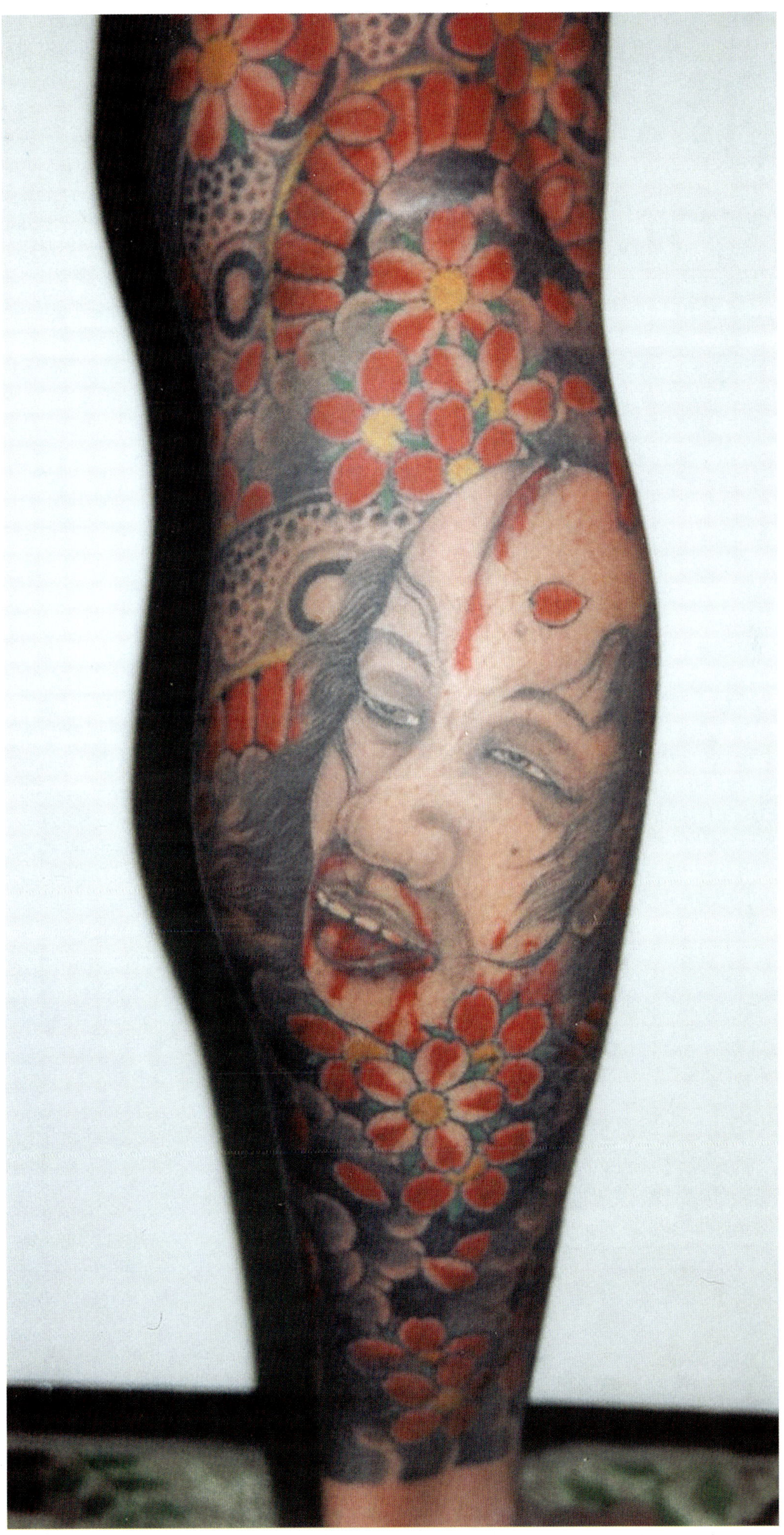

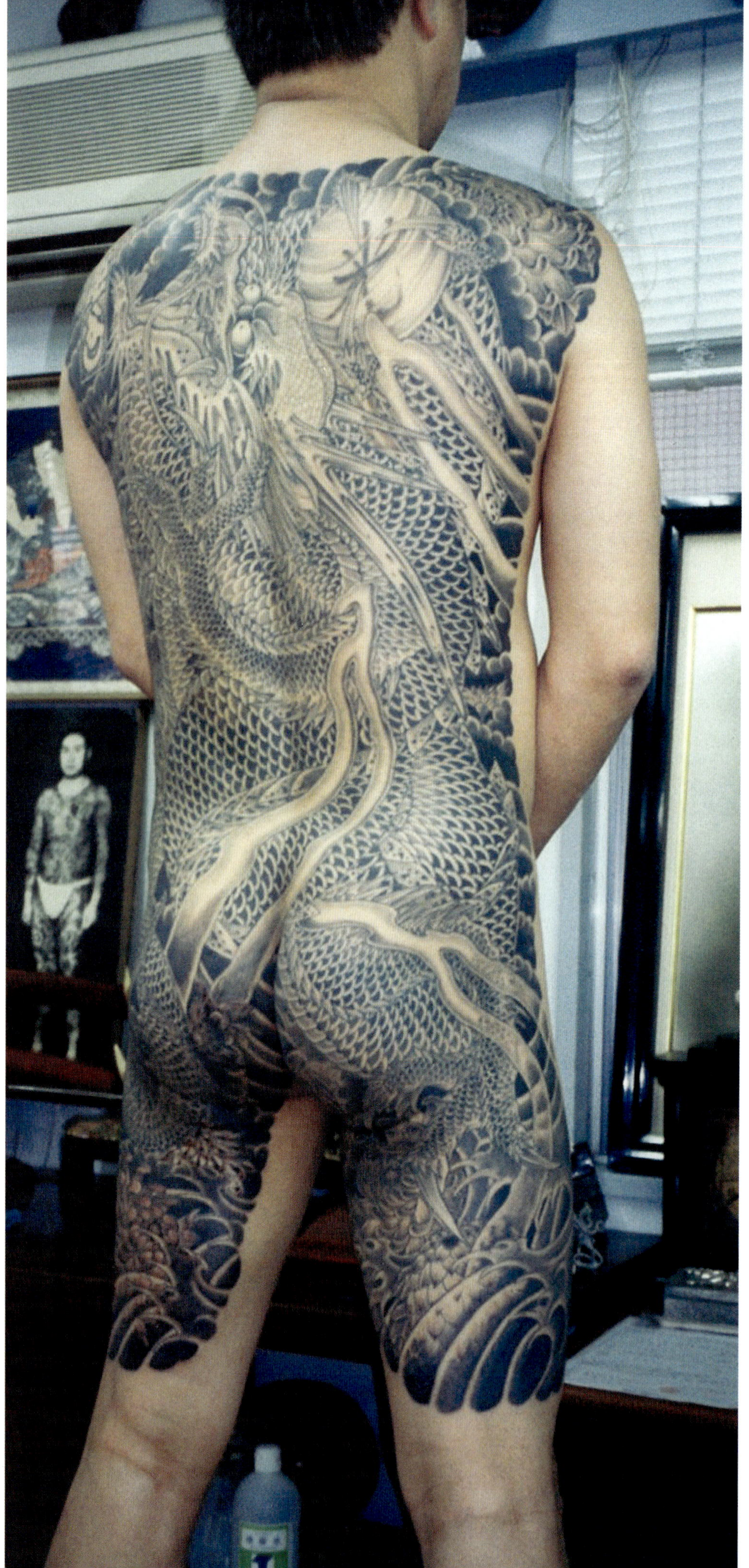

Left:
Ryu, dragon. The dragon, originally a deified snake of Indian mythology, is often represented as a god of the sea with powers governing the sea and tumultuous weather. Edo period firemen often adorned themselves with dragons to protect themselves from fire.

Right:
Tenma-Hajun, the king of Devils. He leads numerous beings and hinders Buddhist practice.

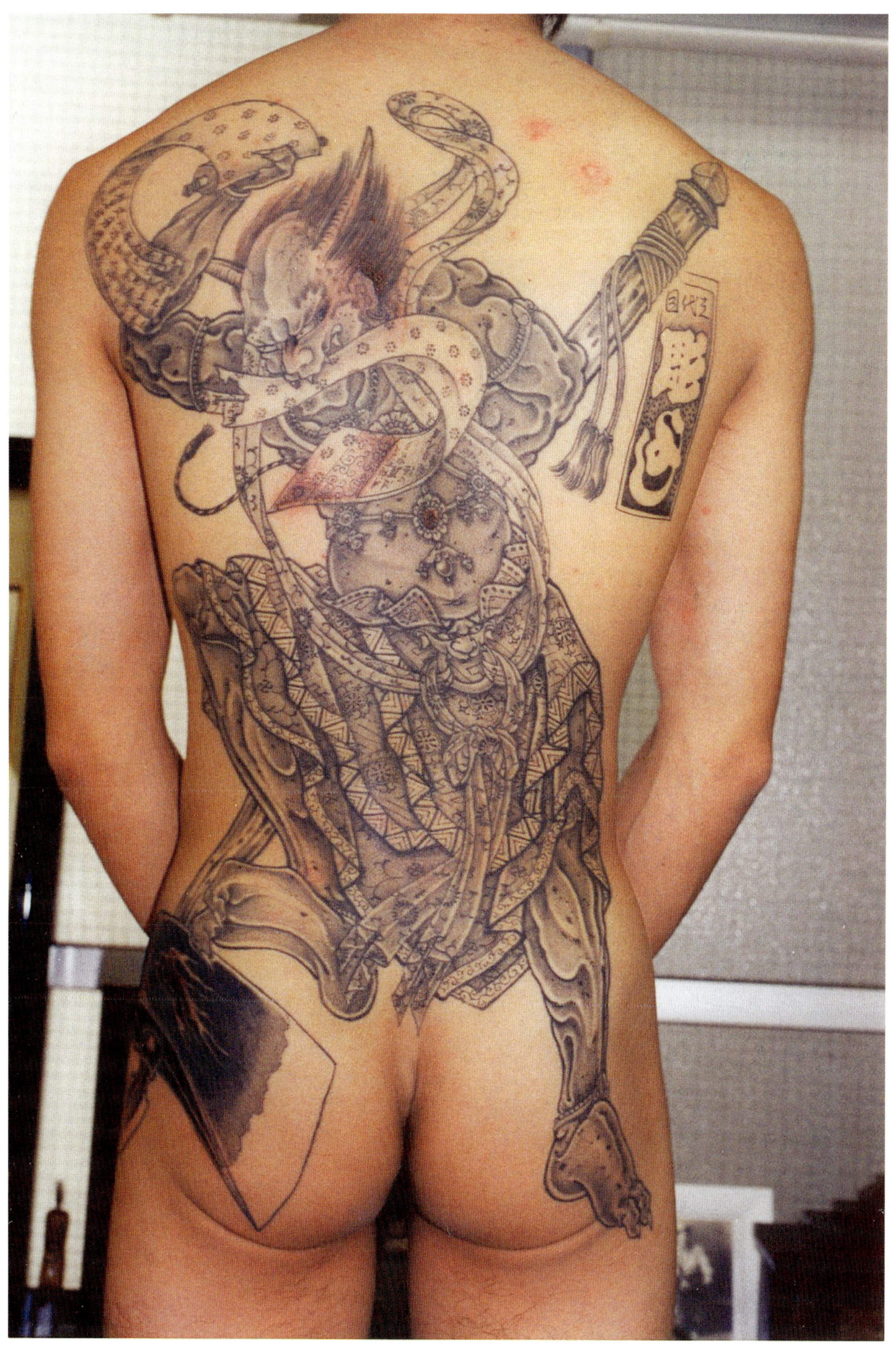
三代目
彫よし

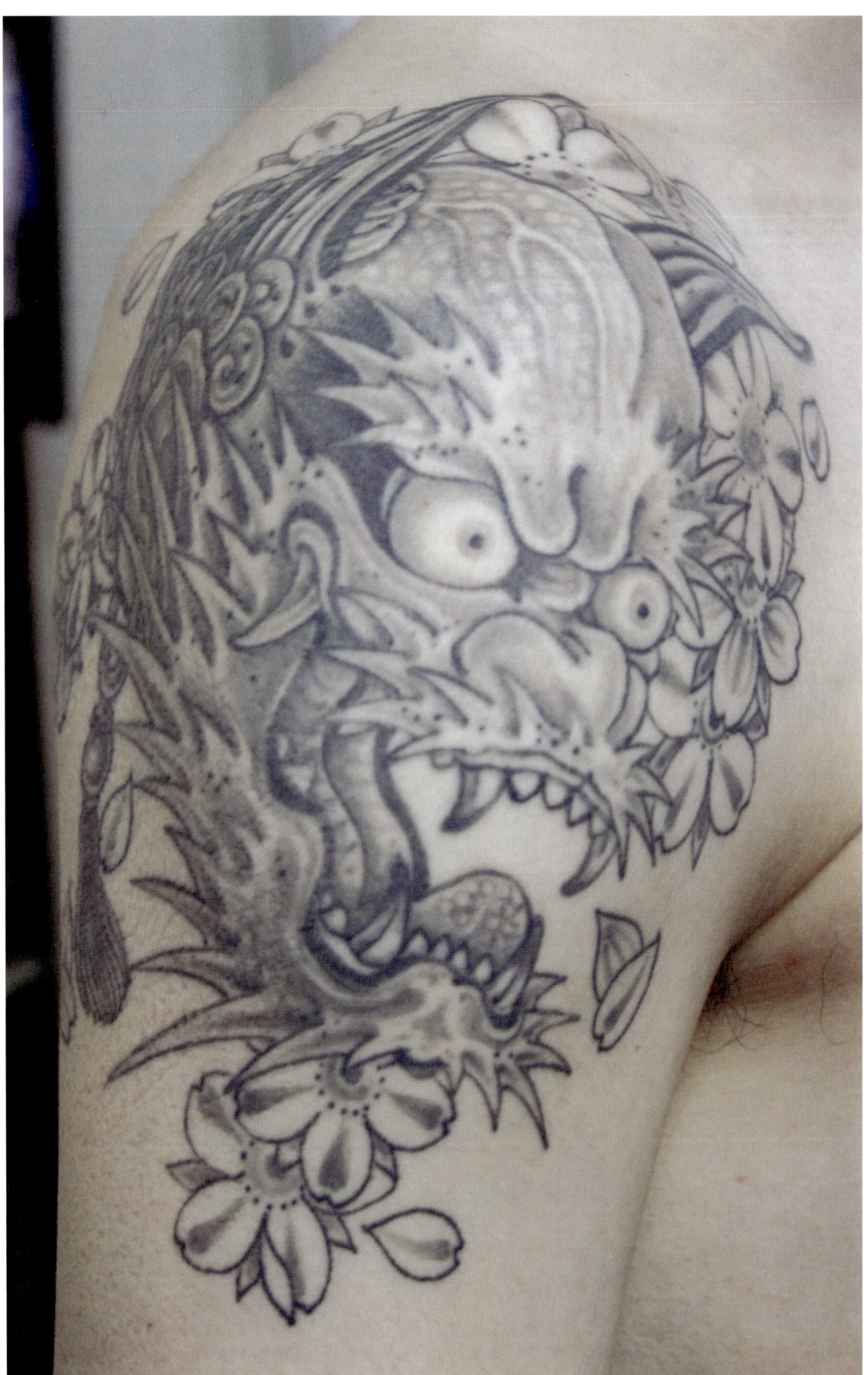

Left:
Oni to sakura. Oni mask and cherry blossoms.

Opposite:
Hannya to momoji. This *noh* mask displays the female demon's simultaneous anger and grief. It is surrounded by maple leaves.

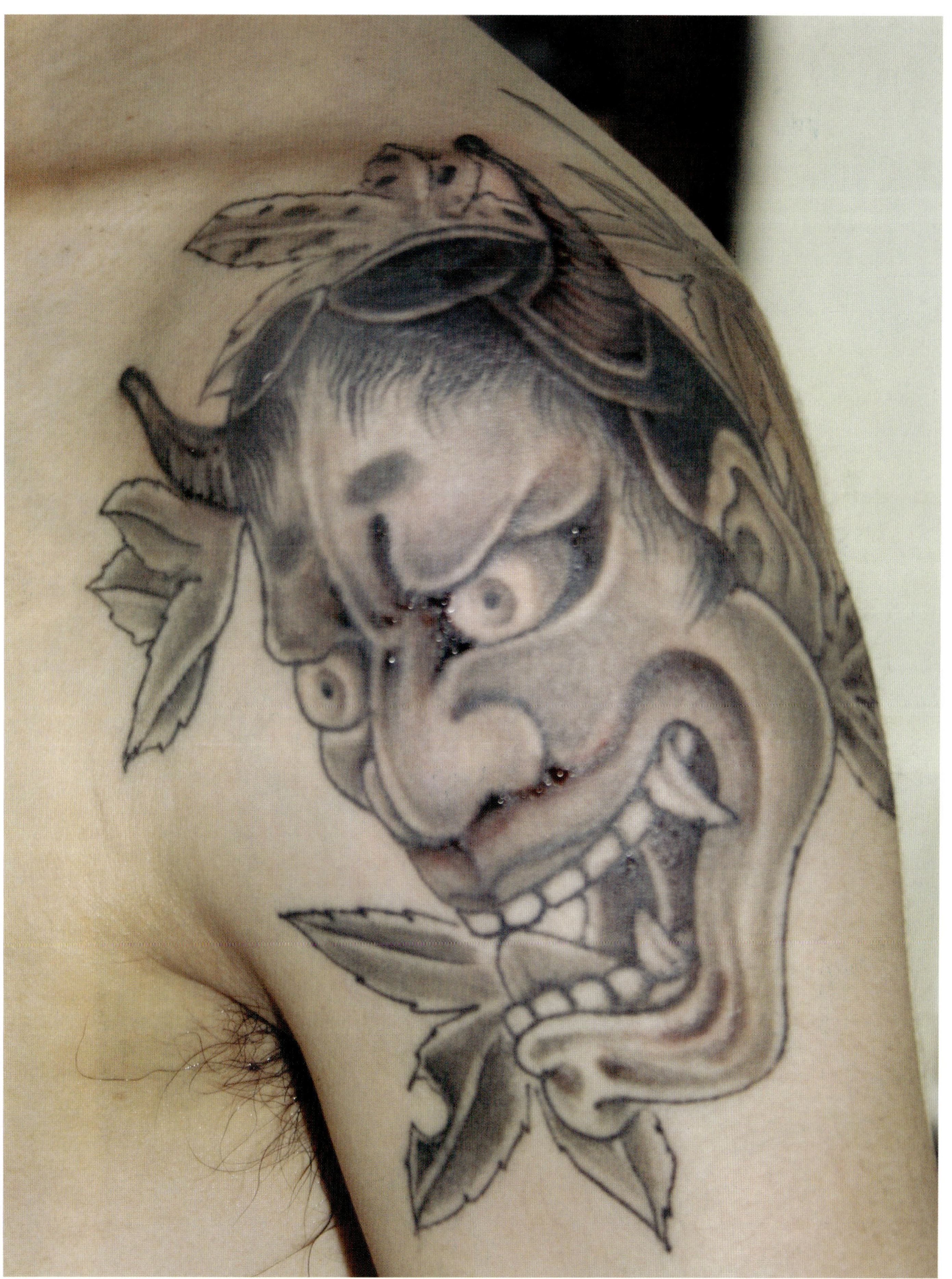

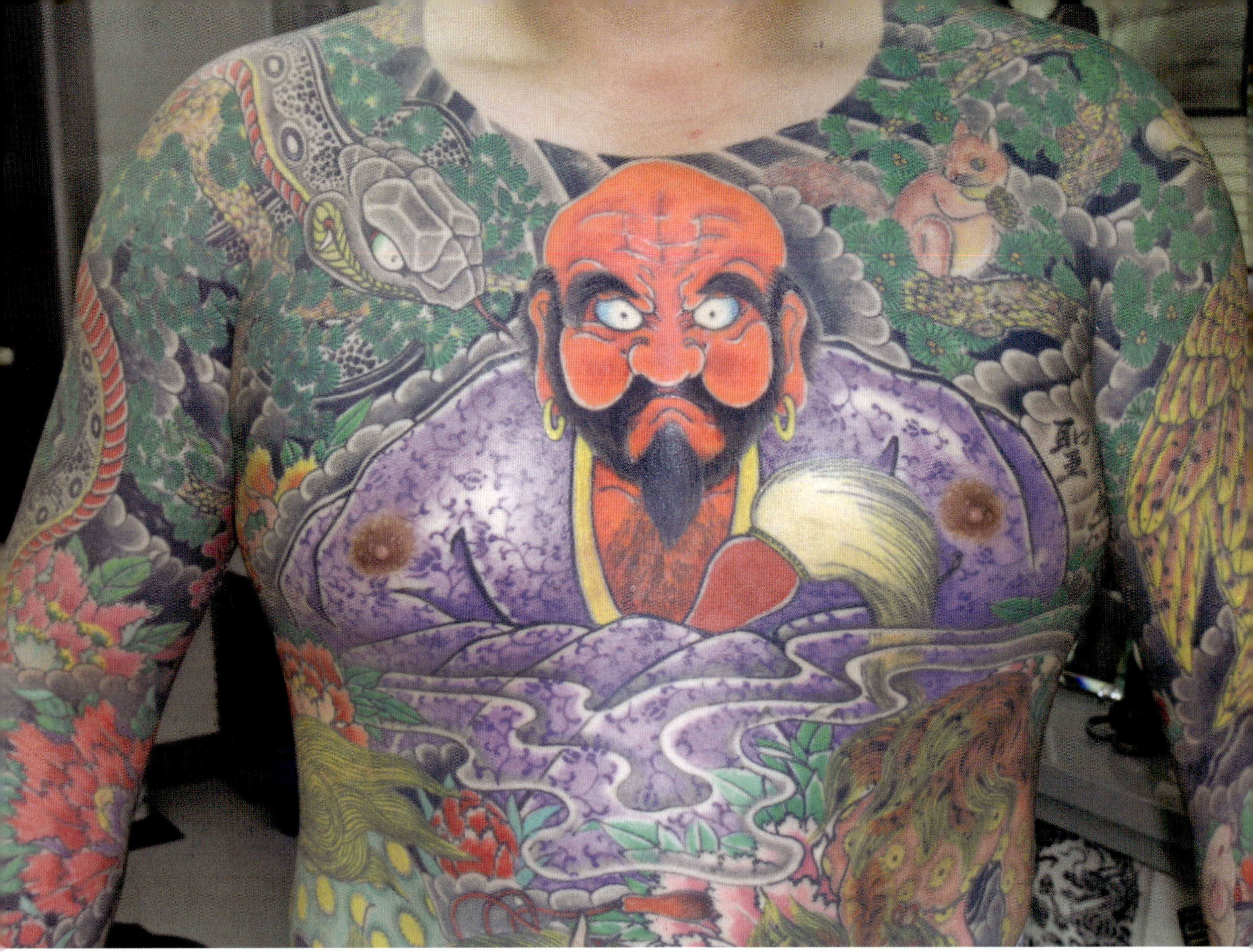

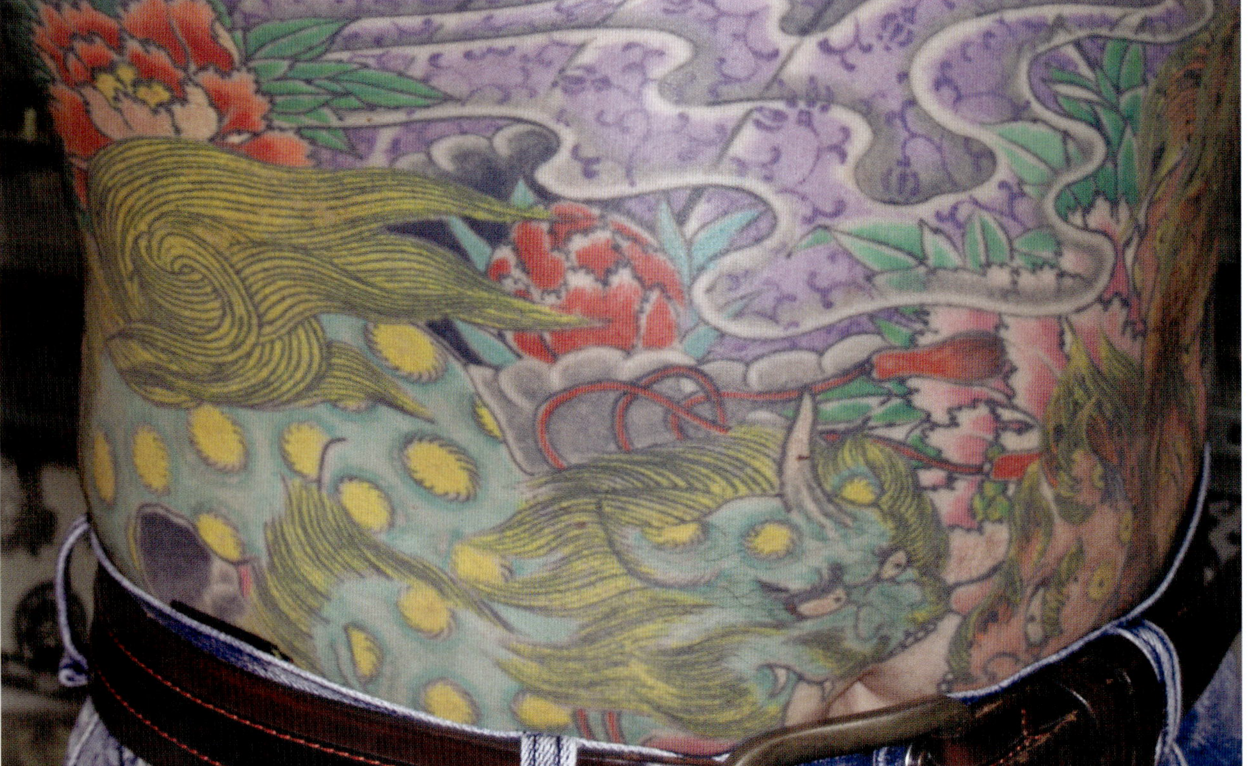

Above:
Daruma and animals frontispiece. Horiyoshi III noted the visual impact of a large centrally placed image of a head on the front of the body. He is interested in the interplay of the tattoo and the person's actual head size, created by their close proximity and similar proportions.

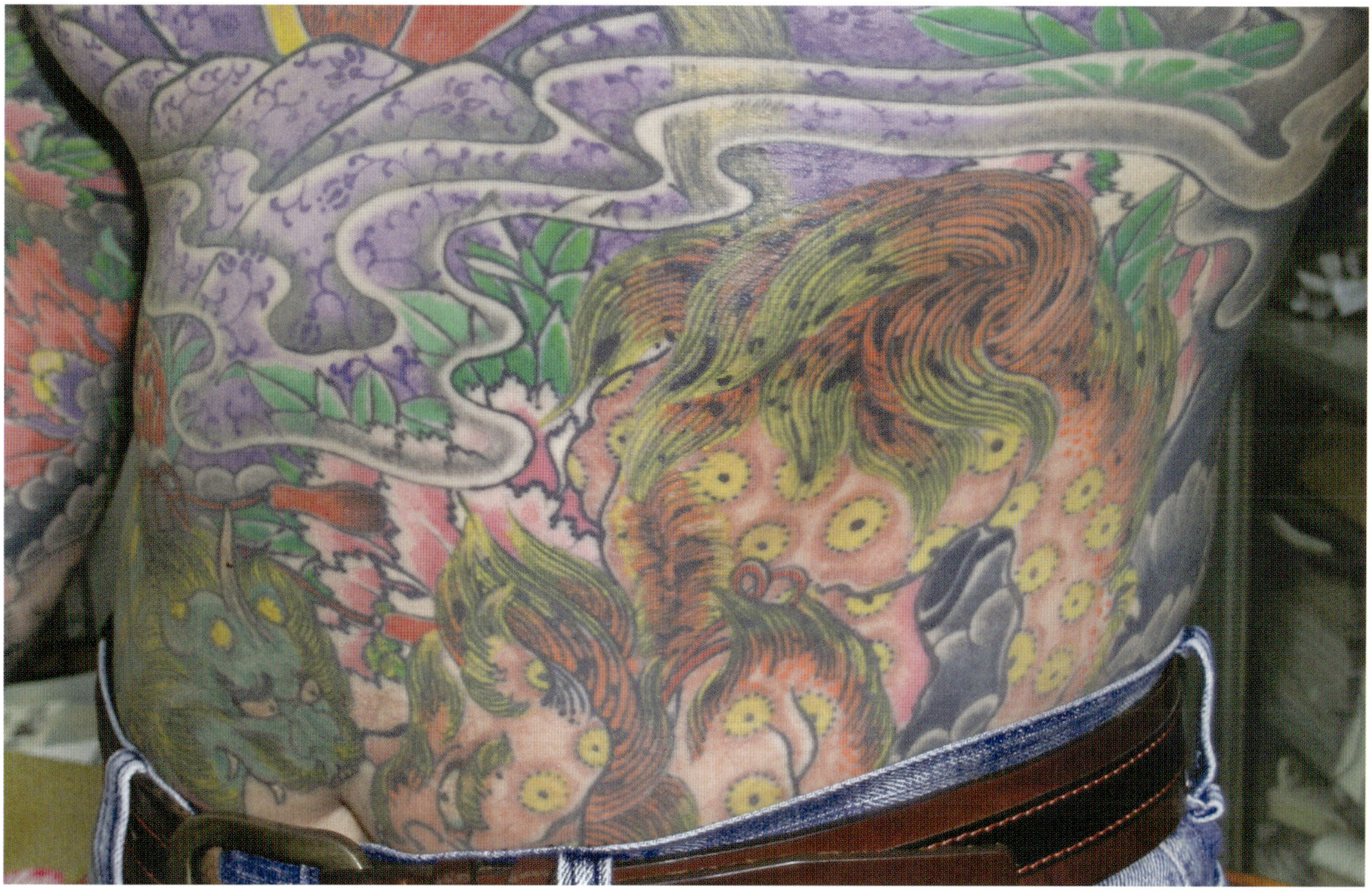

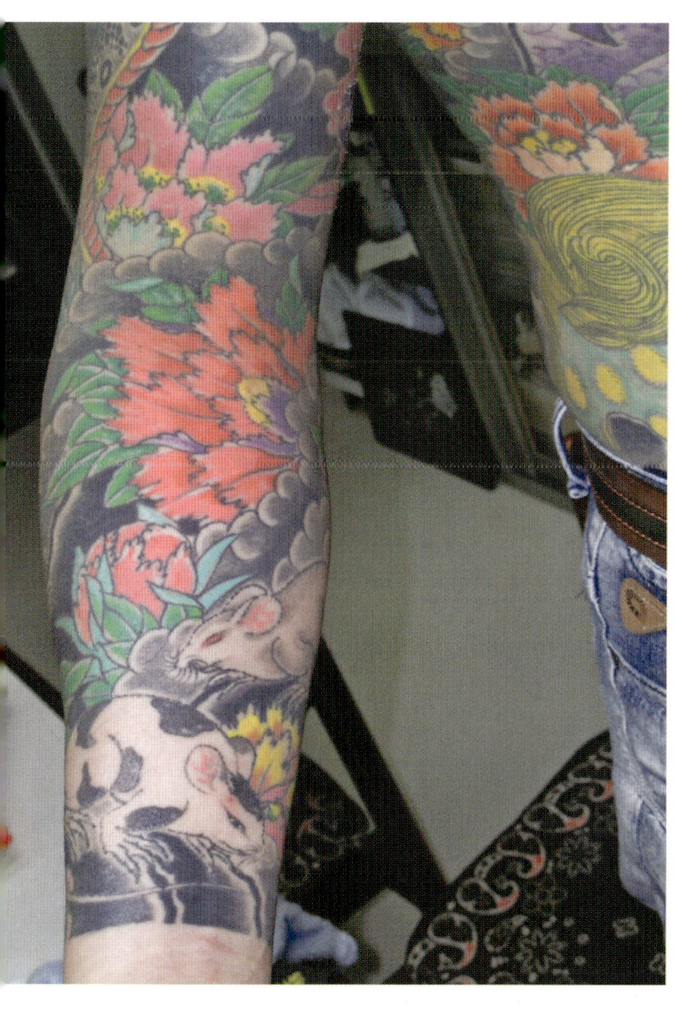

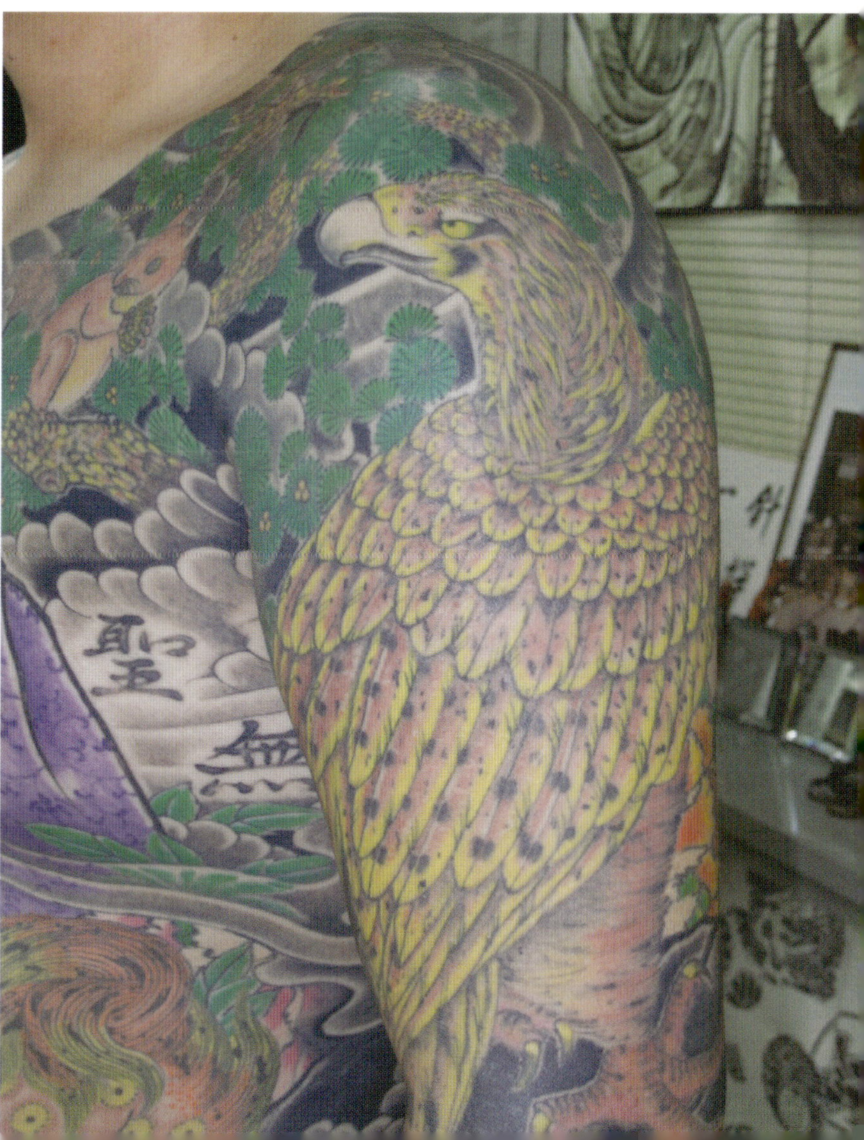

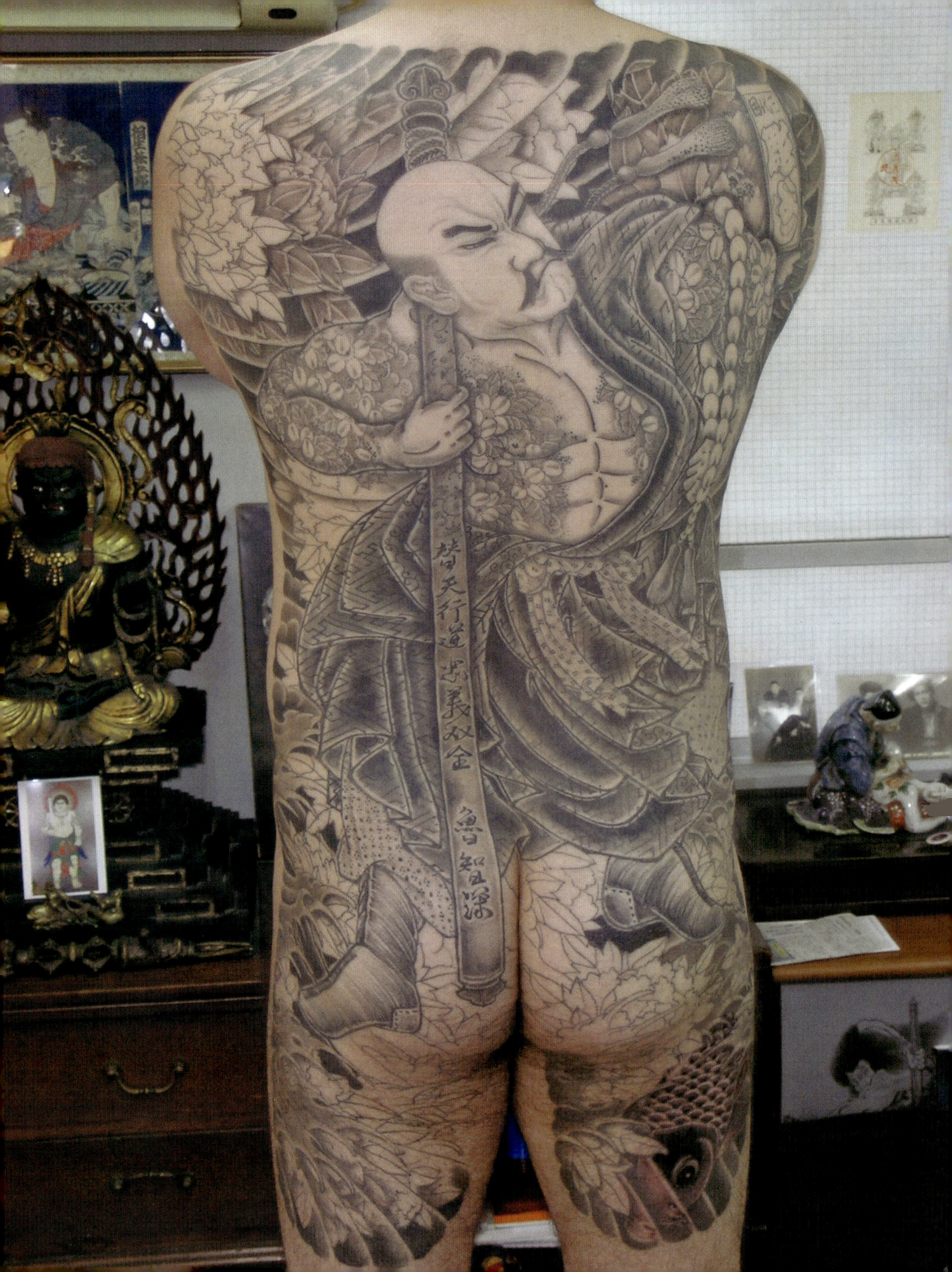
替天行道 忠義双全
魯智深

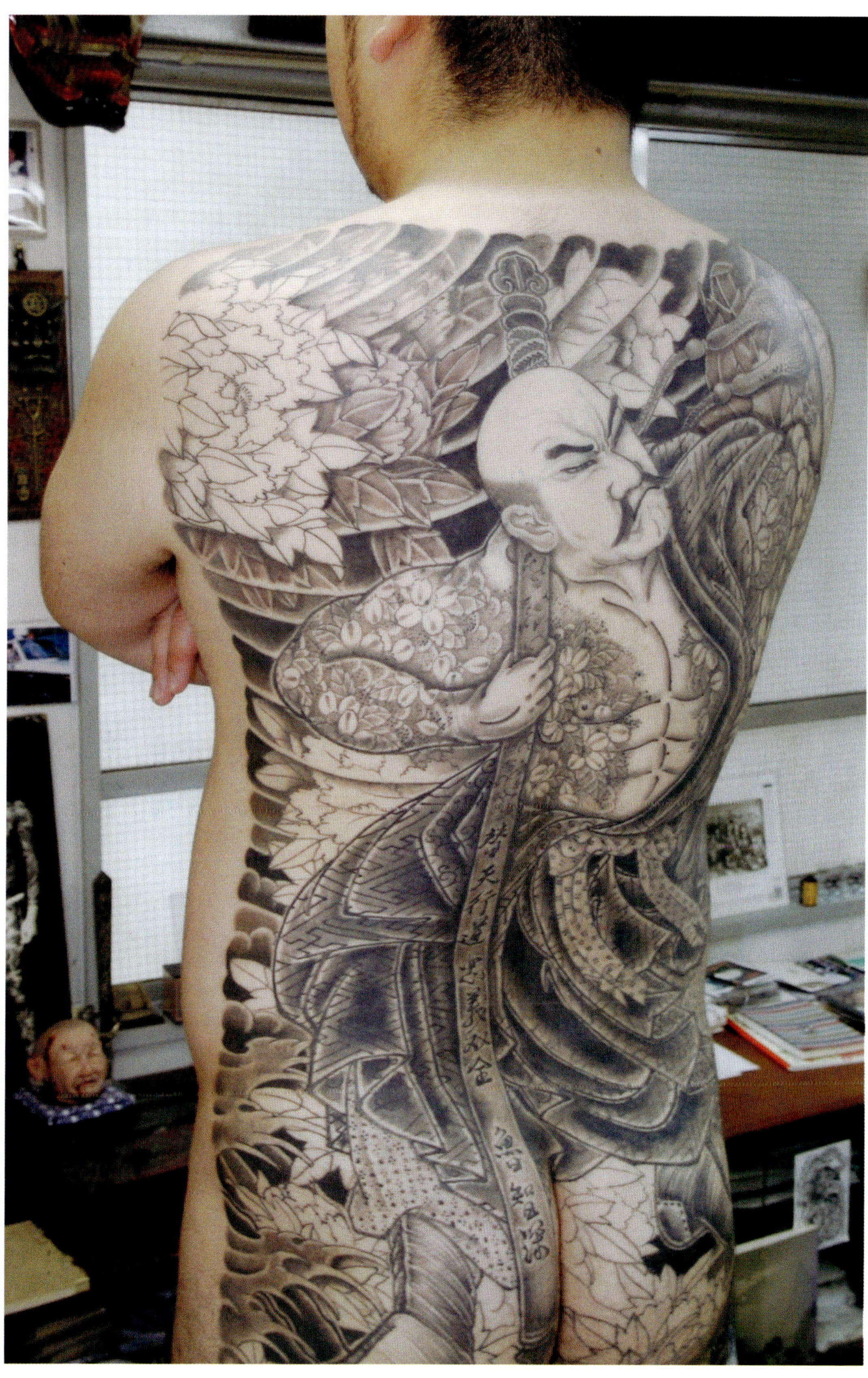

Both:
Suikoden hero, Kaosho Rochishin.

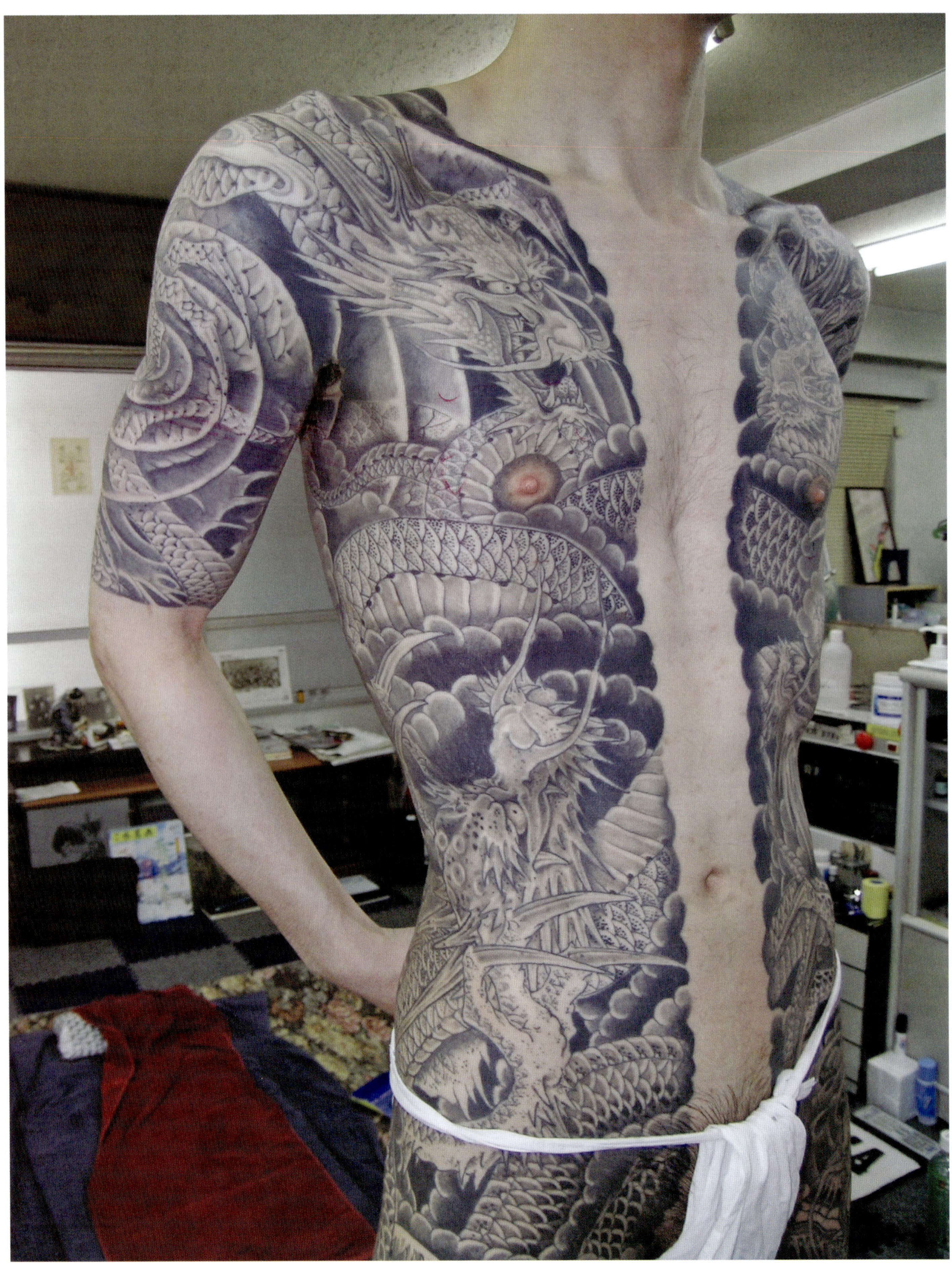

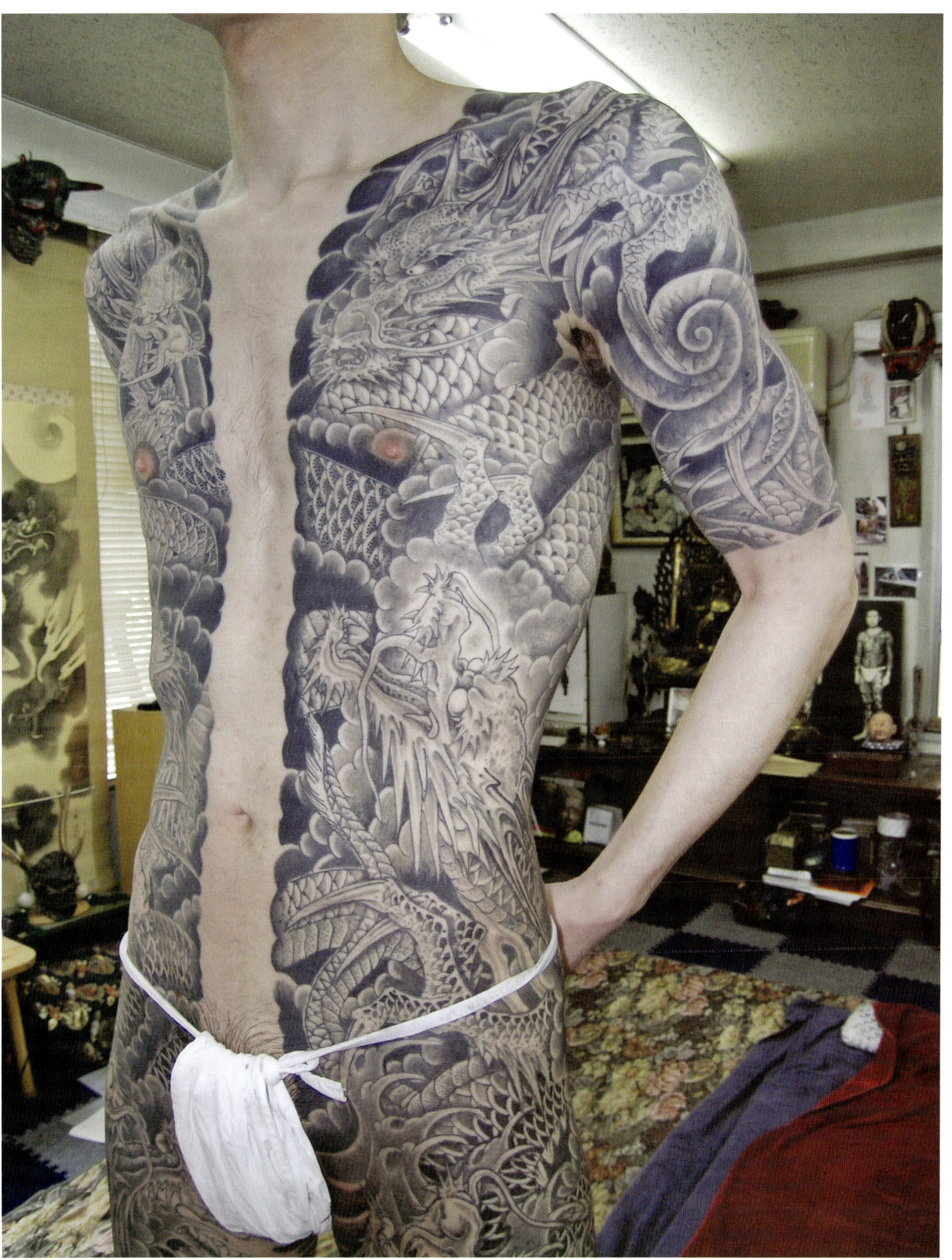

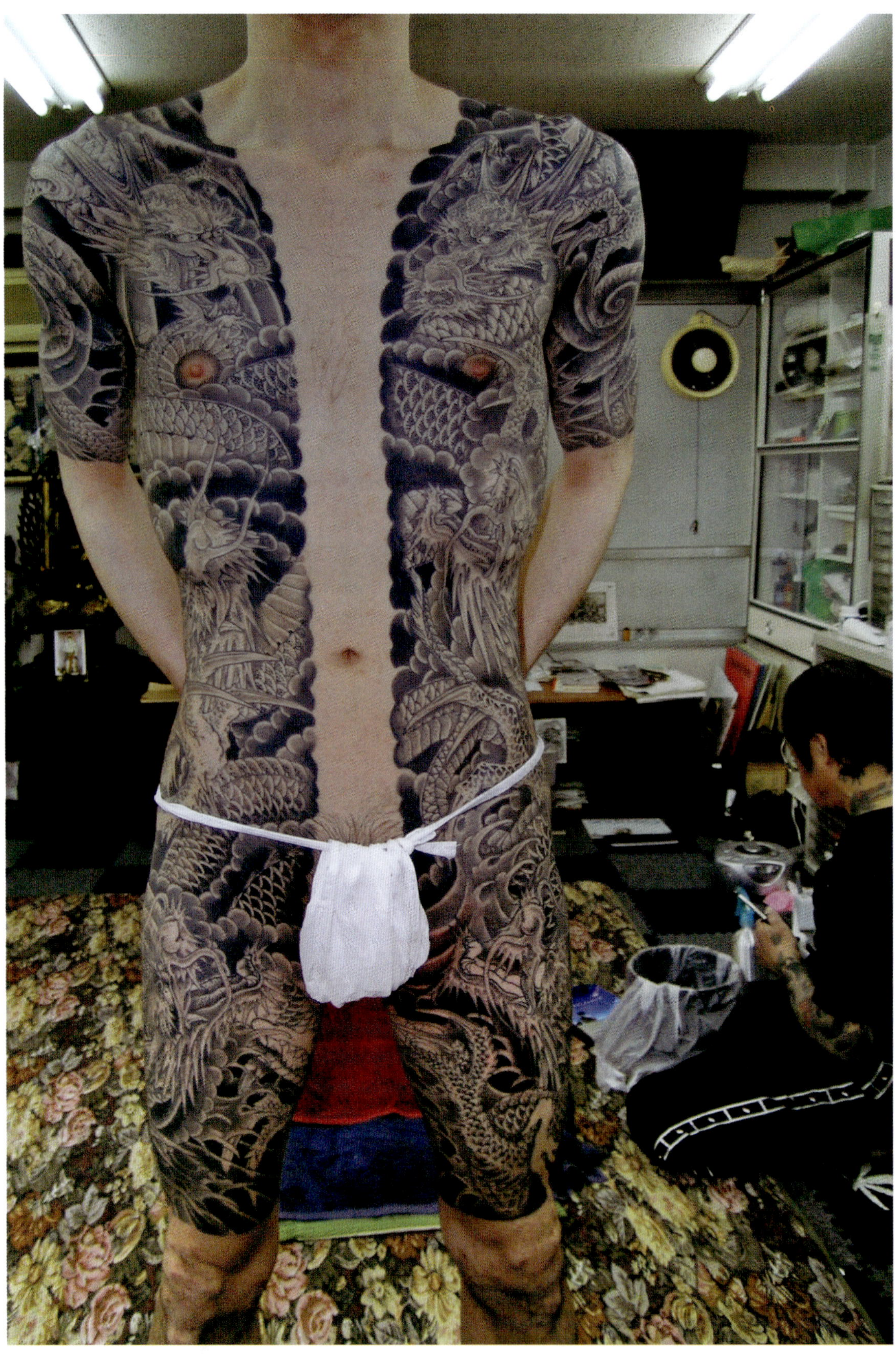

Both: *Ryu munewari*. *Munewari* denotes the split-chest bodysuit style of tattooing.

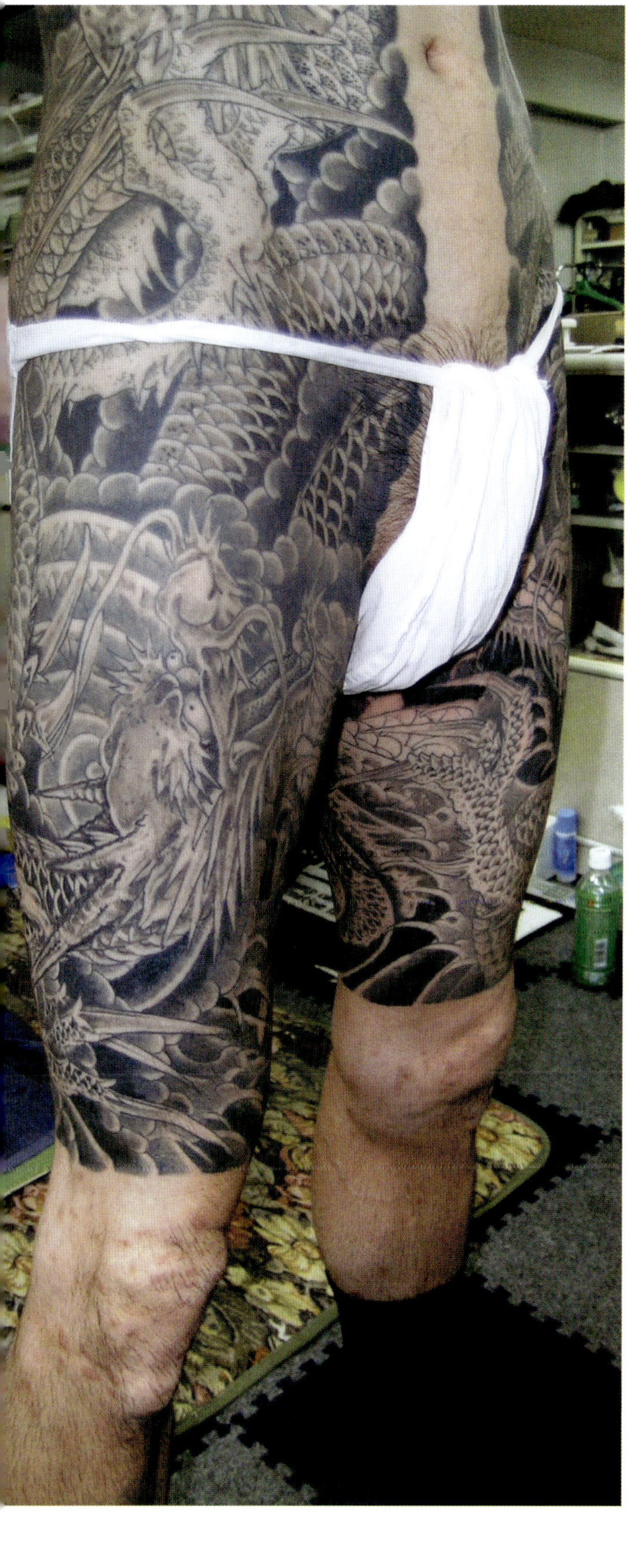

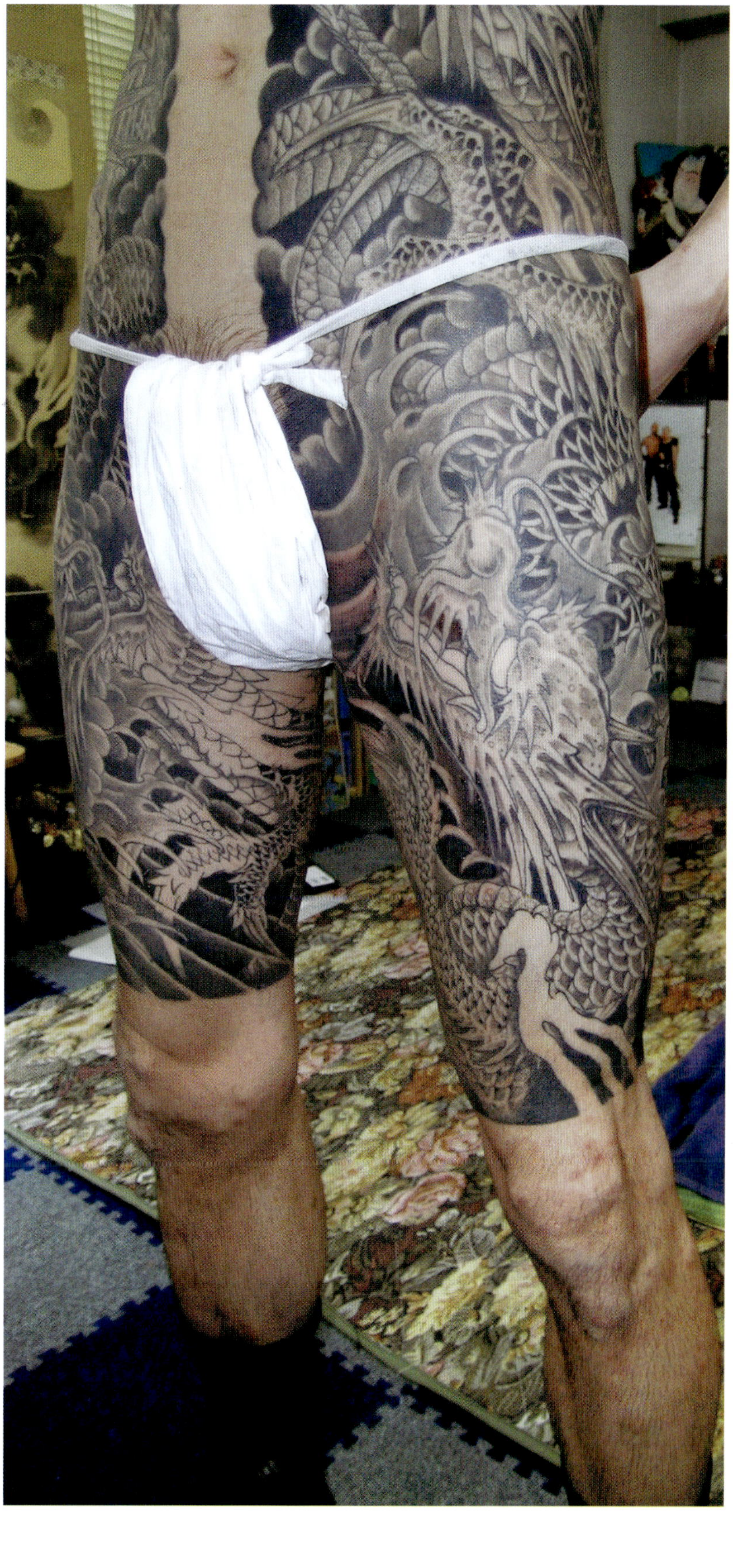

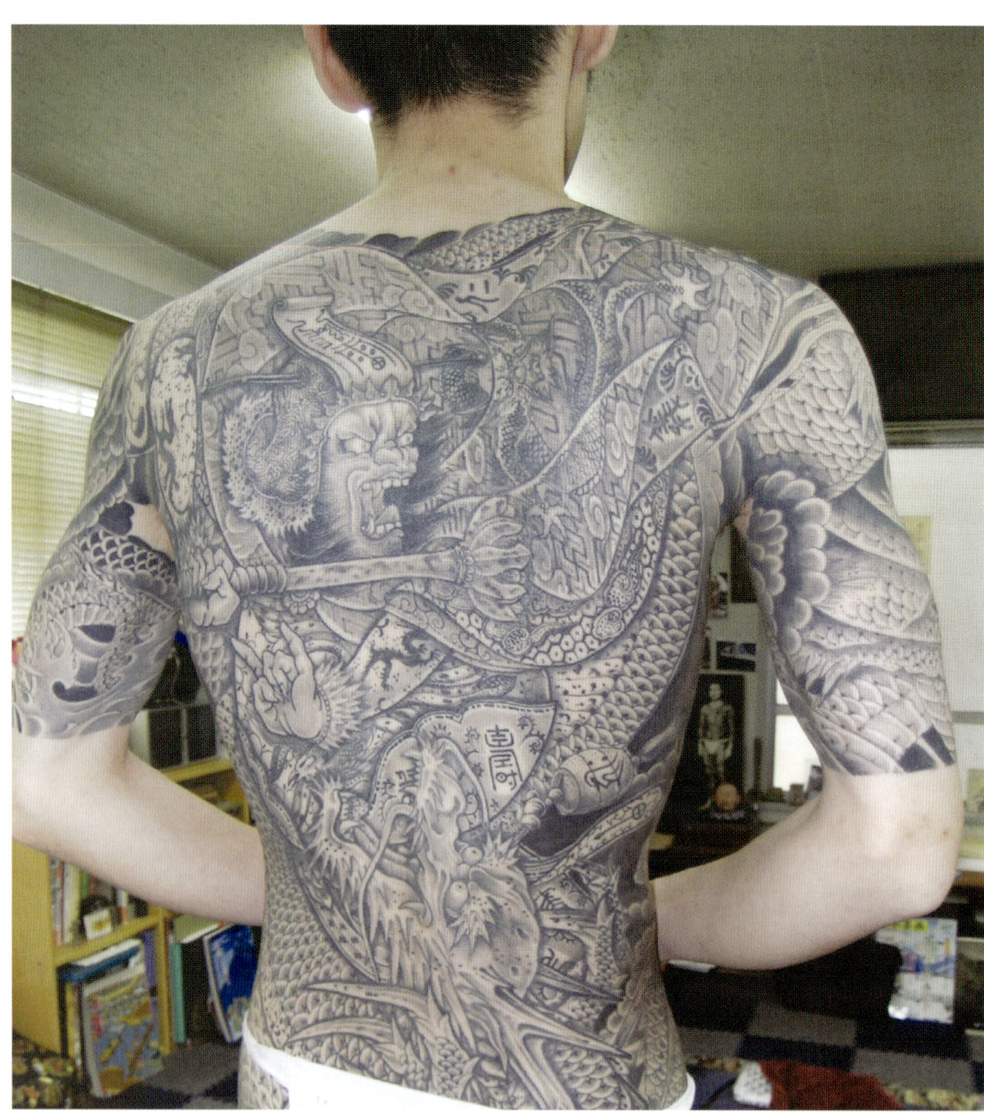

Left and opposite:
Rai-tei, the Taoist supreme god ruling over all thunder gods. He governs happiness and calamity, earthly life and death; superior to both emperors and the master of hell.

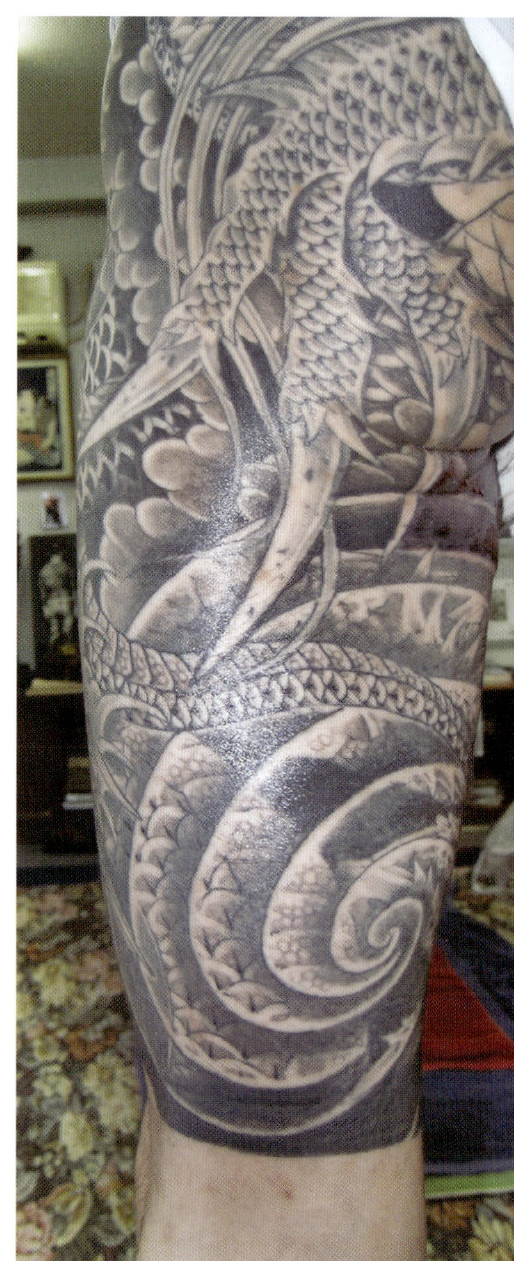

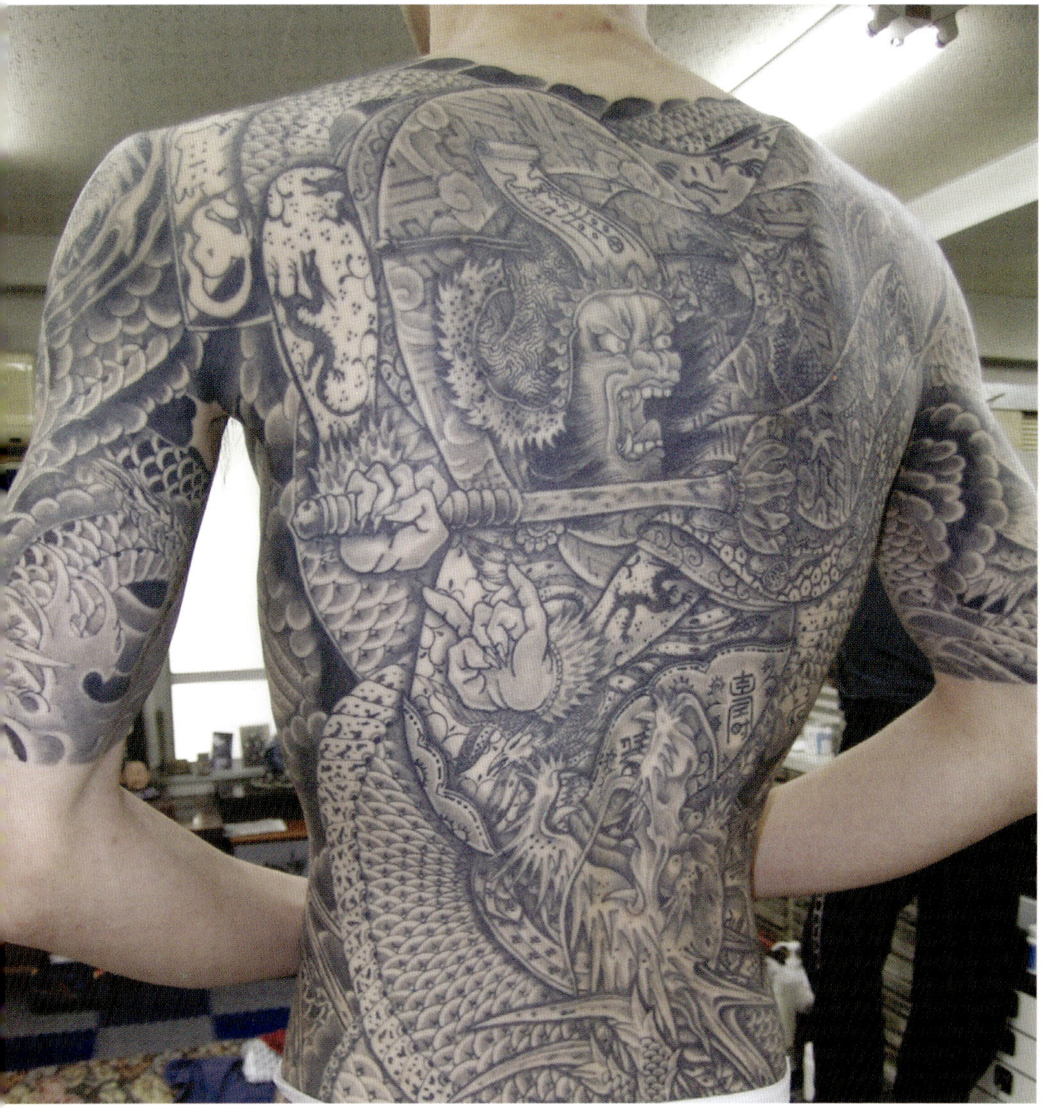

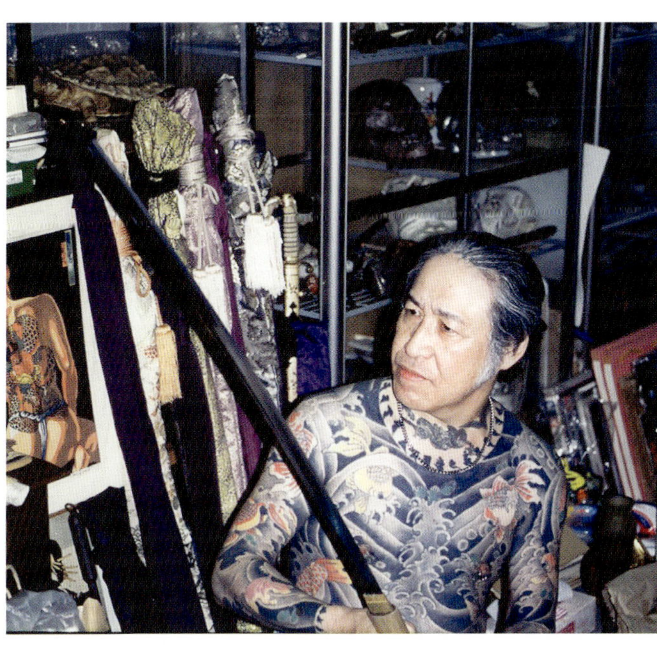

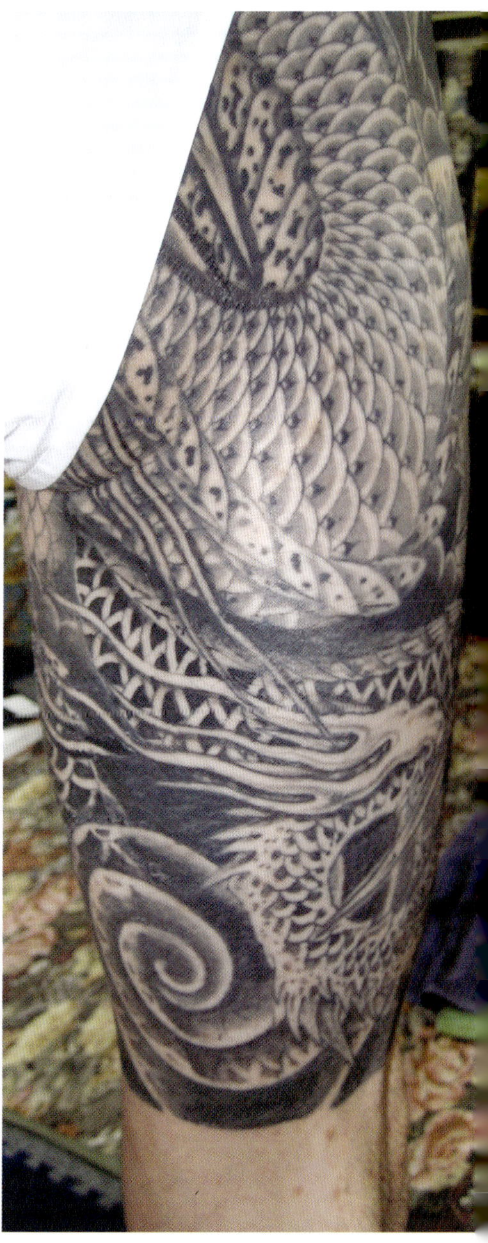

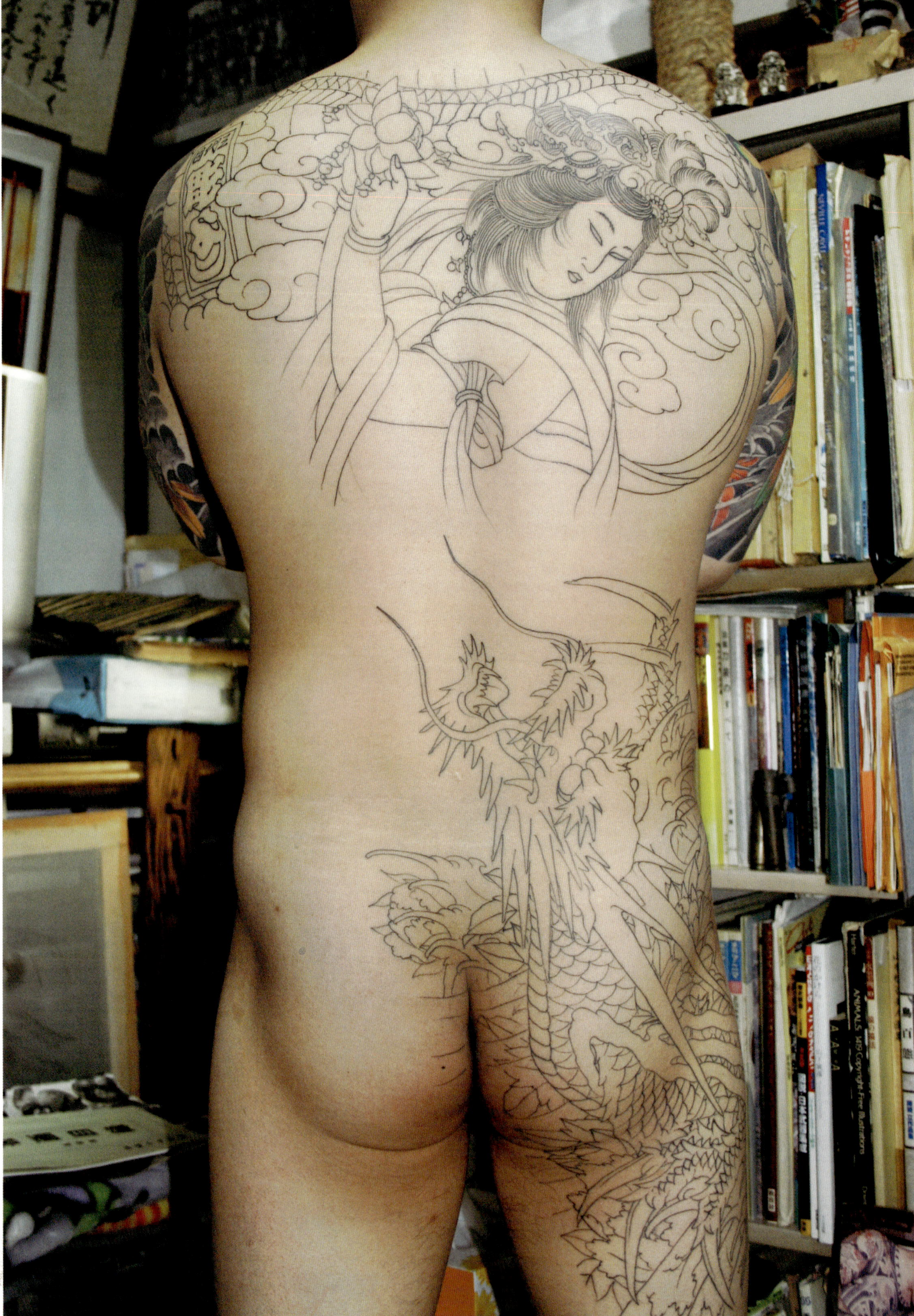

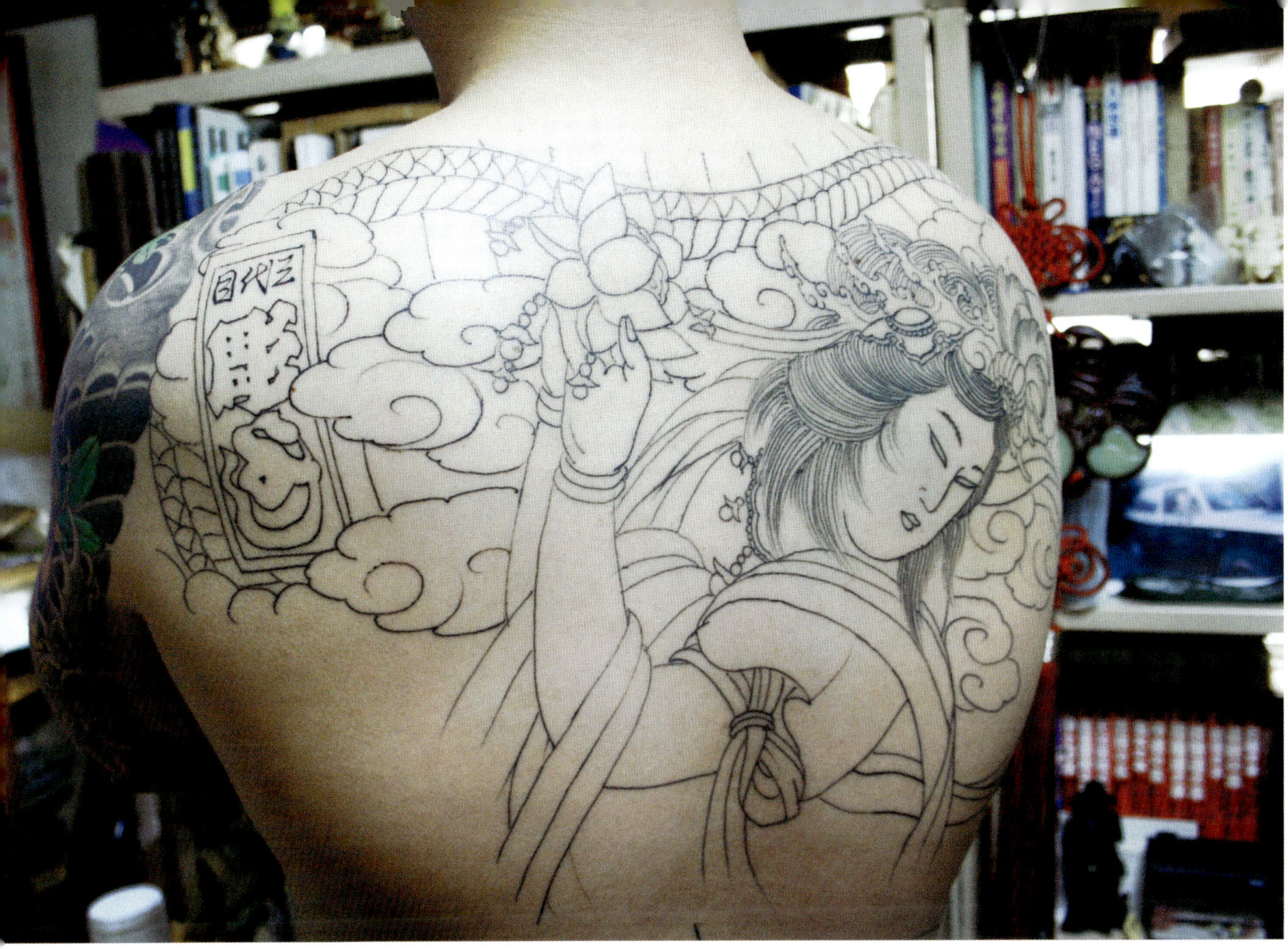

Left and above:
Tennyo sugibori. *Tennyo* outline, “in progress.”

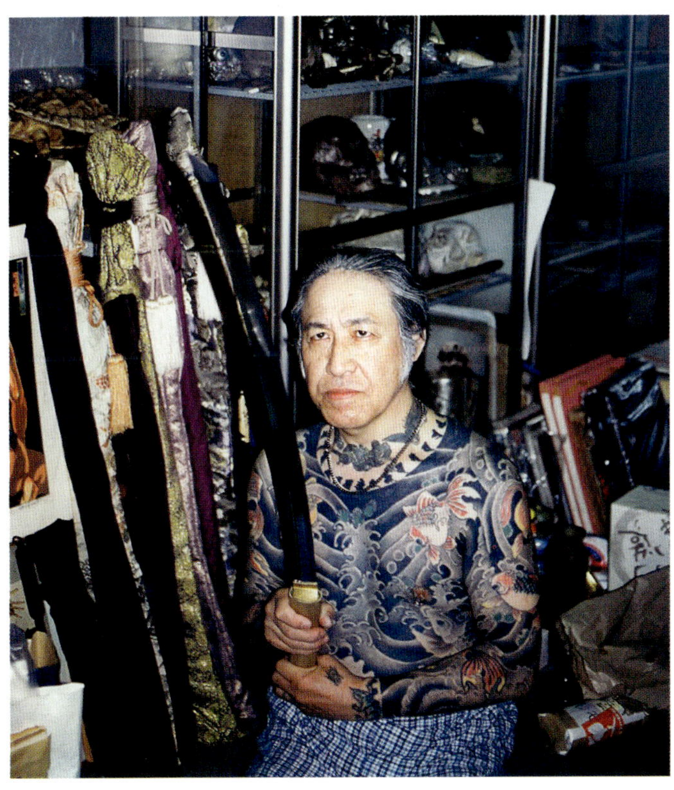

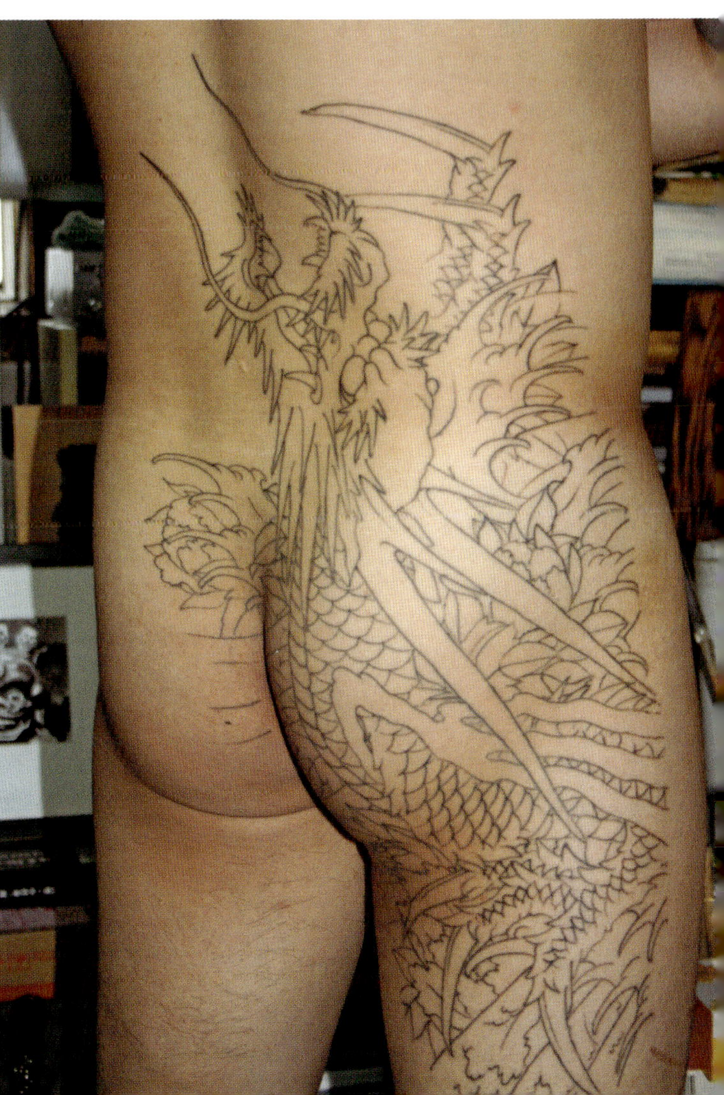

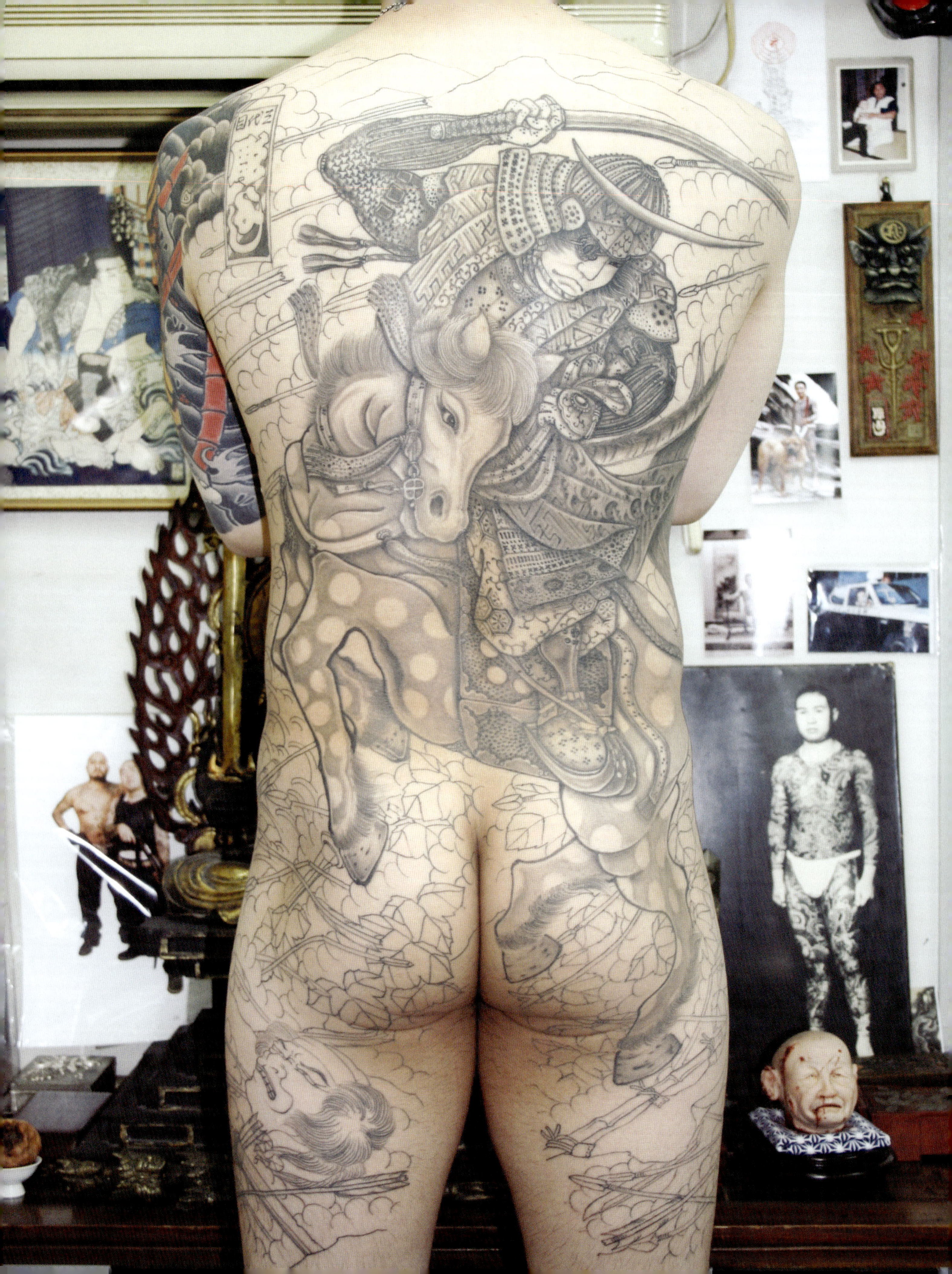

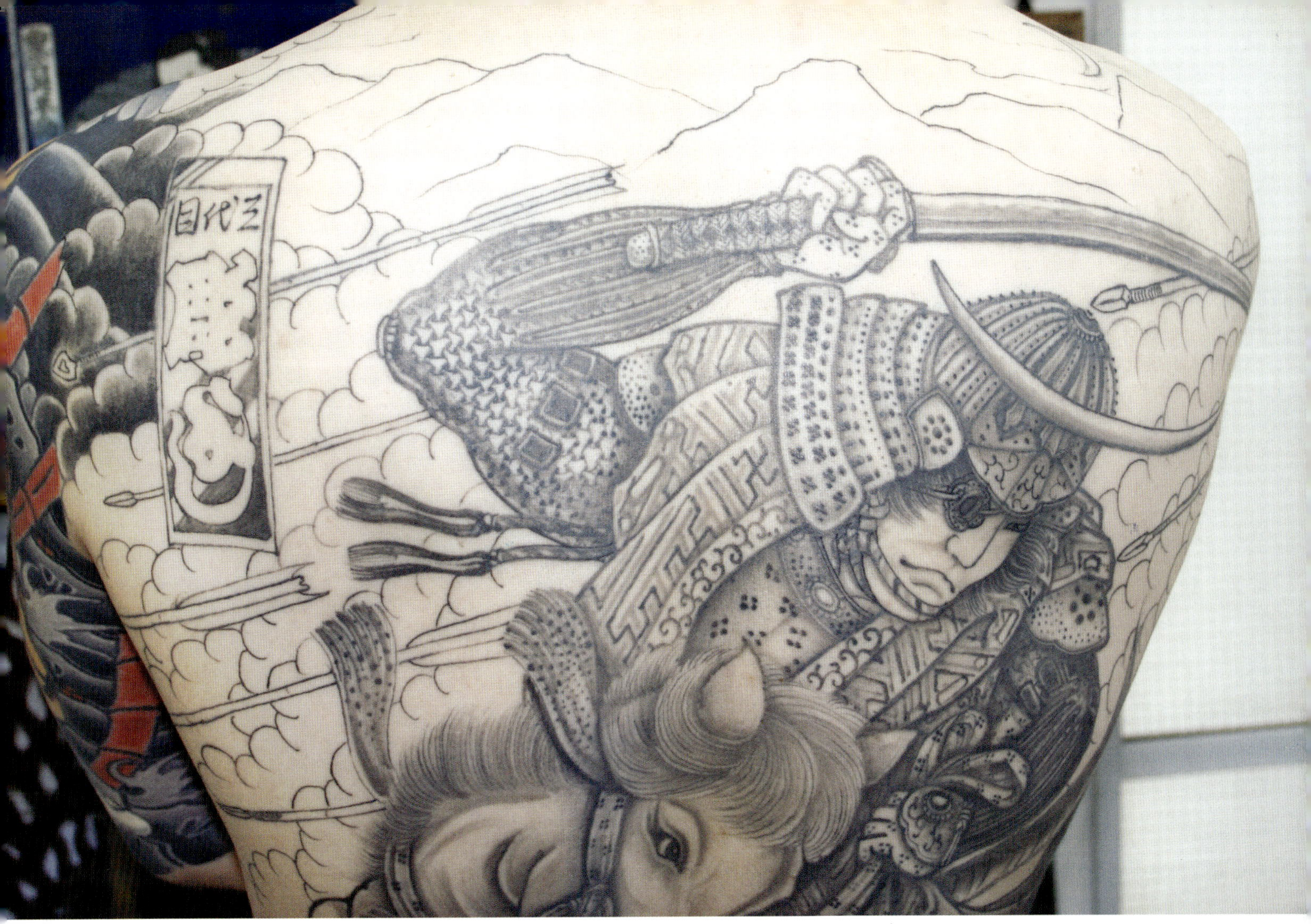

Date Masamune (1567-1636), a historical figure shown on horseback. Having lost an eye to disease, he was nicknamed "Dokugamryu Masamune." Dokugamryu translates to "one-eye dragon."

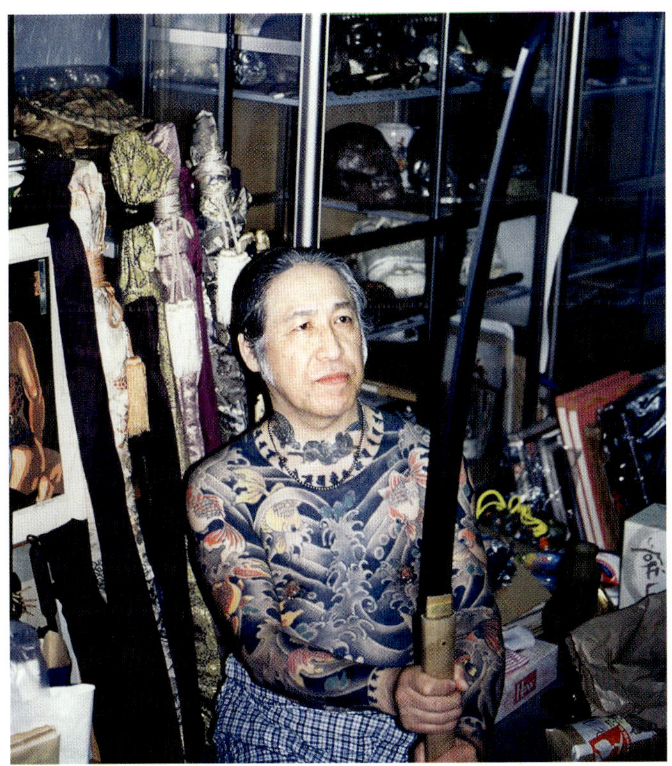

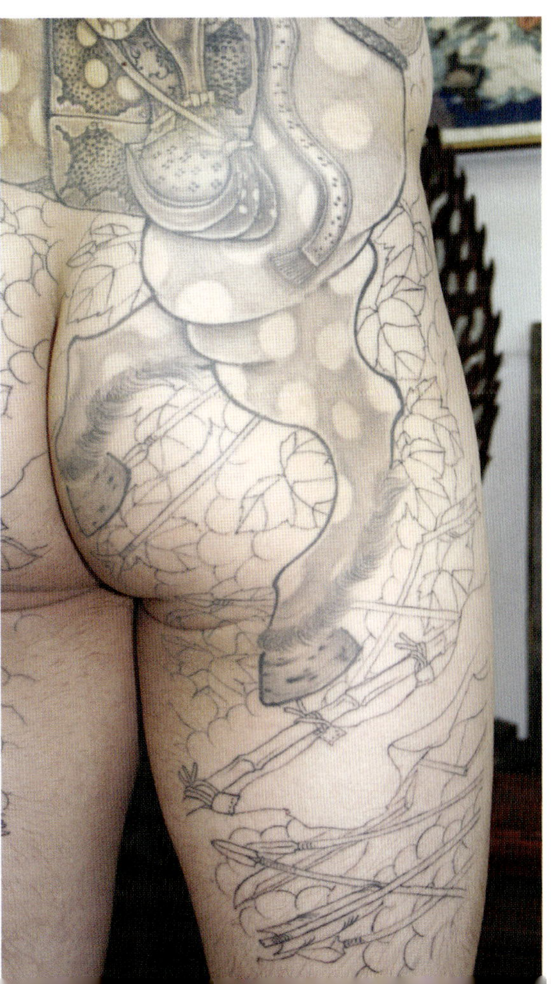

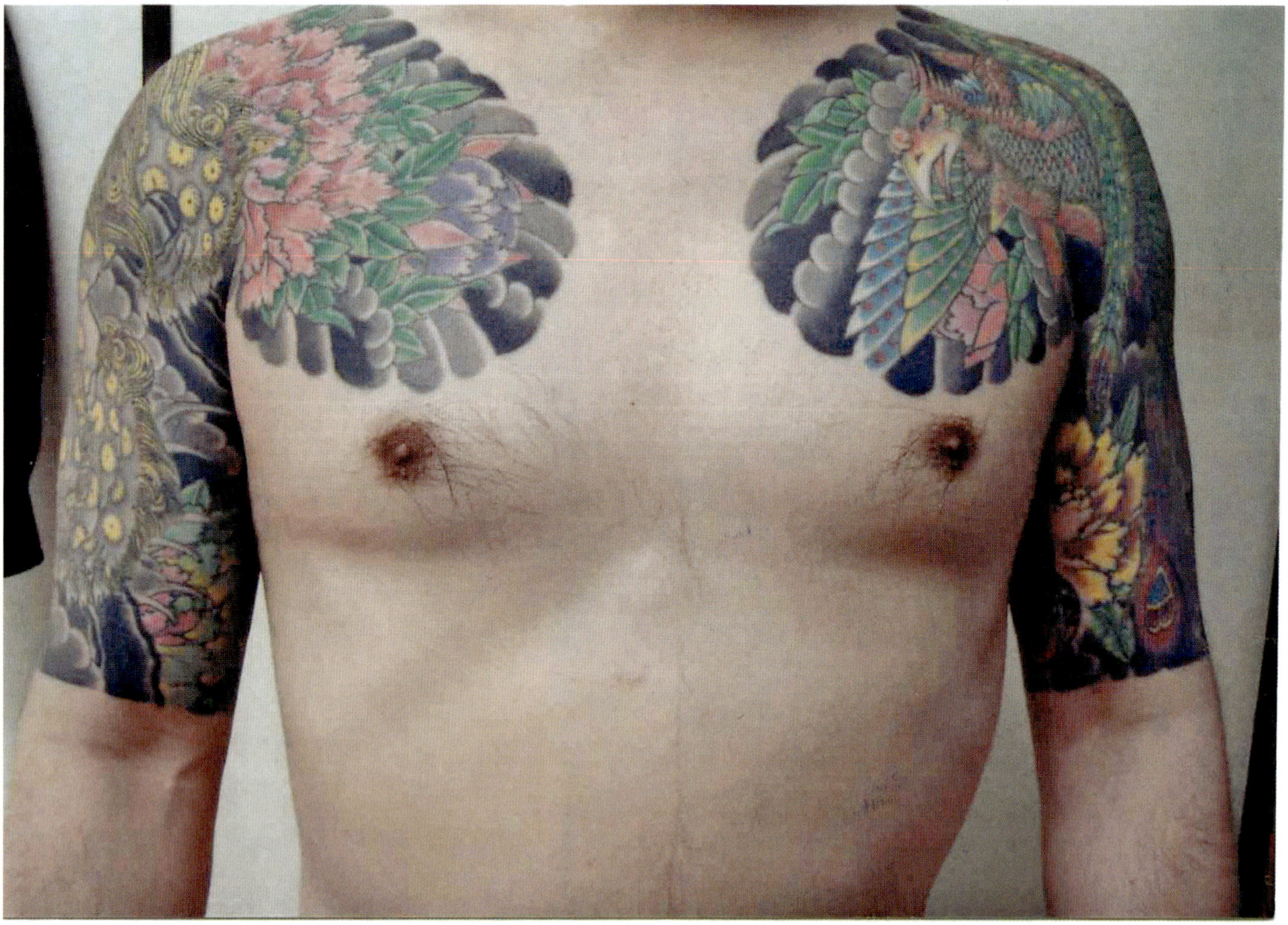

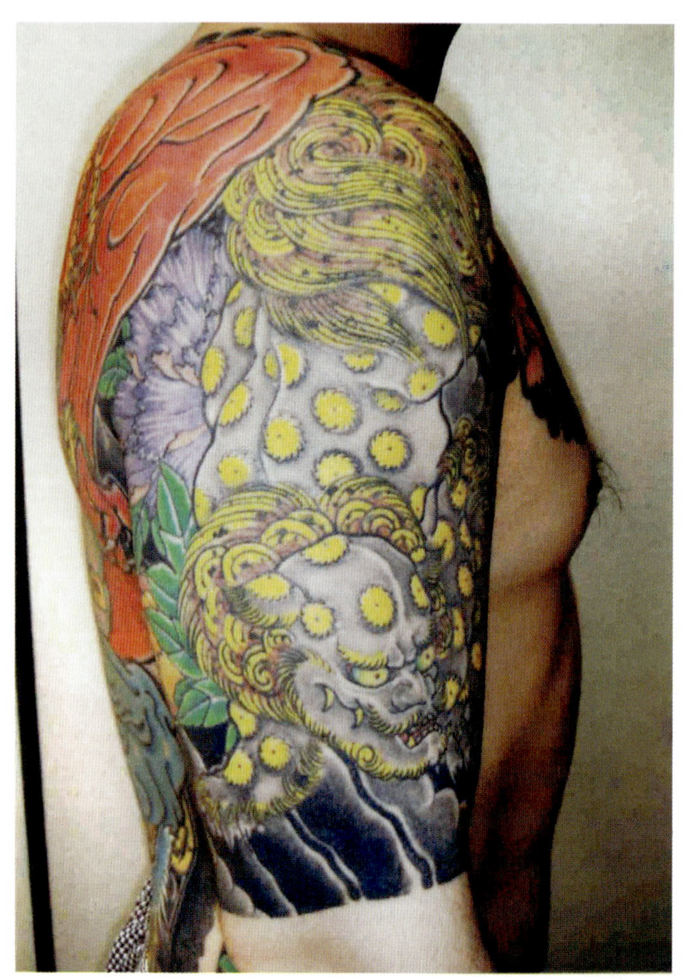

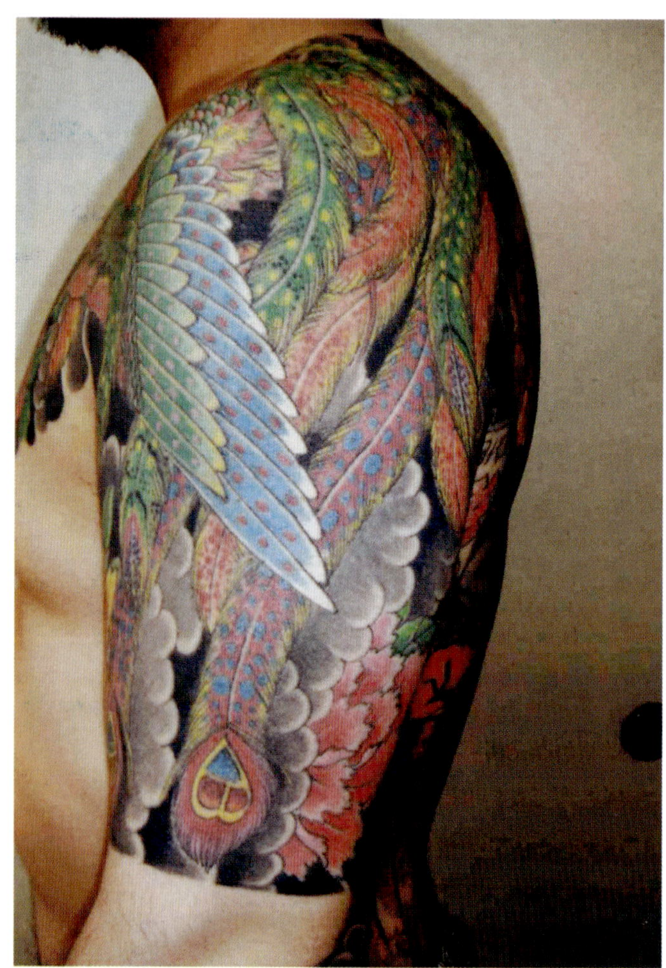

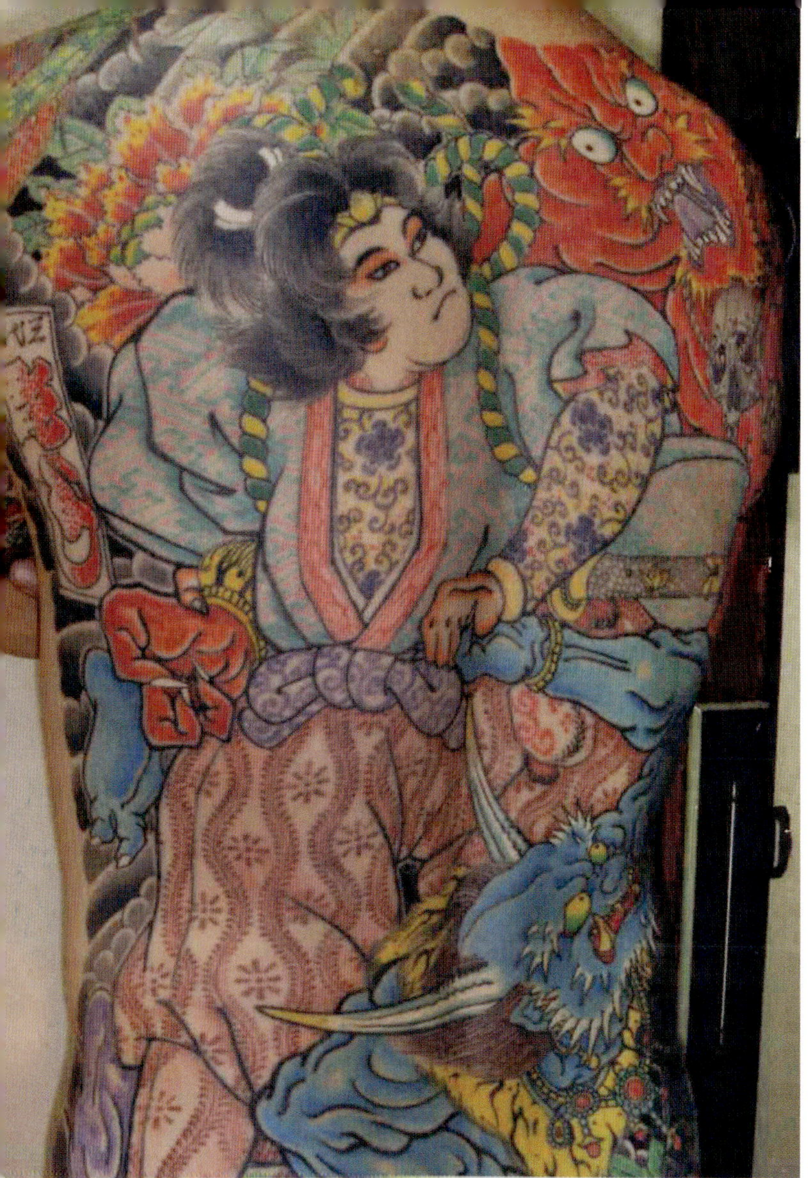

Opposite:
Karajishi to ho-o, Chinese lion and phoenix half-sleeve and chest panels.

Left and Below:
Momotaro subduing an *oni*. In a famous folktale Momotaro was born of a peach and raised by a woman who found him while doing her laundry. His strength was supernatural. With the aid of a dog, monkey, and pheasant he conquered Onigashima, "the island of Ogres."

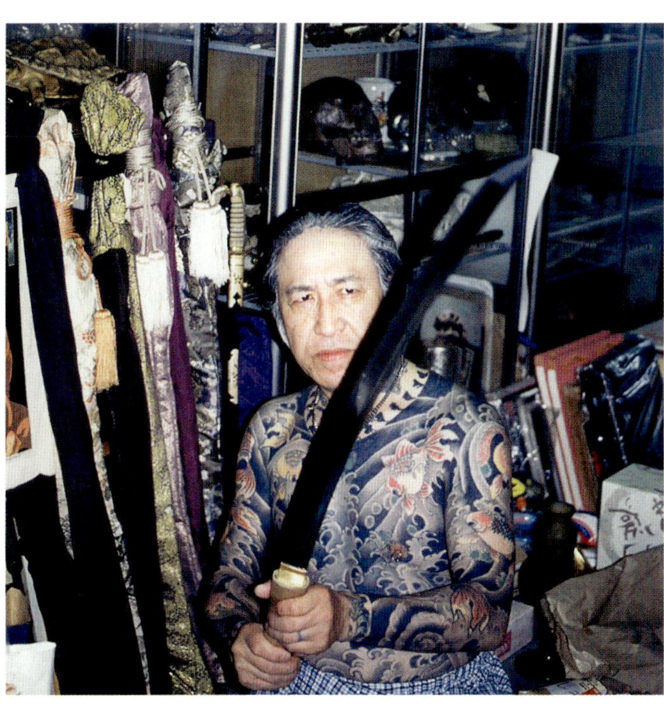

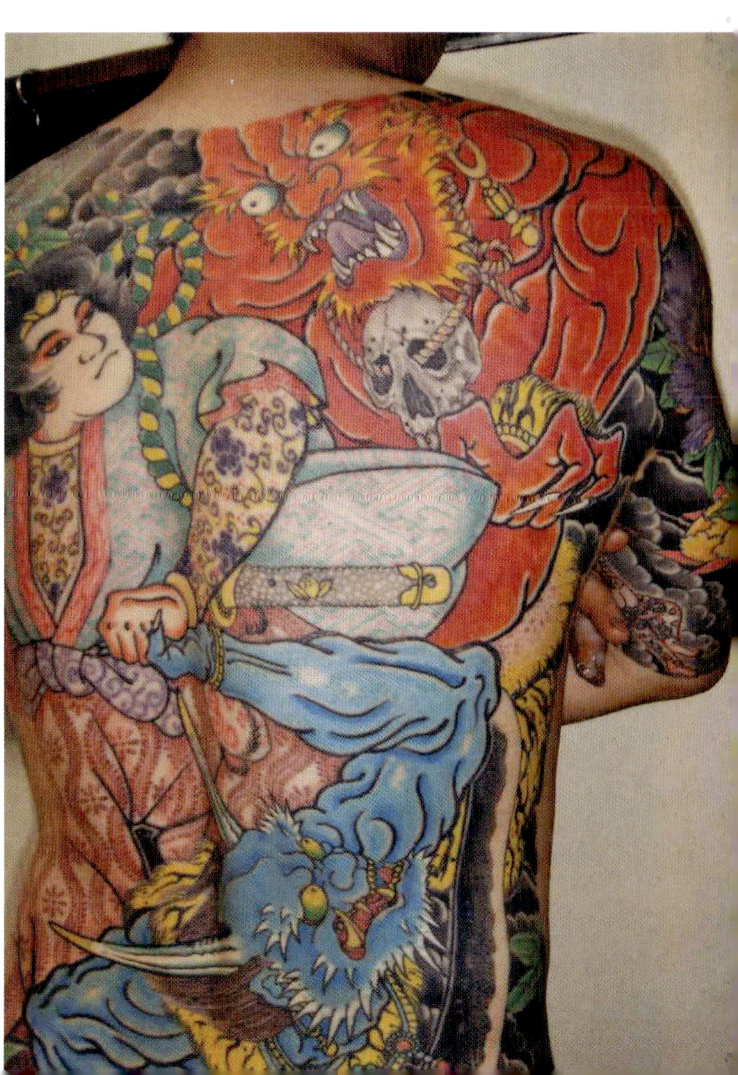

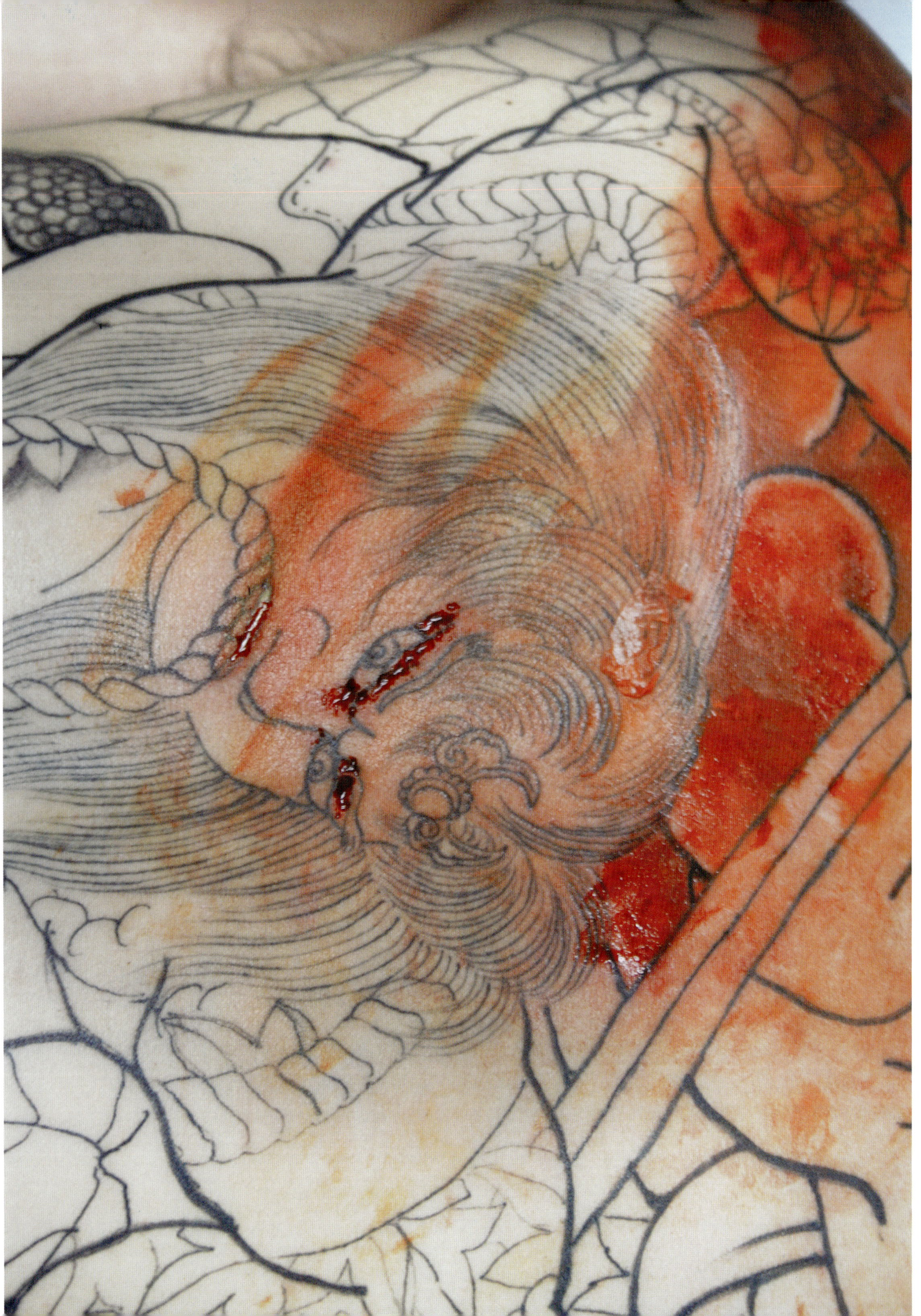

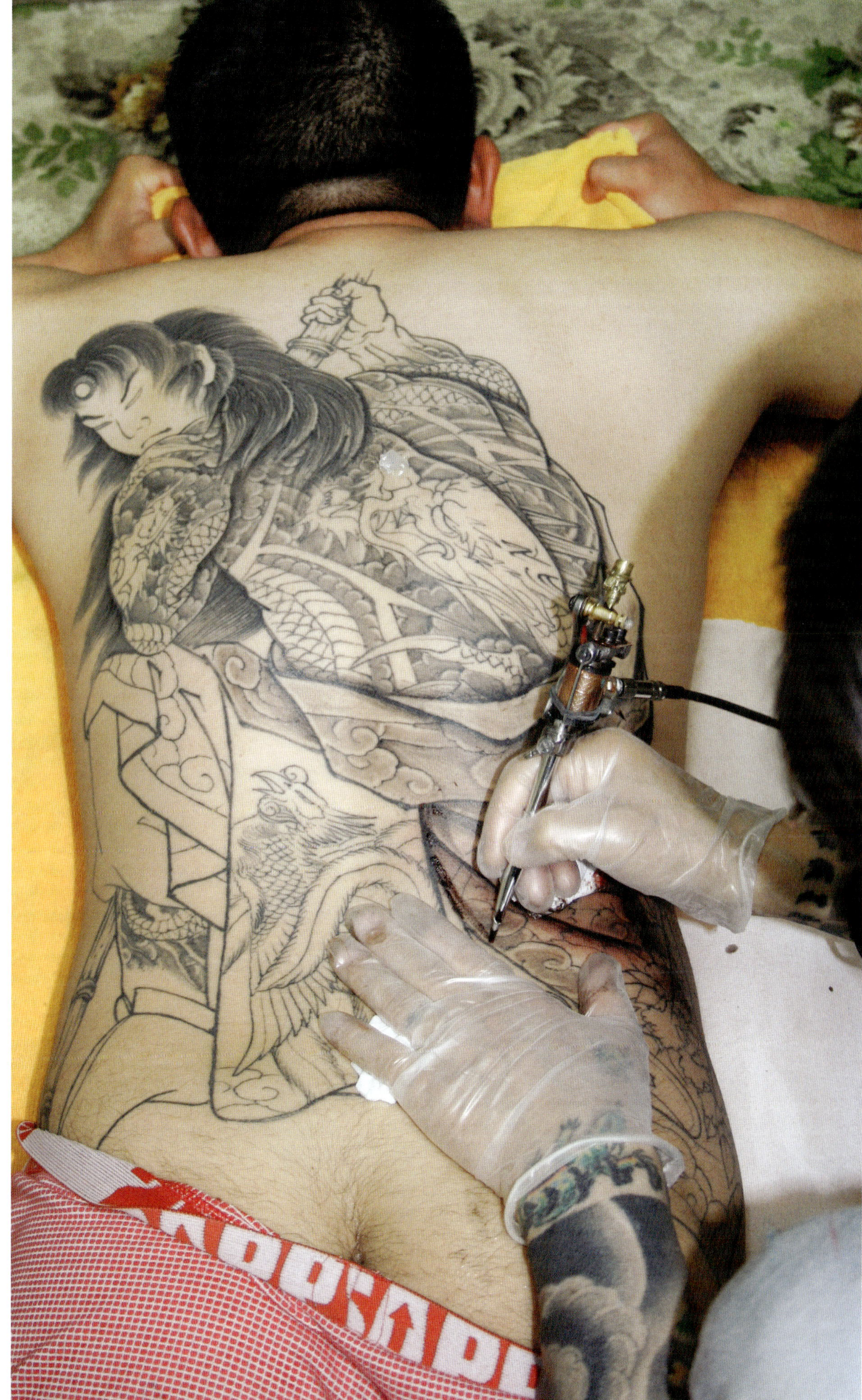

Right:
Kumonryu Shishin, "in progress." Kumonryu is among the most popular of Suikoden warriors. His name literally translates to "nine -dragoned," referring to the nine dragons tattooed on his body. Also adding to his popularity was his choice to reject his noble birthrights in favor of justice and brotherhood. An exceptionally skilled warrior, he was finally felled in an ambush of arrows at the Battle of Yu-ling Barrier.

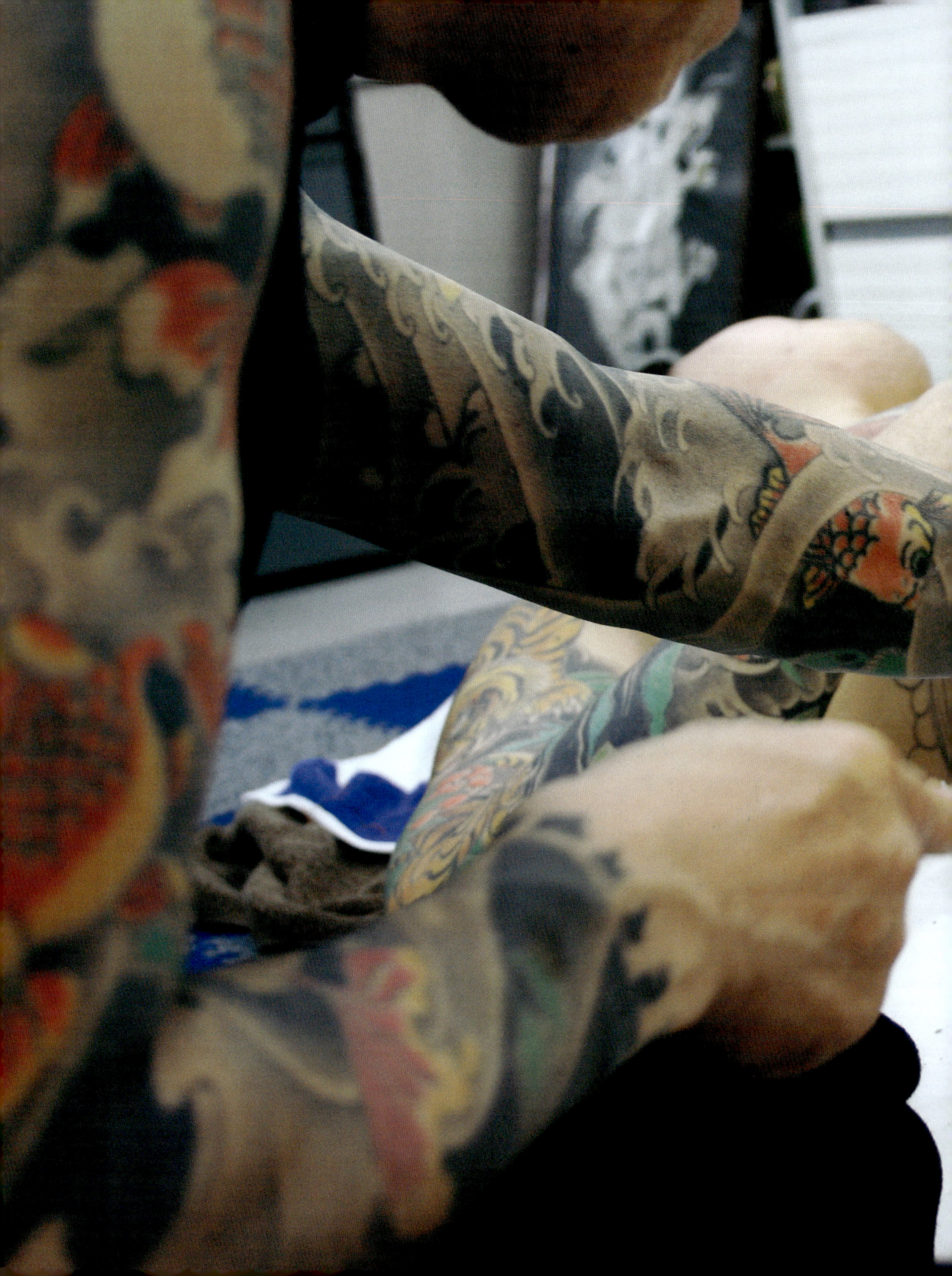

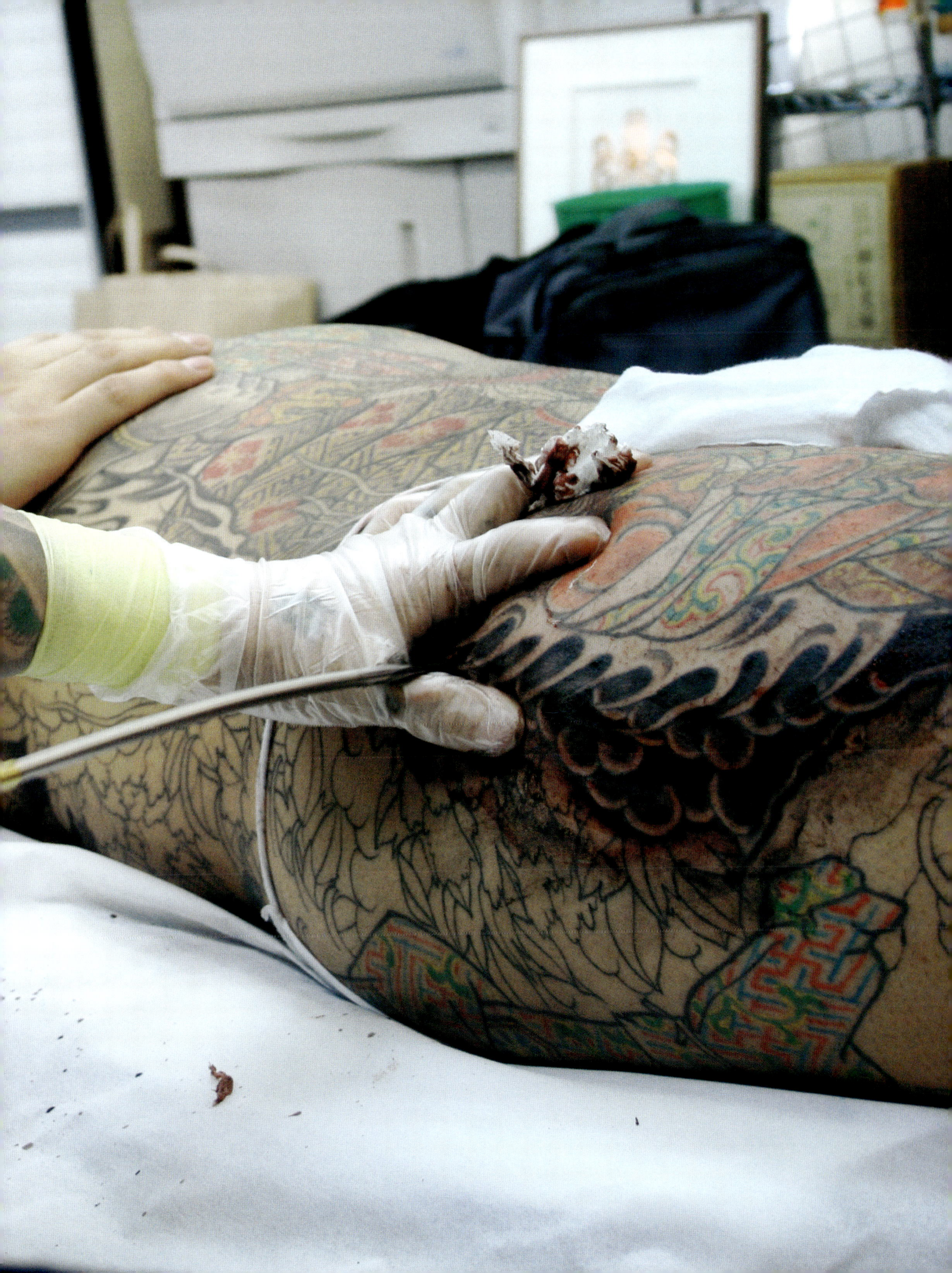

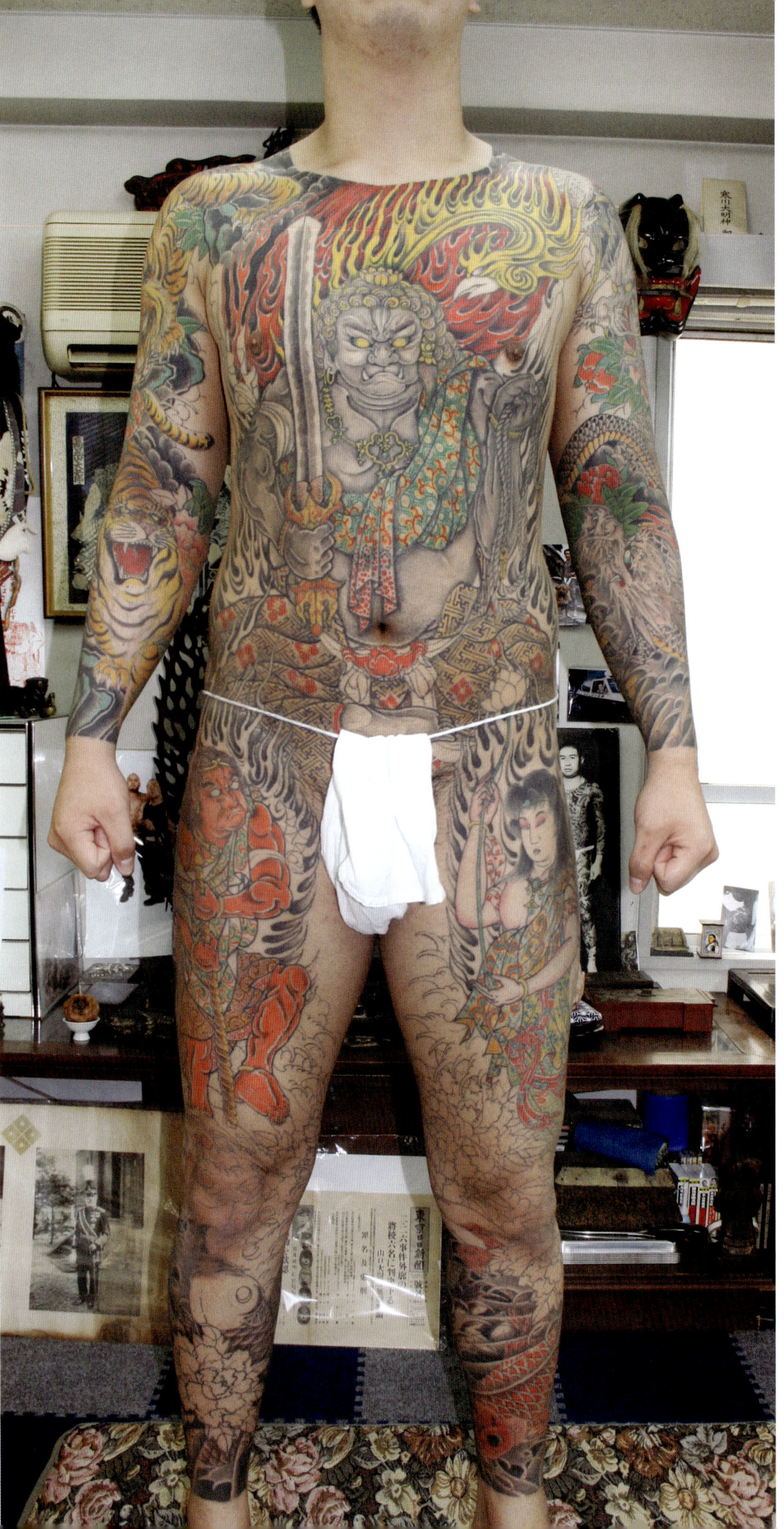

Left:
Japanese tattoo iconography is shrouded in mystery; many motifs have specific meanings, as well as cultural significance. Common misinterpretations of mythology are prevalent in the mind of the general Western public. Oftentimes *gaijin* project an idealized mysticism because they are eager for something different or special, an escape from the monotony or familiarity of their own culture. Japanese tattoo iconography encompasses mythology, history, and superstition. It is presented in an unparalleled visual format.

Another misunderstanding of many *gaijin* is a lack of free will on the part of the client. While there is a heightened respect for the tattoo master, I think it is unfair to discount the participation of the client. Maybe this image has to do with years of film and notions of ultra-loyal samurai and subservient, docile women, but I have found Japanese tattoo clients to be just as interactive if not more so than their Western counterparts. The clients pick their motifs, often discussing the idea with the Master. The final product is usually a joint effort.

Right
Seitaka. Seitaka and Kongara are attendants to Fudōmyō-ō.

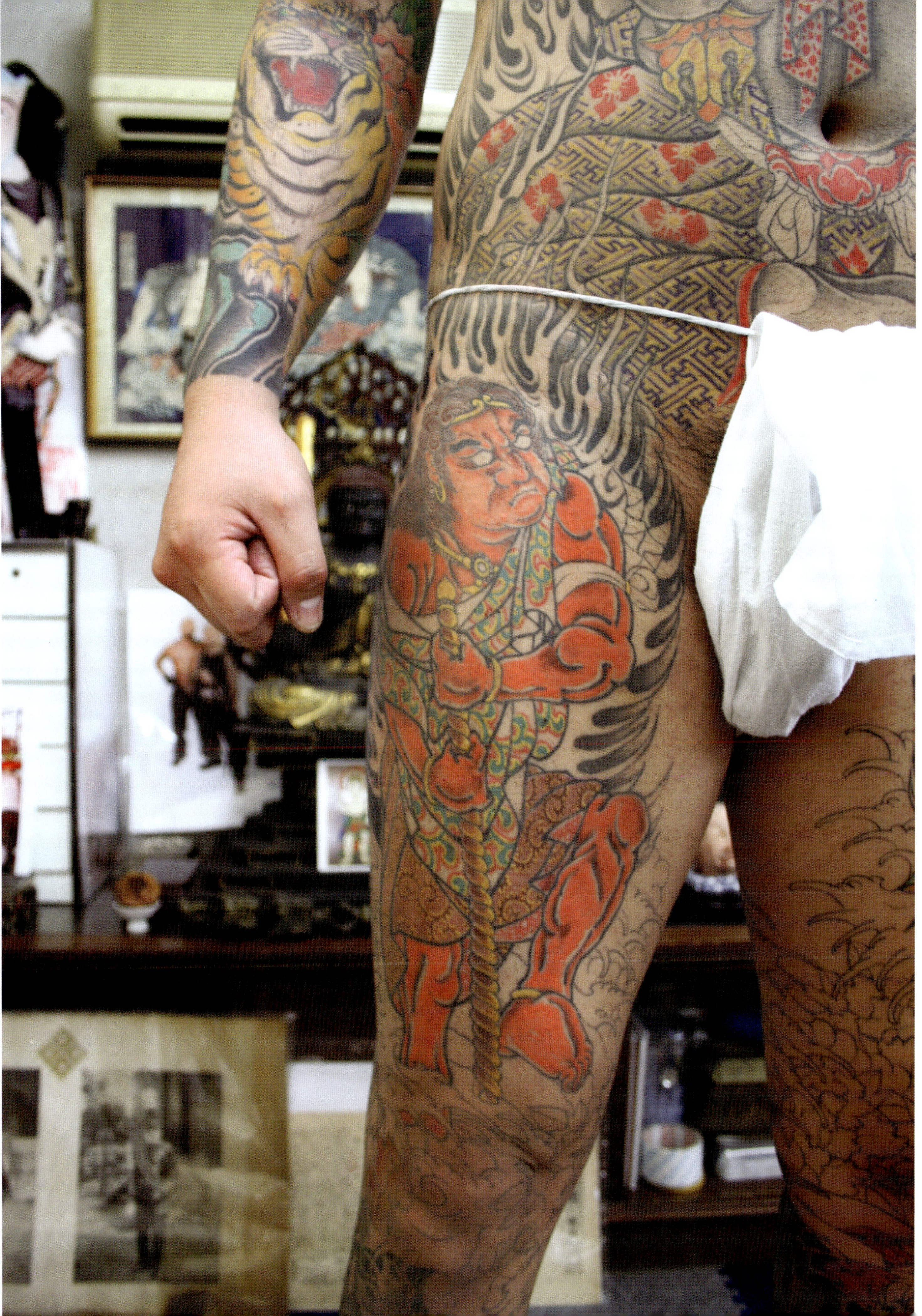

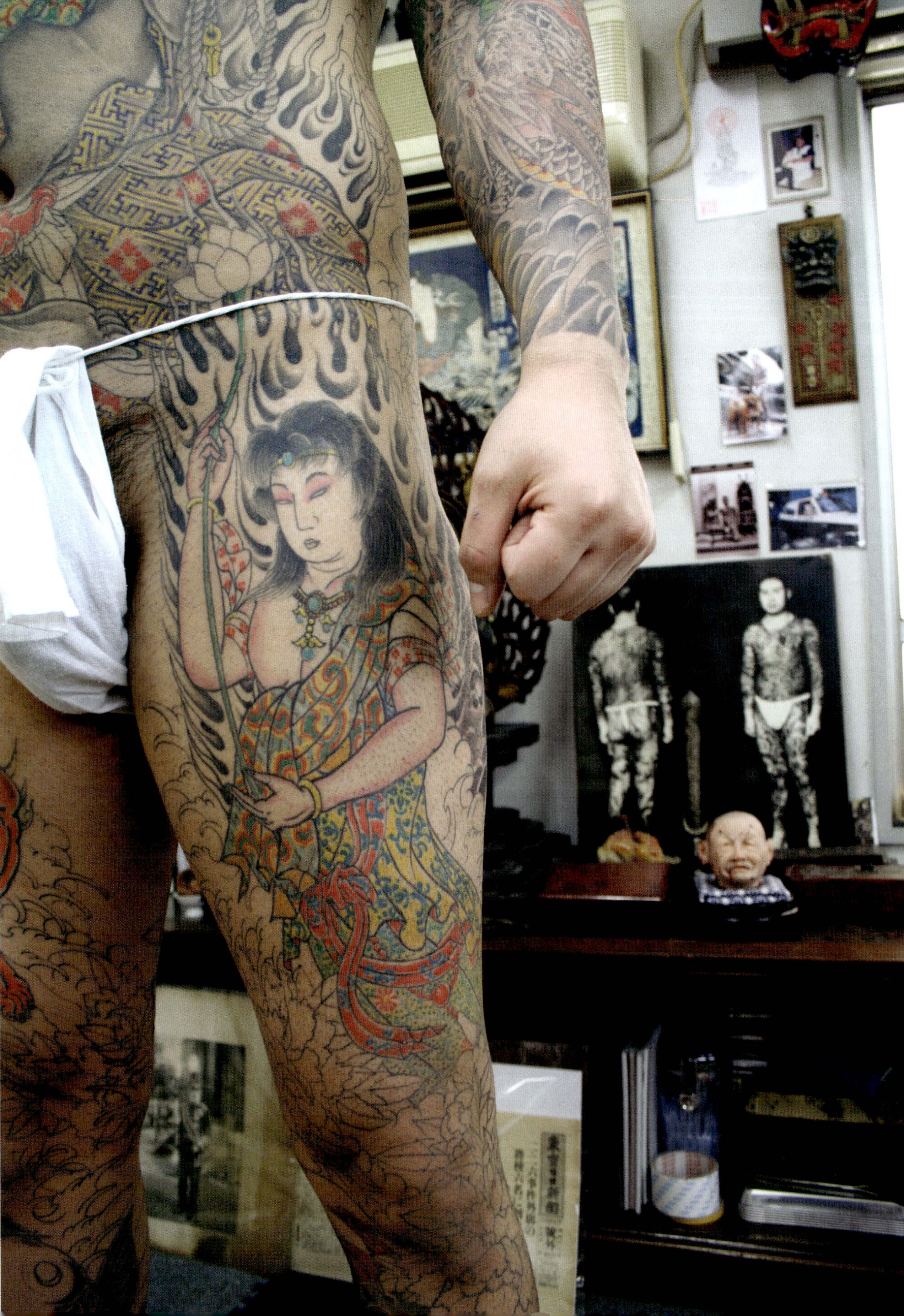

Left:
Kongara.

Right:
In this historic battle, the celebrated swordsman and author of *The Book of Five Rings*, Musashi Miyamoto defeats Kojiro Sasaki with a wooden sword carved out of an oar on the beach of Ganryu Jima.

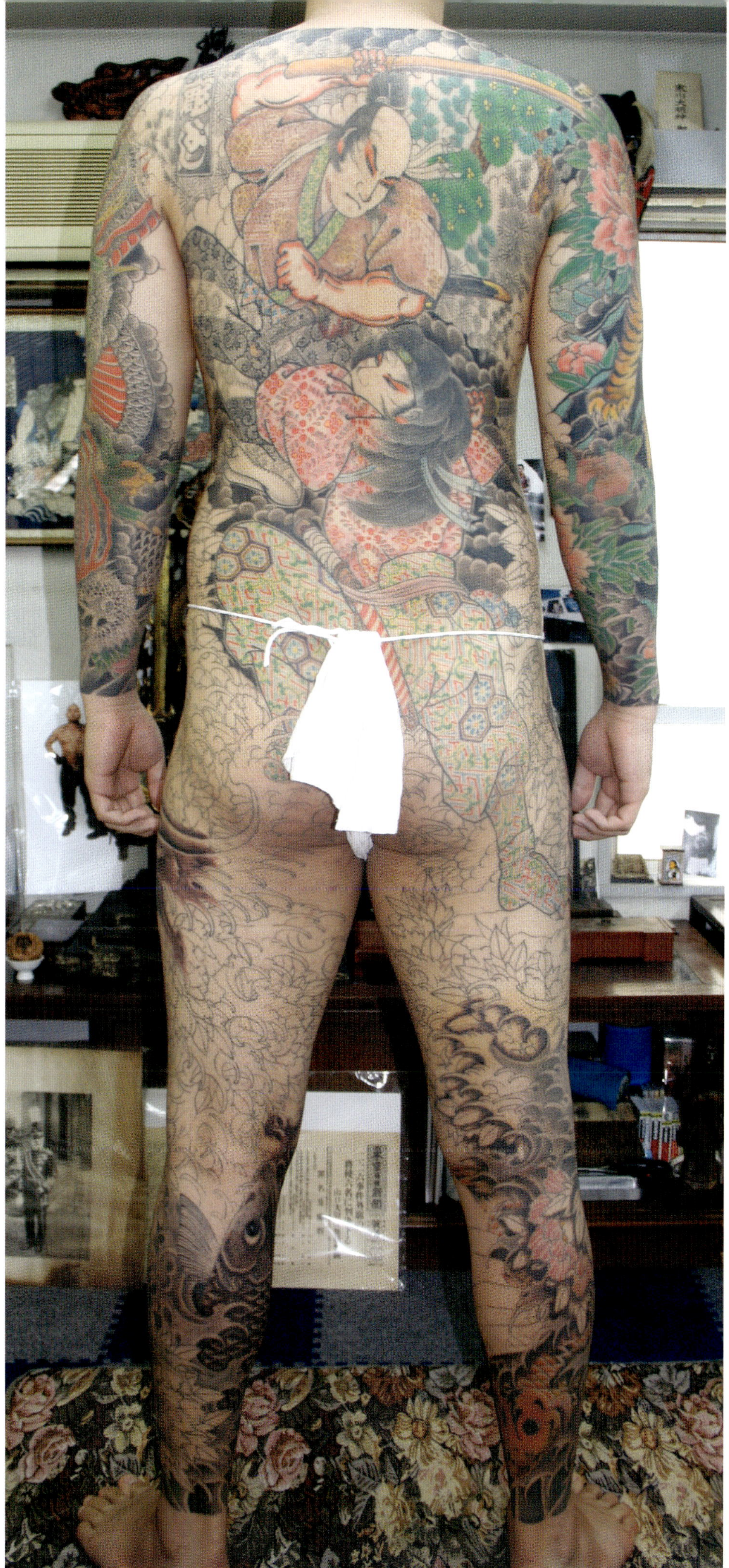

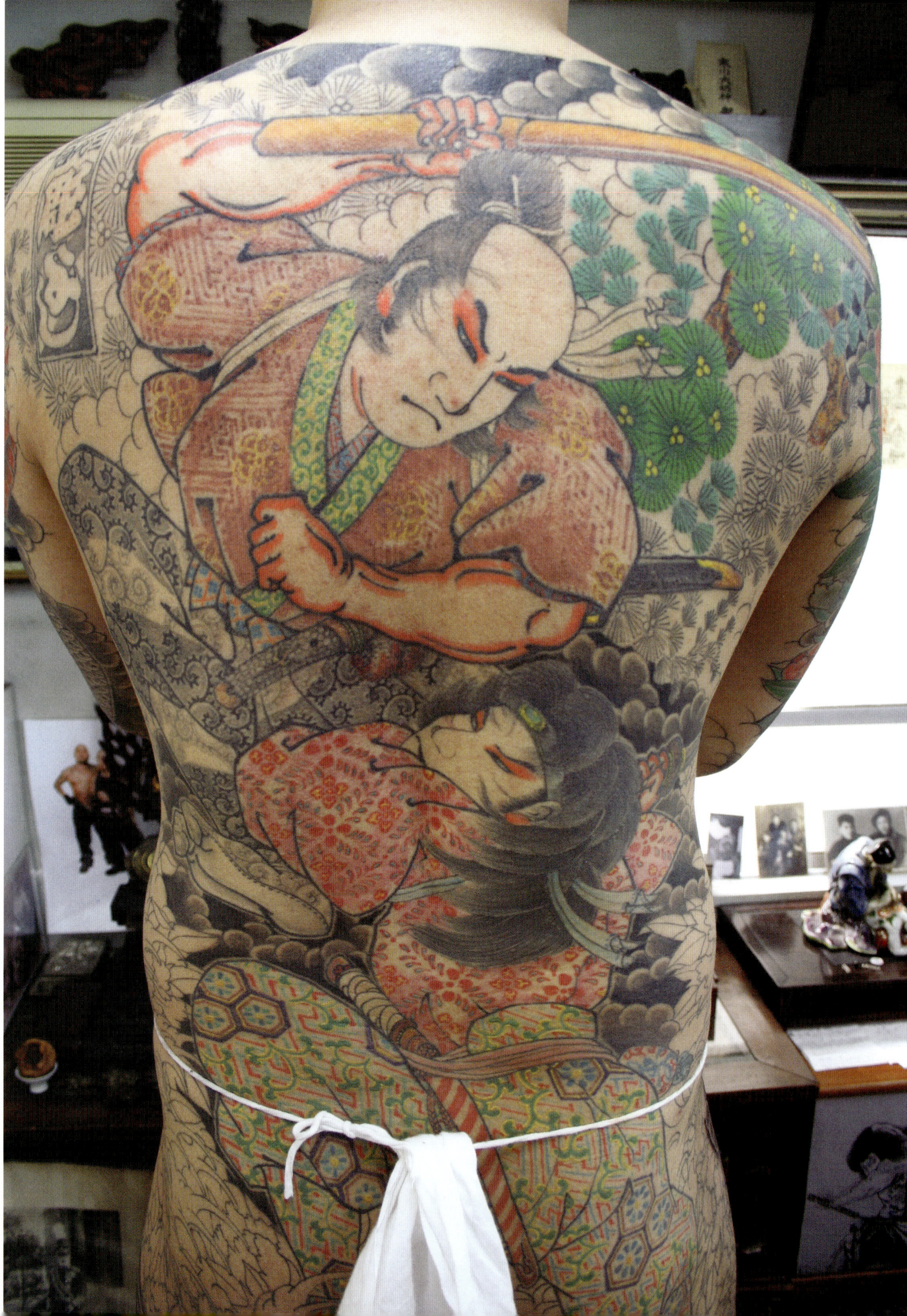

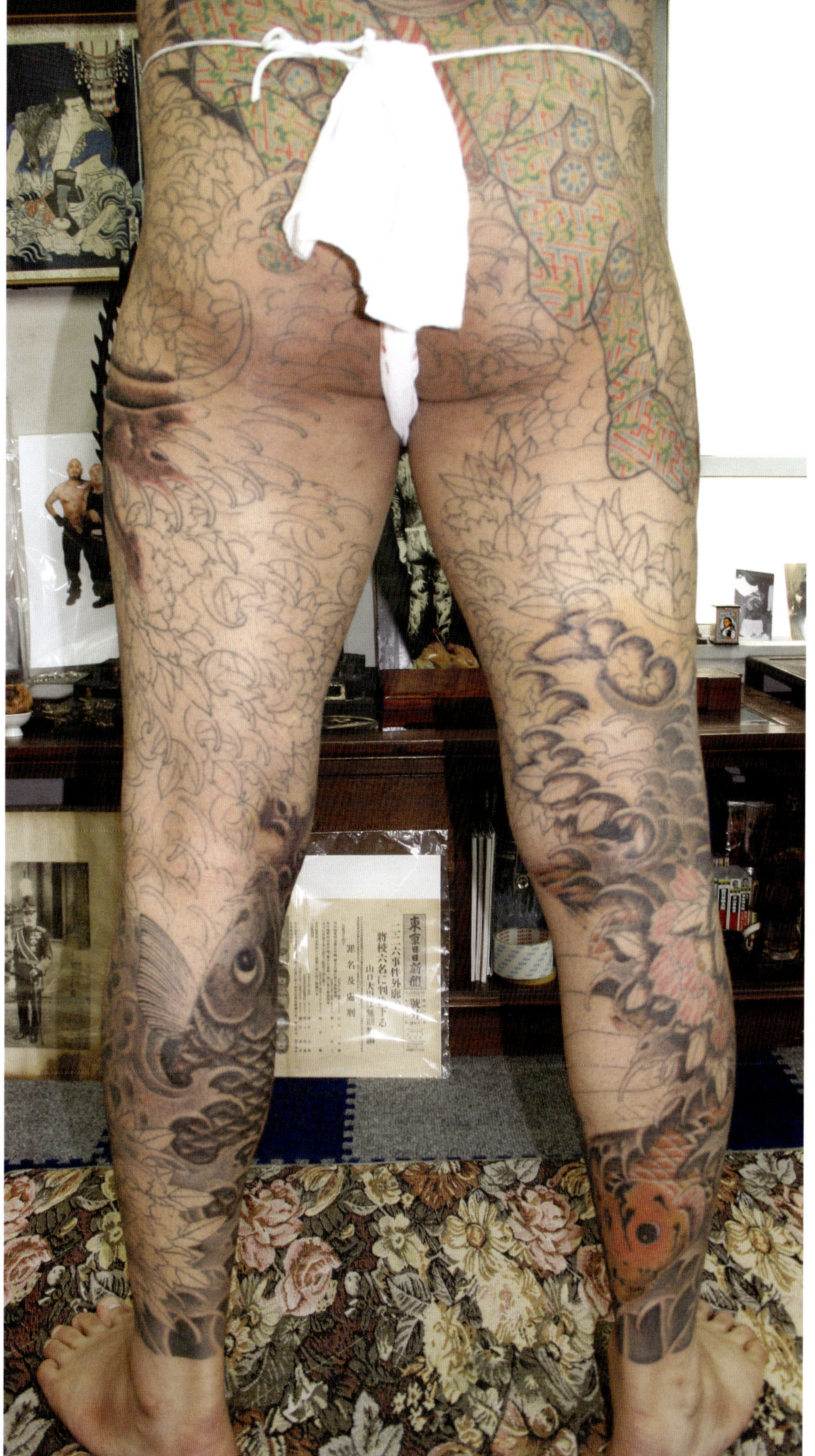
東京日日新聞

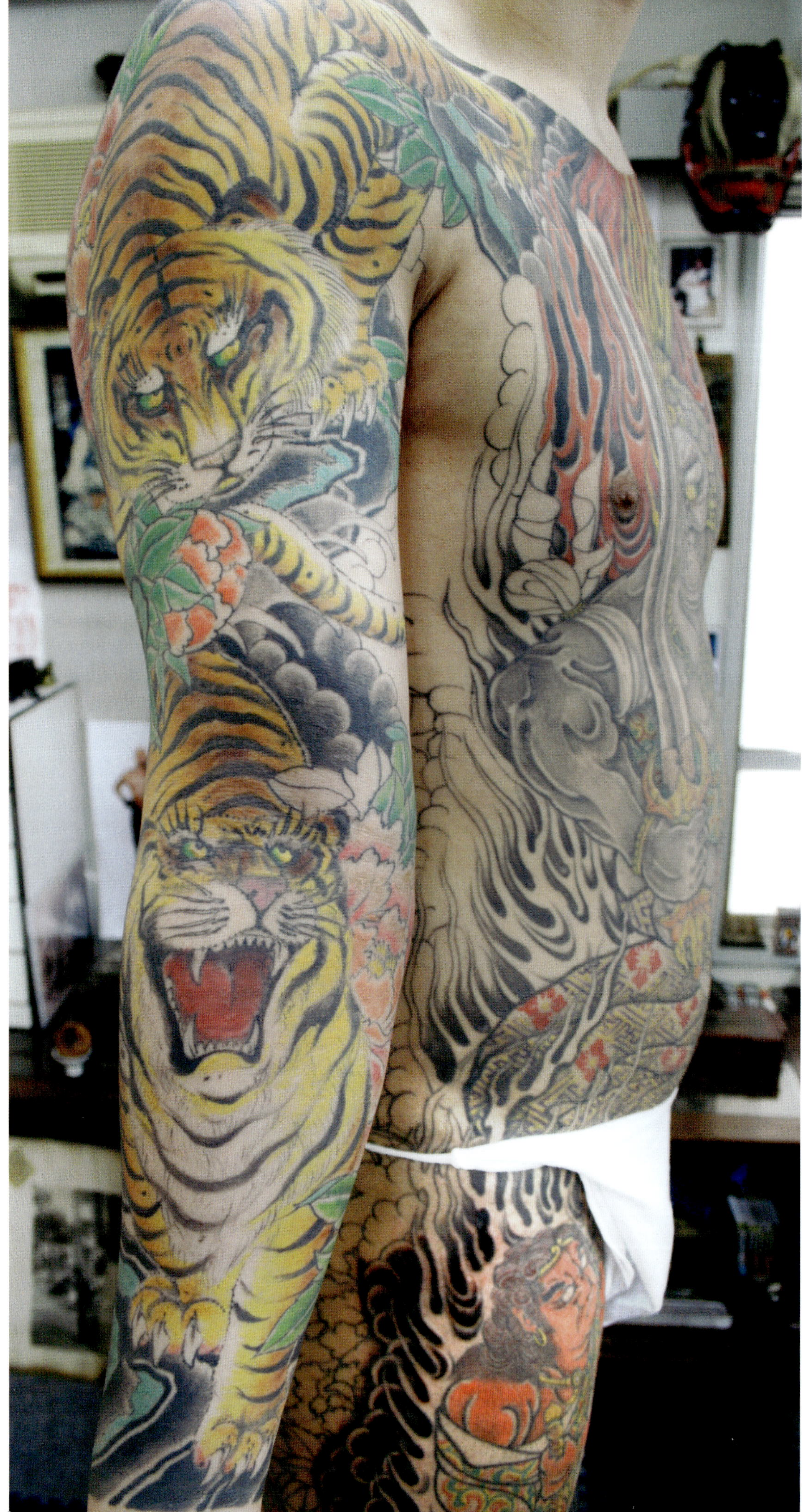

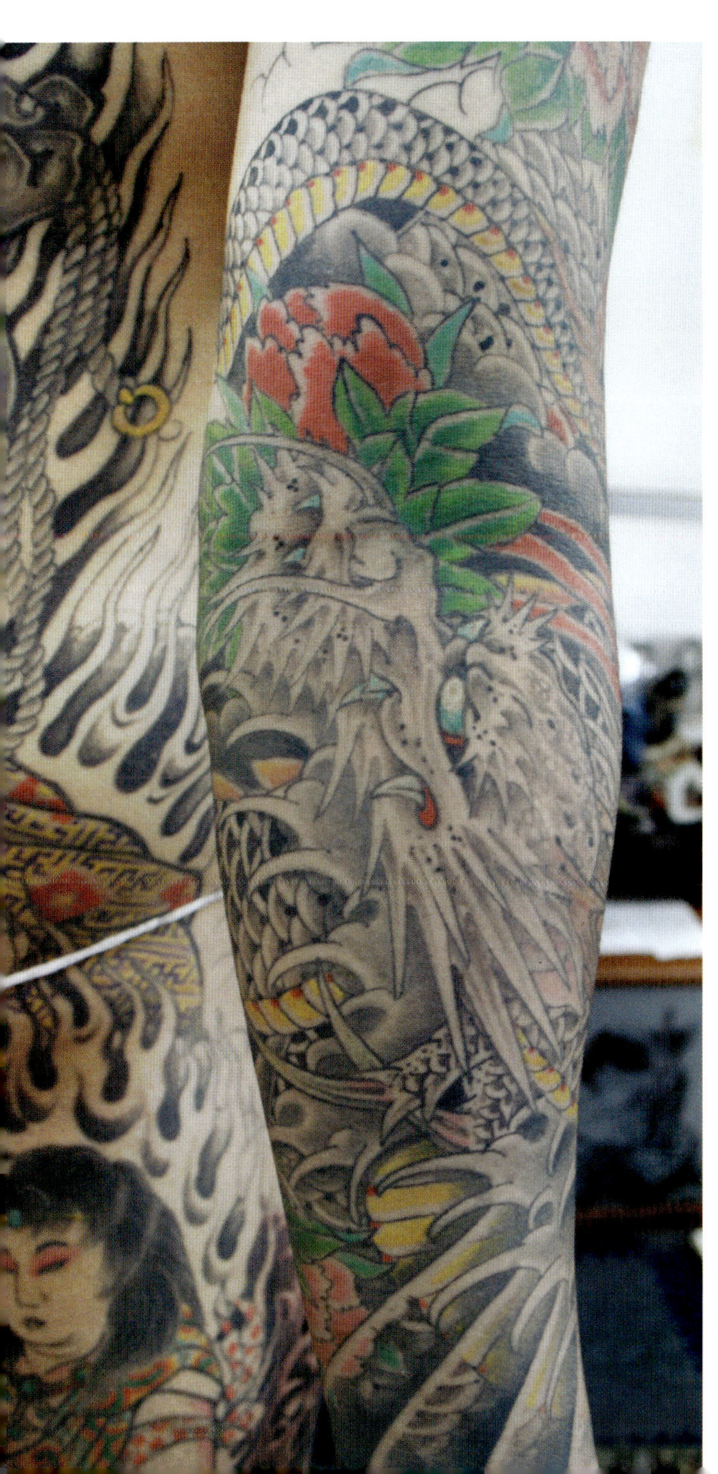

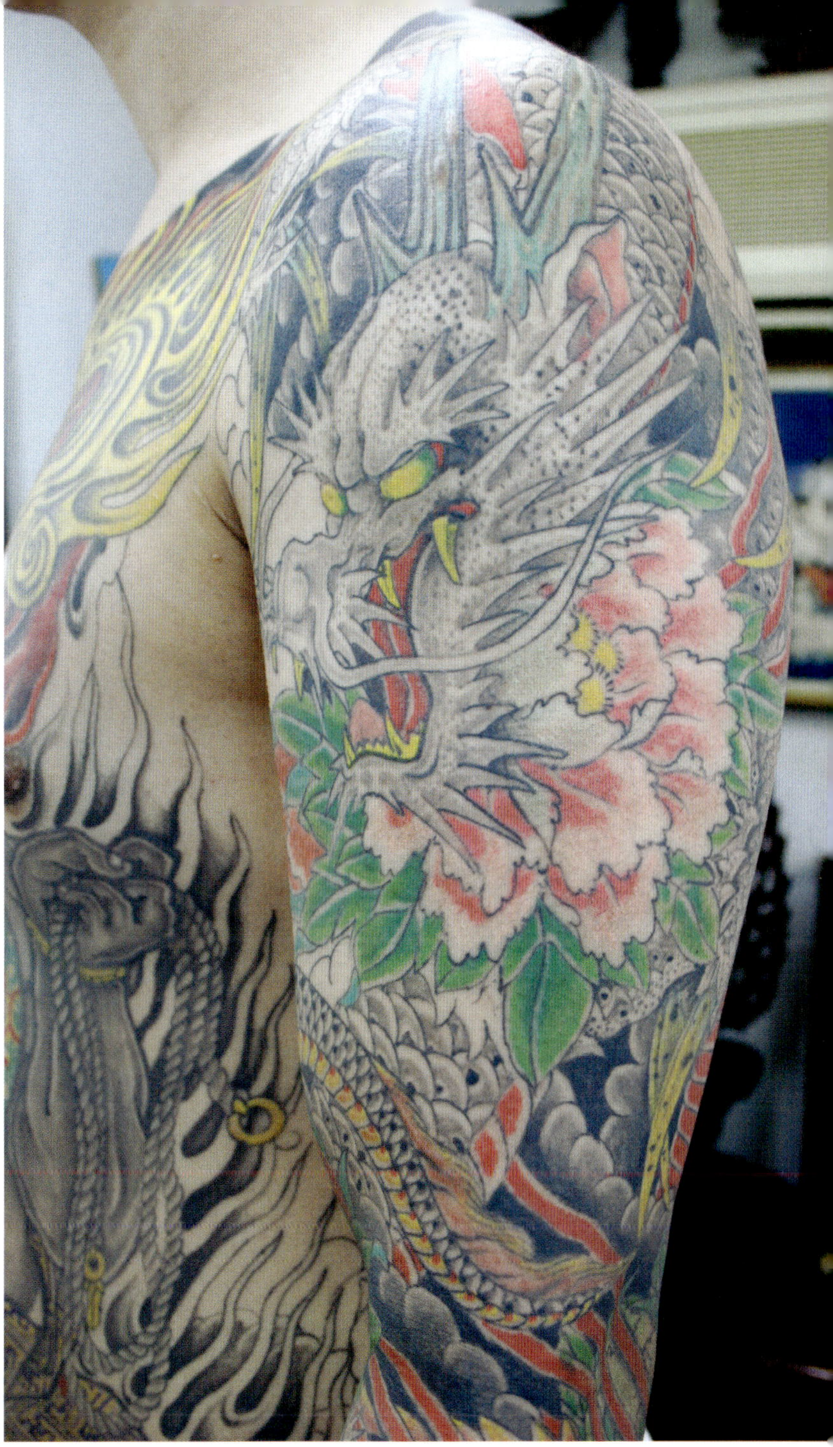

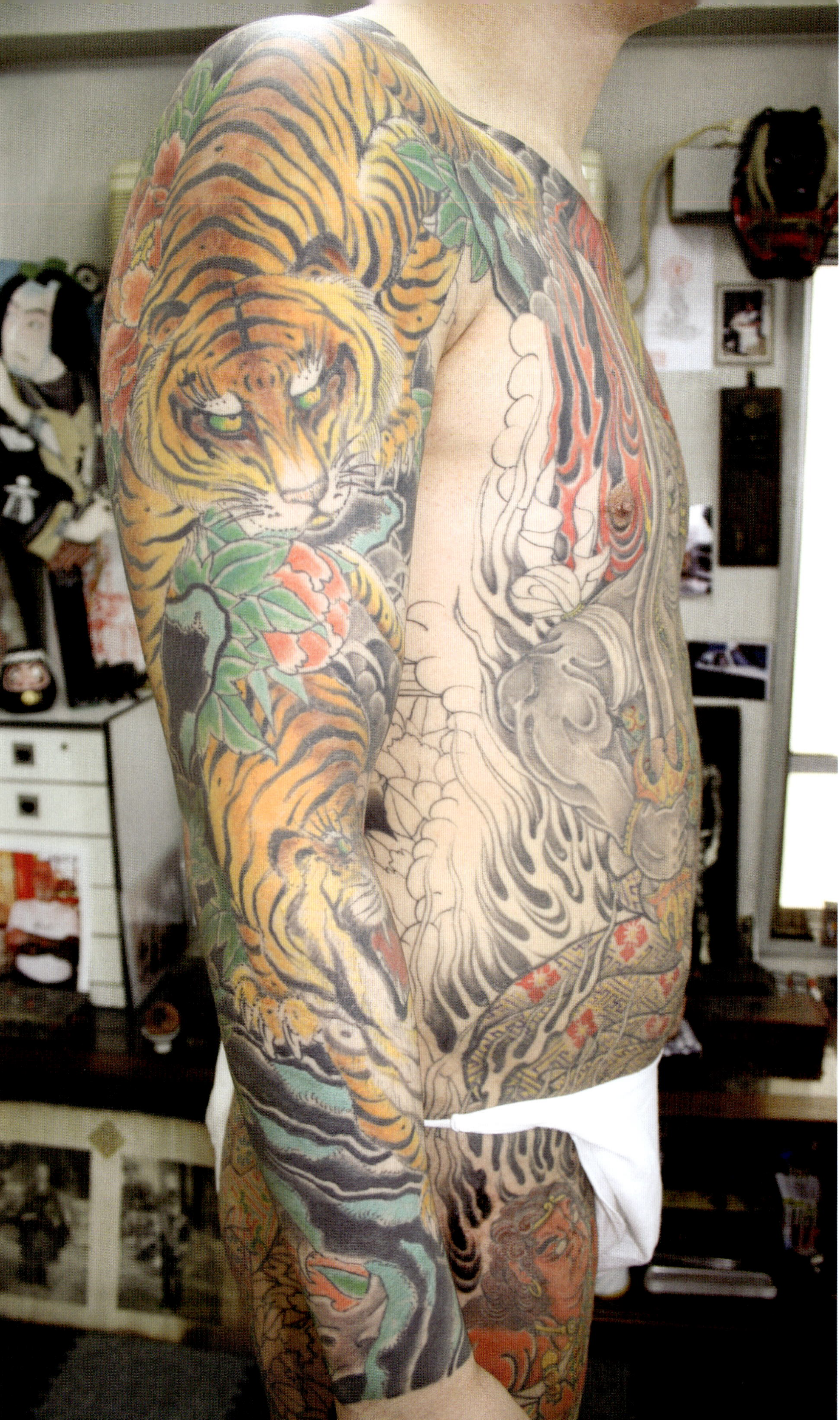

Right:
Sumizome Dayu, she is the spirit of a cherry blossom tree and a character in a *kabuki* play.

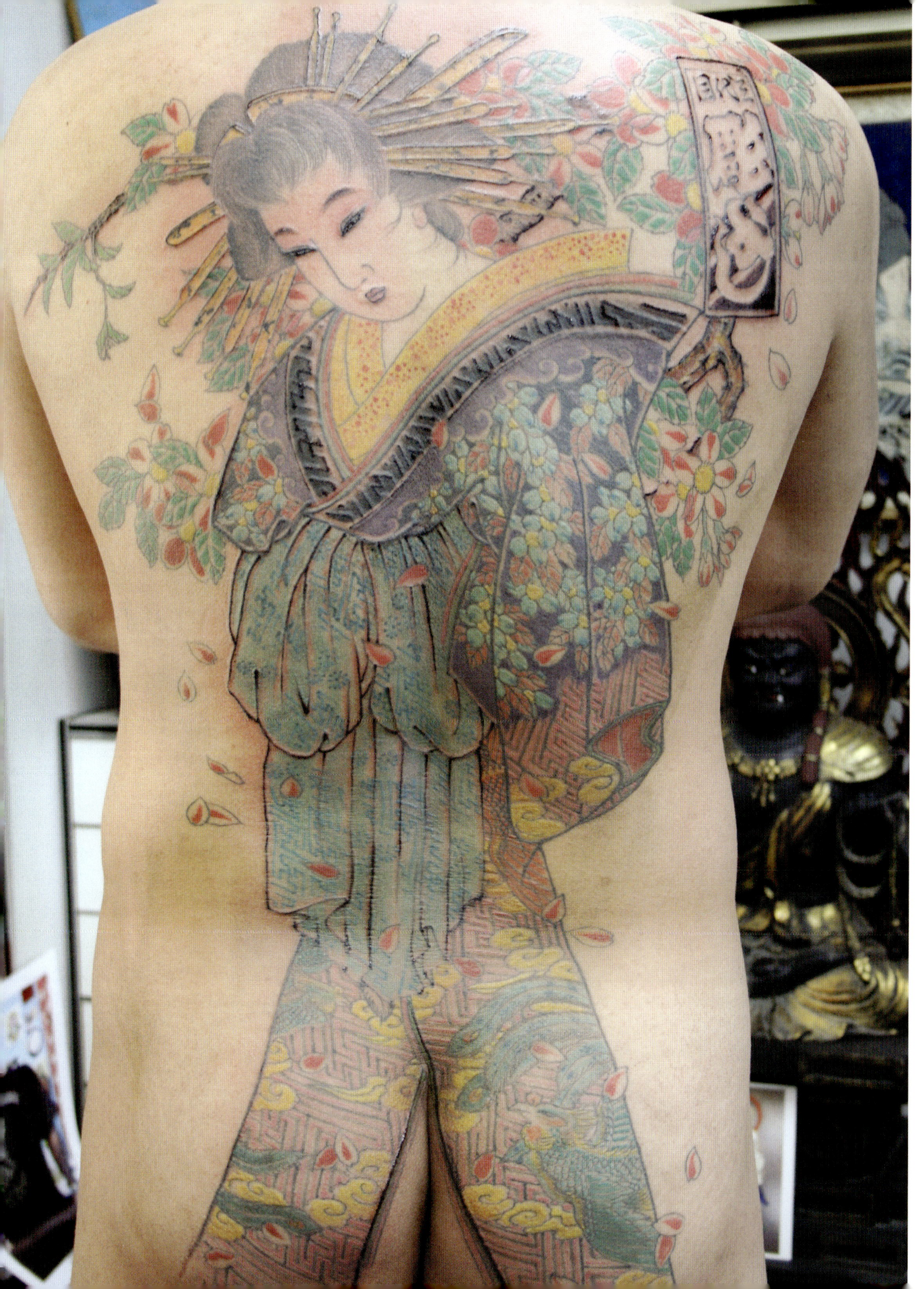

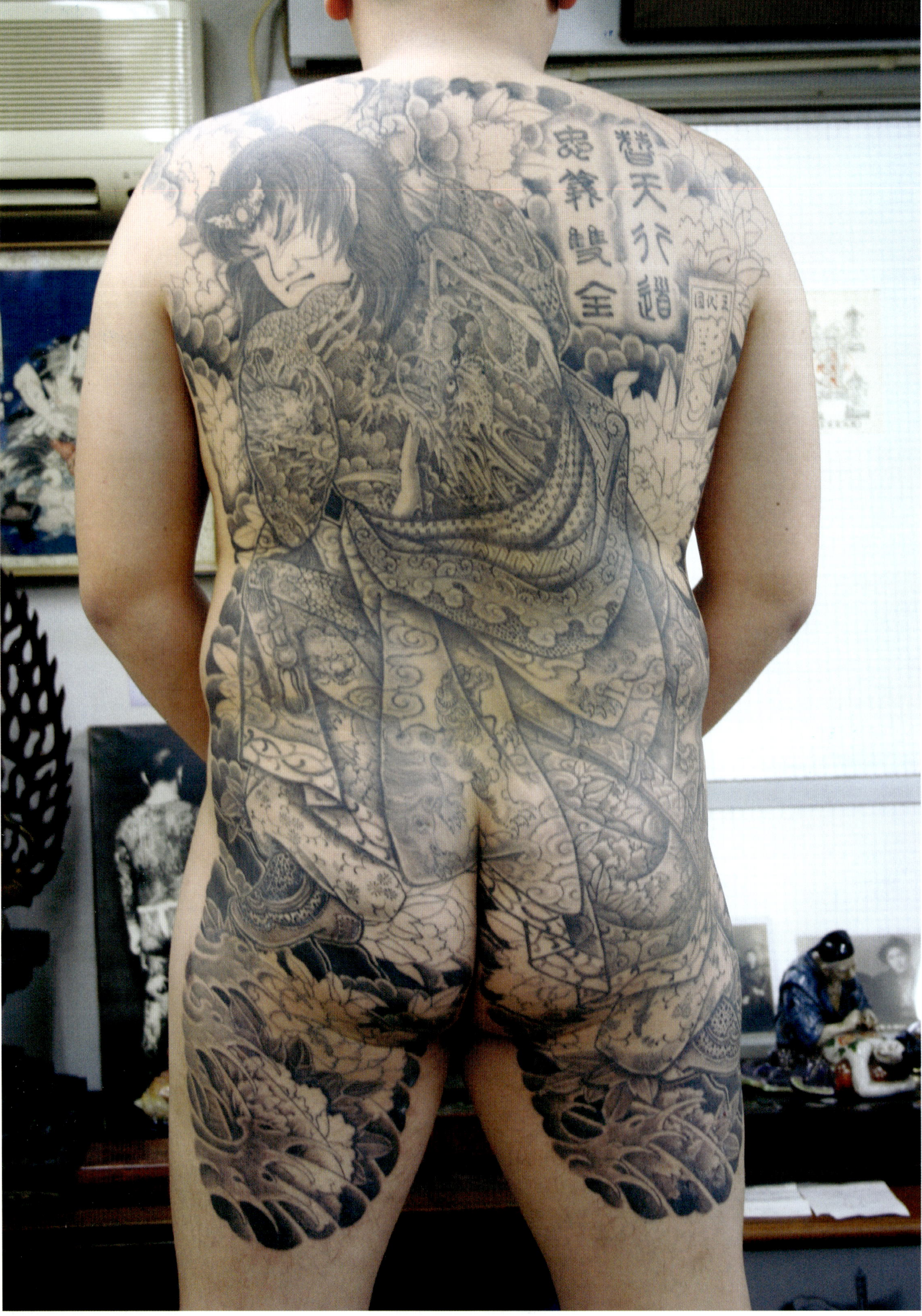
替天行道
忠義雙全

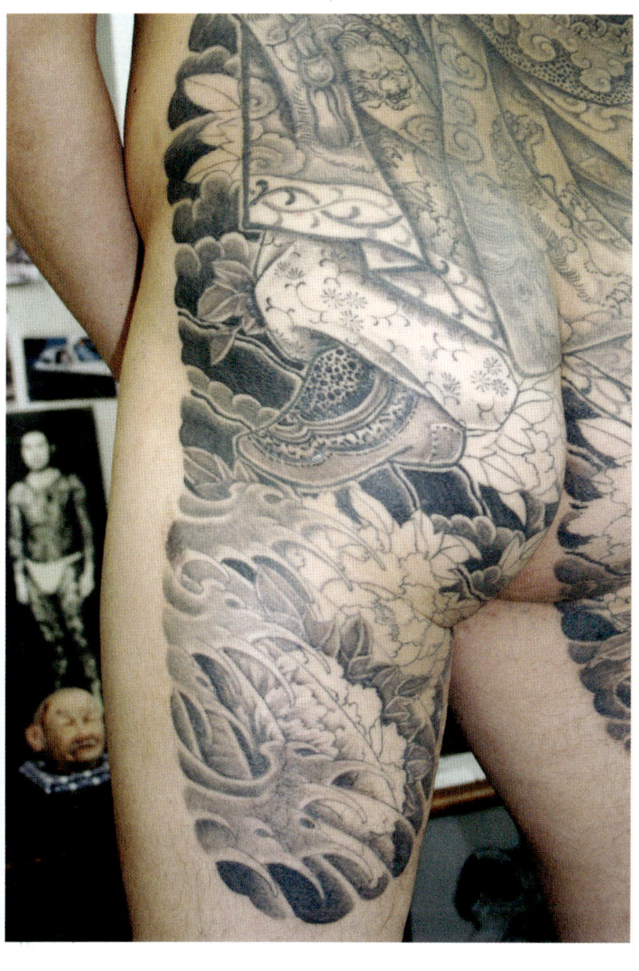

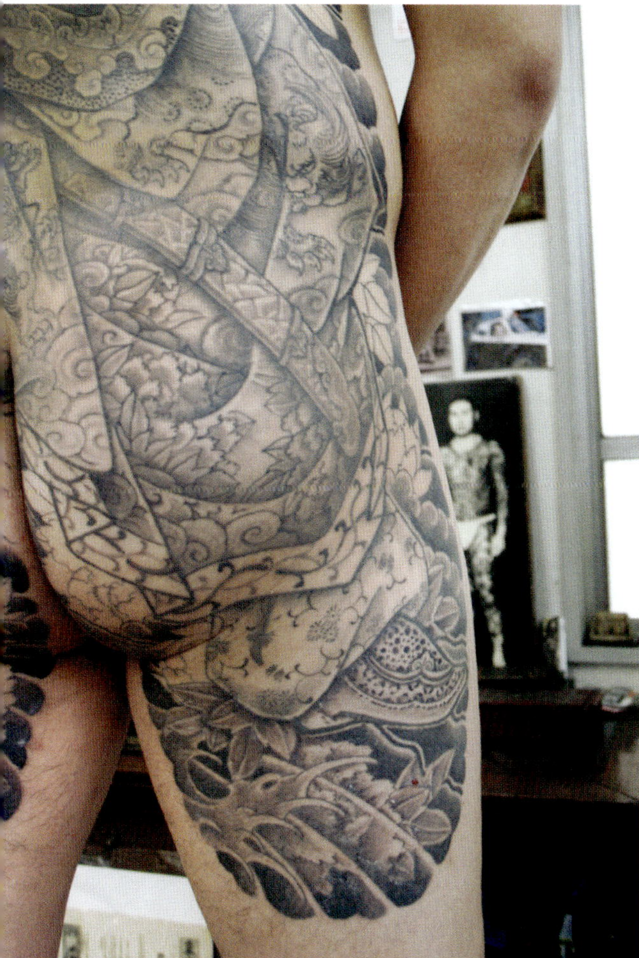

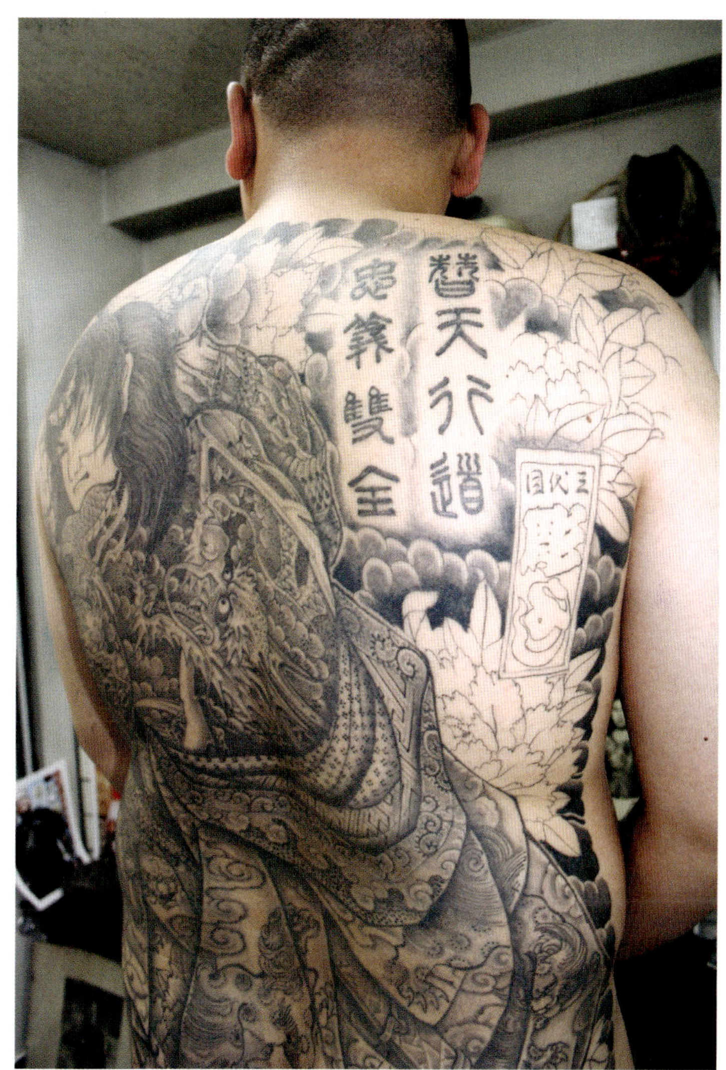

Opposite:
Kumonryu.

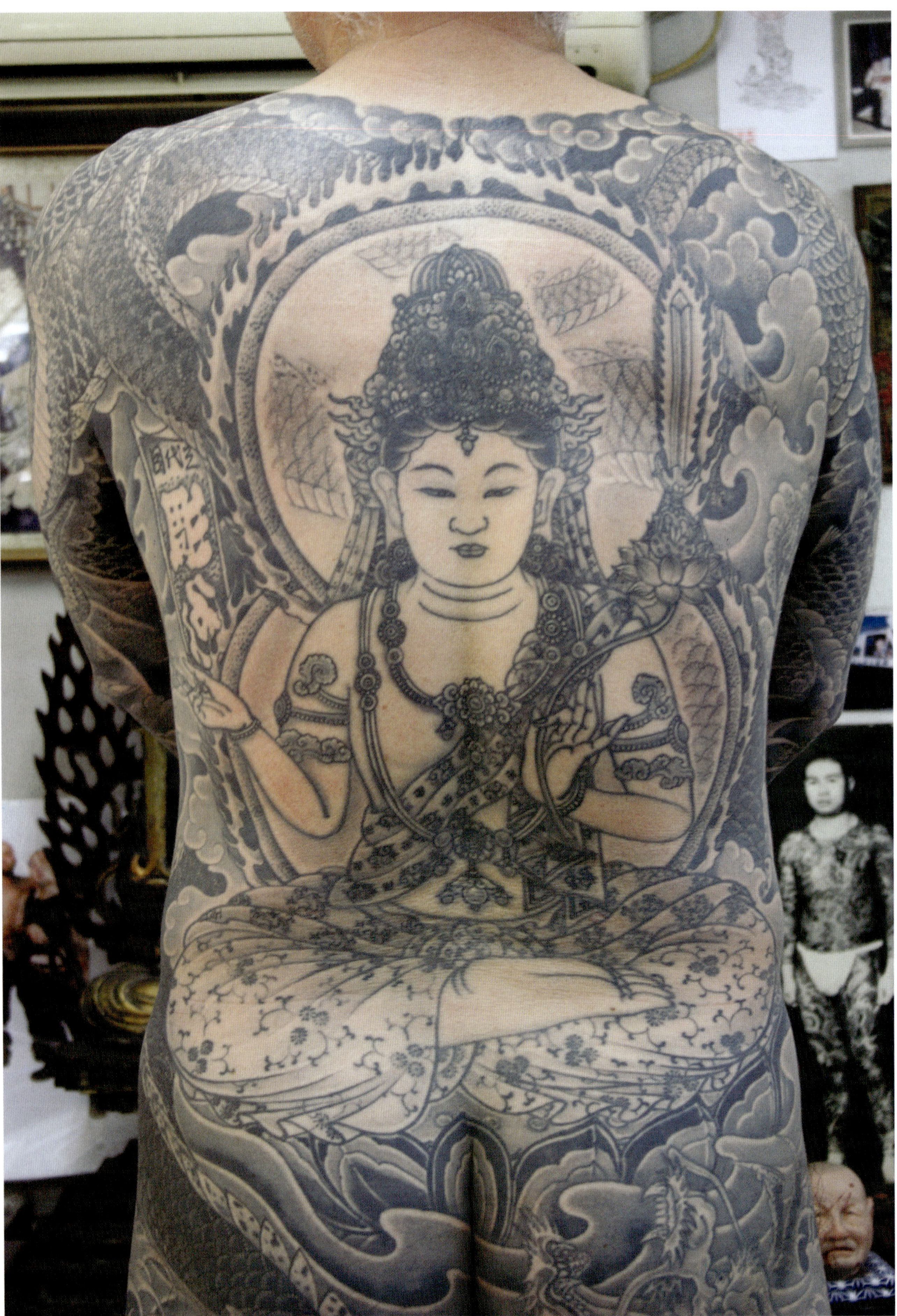

Left:
Kannon Bosatsu. Kannon Bosatsu is the very expression of divine compassion and mercy. Born from the Amida's right eye, she is often perceived as female in Japan and China. She holds a lotus flower and her headdress is decorated with an effigy of Amida.

Right:
The legs are covered with a depiction of 16 Rakan. Rakan are sages who have purged themselves of passion and evil and thereby are liberated from the Buddhist cycle of death and rebirth. These 16 Rakan are commanded by the Buddha to save every living creature.

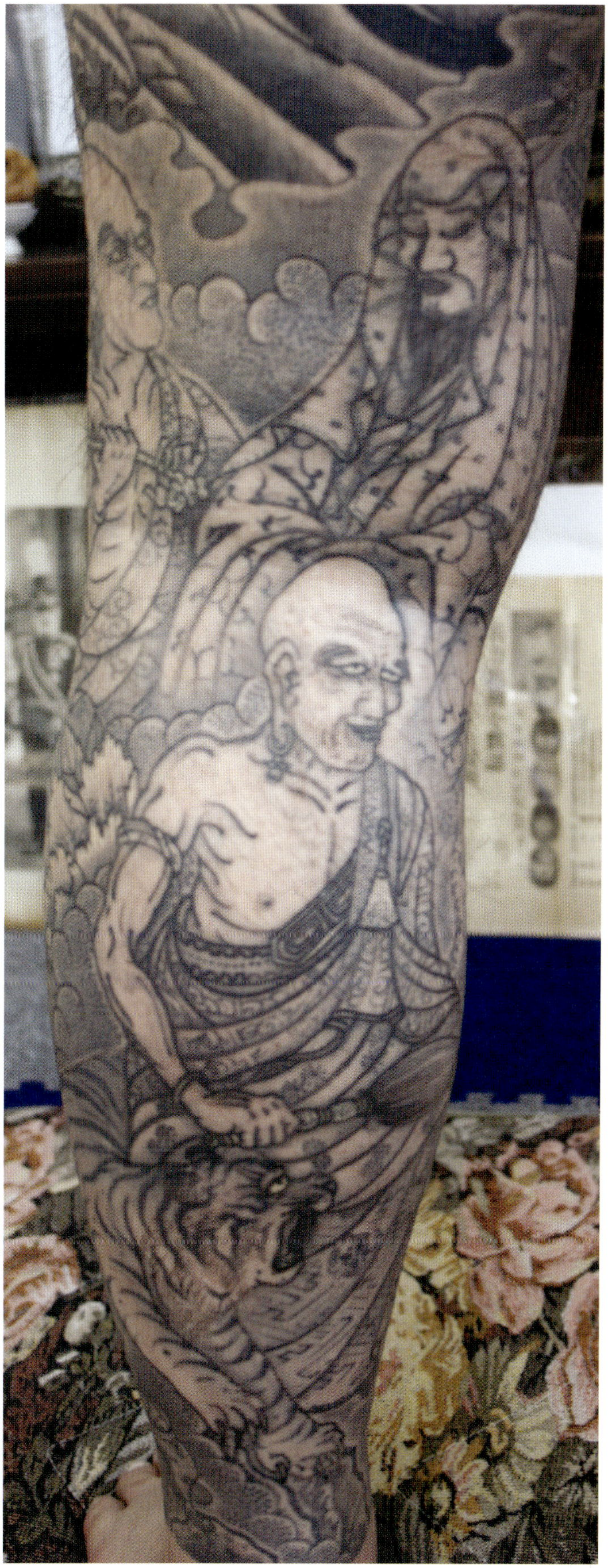

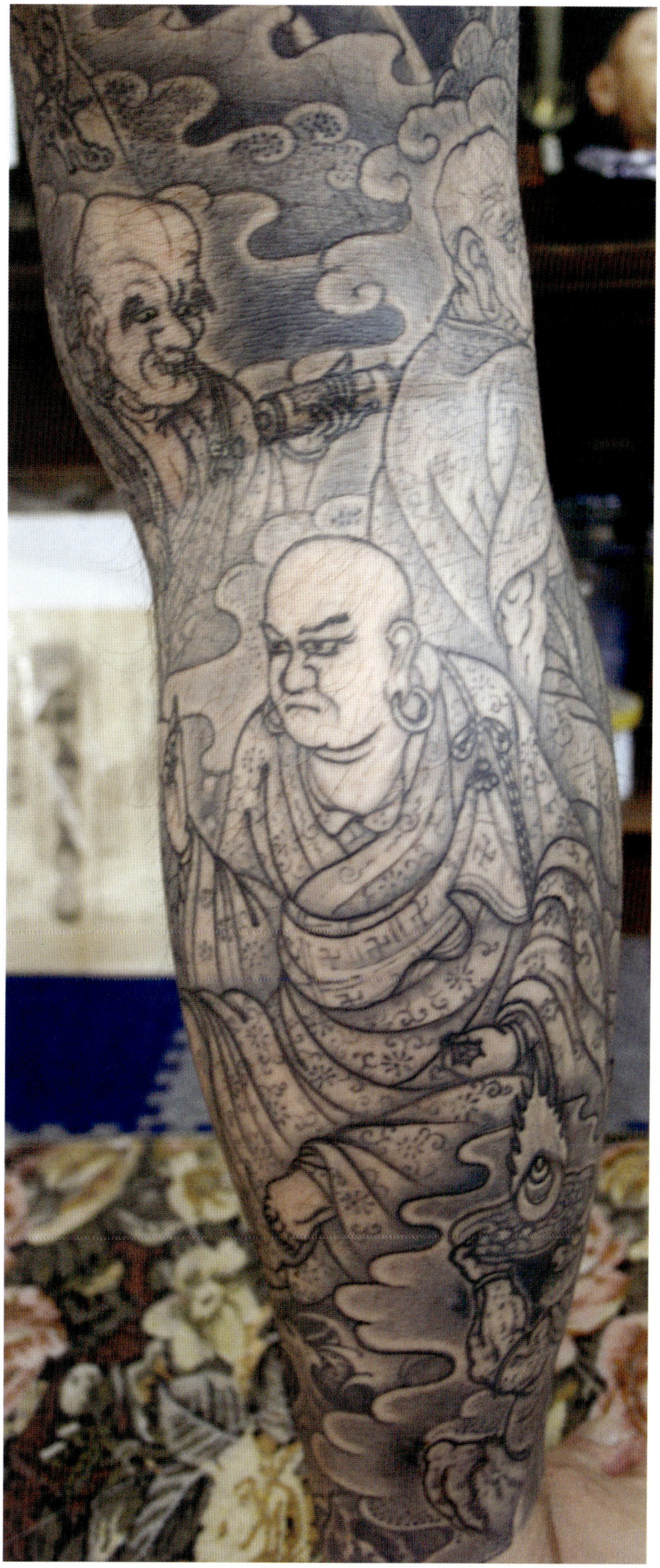

Right:
Kongo.

Far right:
Rikishi. Together Kongo and Rikishi are called Ni-ō. Ni-o are a pair of sentinels that watch over Buddhist temples and denote the beginning and end of all things. The closed mouth of Kongo represents latent power and the open mouth of Rikishi denotes expressed power. They are often depicted as statues at a temple's gate.

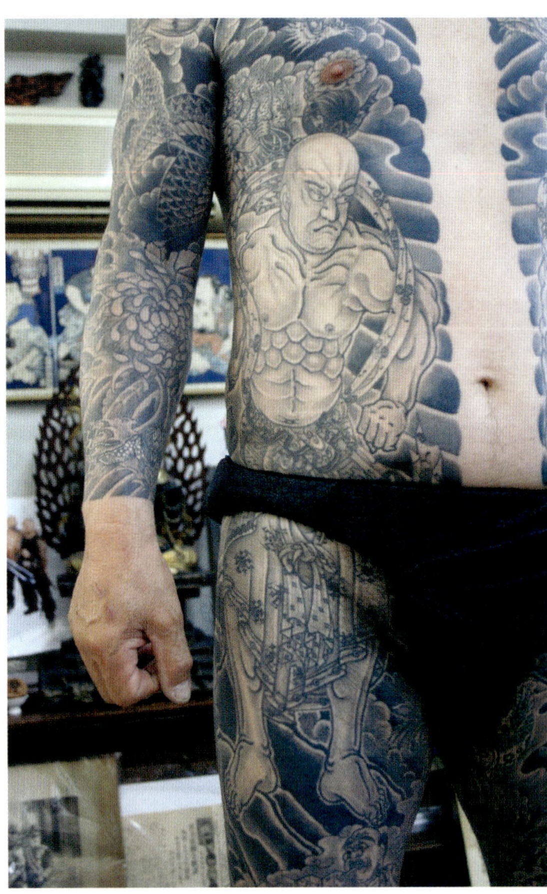

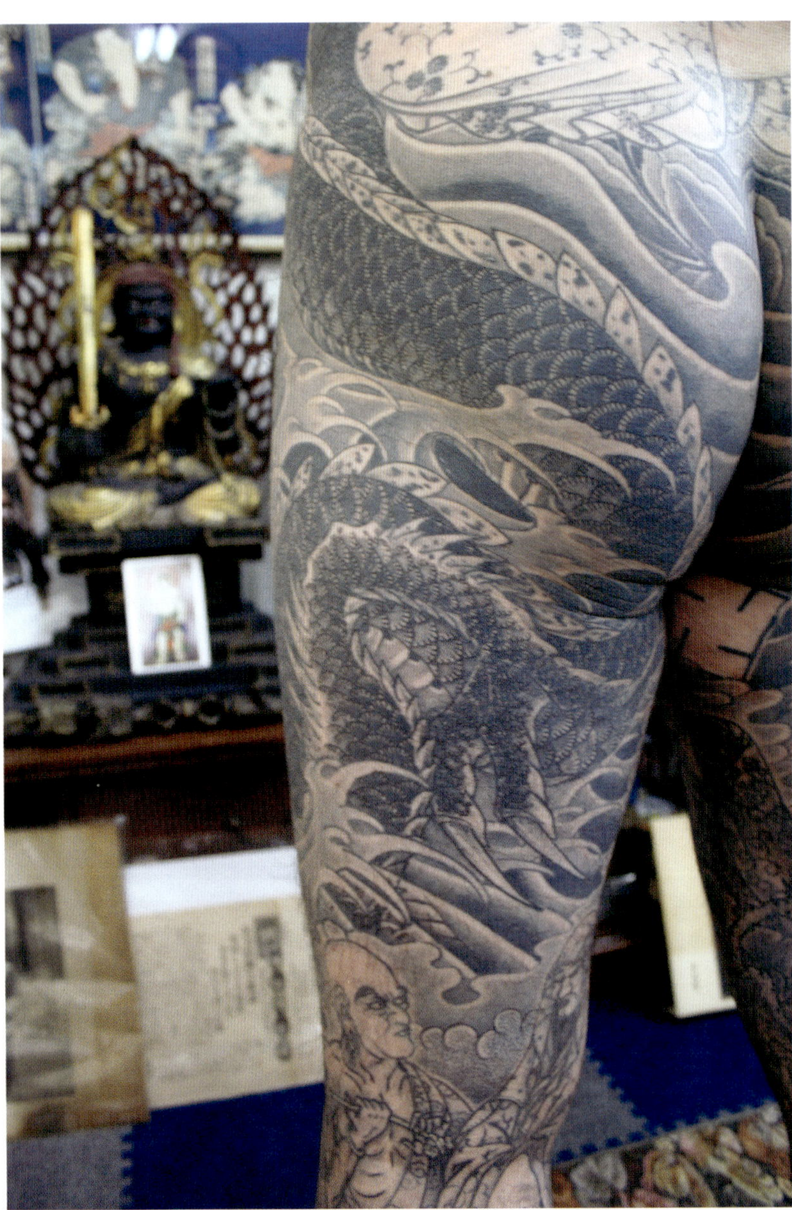

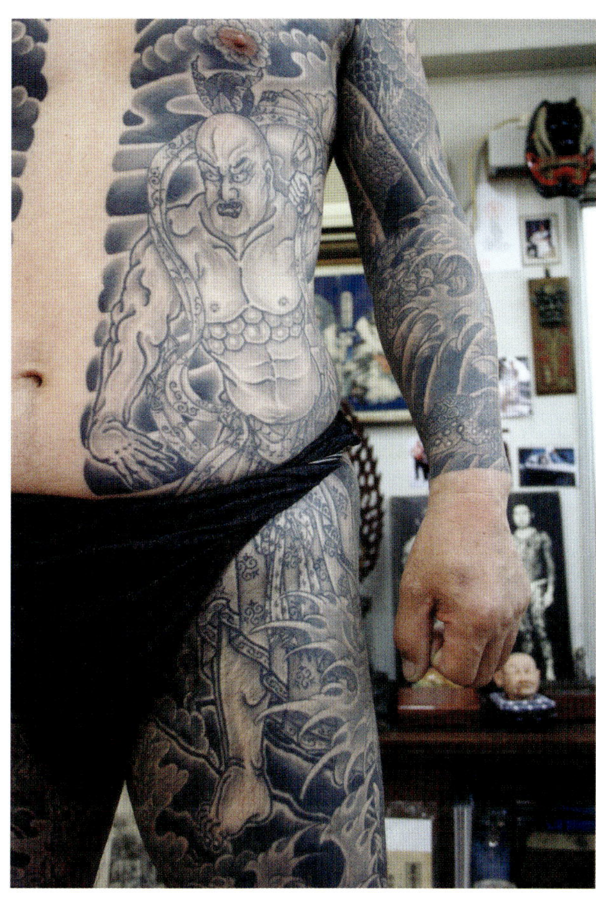

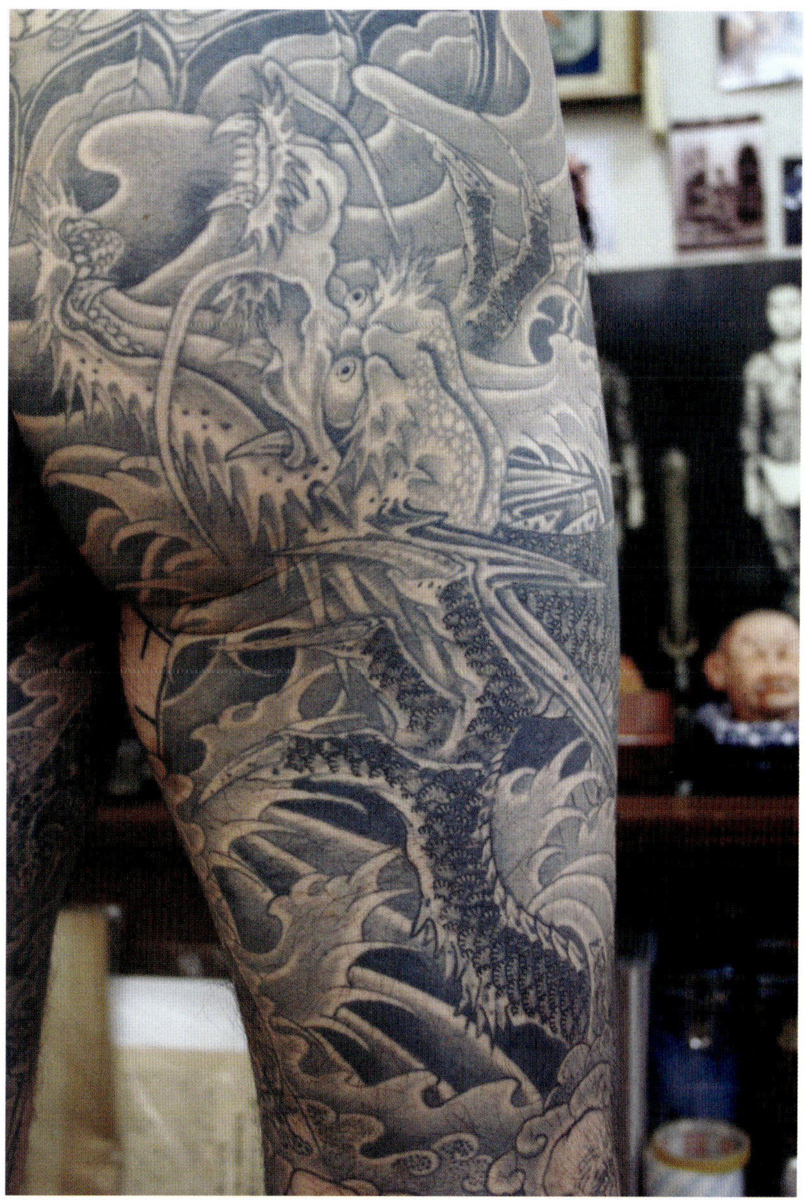

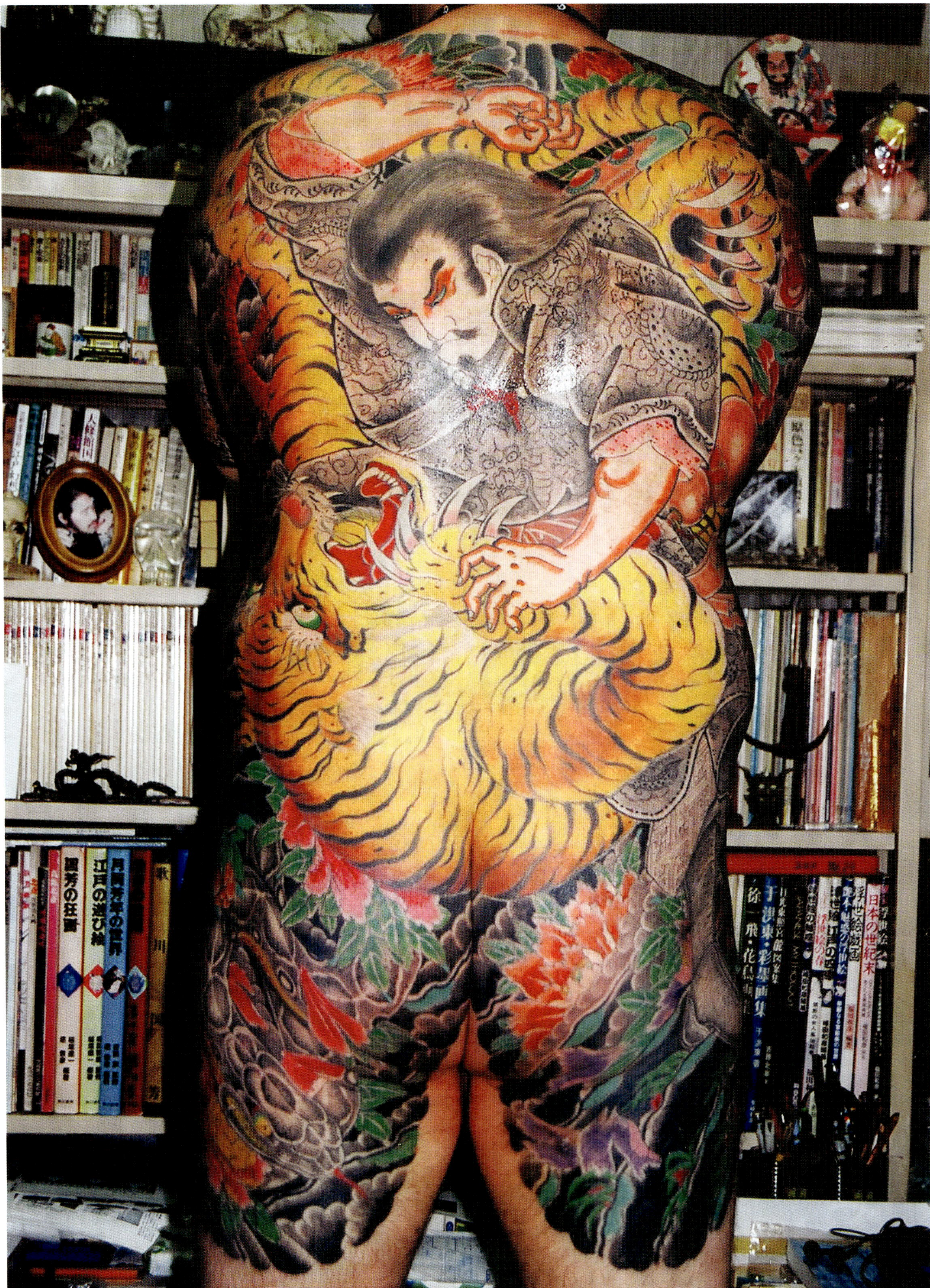
国芳の狂画
江戸の遊び絵
月岡芳年の世界
日本の世紀末

Left:
Gyouja Bushou. A Suikoden warrior and infantry leader from Qing-he Province. He was nicknamed "The Ascetic" because he dressed like a novice monk. He fled his hometown fearing he had killed a man and eventually joined the Ryo-Zan Paku gang of bandits. He gained fame from slaying a man-eating tiger on Jing-Yang Hill and for avenging the death of his brother. He also killed fifteen men that had betrayed him into arrest. Eventually Bushou became a monk and was dubbed "Royal Father" by the imperial government.

Right:
Fugen Bosatsu. "Bodhisattva of Longevity" and attendant to Dainichi Nyorai representing the supreme intelligence of Buddhist Law. Fugen Bosatsu is often depicted atop an elephant and teaches the value of action and conduct.

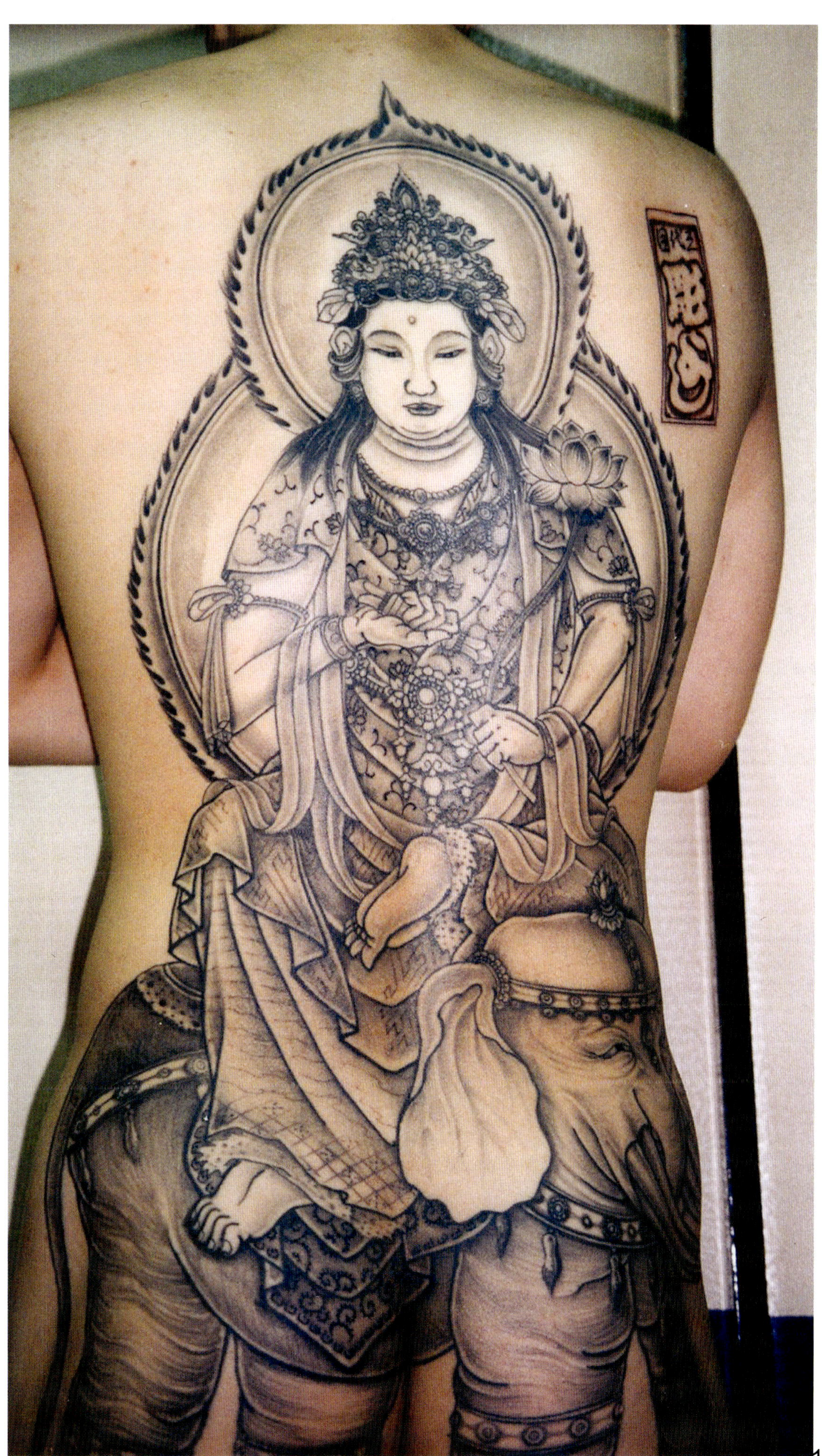

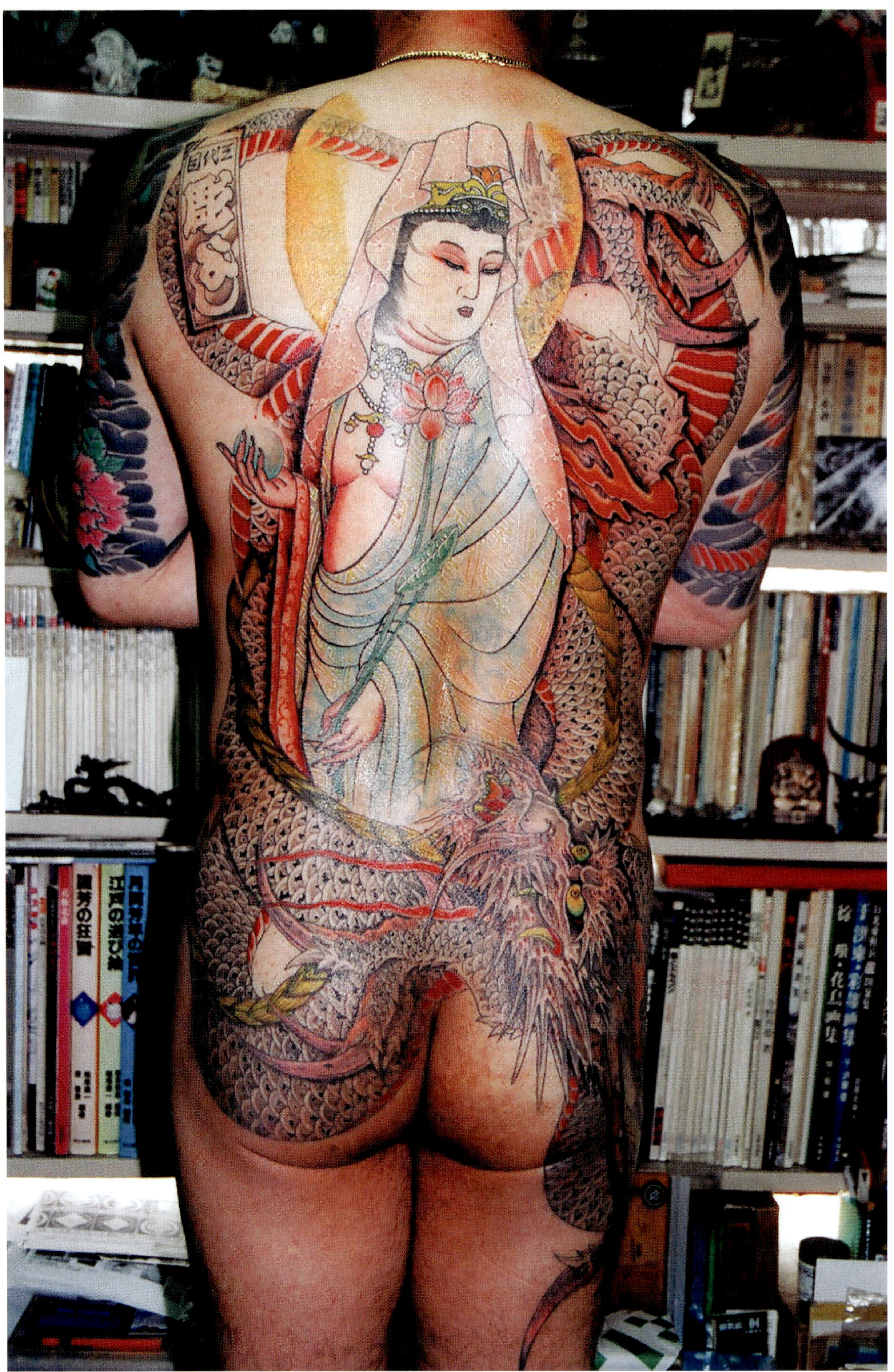

Left:
Kannon Bosatsu.

Right:
An original Fudōmyō-ō design, composed by Horiyoshi III.

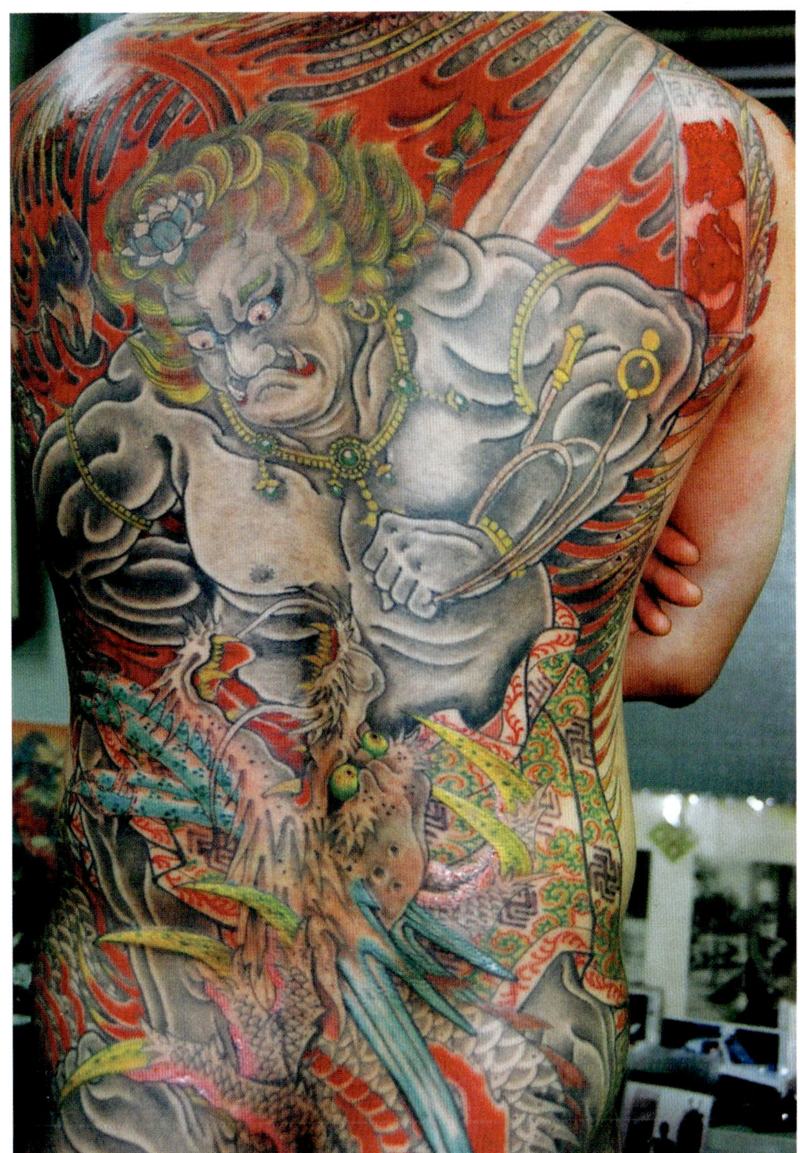

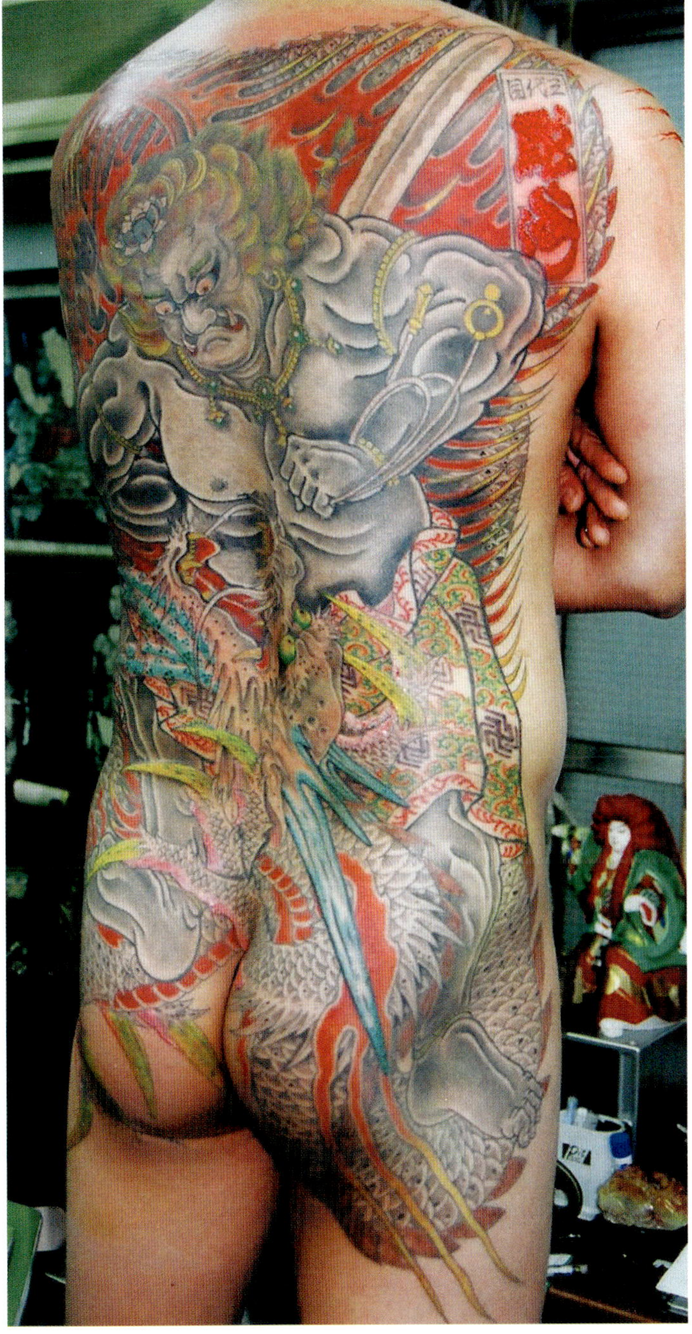

Tattoos by Horiyuki

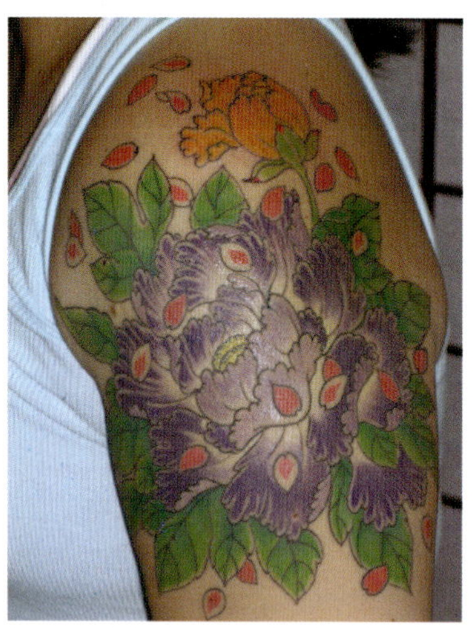

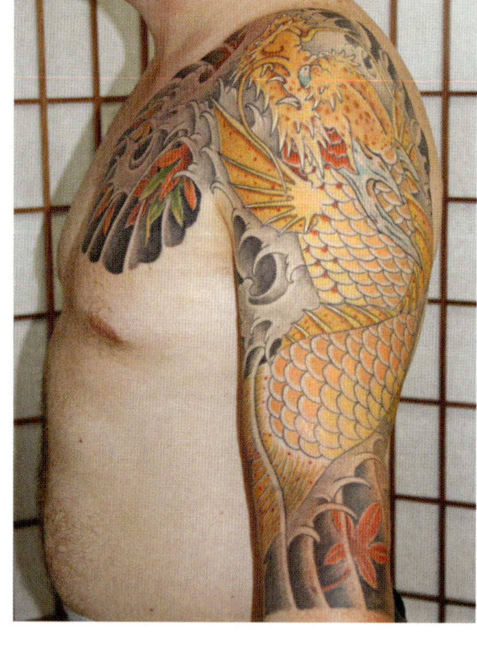

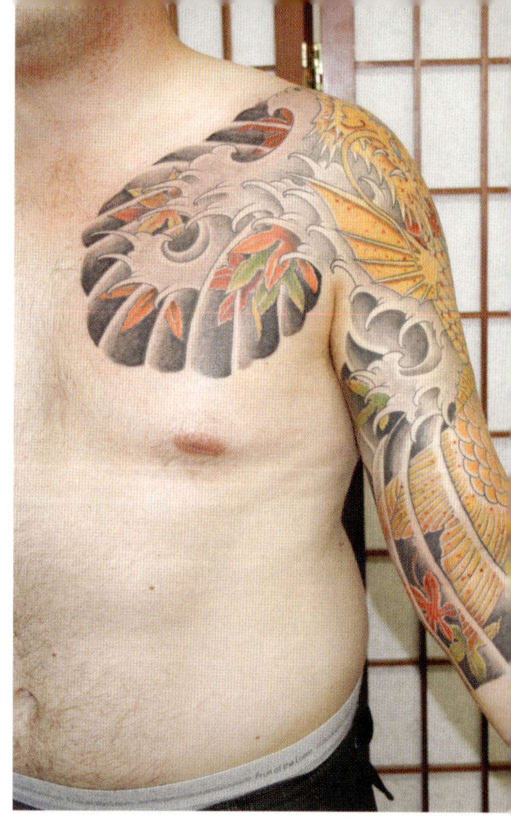

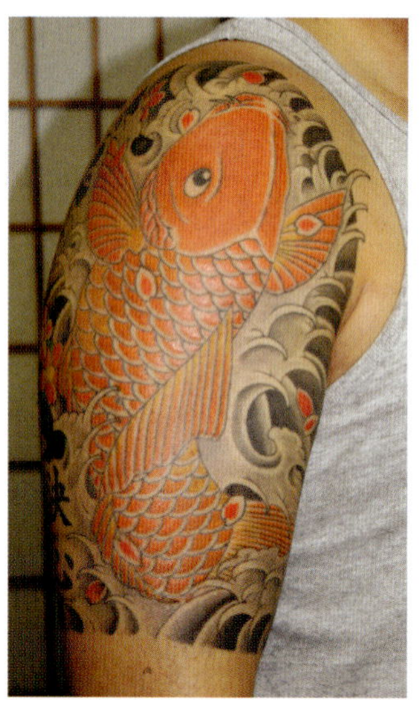

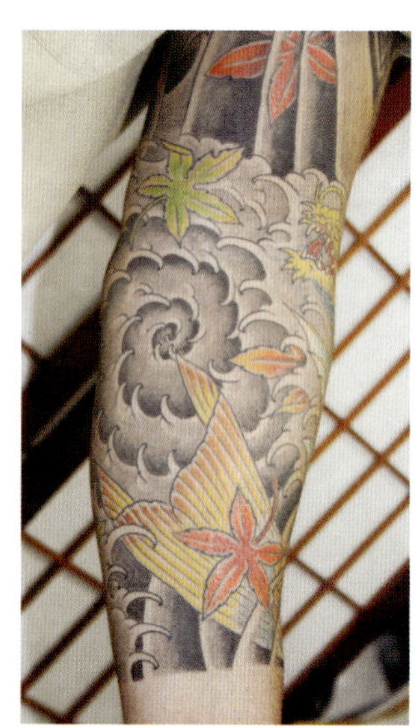

"The following are my most sincere attempts to replicate the Horiyoshi III style."

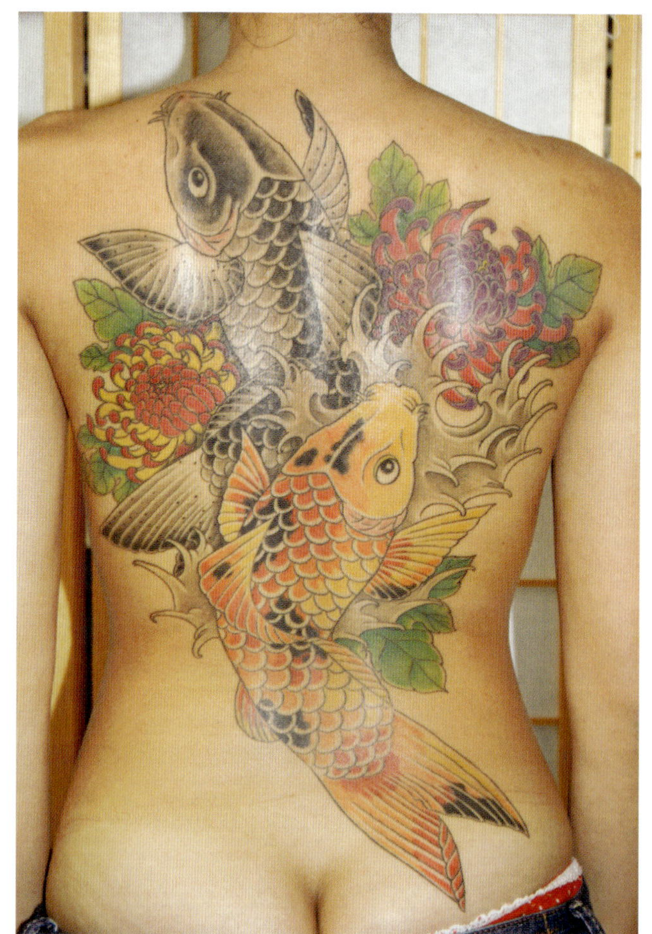

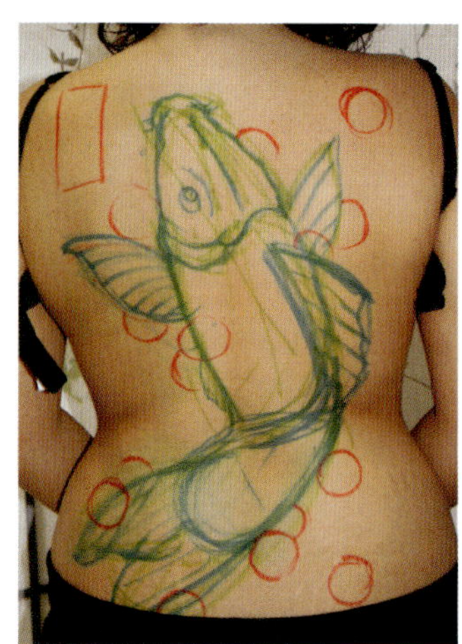

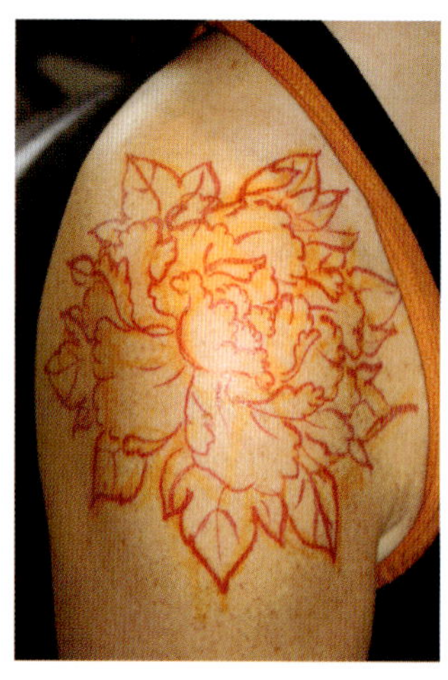

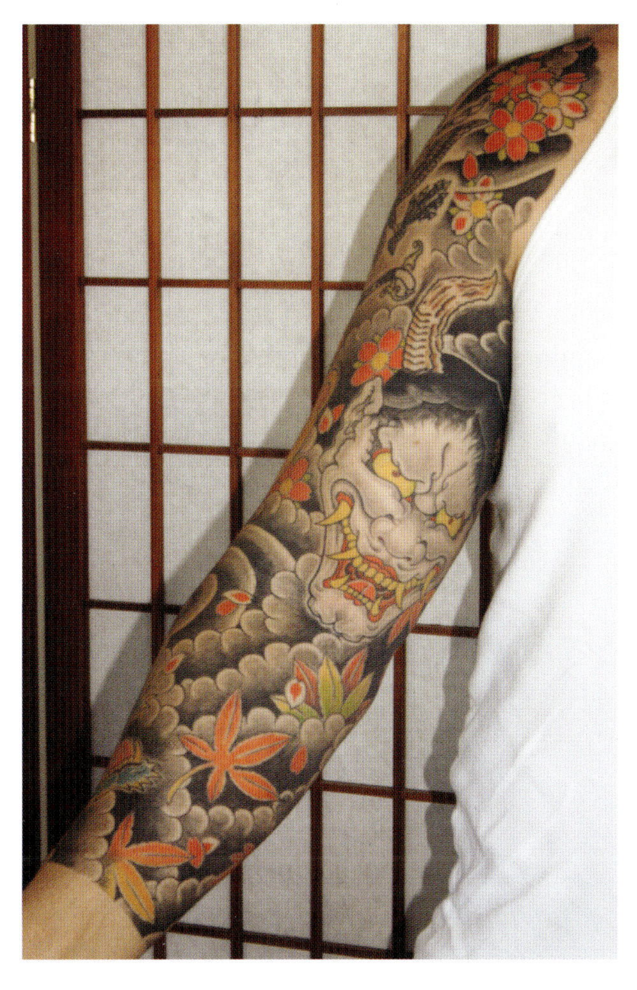
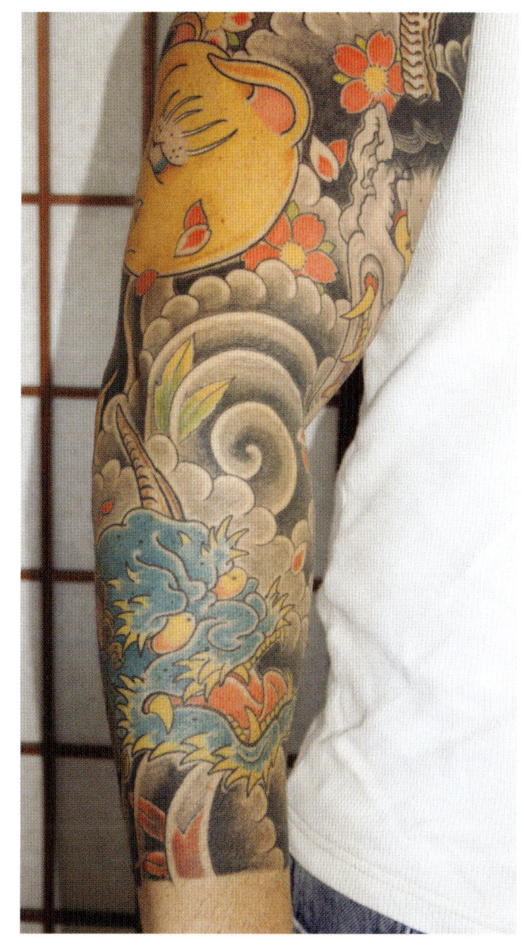
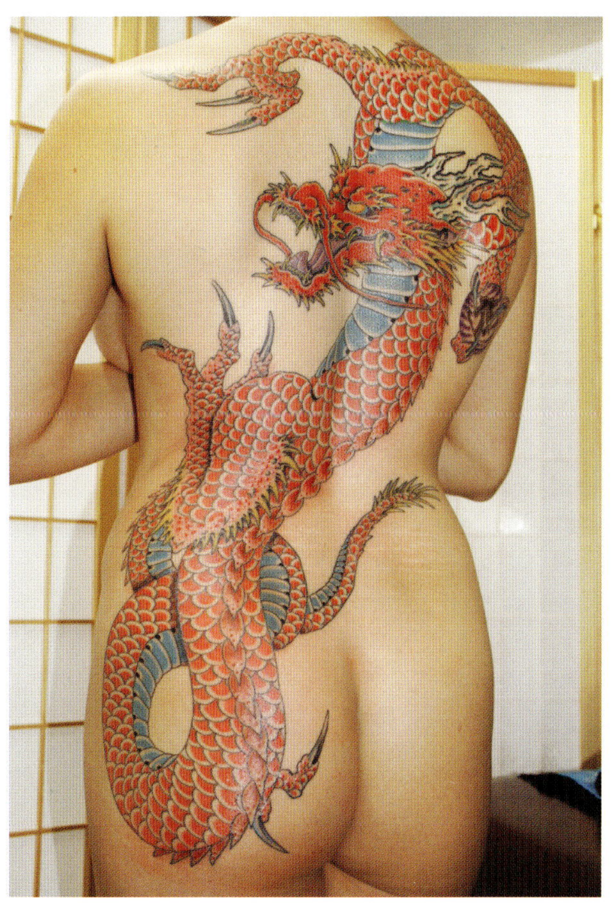
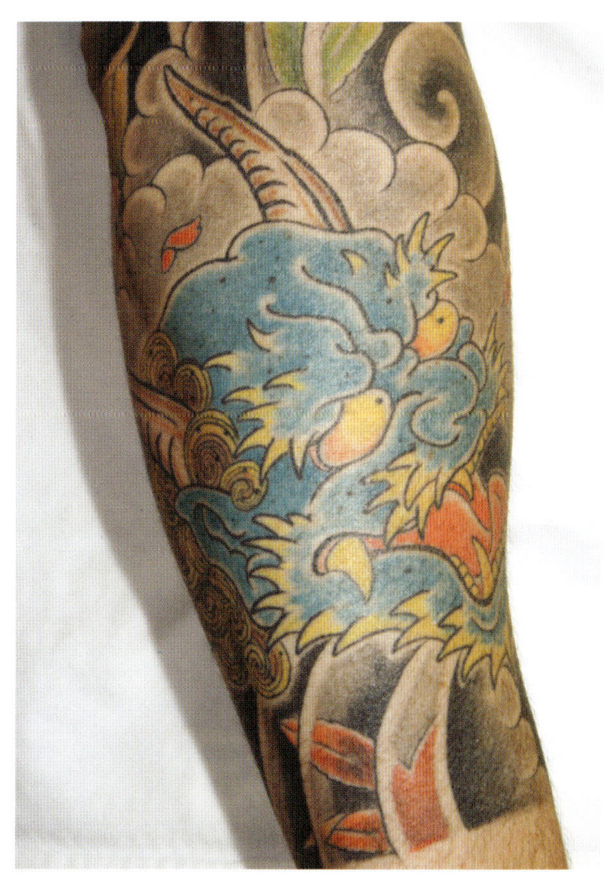

Tattoos by Horiyuki

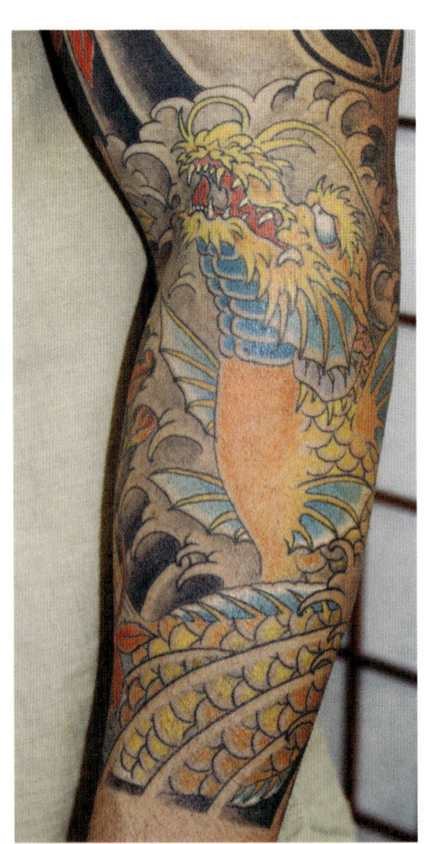

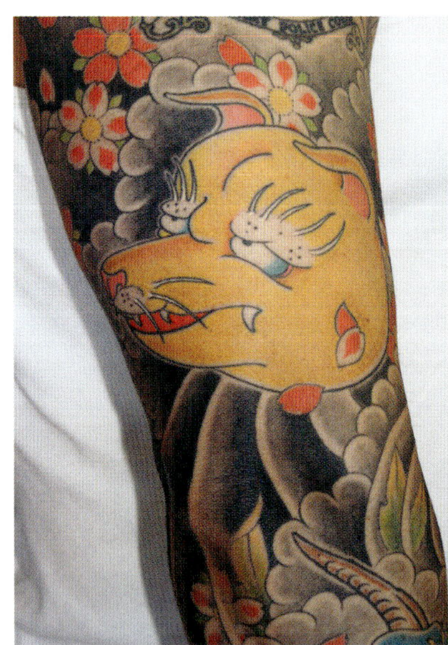

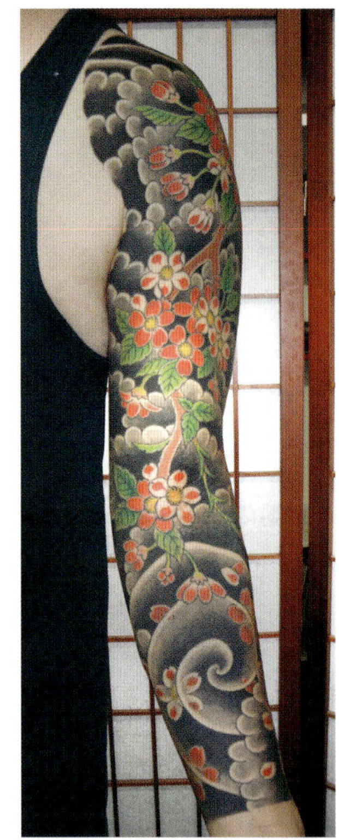

Right:
Ryu after Soga
Shohaku.

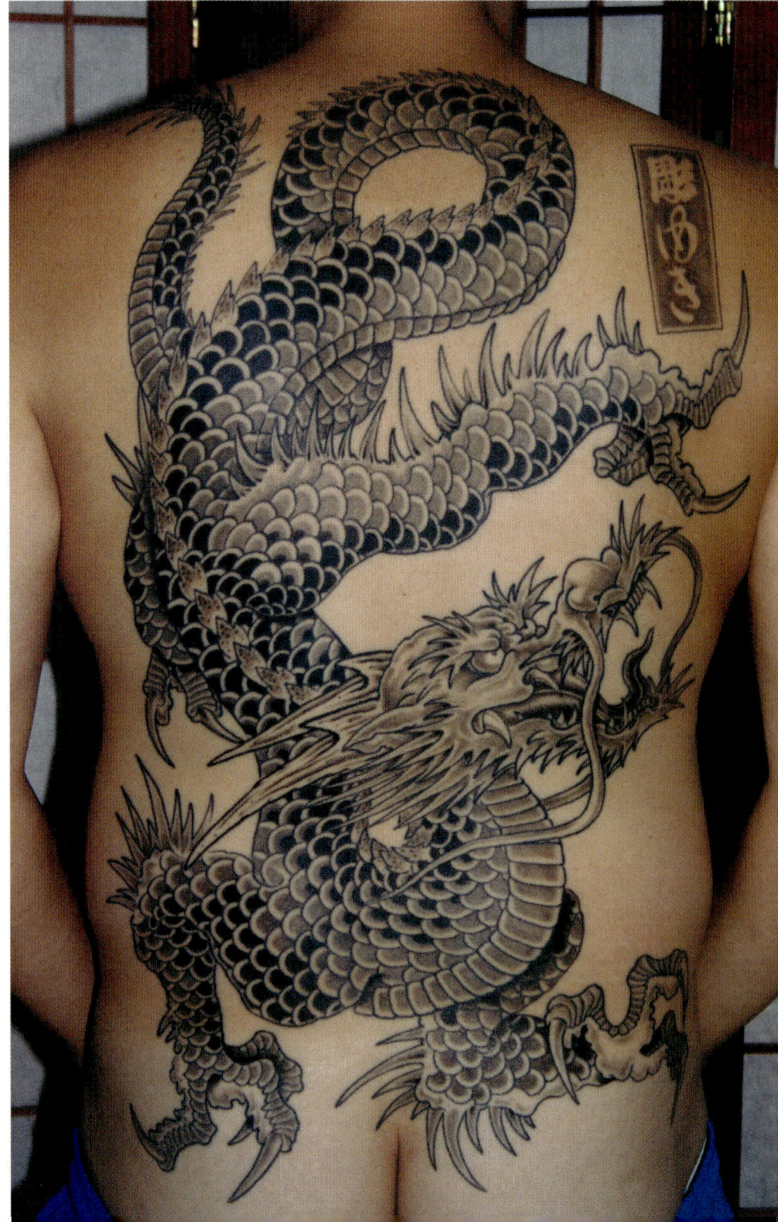

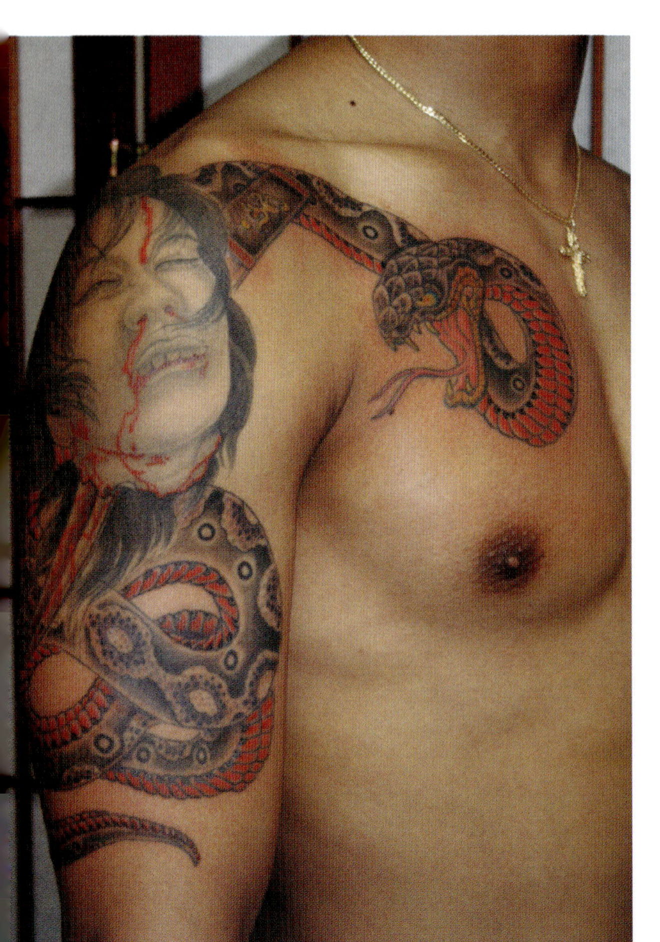

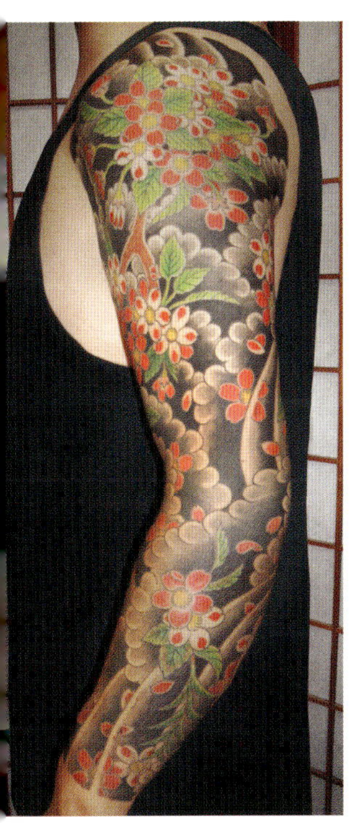
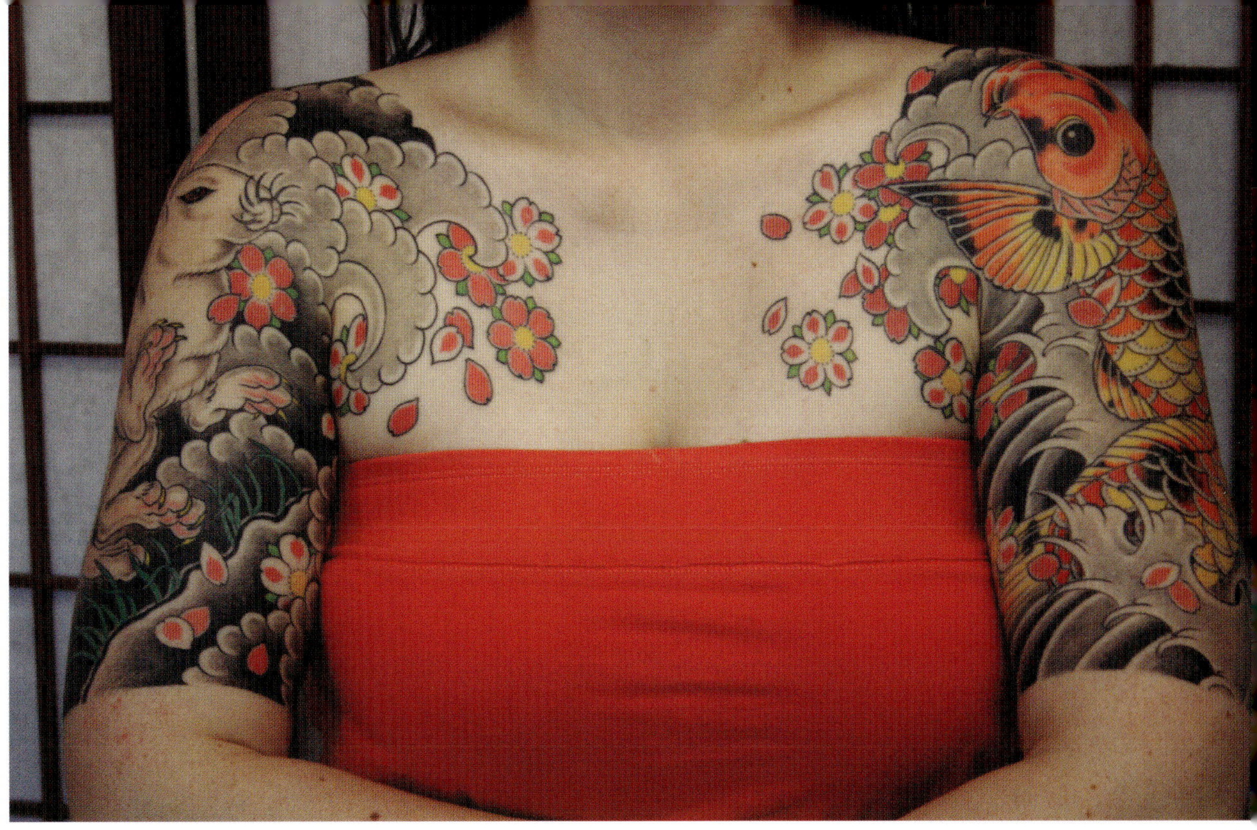
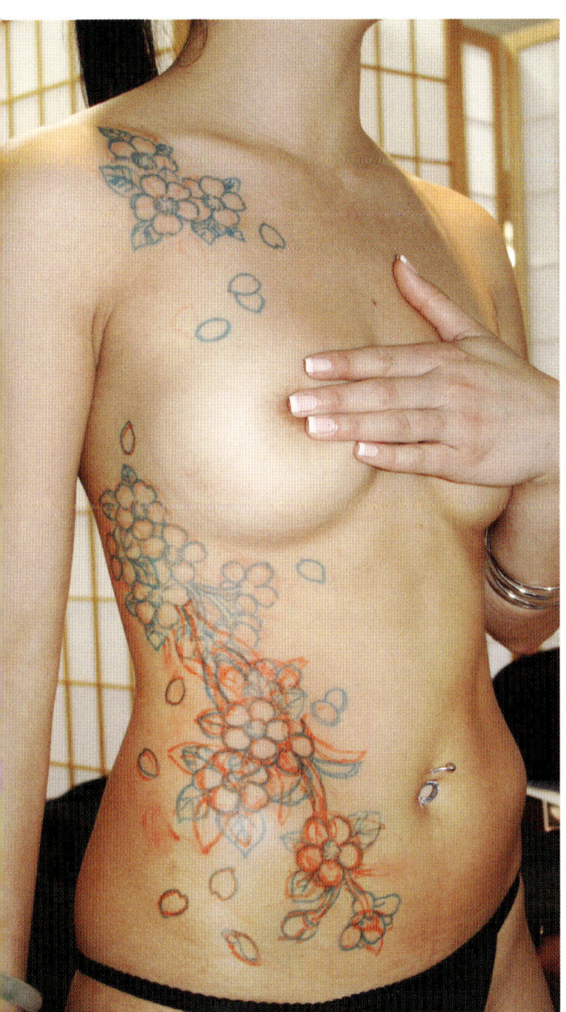
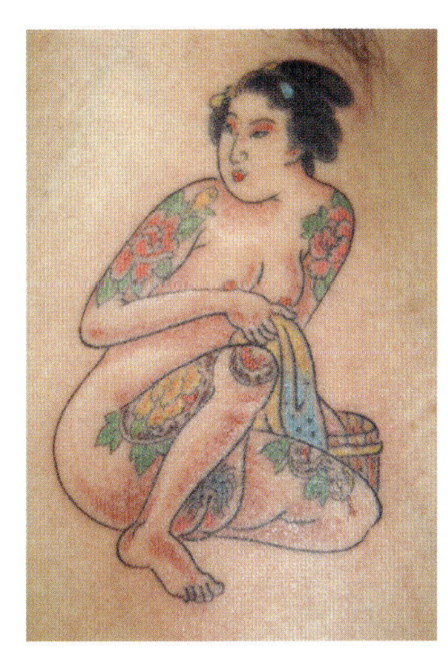
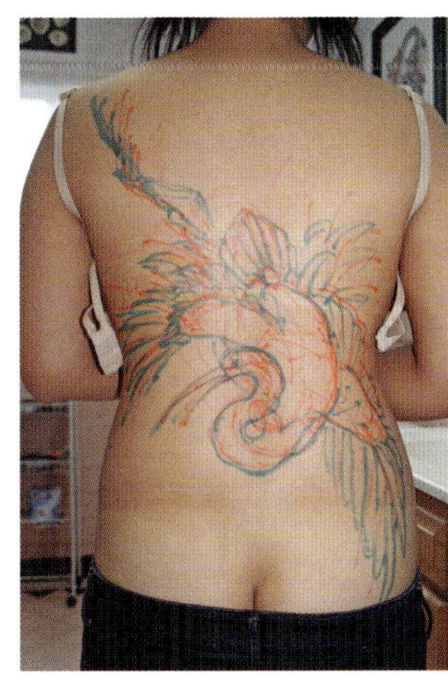
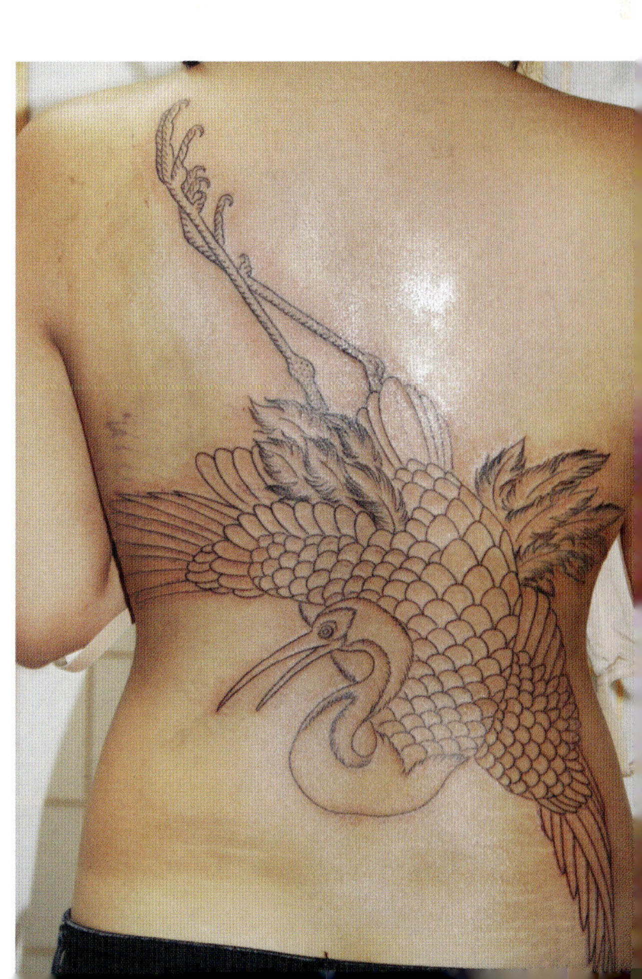

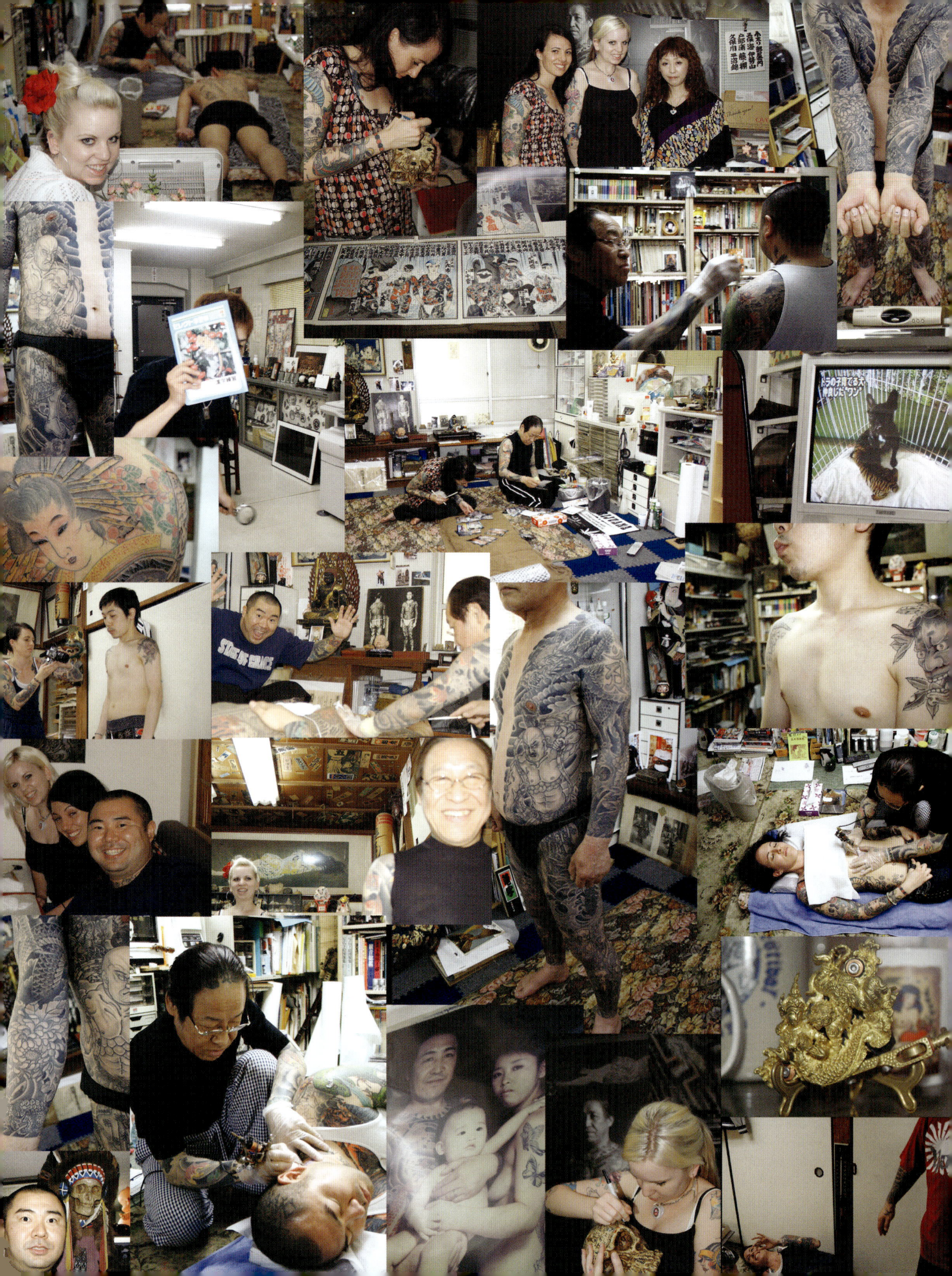

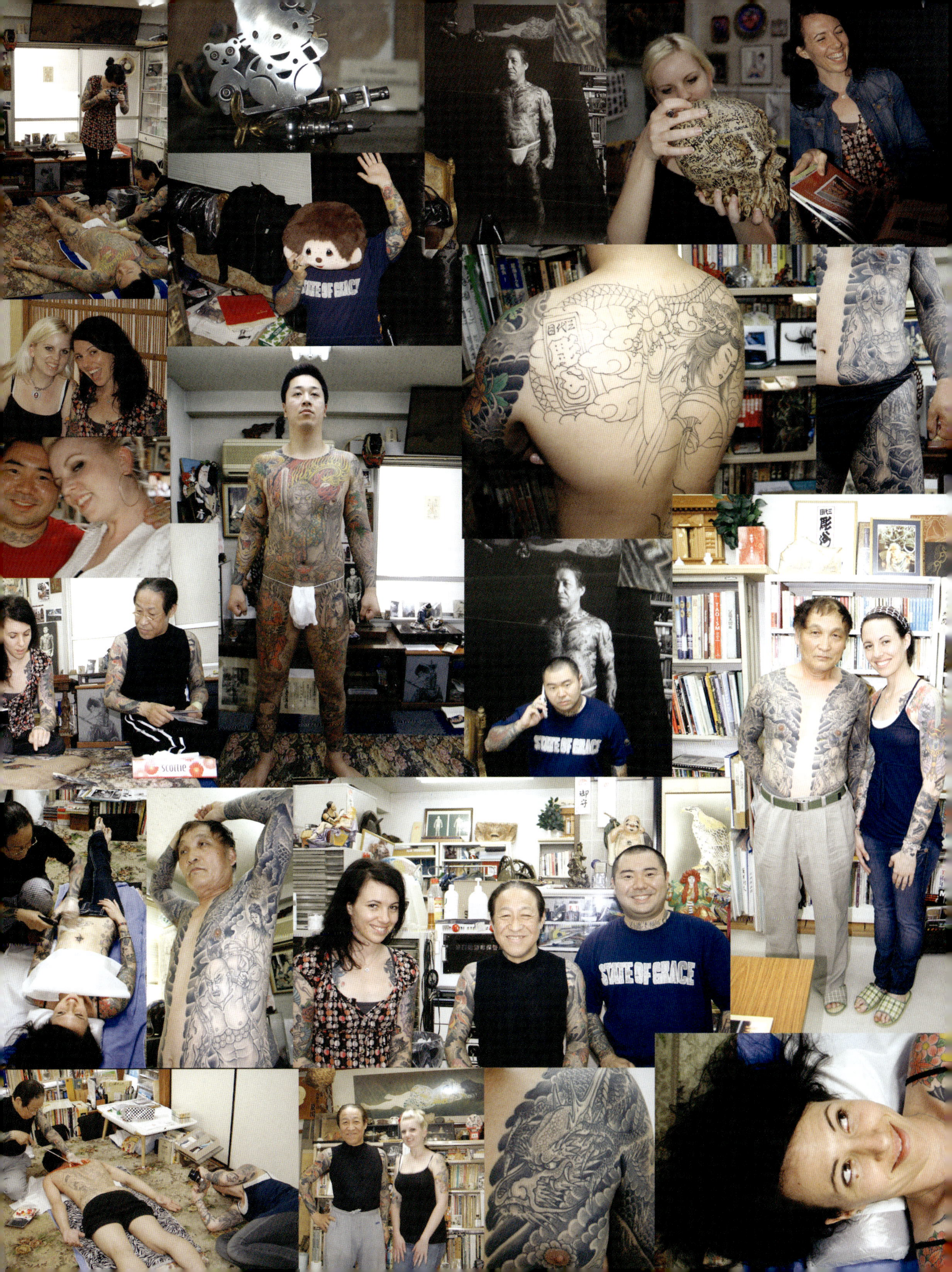
STATE OF GRACE
scottie
STATE OF GRACE
STATE OF GRACE

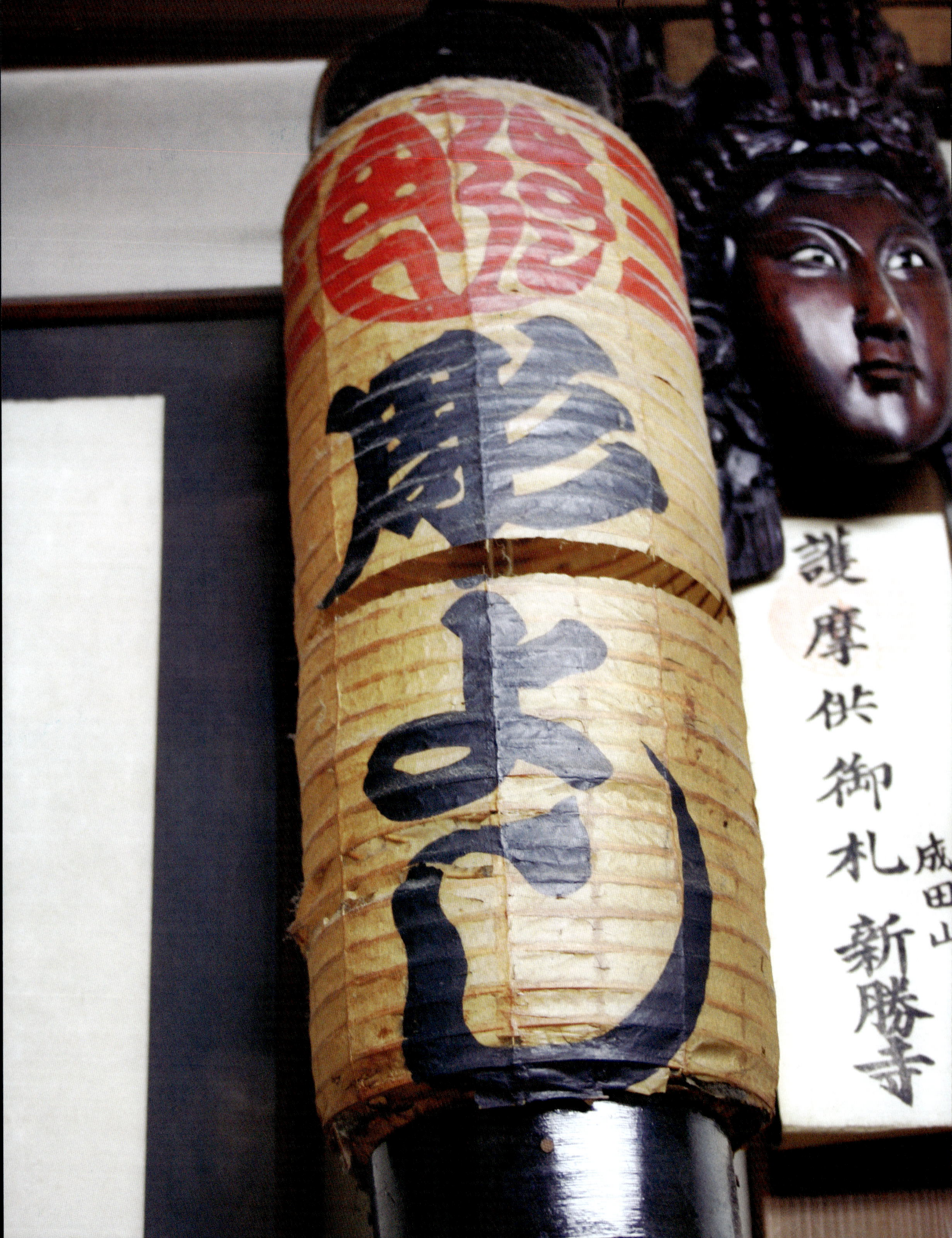

護摩供御札
成田山
新勝寺

Chapter 3
Getting Tattooed

Horiyoshi III has two studios. One is called Noge and the other Ise-Cho, both named for their respective neighborhoods. Ise-Cho is the second floor of a house tucked away in a residential neighborhood. In fact, Shodai Horiyoshi, Yoshitsugu Muramatsu, tattooed here years ago and his widow still lives downstairs. Years after the passing of Shodai Horiyoshi, Horiyoshi III continues to support and care for his master's widow. While Ise-cho is buried in a maze of congested houses, with the entrance in a small alley, Noge is larger and located on a busy street in a lively restaurant and night life district near a major train station. Finding Noge is easy; Ise-cho is a bit trickier, with no outside signage or marking. Horitaka has often joked that if you are a foreigner with an appointment at Ise-Cho; "half the fun is finding it." Even though Horiyoshi III offers the same service at both studios, the experience of being tattooed is very different at each studio, reflecting his acknowledgement of changing times.

The first time I visited Japan, I was tattooed at the legendary Ise-cho location. I fondly remember the nervous anticipation as I walked down the alley and up the steps to the studio. As is the case for many urban spaces in Japan, I was disarmed by how absolutely tiny the second-story workspace is. The space is put to use though, every usable area houses something. I remember noticing the washed out color of the books on the shelves as well as the many photos and prints on the walls. Images I had seen of this space were taken many years prior to my visit, and time had certainly aged my surroundings, yet many familiar details remained intact. Certain masks and posters were still hanging where

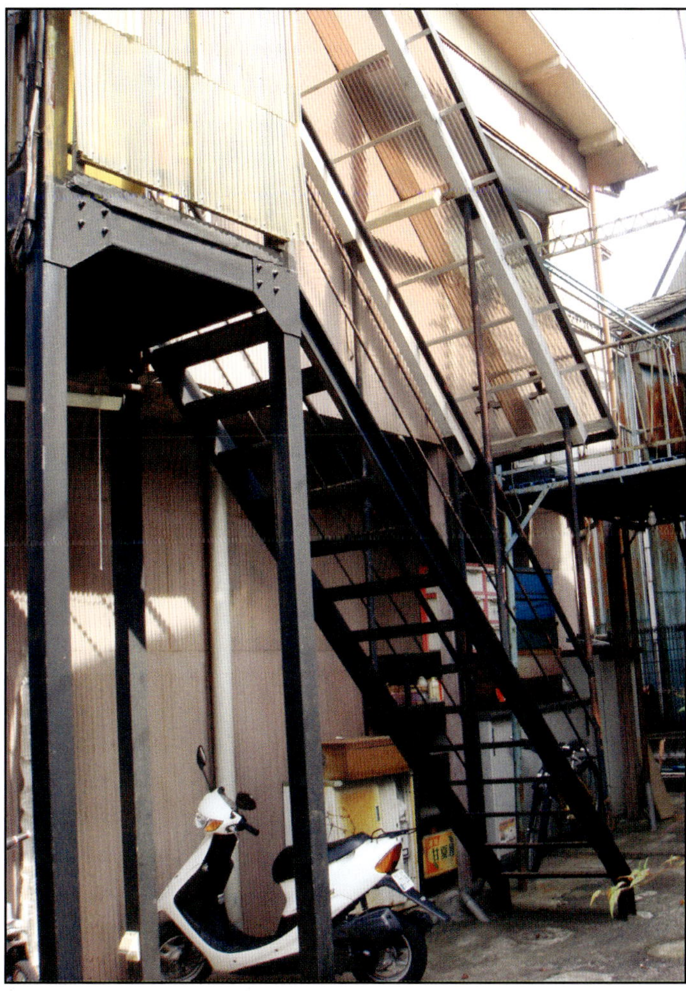

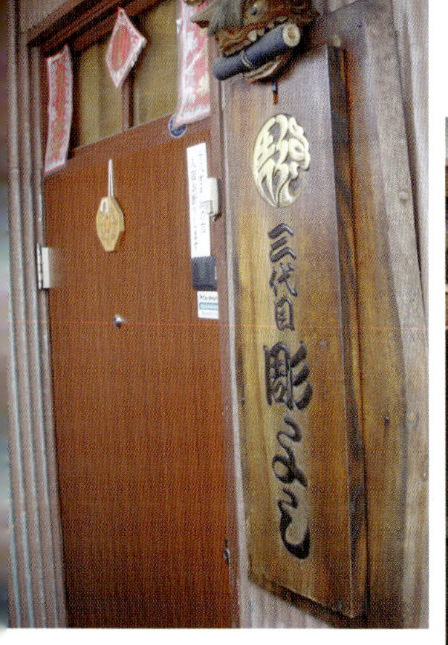

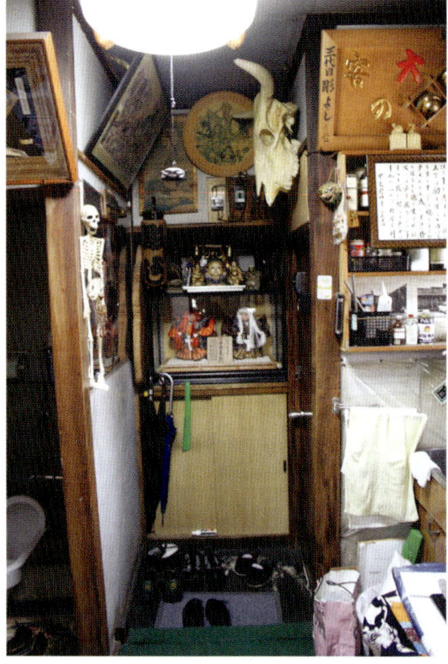

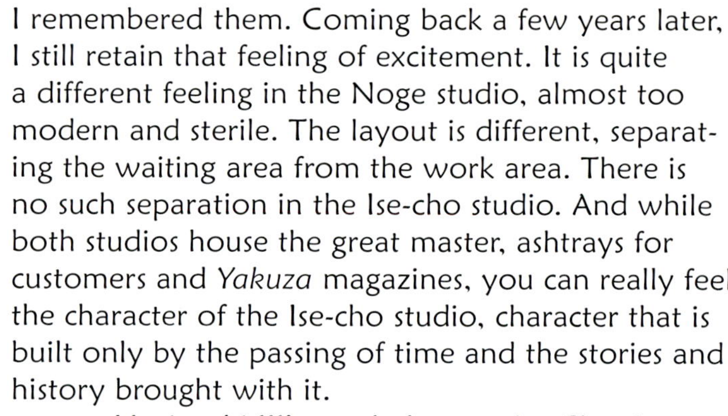

I remembered them. Coming back a few years later, I still retain that feeling of excitement. It is quite a different feeling in the Noge studio, almost too modern and sterile. The layout is different, separating the waiting area from the work area. There is no such separation in the Ise-cho studio. And while both studios house the great master, ashtrays for customers and *Yakuza* magazines, you can really feel the character of the Ise-cho studio, character that is built only by the passing of time and the stories and history brought with it.

Horiyoshi III's workplace, at Ise-Cho, is simultaneously an expression of his taste, source of inspiration and personal history. Nearly every surface of the studio is decorated with some sort of iconic image. Art and tattoo supplies clutter the entry and small room. Every inch of wall space is utilized. The studio is enshrined with relics of tattoo culture and history, but to him they are simply records of his life. We joked about how "young everyone looks" in faded snapshots of Horiyoshi III with Western tattoo masters; our elders, his old friends. A focal point of the room is a painting by his close friend of many years, Kaname Ozuma, a very well known artist most recognized for his paintings of tattooed women. Ozuma sought inspiration from

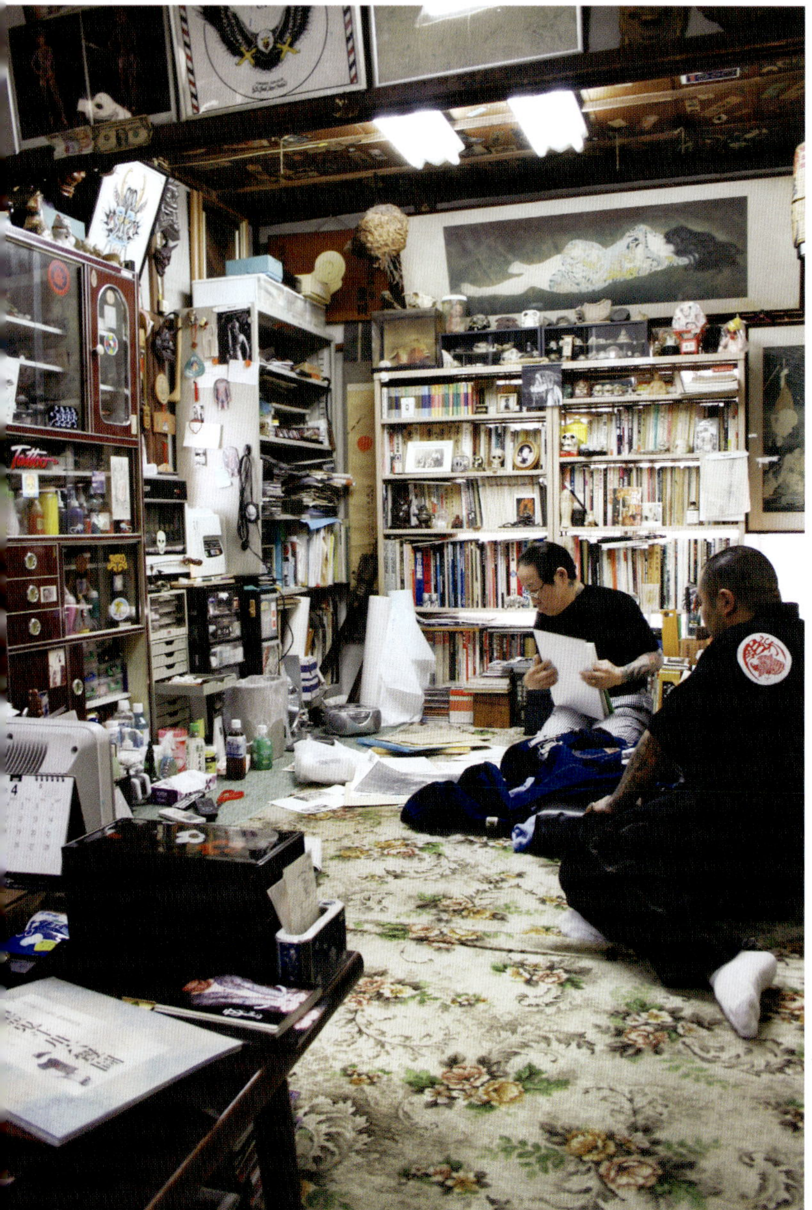

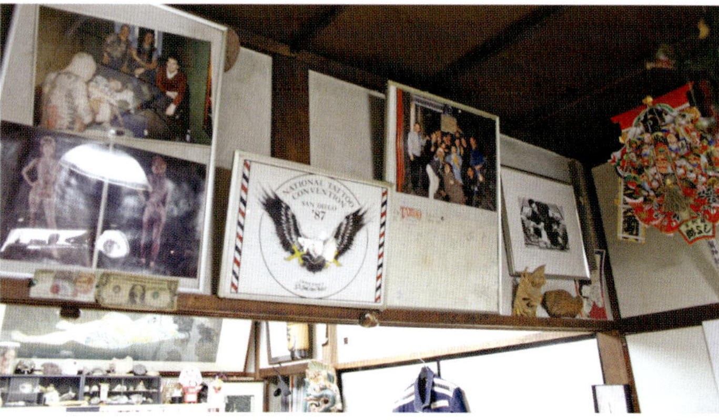

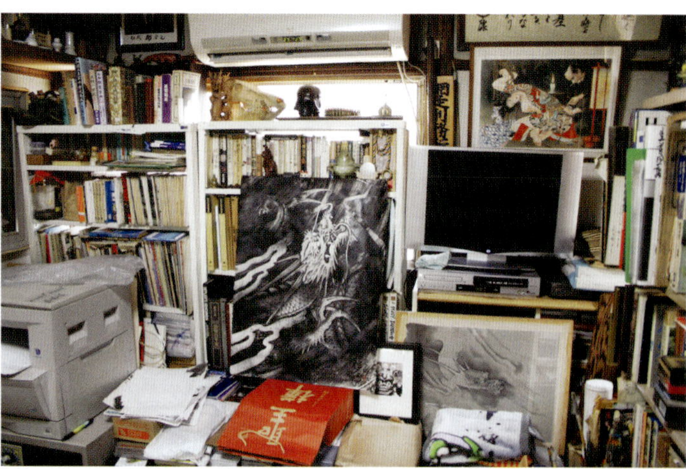

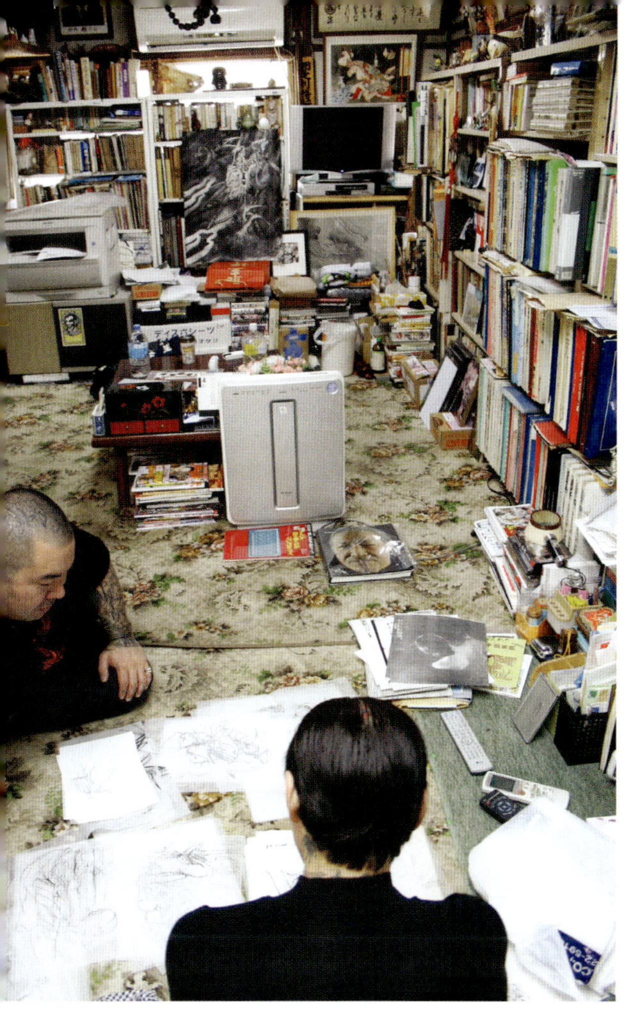

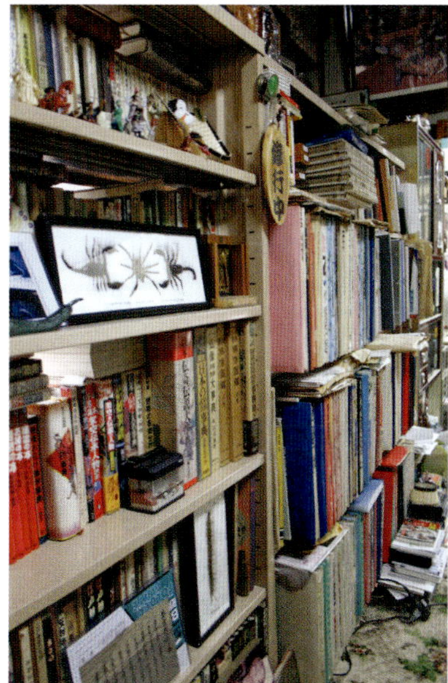

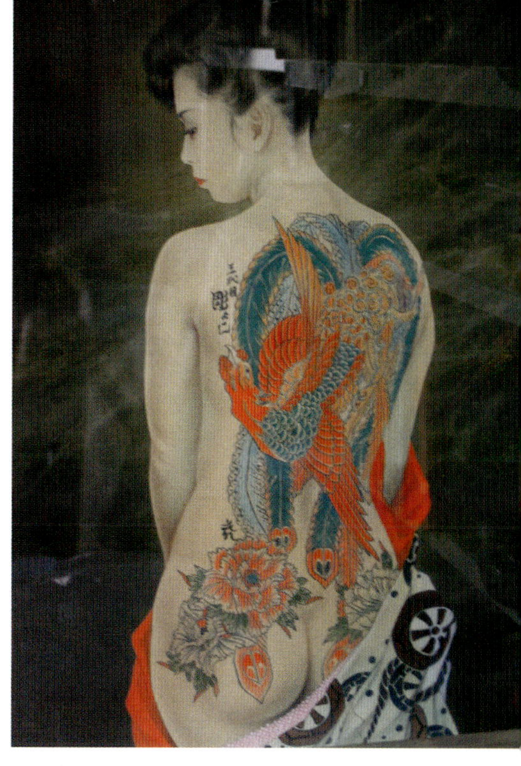

Above right:
Mayumi painted by Kaname Ozuma.

Below right:
"Just in case!"

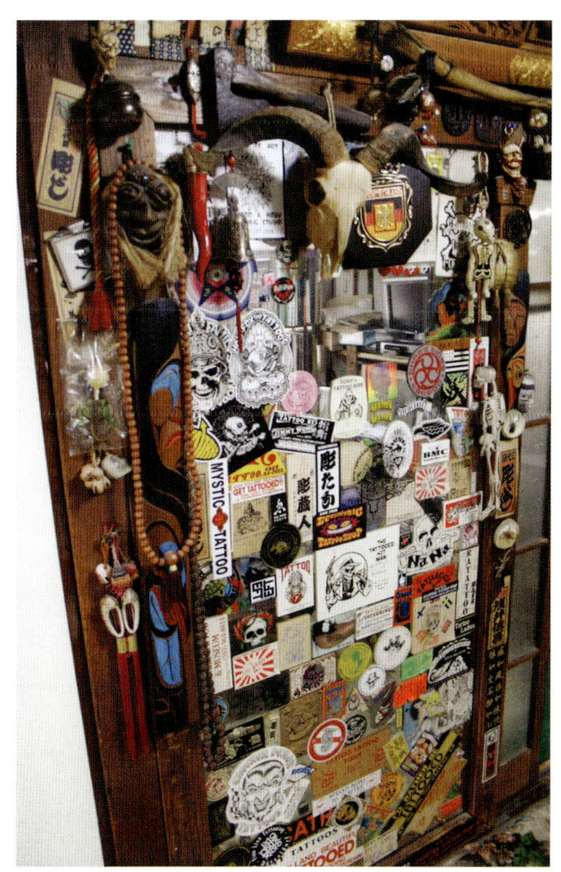

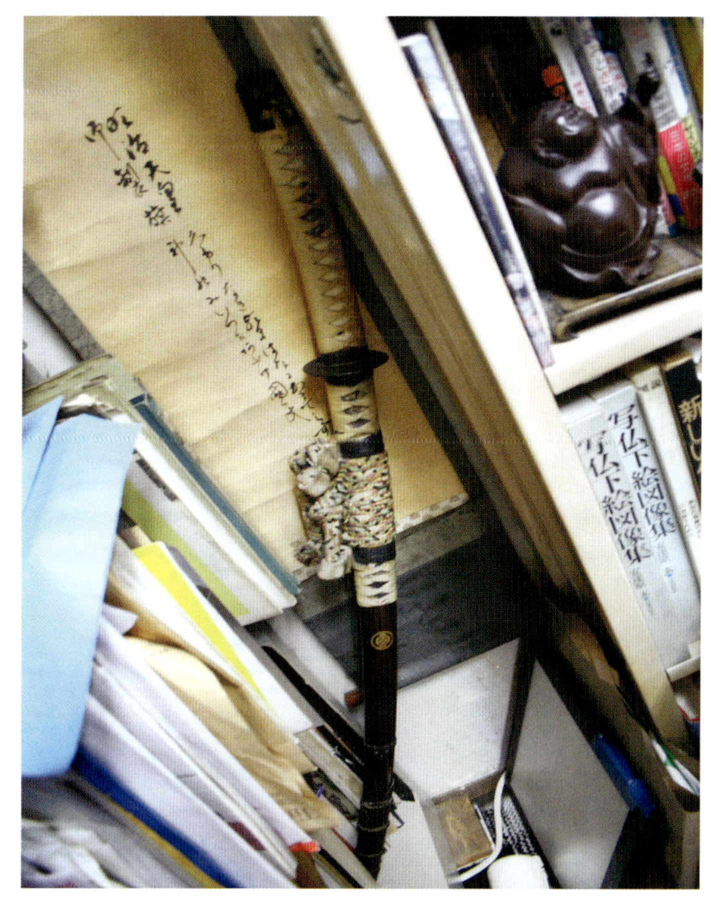

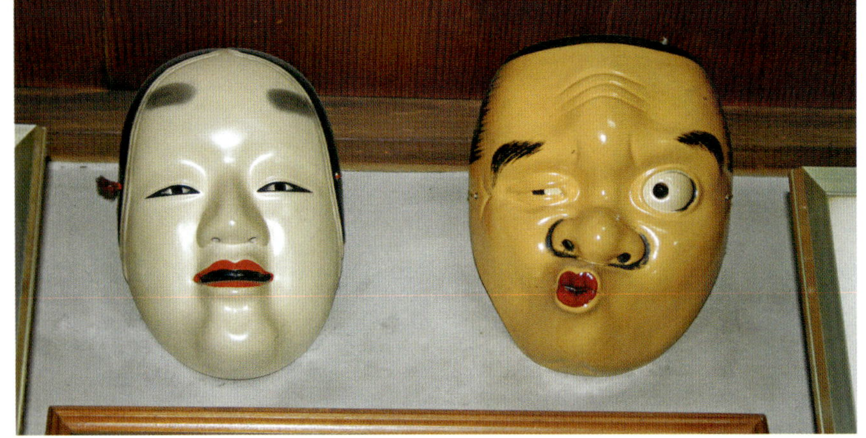

Above:
Kyogen masks of Okame (left) and Hyottoko. Often paired together, Okame is an "ugly girl" and Hyottoko is literally a "fire-man". His strange expression is the result of using his breath to fan the flames of a fire. *Kyogen* is the comic relief between *noh* plays.

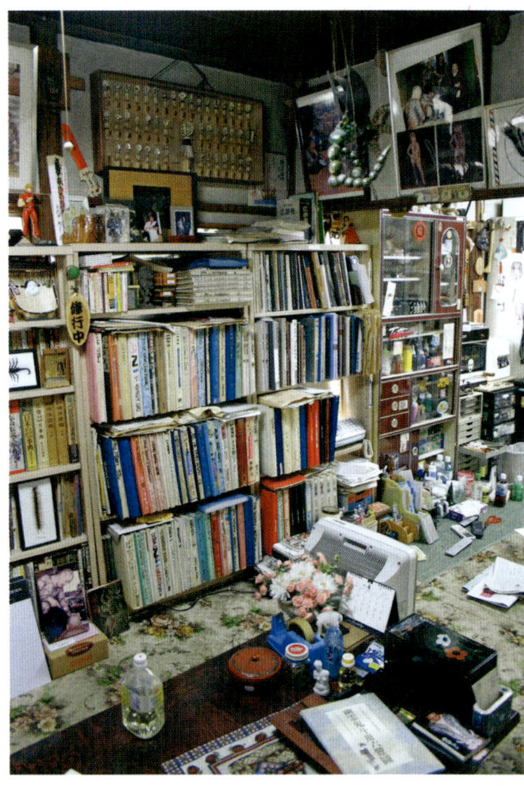

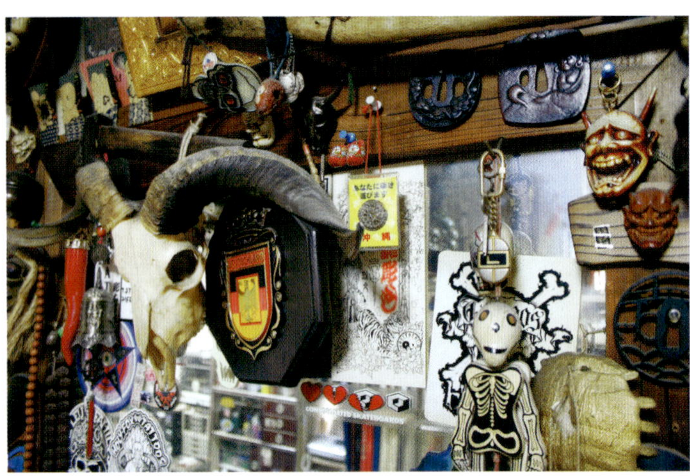

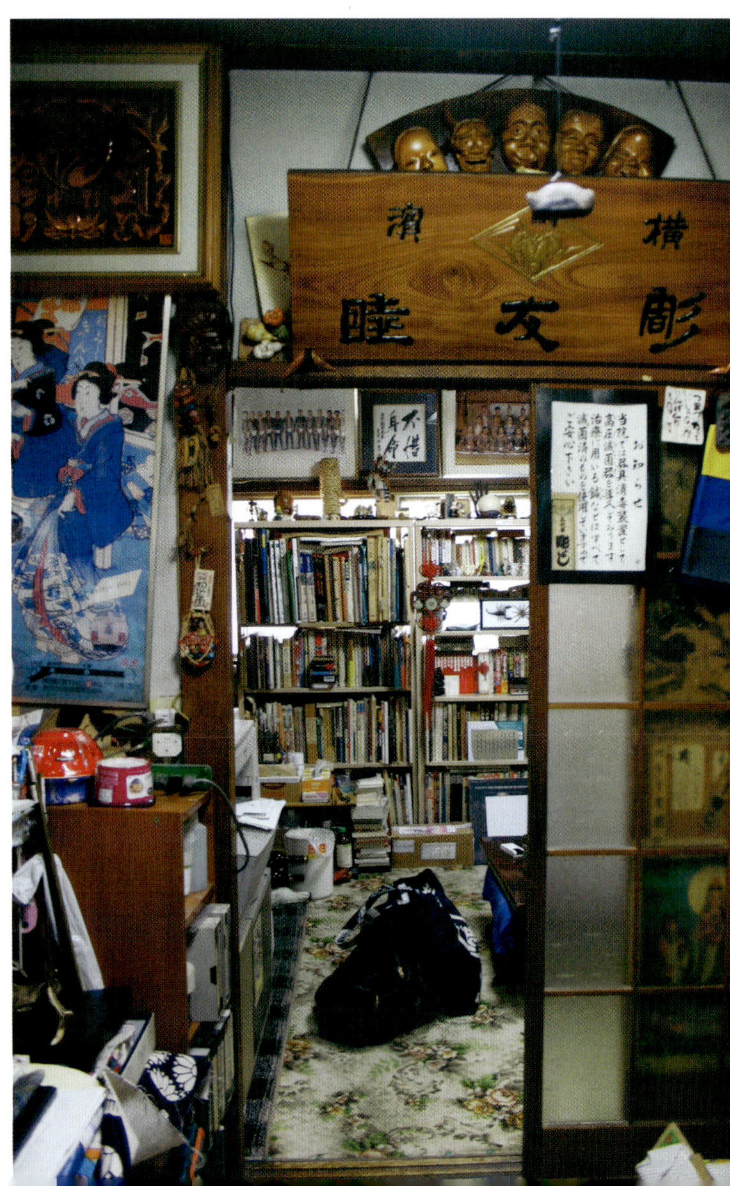

Horiyoshi III and over the years, many of Horiyoshi III's female clients, including his wife, have served as subjects for paintings. A large painting of a tattooed woman in repose hovers over the workstation, the red ink faded. Horiyoshi III acknowledges the two decades that the painting has hung there and jokes that "red is the weakest." He continues, explaining that good red ink is mineral based, -not vegetable-. Many of the decorations have been collected and displayed over the last thirty years. Every wall is lined with books, a library any tattooer would envy and one befitting the most knowledgeable man in Japanese tattooing. Aside from his personal albums covering his whole career, he has many albums containing work from other tattooers. The names on the spines show who has written, who has been here and hearken back to a time when letter writing and photo exchanges were paramount and valued. Before cheap plane tickets, before the Internet, this studio was here and still serves as a vessel to a different time.

Nestled between countless tattoo artifacts are religious objects, various representations of deities and characters of Japanese legend. Among

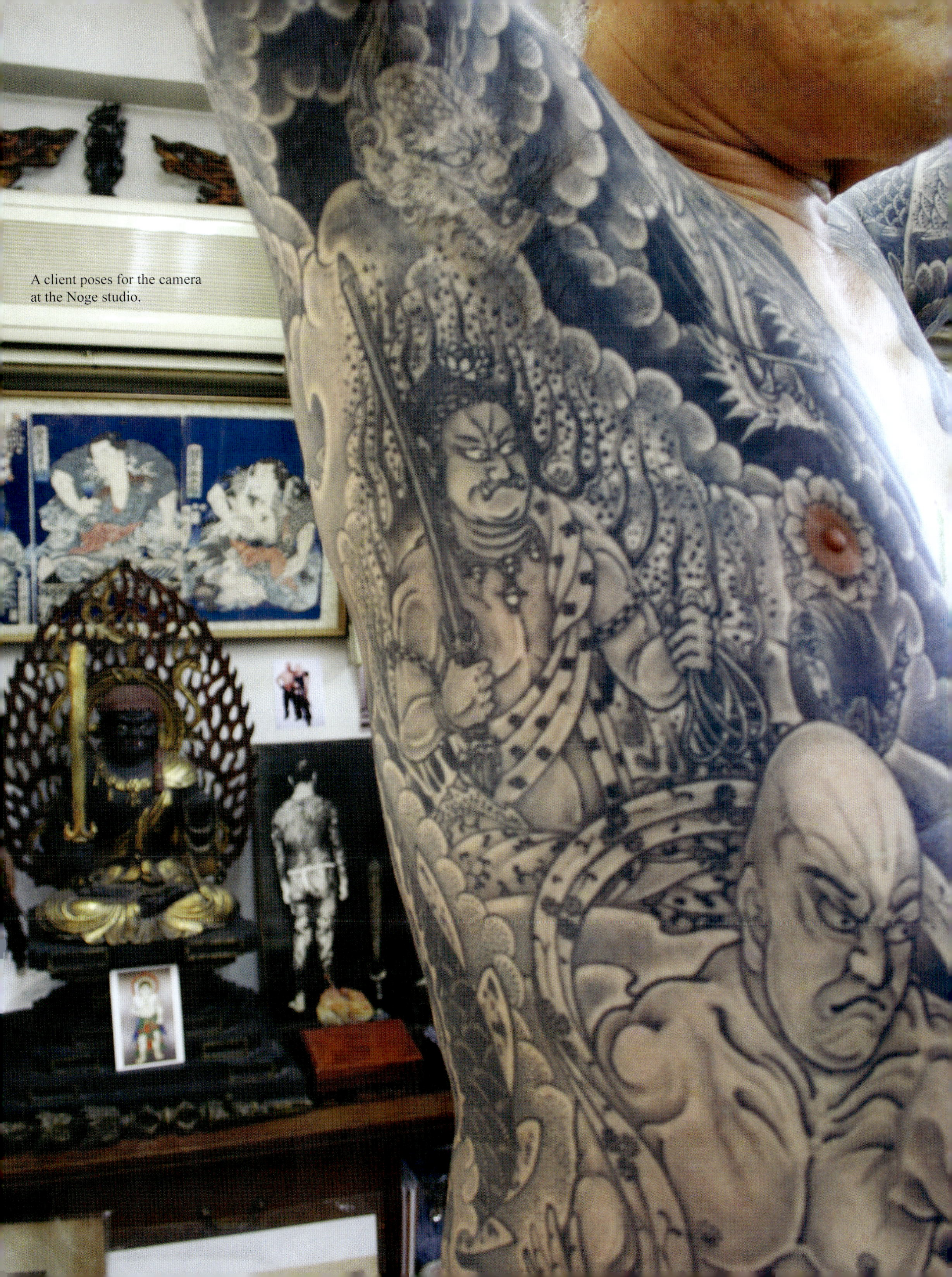

A client poses for the camera at the Noge studio.

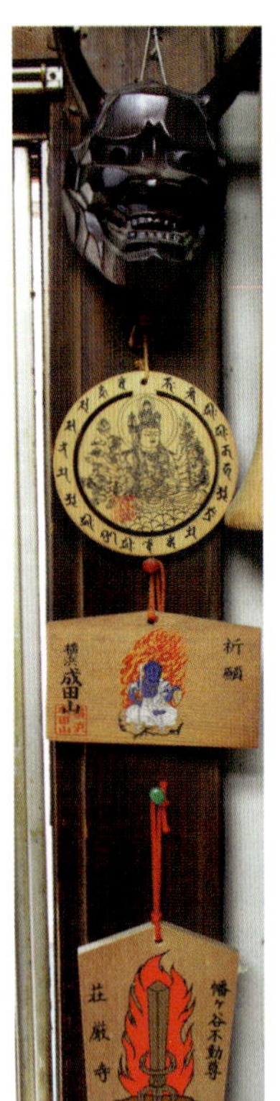

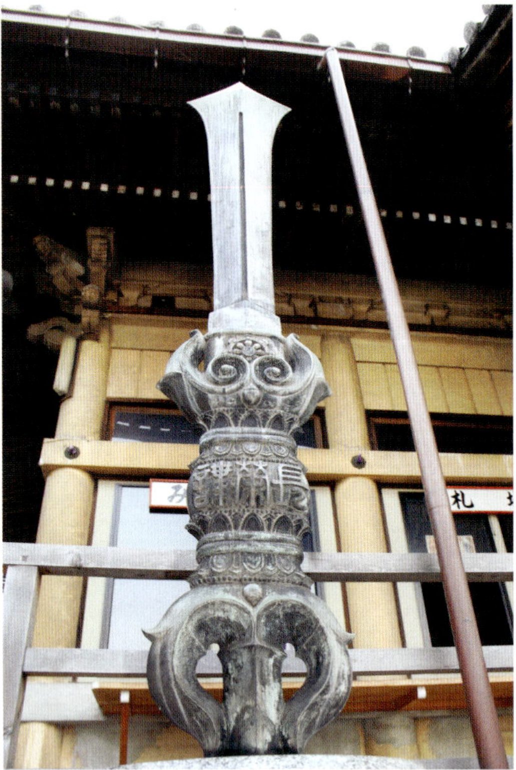

Statue of *kurikaraken*, sword of Fudōmyō-ō.

these, I noticed many images of Fudōmyō-ō. Horiyoshi III shows quite a liking to Fudōmyō-ō, described as the manifestation of the anger of the Dainichi Nyorai, the supreme Buddha in esoteric Buddhism. A three-foot tall wooden Fudōmyō-ō adorns, or maybe guards, the entry to his home and there is also a large wooden statue at the Noge studio. There is also a temple honoring Fudōmyō-ō in very close proximity to the Ise-cho studio and we felt it necessary to visit and pay homage. I asked Horiyoshi III if Fudōmyō-ō was his personal patron saint, and he smiled, answering that he did not want to be "restricted to just one god."

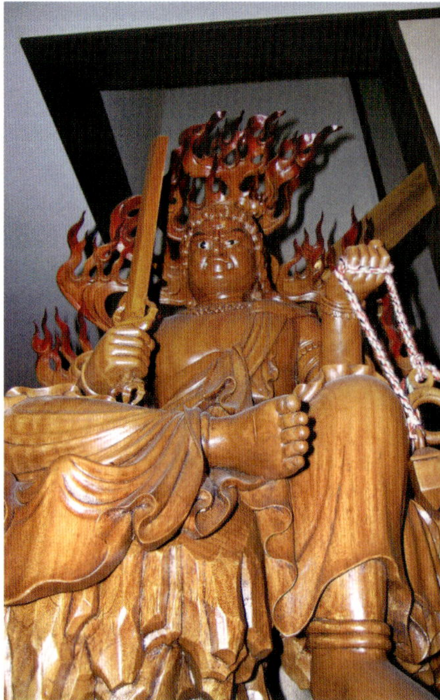

Wooden effigy at the entrance of Horiyoshi III's home.

Enclosed by these assorted religious relics and art pieces of all disciplines, I found myself humbled by my surroundings. I thought back on my first visit to the historic studio. The first time I was at the Ise-cho studio, I felt that simply having the chance to get a tattoo at Ise-cho, the mere notion of the opportunity, was a privileged experience in the tattoo world. I was definitely adding an important piece of tattoo history to my collection in receiving a tattoo from such a living legend. During the session,

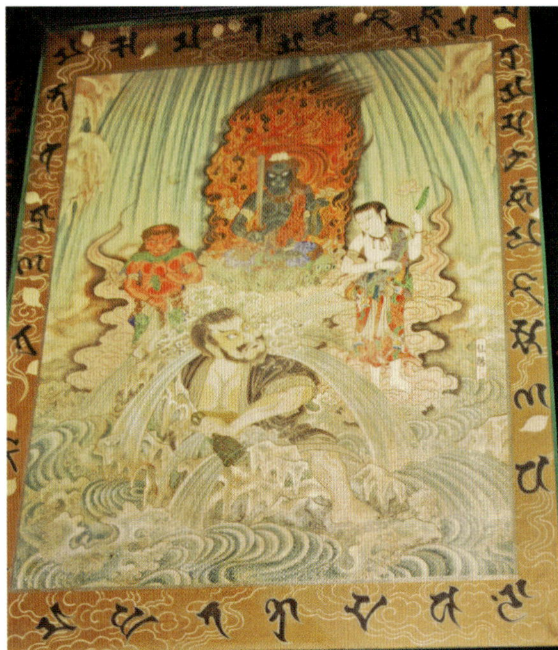

The samurai Endo Morito mistakenly took the life of his mistress in a murder attempt on her husband's life. Devastated, he took the Buddhist name "Mongaku" and, seeking penance, prayed to Fudōmyō-ō under a waterfall. After three days Fudōmyō-ō was convinced Mongaku's repentance was true and sent his attendants Seitaka and Kongara to rescue the frozen man. This painting hangs next to the altar dedicated to Fudōmyō-ō at the temple in Yokohama.

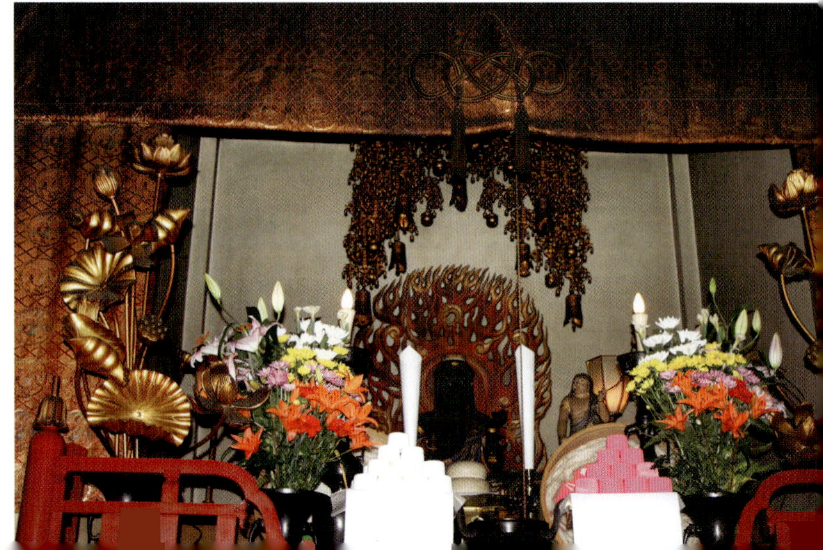

I thought of the many photos of him working and the many clients that had preceded me. There I was, on the same floor that hundreds of people had been tattooed on, lines hand outlined, bodysuits completed. These were the bodysuits that would become legendary in the minds of my colleagues and myself alike, that we would so fervently study thousands of miles away, decades later. I was on the same floor shared by carpenter and *Yakuza* boss alike and the sheer enthusiasm dulled the pain. This statement should be qualified by the fact that I was getting my ribs tattooed, which is easily among the more painful areas to tattoo. Even years later the aura of this place has not faded. It, much like Horiyoshi III himself, is an eclectic place, expressing his taste and reflecting the variety in his clientele.

For several months leading up to our trip, I had been entertaining the idea of getting a tattoo that commemorated my lifelong passion for tattooing. It was a vague idea and sounds somewhat silly when explained. I wanted a tattoo of the word tattoo, much in the way people venerate loved ones by getting their names tattooed on them. During the nineties, it was a popular trend for tattoo artists to get images of tattoo machines on them. Although this idea is dated, I adore the sentiment. I didn't come to Japan this time with the expectation of receiving a tattoo from Horiyoshi III but the feelers were out seeking inspiration. Looking at the drawings for the ghost series days prior, there was an image that spoke to me. It was the glyph that he had etched into his own tombstone. He had taken the *hiragana* symbols for *irezumi* meaning tattoo, and manipulated it to appear to be a *bonji*, the Japanese versions of Sanskrit. In Japan bonji are used as prayers and to symbolize deities-- they are holy symbols. Thus, Horiyoshi III had created a sacred symbol for tattooing. Horiyoshi III is widely recognized for his incredible mastery of calligraphy and only a mind with his talent and wit, coupled with his extraordinary hand, could have conceived of such a complex and beautiful character. Upon encountering this image, I was immediately attracted to it. This was exactly the symbol I was looking for, to place center mast on my sternum. As I walked through Yokohama with Horitaka, I explained how I felt and asked him if he would do the honor of putting this tattoo on me when we got back to San Jose. He thought for a moment and being of like mind, thought it was a great idea, but one that should be given by the man himself. We had plans to spend the whole day in the Ise-cho studio draw-

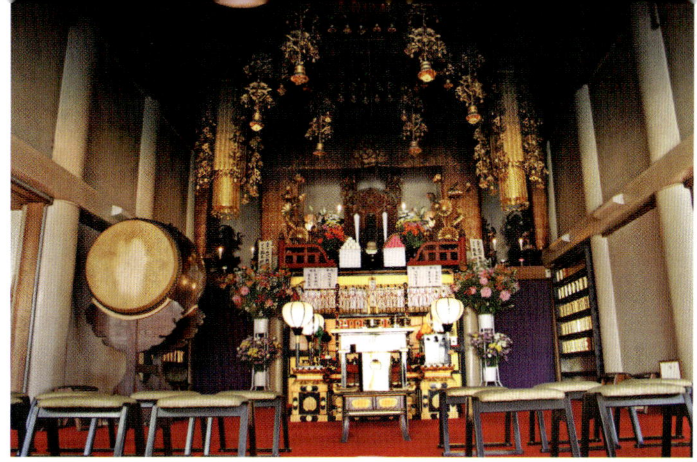

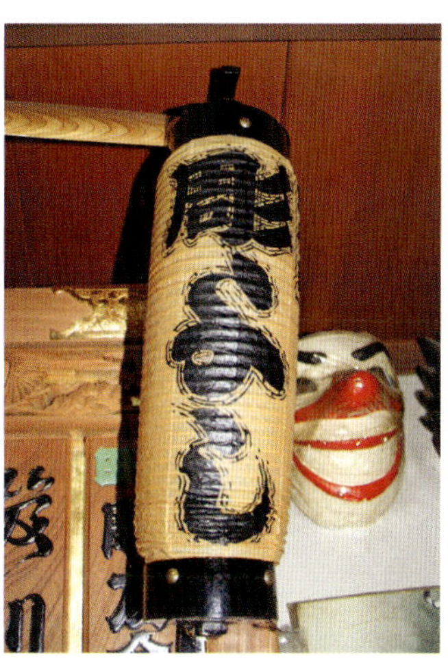

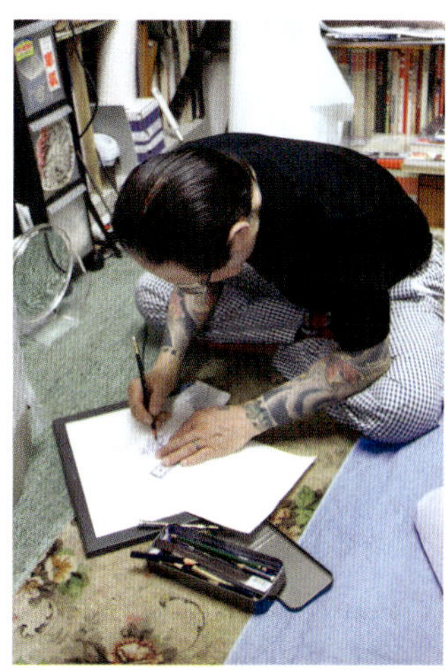

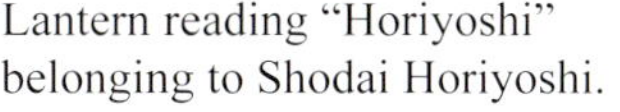

Lantern reading "Horiyoshi" belonging to Shodai Horiyoshi.

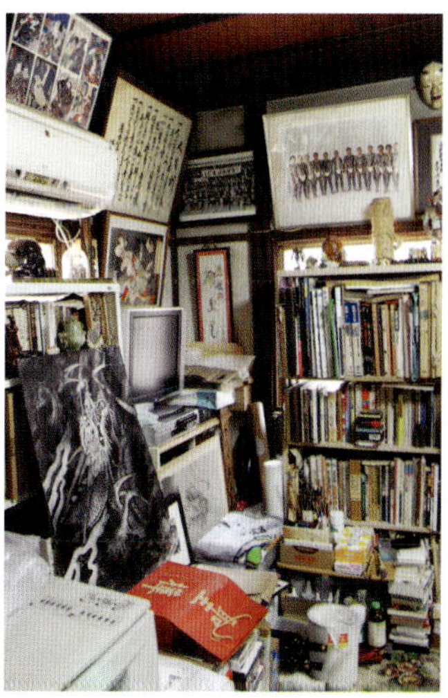

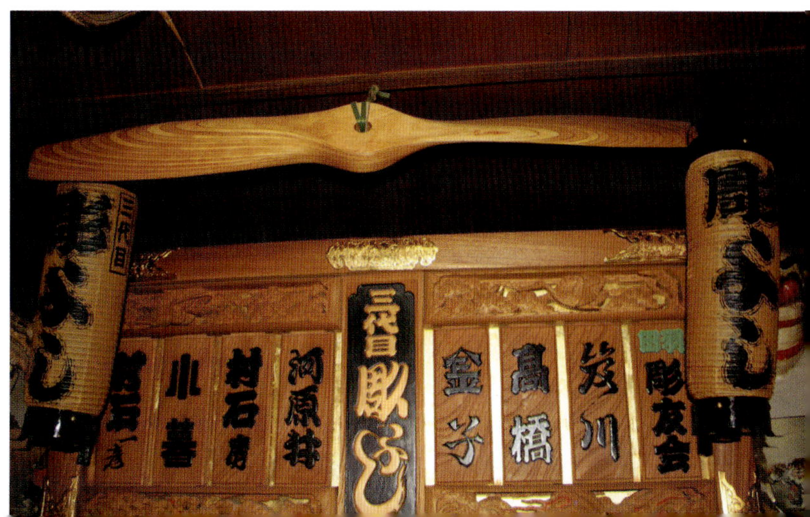

ing and working with Horiyoshi III that Saturday, and Horitaka asked "Big Man" if he could possibly do these tattoos for us during that time. He agreed and the appointment was set!

While the Master was setting up his machines, he told us that he was going to draw a new character just for us. He wanted us to have something original since the image I had seen was from his new book and soon to be published. It was a real honor and pleasure to watch as he recreated the characters, deftly commanding the brush... it was truly beautiful. Once the symbol was ready, it was tattoo time! Horitaka planned to put the symbol on his neck, a decision he knew he would have to negotiate with his master. Horiyoshi III has discouraged Horitaka from tattooing himself outside the confines of the Japanese style bodysuit, namely marking his hands, neck, and face as off limits. Horitaka has followed Horiyoshi III's lead in covering his entire body in tattoos and is committed to being heavily tattooed. He had a prepared response for Horiyoshi III's protest to the neck tattoo: "I want it in the same spot you have the spider. I want to look like my master!" Horiyoshi III couldn't really argue that point and the tattoo was started. It was a warm and humid day, especially in such a confined place, and four years later back on the floor of Ise-cho, I was no less nervous or excited. No matter how often I get tattooed, I always find myself trembling moments before. The finished product far surpassed any hope that I had for this tattoo. Having the opportunity again, to be a client in this notable setting and receive such a meaningful tattoo was an experience that was both humbling and overwhelming. Horitaka and I have debated whether Horiyoshi III is a painful tattooer, and I have always joked that his tattoos don't hurt. Perhaps at that moment my reverence countered the sting of the tattoo needle.

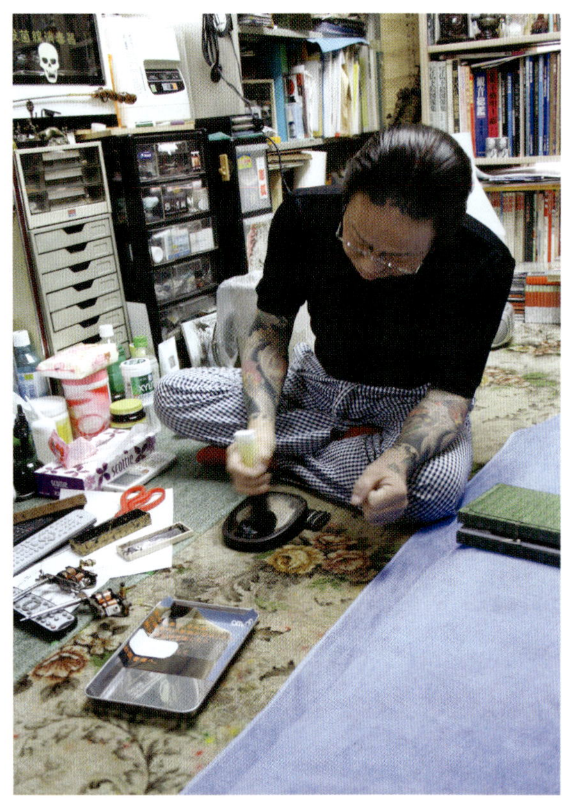

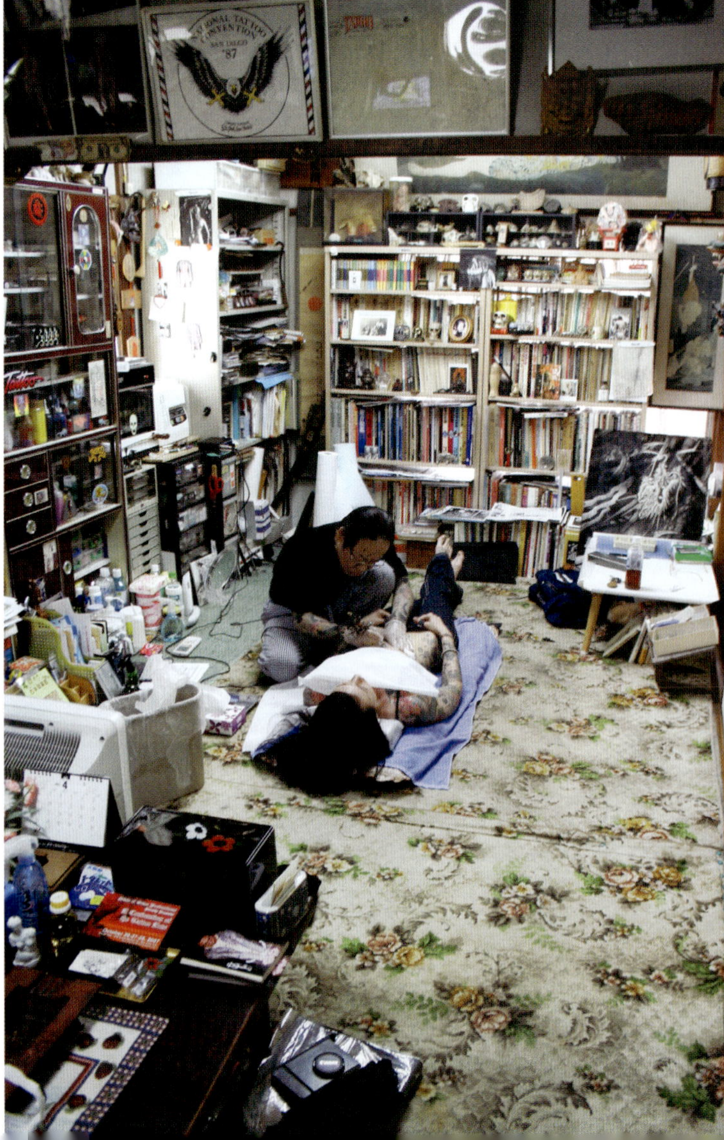

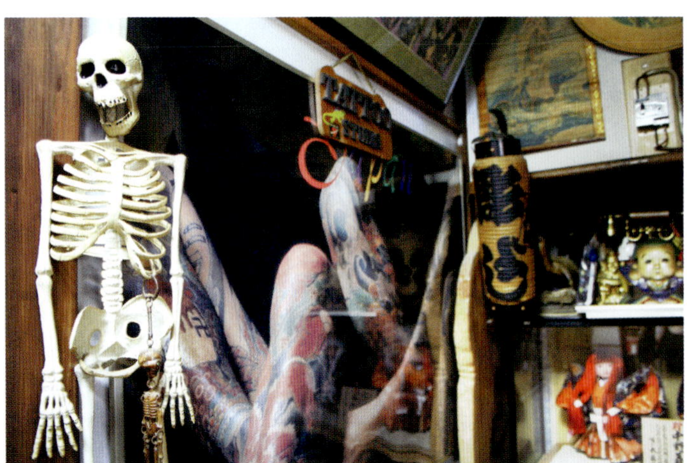

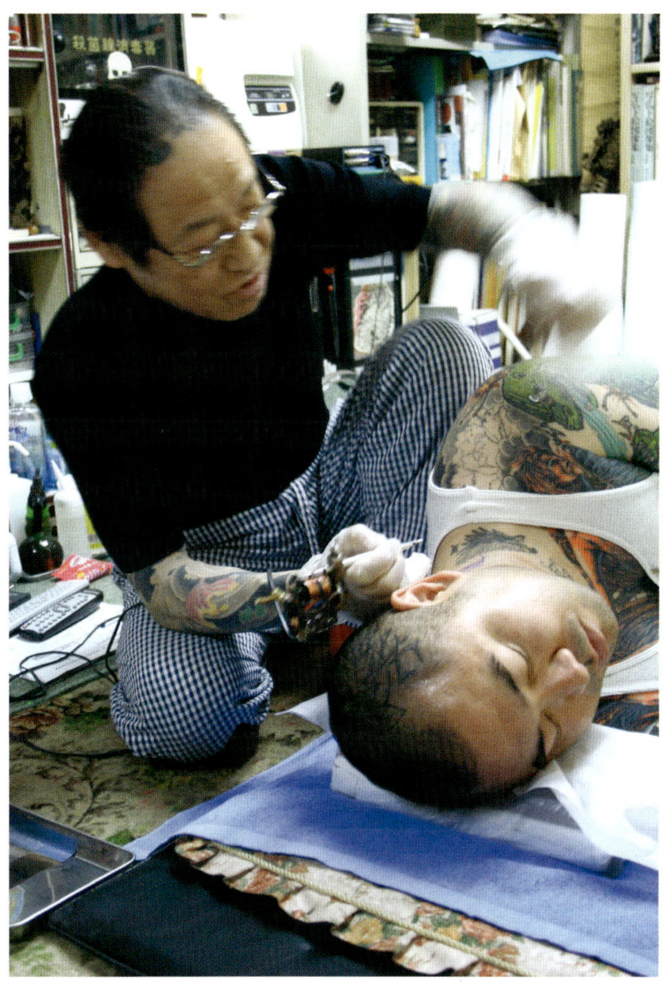

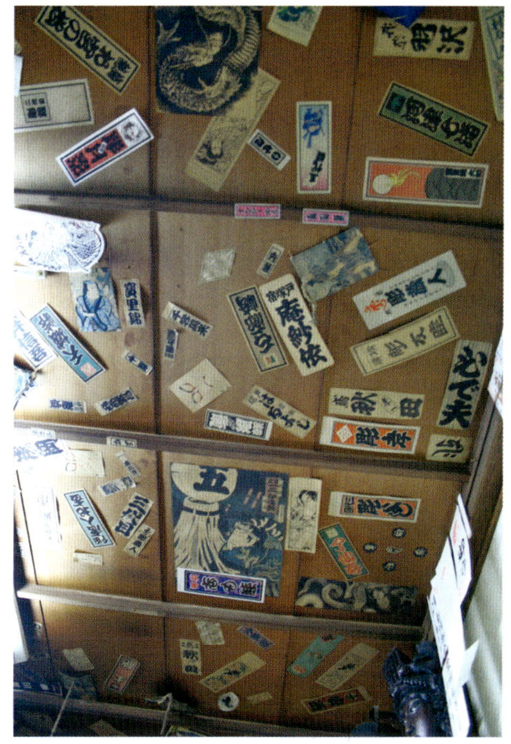

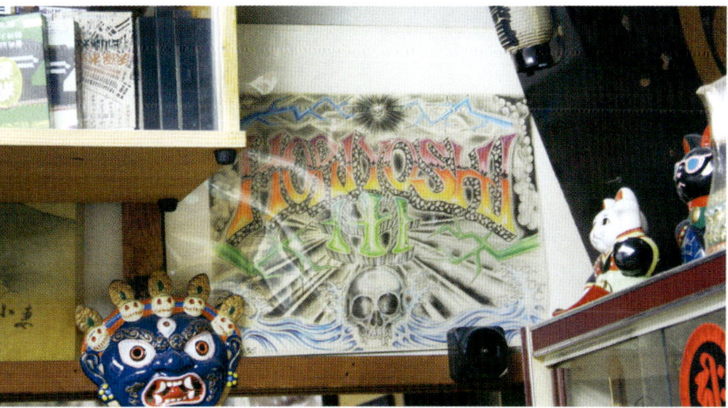

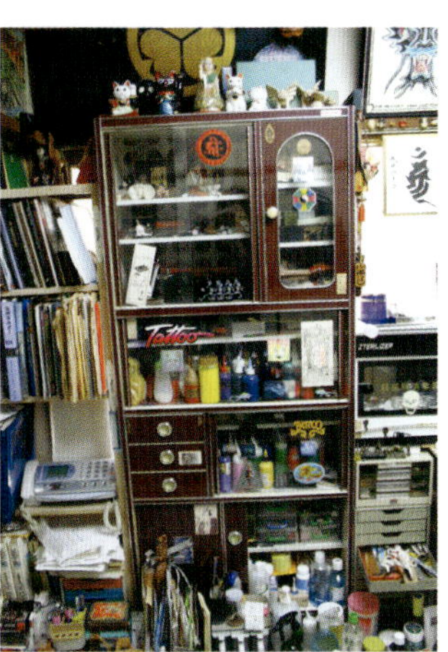

Below:
"*Otsukare sama deshita*!"

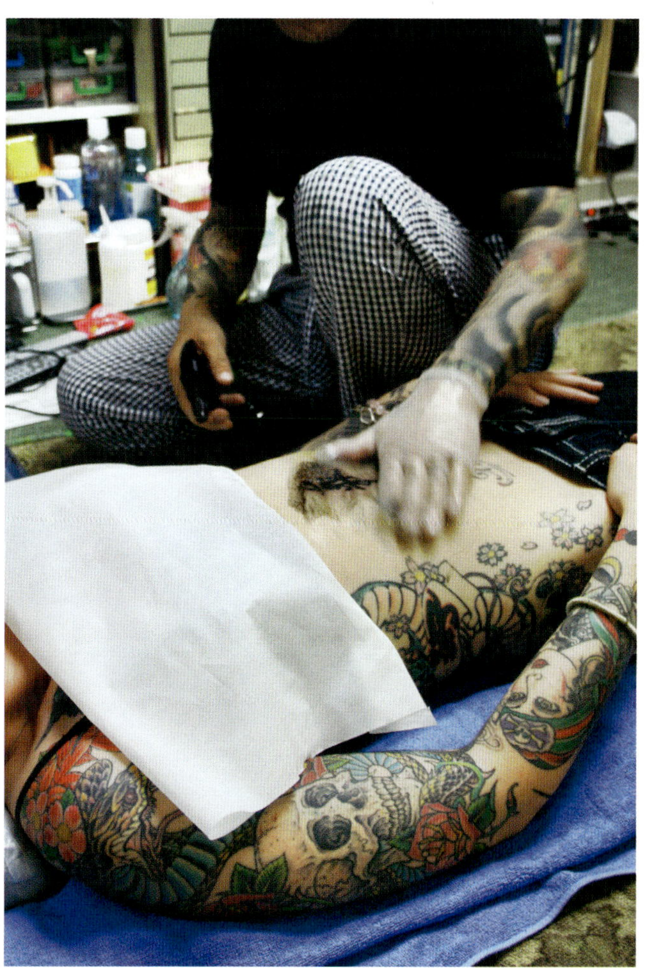

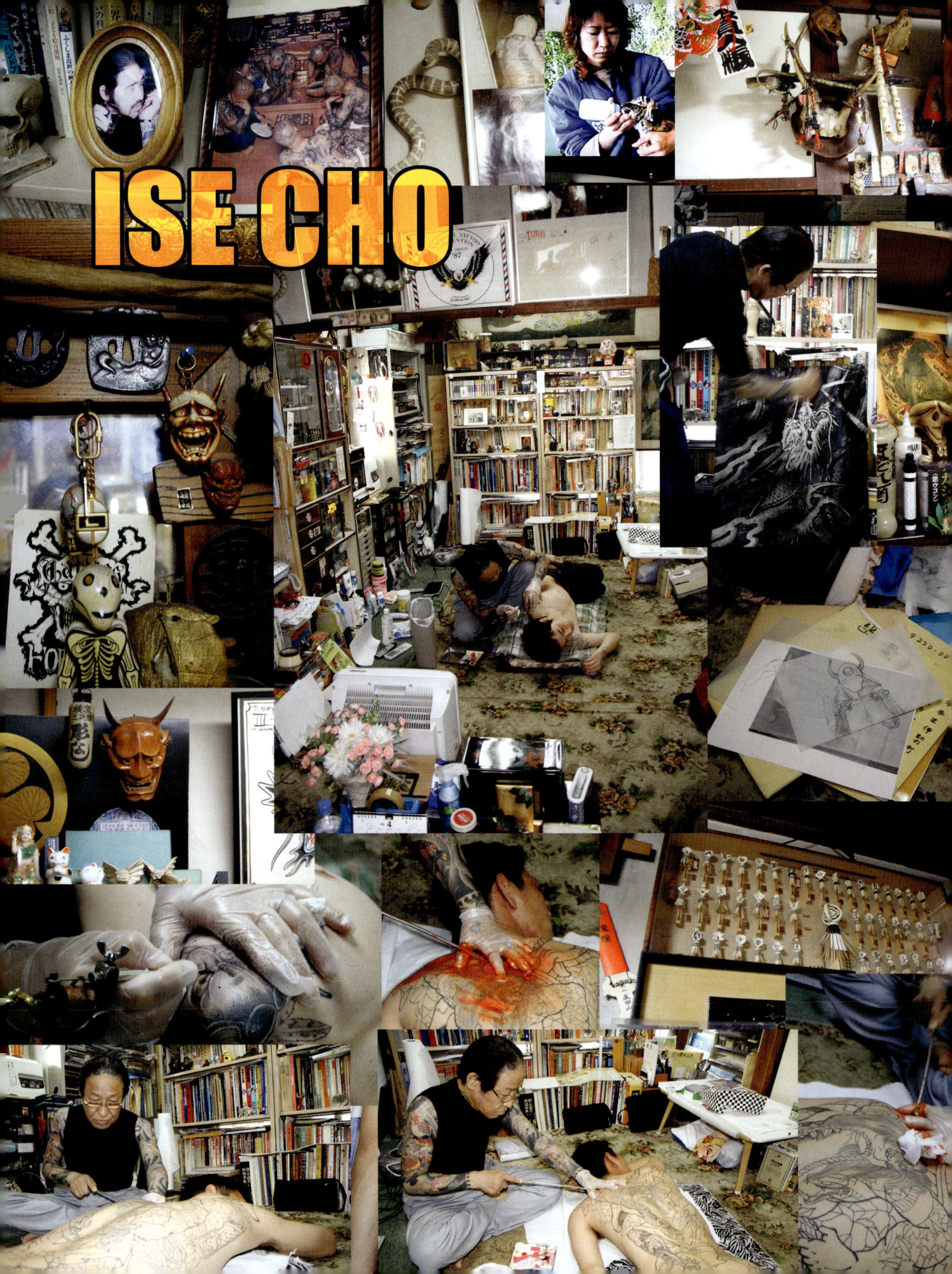
ISE CHO

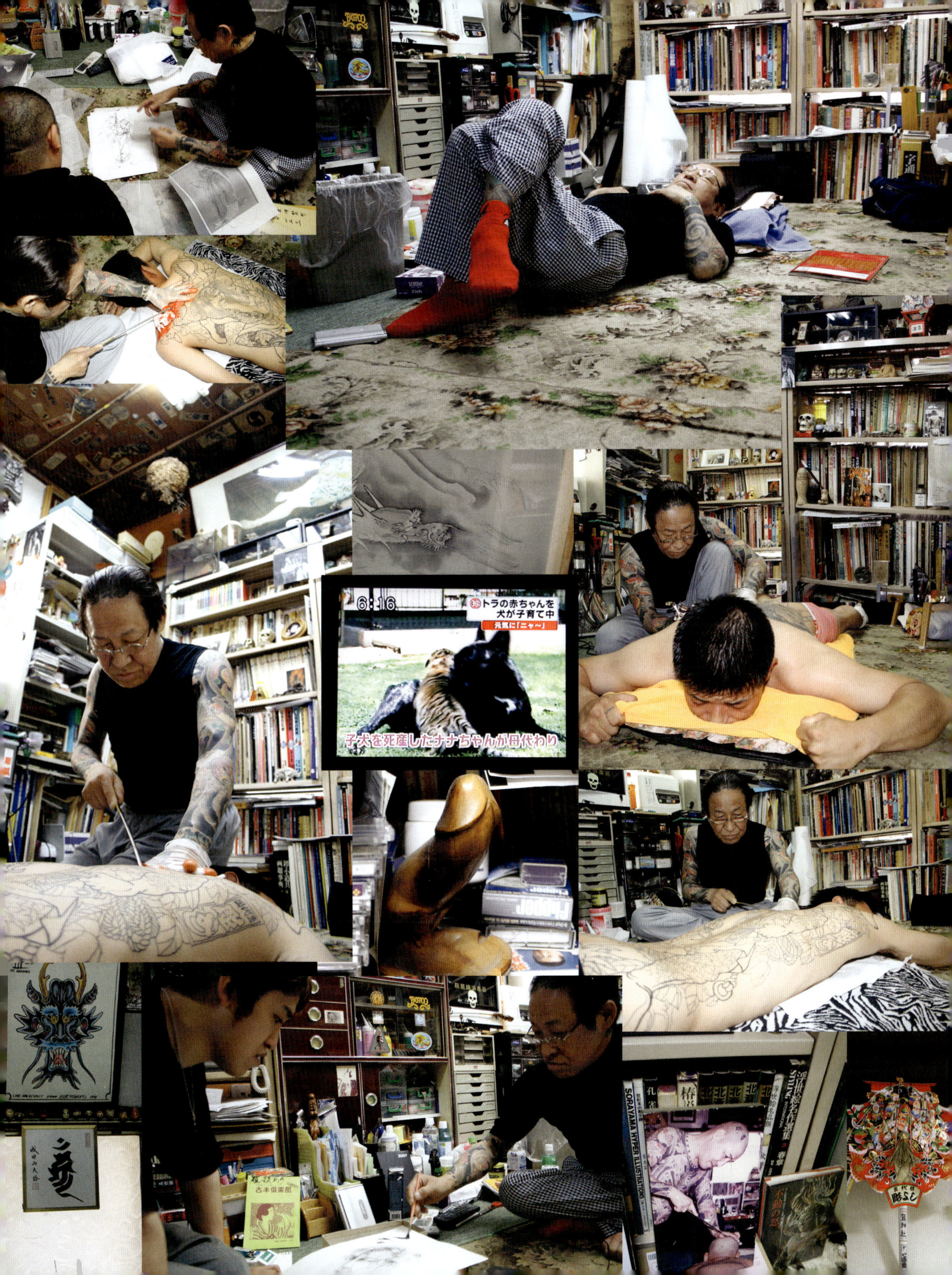
6:16
トラの赤ちゃんを
犬が子育て中
元気に「ニャ～」
子犬を死産したナナちゃんが母代わり
SORAYAMA HYPER ILLUSTRATIONS

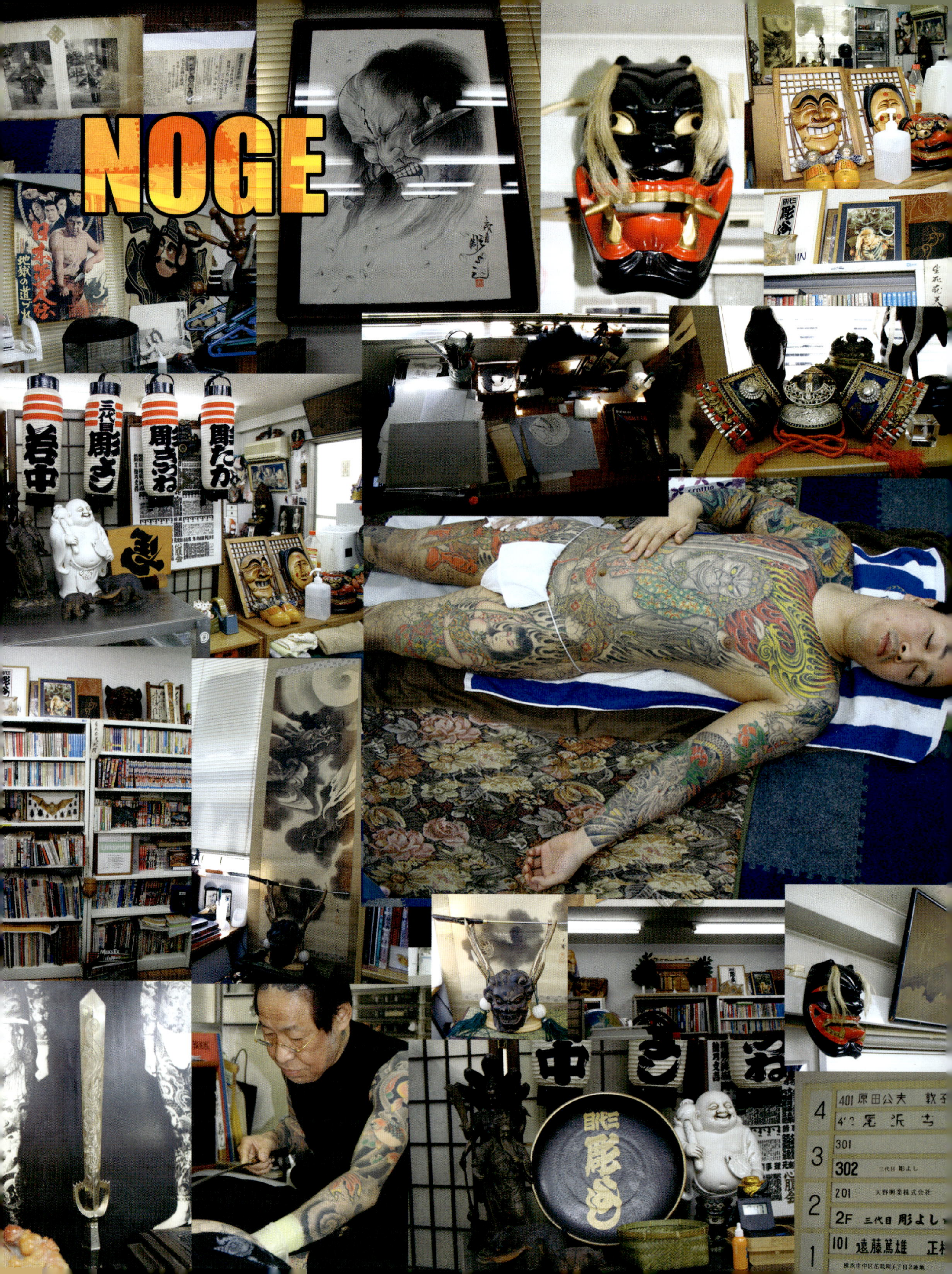
NOGE
三代目
彫よし
4
401 原田公夫 敦子
3
301
302 三代目 彫よし
2
201 天野興業株式会社
2F 三代目 彫よし
1
101 遠藤篤雄
横浜市中区花咲町1丁目2番地

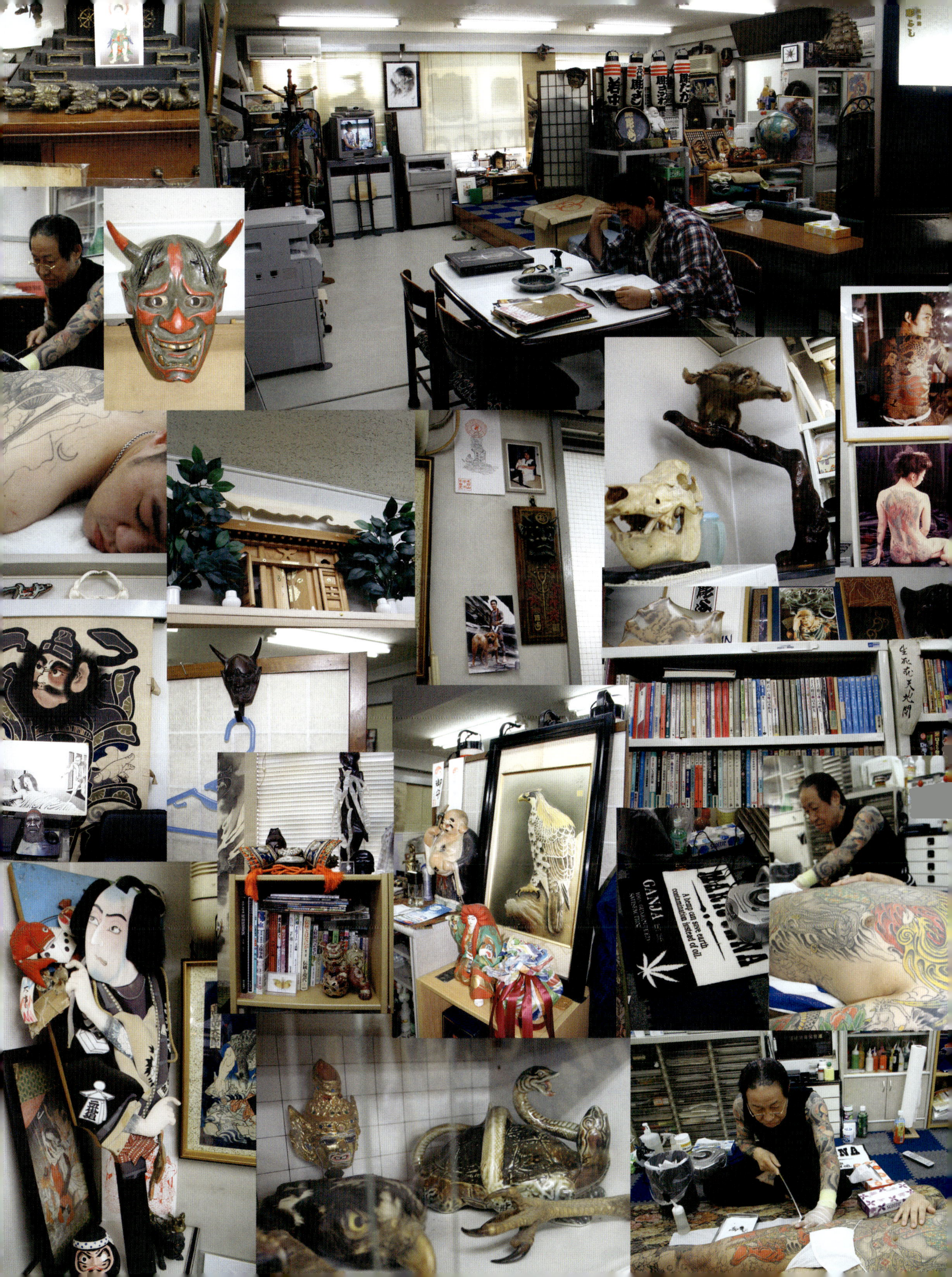
GANJA
A hemp can save earth
contamination instead of oil.

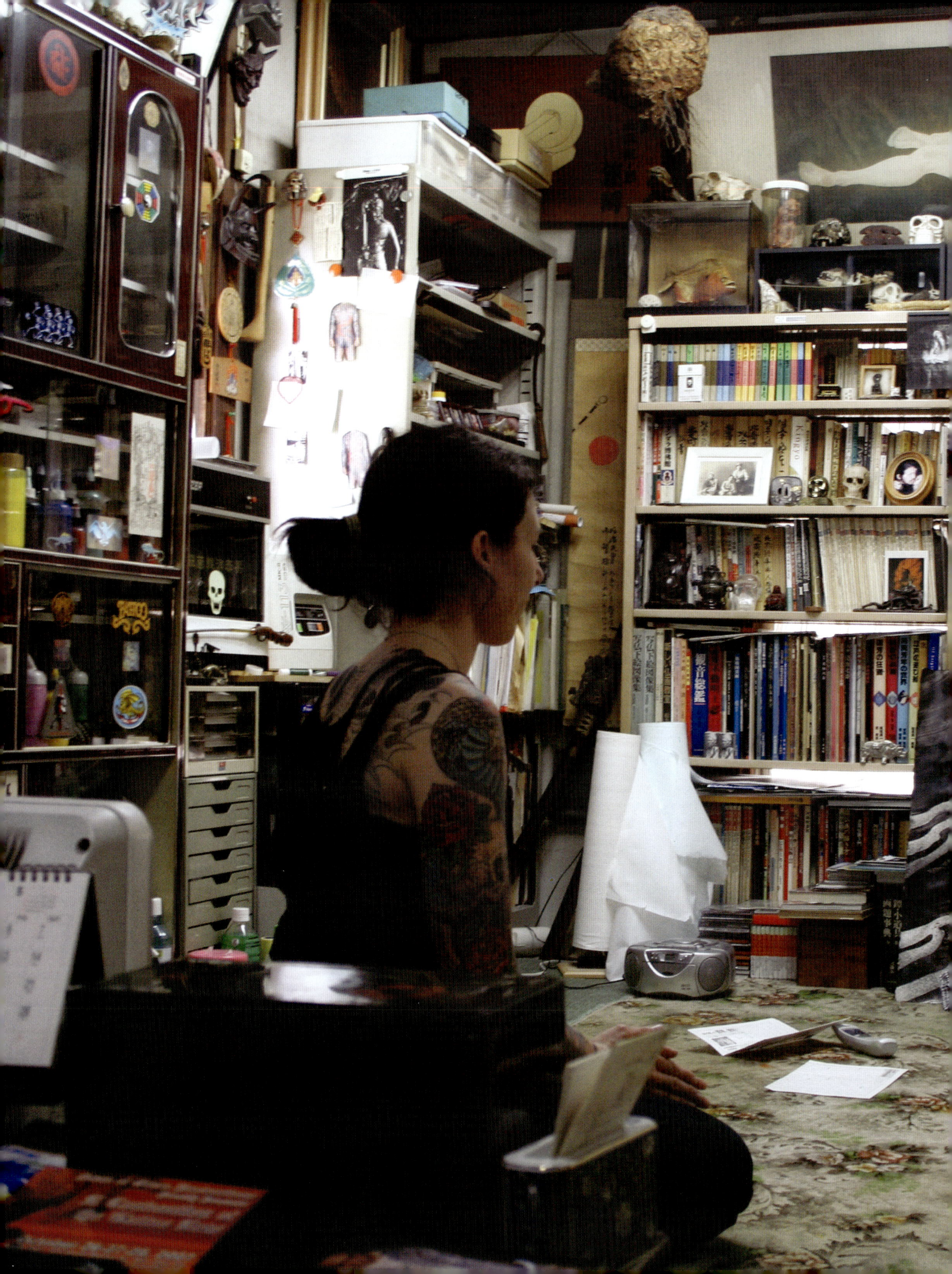

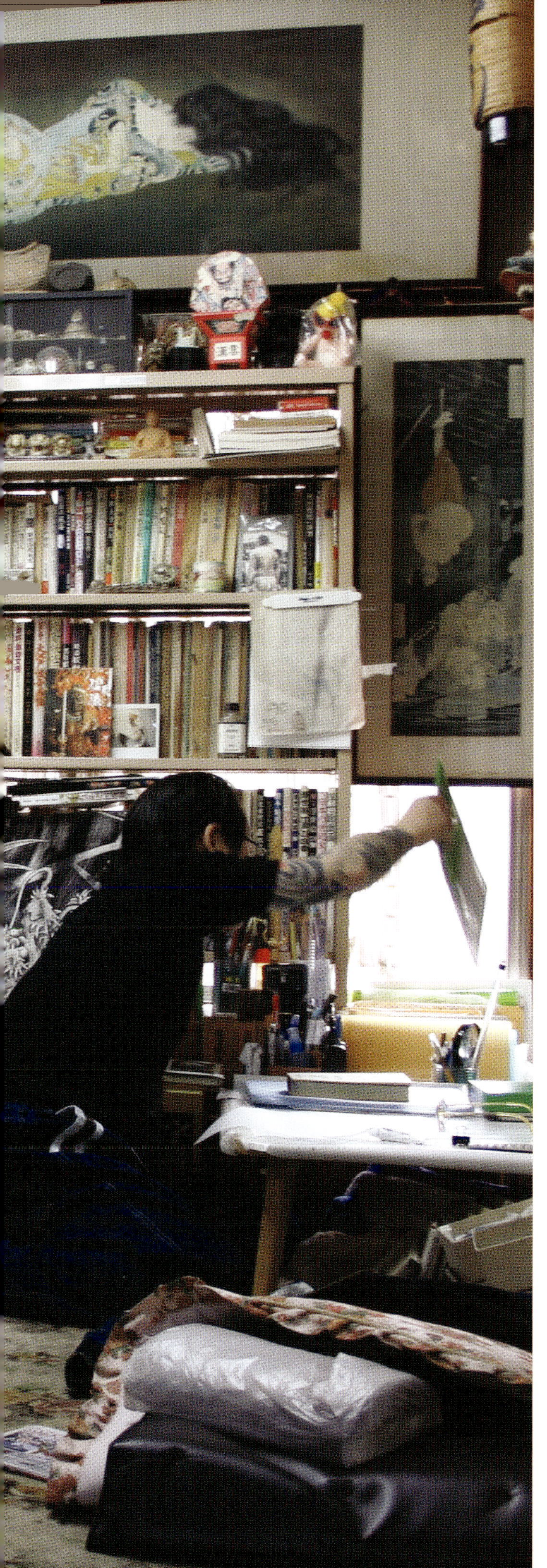

Chapter 4
REIGI

Horitaka did his best to prepare me for the necessary *reigi*, or etiquette involved in daily interactions in Japan. As compared to American culture, Japan feels much more formal. From the perspective of a tattooer, I am especially sensitive to this within the subculture of tattooing. This is an interesting dichotomy since Western tattoo subculture often appears less governed by manner and etiquette. It is similar to the Western notion of the "outlaw". In truth, tattoo subcultures worldwide carry their own set of rules and mores and, though different from that of "polite society", are taken just as seriously. Social faux pas might just get your nose broken in some circles. The mingling of tattooers from different backgrounds results in a type of cultural exchange, and draws attention to different ways of displaying respect. Japanese tattooing is entrenched in Japanese culture, not just visually, but also in social interactions. It is easy for foreigners to ignore these formalities. Likewise, Japanese tend to dismiss the discourteous behavior of foreigners and attribute it to their lack of understanding of *reigi*. The explanations given to me concerning *reigi*, or rather the *reigi* I practice around Horiyoshi III, is not exclusive to tattooing. They are common displays of respect shown to elders or higher authorities, a basic tenet of polite behavior in Japanese culture.

Japan is what many consider to be an outwardly polite society, and the concept of *reigi* permeates all aspects of everyday life. Some are as basic as proper greetings or waiting for the master or elder to eat first before commencing a meal. Others are much more involved and alien to the average Westerner. While at the Horiyoshi III studios, I am

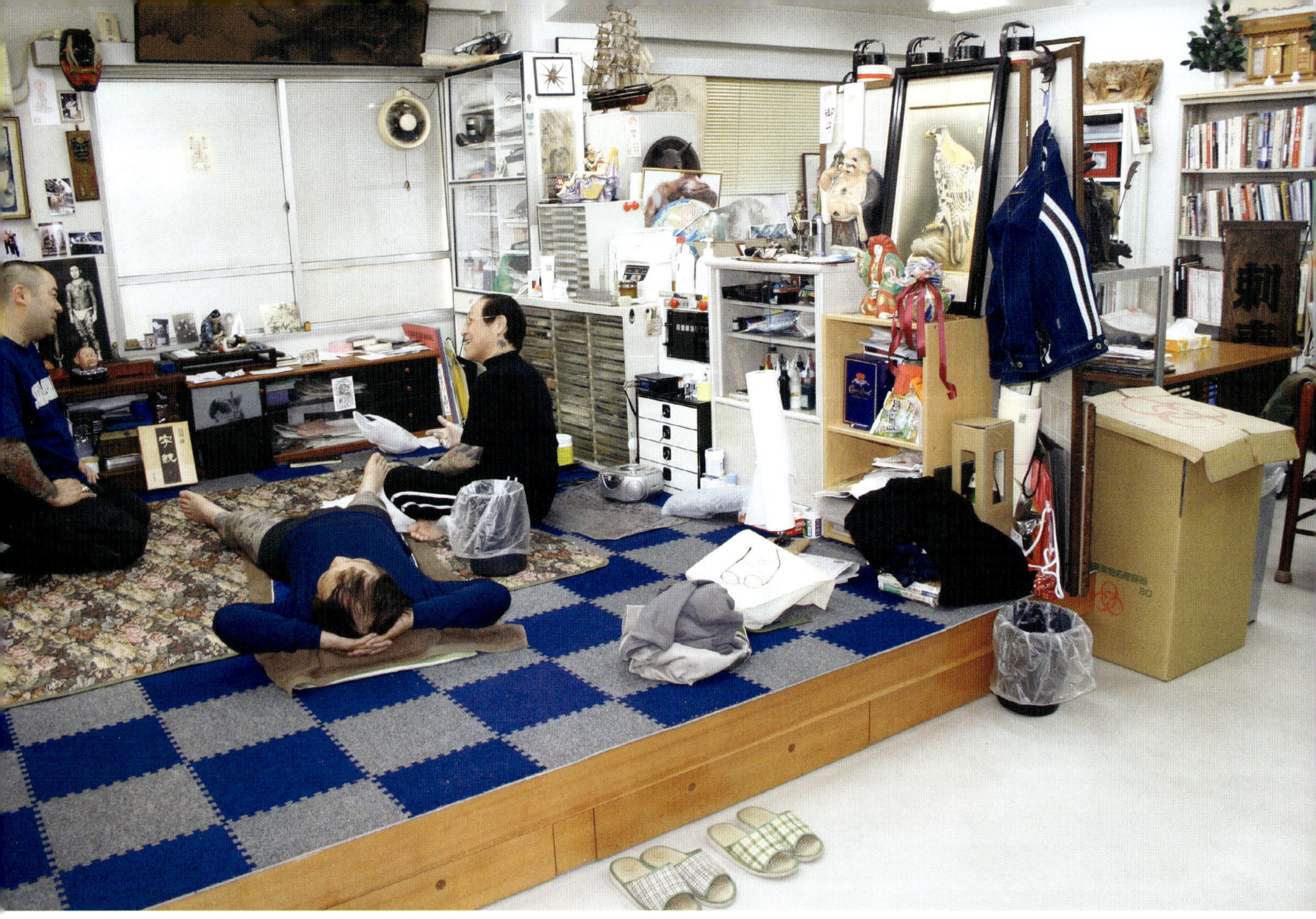

always careful to observe proper protocol. When a client enters, the apprentices stand, bow and announce *ohayo gozaimasu*. Language books will interpret this as a formal good morning, and this is its usage in most of Japan. In my experience in the tattoo sub-culture it is a polite salutation that is said throughout the day. This appropriation is specific to some industries such as tattooing. The greeting is exchanged and then the client removes his/her shoes and puts on slippers for indoor use. When Horiyoshi III or a client steps up onto the work platform, they step out of the slippers. Following Horitaka's lead, I turn the sandals around so that when he returns to them, they are facing him, ready to be worn. This is a practice taught to Japanese children by their mothers called *defune* or "embarking boat", the analogy of a boat facing outward towards the direction it is moving in. Clients at the studio are remarkably polite as well, waiting their turn quietly until summoned. At this point, they walk over to him, bow deeply, remove their slippers, step up and then roll out their own towel to lie down on. The session begins. At the close of the appointment, the customer thanks the master, bowing again, pays and gathers his belongings. The underlings walk him to the door, maintaining eye contact, bow and say *otsukare sama deshita*. This translates loosely to "thank you for your hard work", and is very appropriate for one who has just labored or been tattooed. We continue to stand at the door until the client is gone. Many of Horiyoshi III's clients are well versed in this and oftentimes I have seen clients hurry out, sometimes with shoes still untied, so as not to keep people waiting on them. Many people in Japan focus on the group dynamic whereas in the West, we tend to think of ourselves first.

Horiyoshi III tattoos about seven or eight people a day, six days a week and each time this display of formalities is performed. This may sound exhausting to a foreigner but it is routine in Japan. This can also be seen as a time and place for a client to make a formal display of respect and reverence to the *sensei*. It is a physical language that is a crucial performance of emotion in Japanese culture. Conversely, if these formalities are not performed, it can be interpreted as a sign of disrespect. I always do my best to adhere to the *reigi* expected of me, but I must admit at times it is difficult. It is a restraint that can feel foreign to me, when I bid farewell to Horiyoshi III and his family, I wanted to hug and kiss them in typical American fashion, but knowing that was not what they were accustomed to, I opted for a respectful bow and my most heartfelt *arigatou gozaimasu*.

The shop is kept tidy, ashtrays are constantly emptied, garbage taken out, portfolios and magazines straightened. When I am around the shop I participate in these chores and focus my attention on the master. I keep quiet and find unobtrusive places to sit so as not to disturb him. The overall atmosphere of the workspace is proper. There is little conversation and clients wait their turn to interact with Horiyoshi III. He has a presence and it is reflected in the respect that his clients show him. There is no shop girl or secretary. The apprentices that are present put his needs before their own out of respect and a trust in his judgment, they do not hold a managerial position or seek greater financial gain with these extra responsibilities. His own master ingrained these practices in Horiyoshi III and he expects nothing less of those around him. He not only carries the tradition of artistry passed on to him, but also perpetuates the social graces of his generation. His demeanor encourages all those around him to hold themselves to a higher standard. As an onlooker it is apparent that Horiyoshi III values the notion of "acting right" and it is clear that the people that are close to him are treated with the respect that they bestow upon him. Respect is a characteristic that he has sought in his apprentices and may even surpass artistic talent in his process of selection. An apprentice is more than a student; they become a member of your family, your crew, they may even carry your name as Horiyoshi III did for his master. They should not embarrass you publicly. Tattoo masters do not run art schools. They teach the culture of tattooing to a select few who will bear their name long after, insuring the future of the Master's legacy. Indeed, much rides on the demeanor of the apprentices for it is not simply about artistic ability. This is a lesson for outsiders in comprehending the social structure of tattooing in Japan as tattooing intermingles with other subcultures, most notably the *Yakuza*. In dealing with

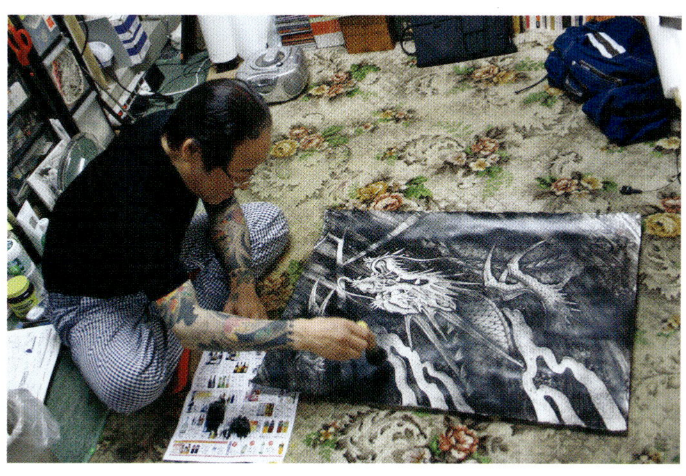

Below:
"*Kanpai*!"

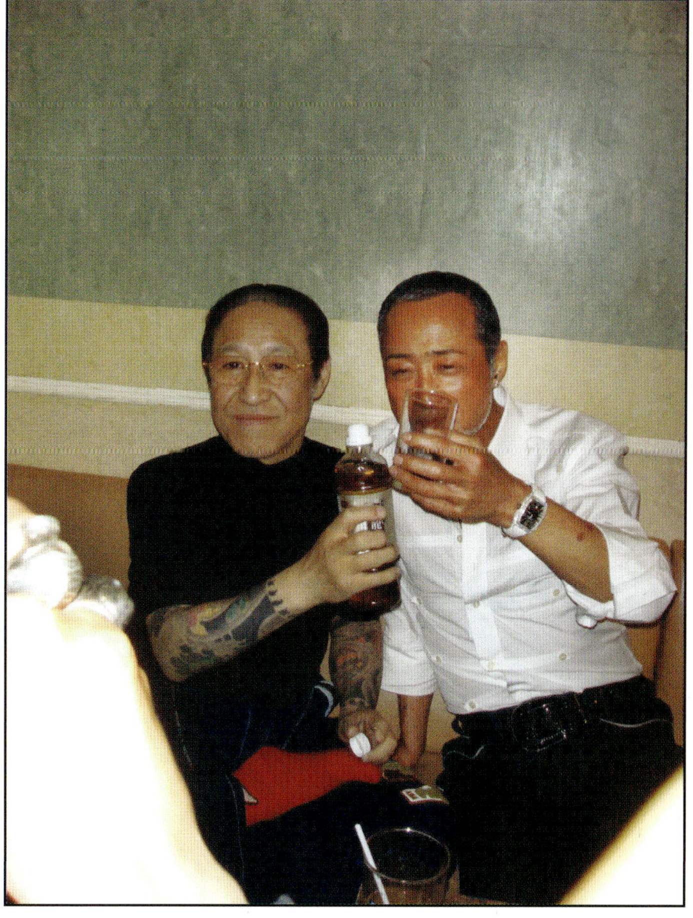

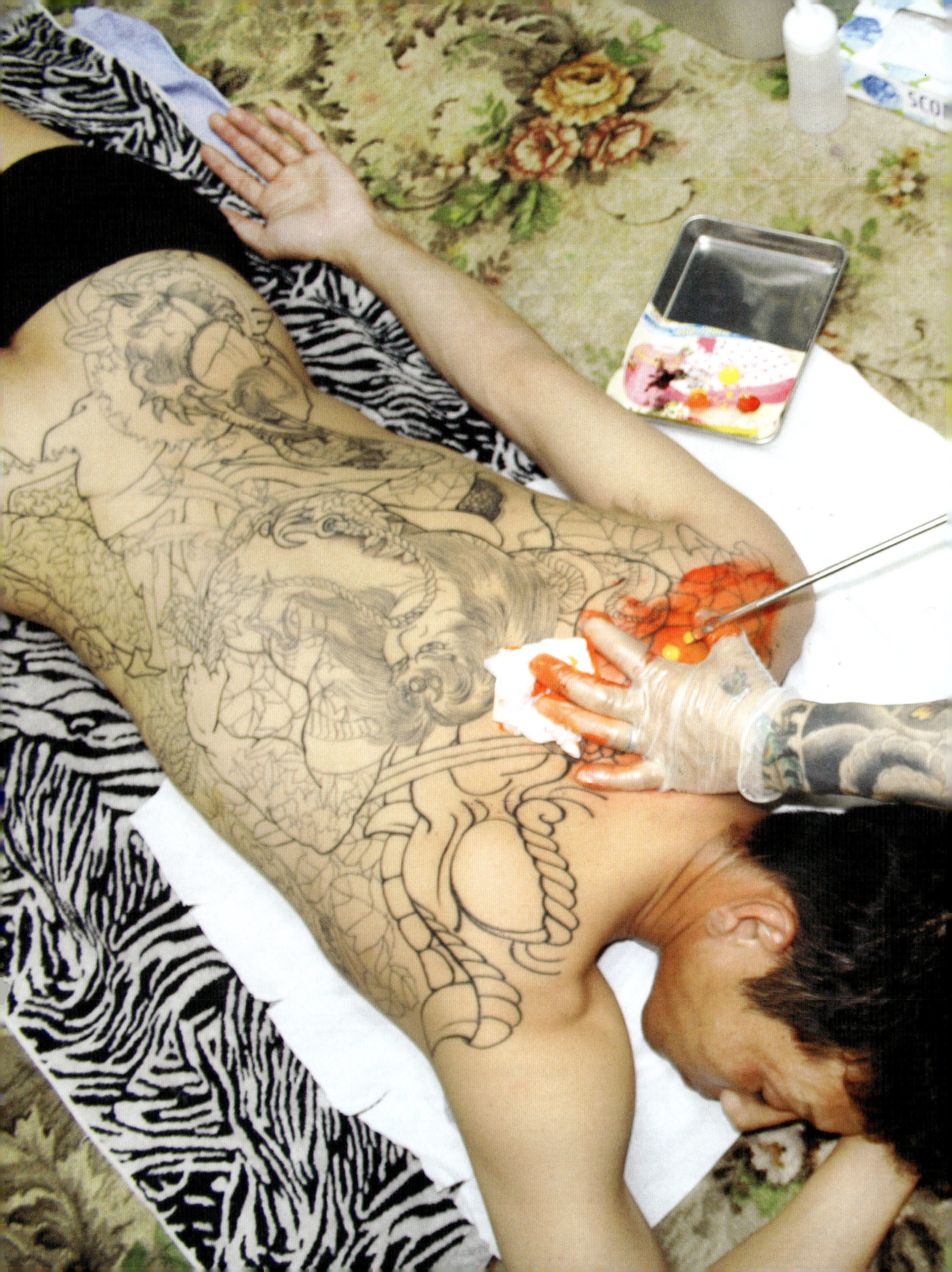

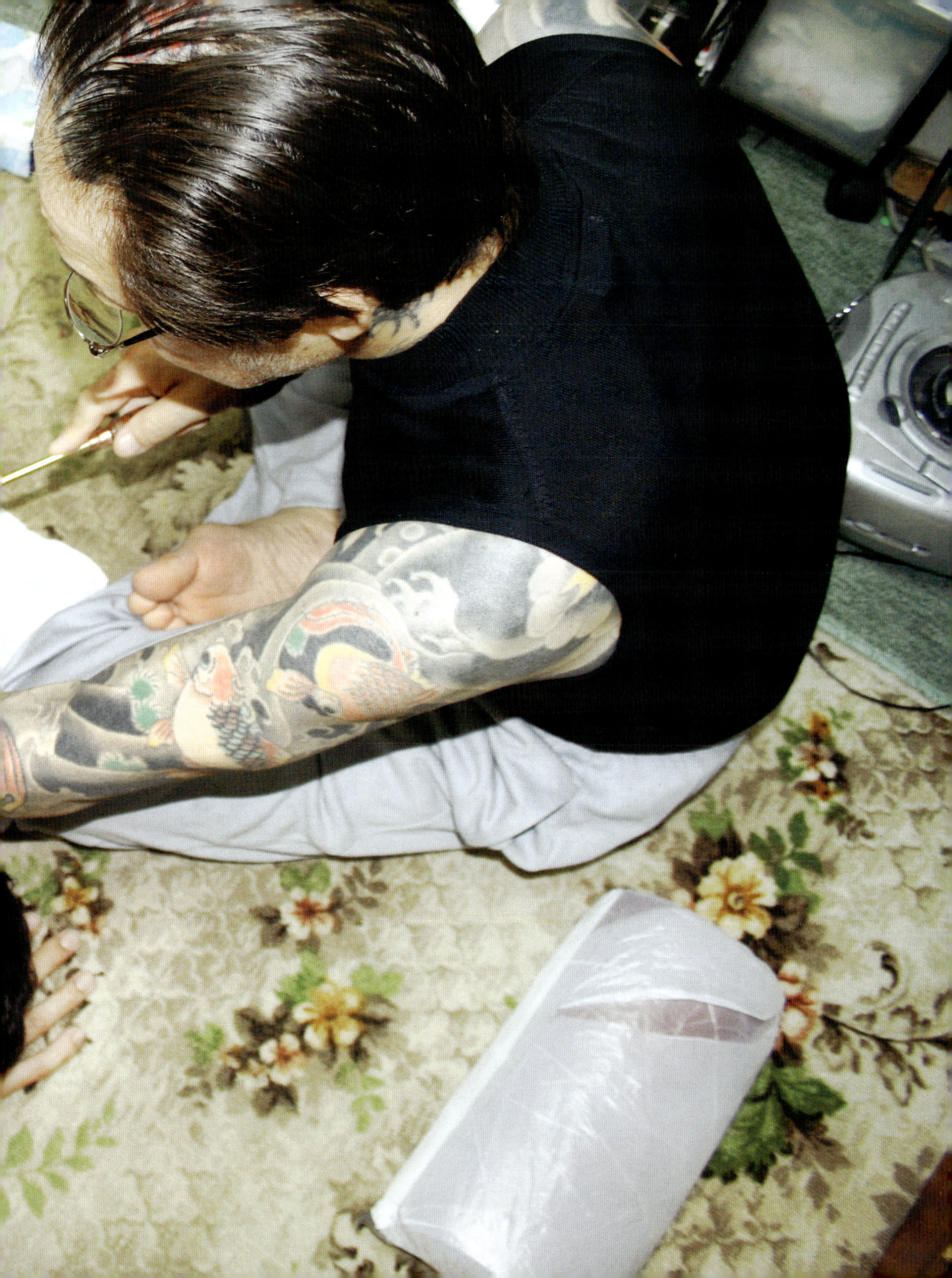

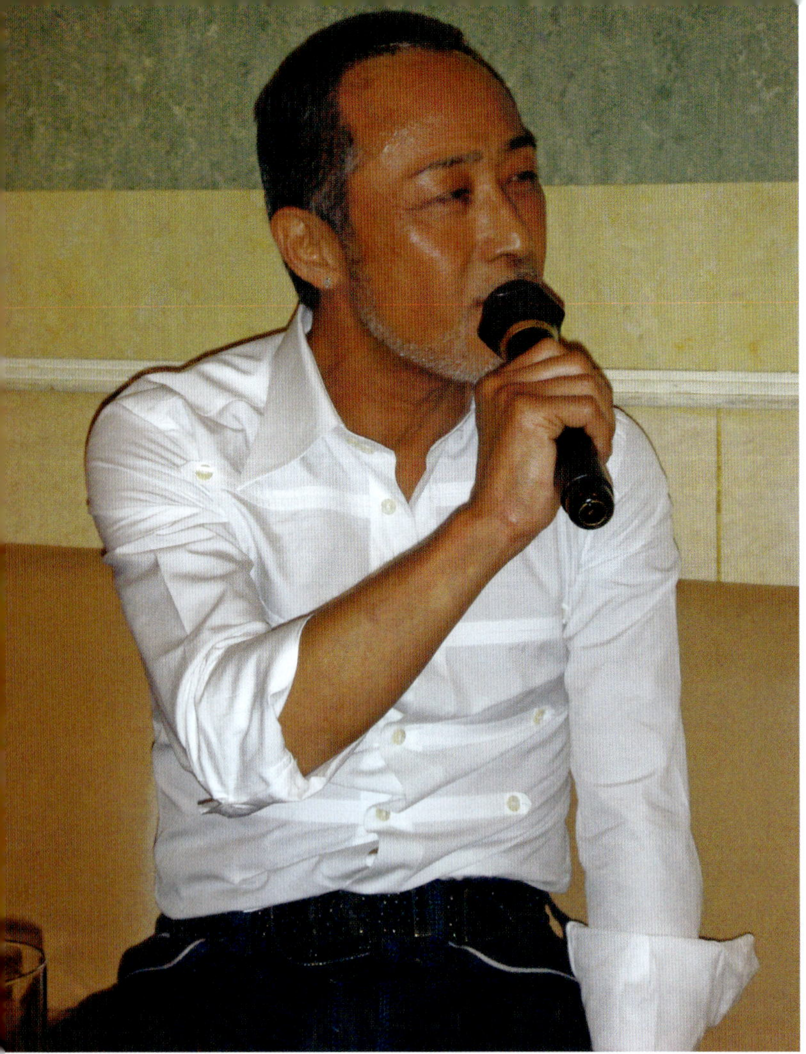

Above:
Horiyasu

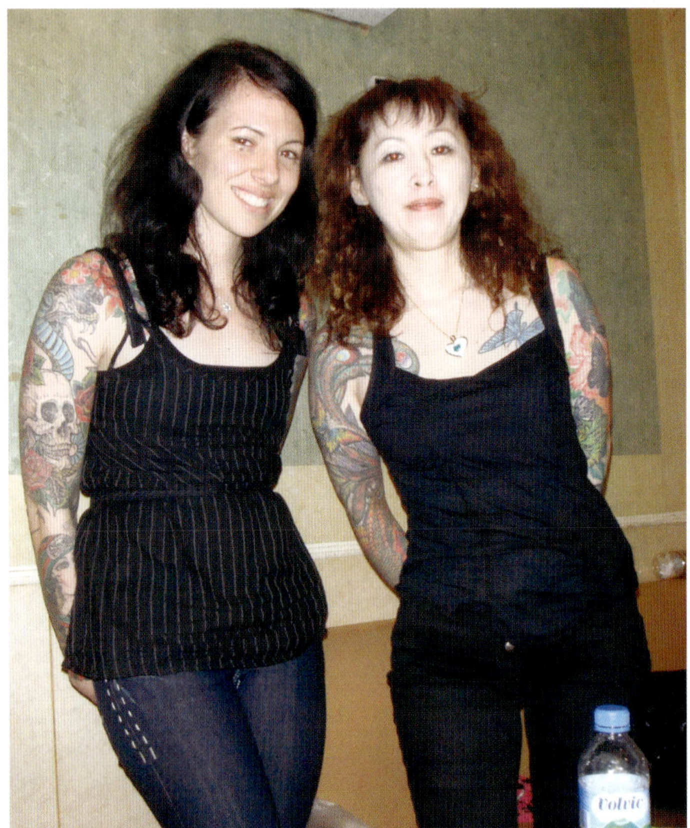

Japan's equivalent of the mafia, it is a top priority that the tattoo artist is of proper social refinement. As times change, many young Japanese tattoo artists ignore these old-fashioned ways in favor of a more casual, Western attitude. Simultaneously there is a changing trend in clientele. While tattooing has always entertained clients who were *katagi* or from the "legitimate" world, it is only in recent times that their presence has equaled that of the gangsters. Tattoos in general, but notably the Japanese tattoo, are still classified as taboo in Japan. Visiting tattoo shops even in a city as metropolitan and modern as Tokyo, we saw no ground level storefronts. These businesses were located off the street level, on higher floors, buried in apartment complexes or in backrooms of other shops.

Seniority is a crucial aspect of *reigi*. The hierarchies are based upon age and rank. The concept of the tattoo family in relation to *reigi* can be compared to the historic "schools" of painting or "family based ateliers" that date as far back as the late Kamakura period. (1185-1333) In these studios, technique was passed down from a master to his sons and talented students.

"Four characteristics definitive of traditional guilds mark the basic organization of the Kano [famous school of painting founded by Kano Masanobu in the latter half of the fifteenth century] house: (1) a basis in familial ties that continued over many generations and was maintained through family handbooks, craft techniques, and trade secrets; (2) the hereditary acquisition of a craft or trade passed through the male members of the family, a system that also permitted the adoption of talented outsiders in order to perpetuate the family's collective prosperity; (3) a single vertical relationship of father-son/assistants, capped by the oldest members as the head; and (4) cooperation on large projects

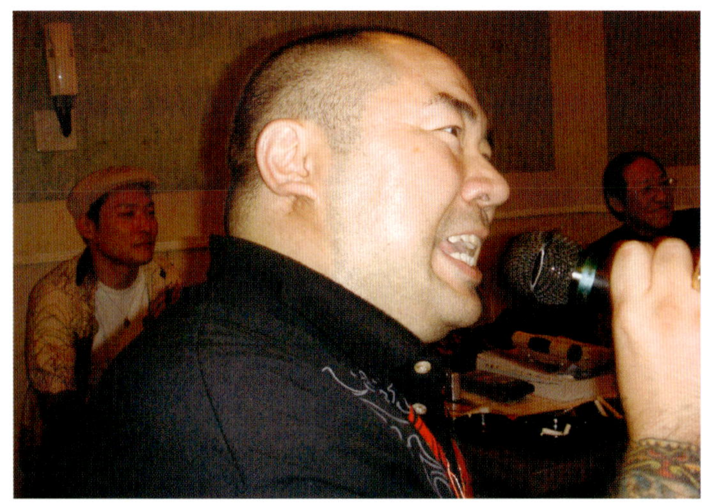

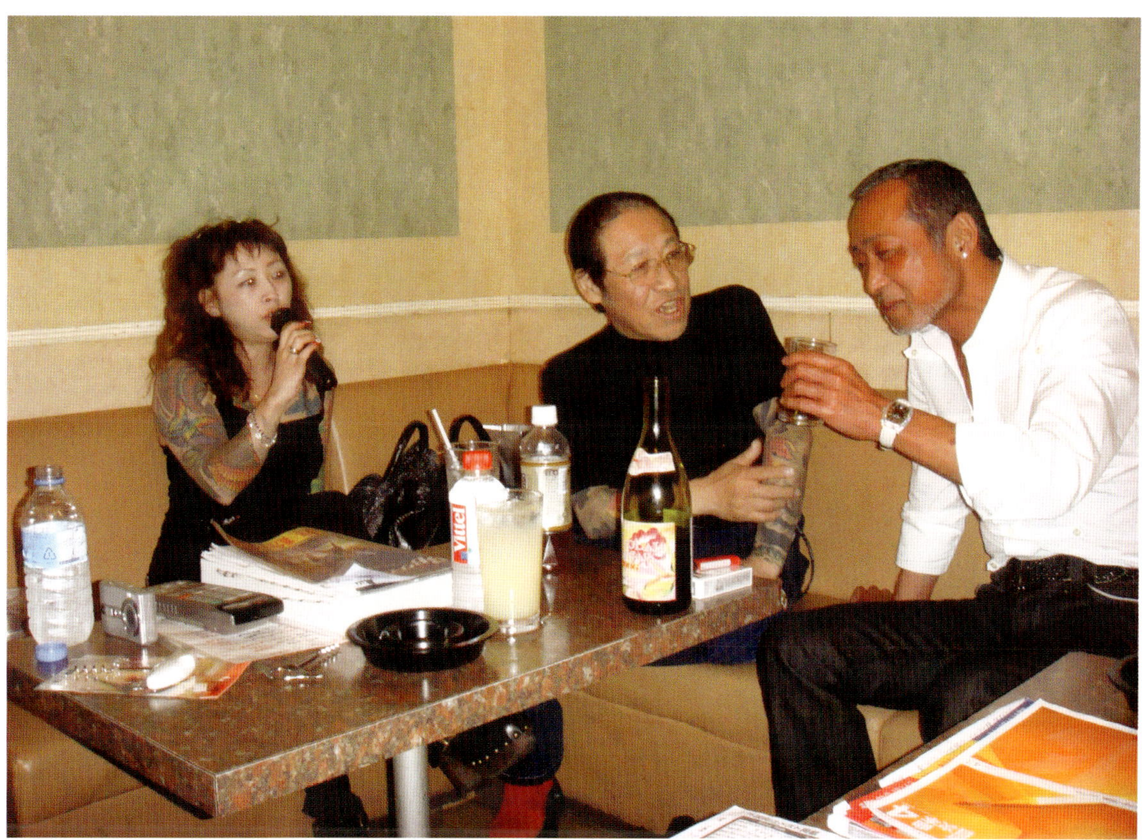

Left:
Mayumi, Horiyoshi III, and Horiyasu at the local karaoke box.

Below:
" Don't stop believing!"

with other workshops and the building of alliances through contract or marriage."[1]

In this example, the system of gathering students is explained, and rank is explored. Seniority, after the master, is attributed first to the "father-son" relationship. The next tier in this hierarchy is determined by age- the older student assumes the higher rank. A comparable arrangement is seen in the structure of the tattoo family. It is the birth-rite of the eldest son to inherit the master's title first. Yoshitsugu Muramatsu, was Shodai Horiyoshi I. His son Yoshiyuki Muramatsu became Ni-Daime Horiyoshi or Horiyoshi II. Yoshihito Nakano, the gifted student of Shodai Horiyoshi became San-Daime Horiyoshi or Horiyoshi III. Horiyoshi III's son Kazuyoshi may decide one day to follow in his father's footsteps and would be entitled to bear his father's name. Generally age is a factor in the ranking system within the tattoo familial structure, but the number of years an apprentice has spent with the master can take priority over the age of another apprentice in rank. Always the innovator and trendsetter, Horiyoshi III is the first Japanese tattooer to take on apprentices abroad. Horitaka, although making frequent visits to Japan, lives and operates State of Grace Tattoo in San Jose, California. He represents Horiyoshi III and promotes his artistic lineage in the United States. Alex Reinke, Horikitsune, lives in Germany. With

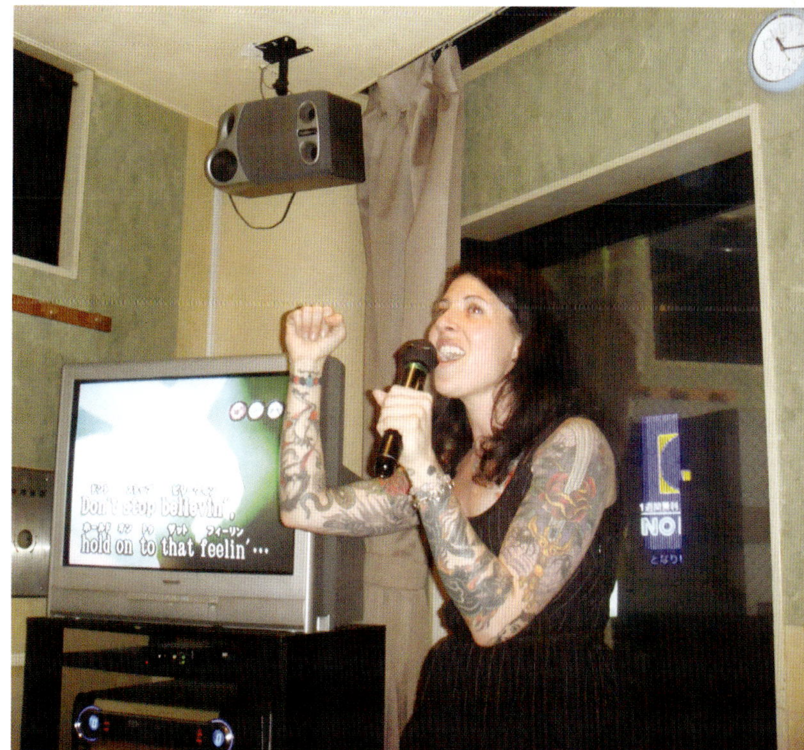

international reach, Horiyoshi III's apprentices help his influence of the tattoo community on a global level.

There are many commonalities in the mode of transference of information in comparing the tradition of tattooing to the structure of these art schools. Although similar in their arrangement of members, there are also decisive differences. While there is a body of information being passed from master to apprentice, there are dissimilar conditions and expectations of the apprentices. It is more than whether or not the crafts person will be successful in executing their craft. The practice of painting has never been illegal, nor has it had a social stigmatization. It has no noted association with the *Yakuza* and has never been considered a tightly knit underground society in the way that tattooing has been forced to be by legitimate society. While in images of Kano schoolrooms, there are dozens of students painting side by side, it is rare for tattoo masters to have more than a handful of apprentices at any given time. Students of tattoo masters do not simply complete an academic course and seek work on their own. They work by their master's side, dedicating themselves through study and service to him until he trusts they are prepared to open their own shops. After a certain unstipulated amount of time the student goes through a type of graduation. Although there is no degree, nor pomp and circumstance, they leave the master's side to open a shop of their own. It is now up to the apprentice to carry the flag for the master. In Japanese this is known as to *dokuritsu*. The apprentice breaks away from the master and is not kicked out of the family. The master and apprentice relationship stays intact, while the apprentice is encouraged to pursue his/her own career.

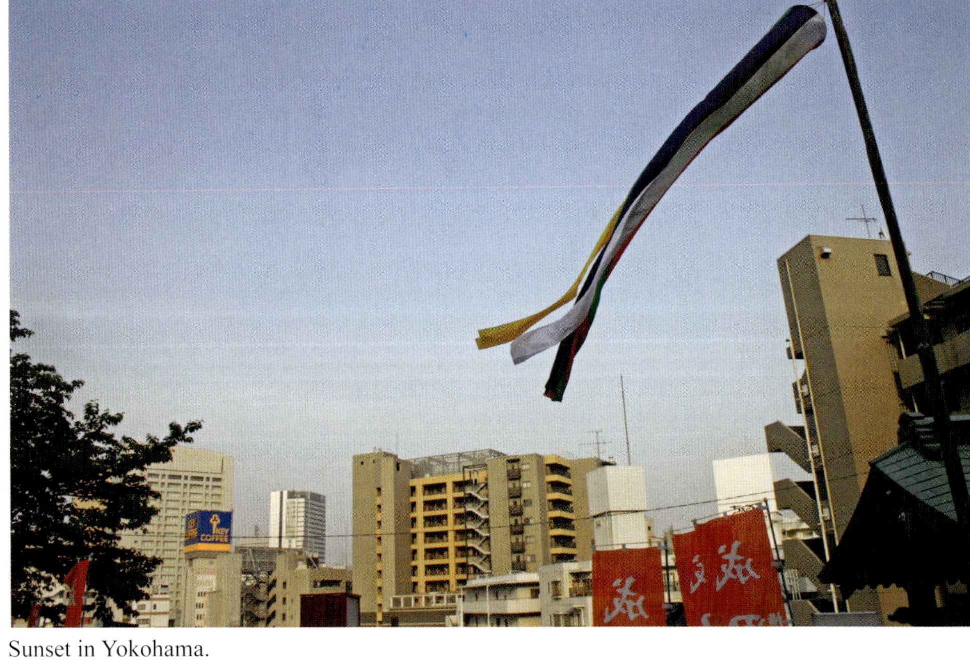

Sunset in Yokohama.

This can include receiving the title of *shodai*. A *shodai* is entitled to collect apprentices and have his own shop and crew, he is essentially first in a lineage. Not all apprentices receive this title. When the apprentice opens his own shop, even with independence from the Master, he continues to carry and perpetuate the traditions he has learned. The new studio remains affiliated with the master as a branch of his tutelage and most likely pays a percentage of their income to him each month. For the master, he is creating employees and expanding his domain while perpetuating his artistic legacy, and the apprentices are guaranteed work after their education. It is a symbiotic relationship that is financially beneficial for both parties. As a professional tattooer and even after receiving the title *shodai*, an apprentice maintains the status of "apprentice" as a sign of respect to the master. This is a way one can acknowledge the person who has brought them into the business and taken that chance on them. Horitaka has vowed his loyalty to Horiyoshi III, and finds satisfaction in referring to himself as an apprentice to Horiyoshi III. His studio in San Jose embodies the spirit of Horiyoshi III and expands his reach to California and America in reflecting his style of tattooing and in the conduct of his tattoo shop.

When members of multiple tattoo families are present, the issues of status and rank is further defined. Each family has their own unique ranking system, specific to their crew. When there are different tattoo families present, or multiple masters together, ranking takes into account age, experience, prestige and power. I observed this evolved order at a dinner I attended with Horiyoshi III, Horitaka and Horiyasu. Horiyasu is an old friend, colleague and client of Horiyoshi III, and is quite an accomplished tattooer in his own right. He had a younger associate with him who exhibited perfect discipline and *reigi*. He did not speak unless spoken to. His attention was focused on the rest of us; he made frequent trips to the drink bar making sure that our drinks were always full. He emptied Mayumi's ashtrays in between cigarettes. Overall, his presentation was flawless; he catered to everyone's needs without drawing any attention to himself and did not eat until everyone else had been satisfied. Horiyoshi III was unquestionably the highest rank at the table and thus determined the seating arrangement, in this case placing Horiyasu across from him and Horitaka at his own side. Normally it is Horitaka's role to accommodate the master during dinner, what with lighting his cigarettes when he was a smoker, refilling drinks, calling the waitress and so forth. At this dinner the younger man that had accompanied Horiyasu assumed this role, not just for Horiyasu and Horiyoshi III but also Horitaka. Horitaka was not quite ready for this and tried to refuse the gestures but at the young man's insistence, allowed him to continue. But as they say, those that give respect get respect.

Dinner conversation was enjoyable. It had been a long time since the two masters had spent time together and they reminisced over shared drinks. I found out that Horiyoshi III had tattooed Horiyasu by hand over twenty years ago. The two masters discussed and joked about how times had changed. They spoke of the changing clientele, the influx of *katagi* or non-gangsters getting tattooed as well as the increase in non-Japanese, *gaijin*. The non-Japanese present issues of their own, the most notable issue being the cultural barriers of language. Both masters vented about dealing with phone calls from clients that didn't speak Japanese. Horiyasu recounted a story of a seemingly endless phone call where he tried to communicate, Japanese-English dictionary in hand. He wondered why it was his responsibility to speak English in his own studio and not the other way around. Horiyoshi III agreed. Perhaps this communication barrier encourages a stigma associated with a Westerner's sense of entitlement. While both masters had their share of complaints, they did acknowledge the positive aspects of overseas customers, discussing the pleasure they find in receiving attention from a wider audience. Horiyoshi III takes pride in putting Yokohama on the map. It is his hometown and he does appreciate that people travel there from all corners of the globe just for his tattoos. He concedes that foreign clients, while difficult, are "cool".

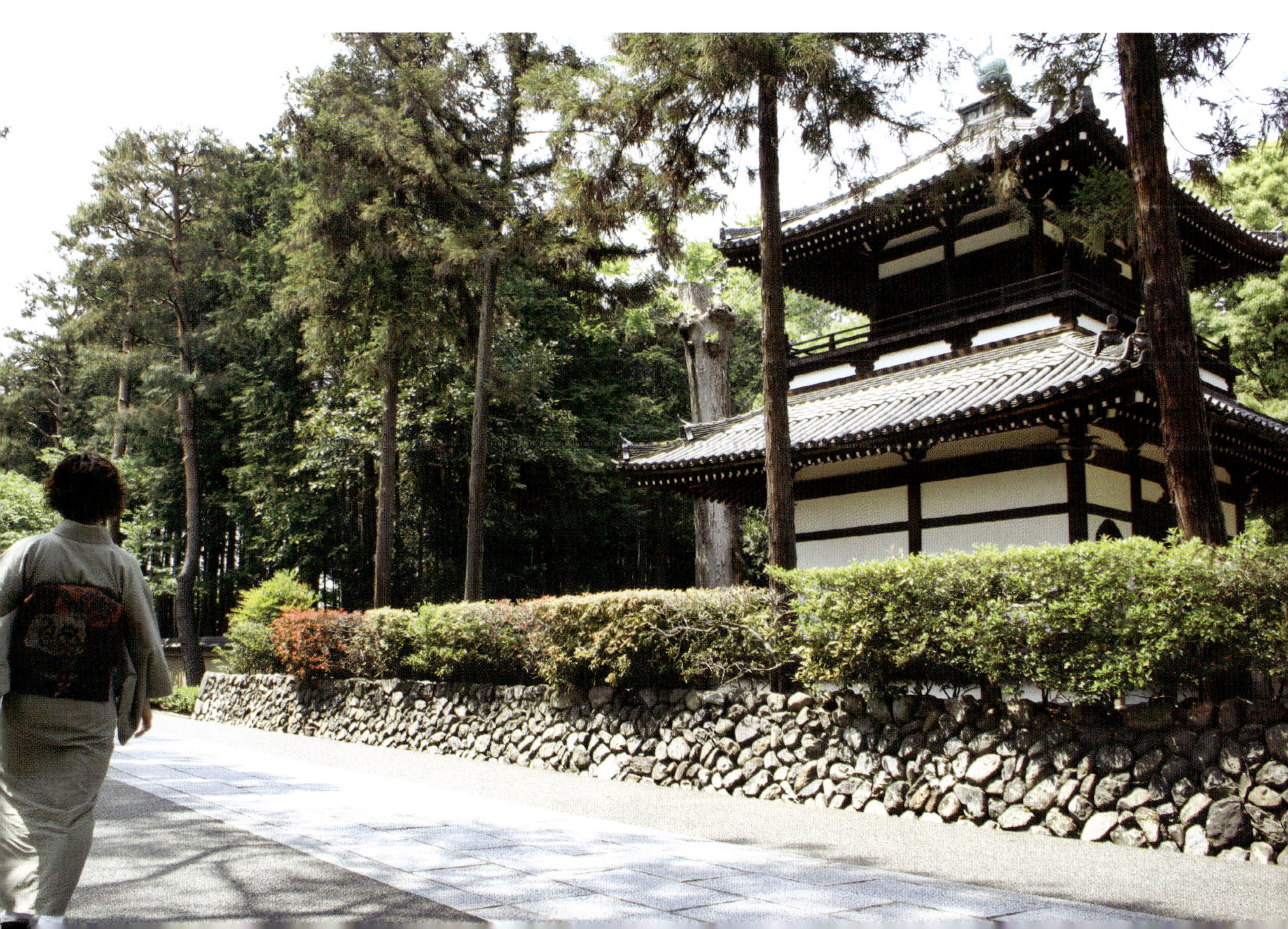

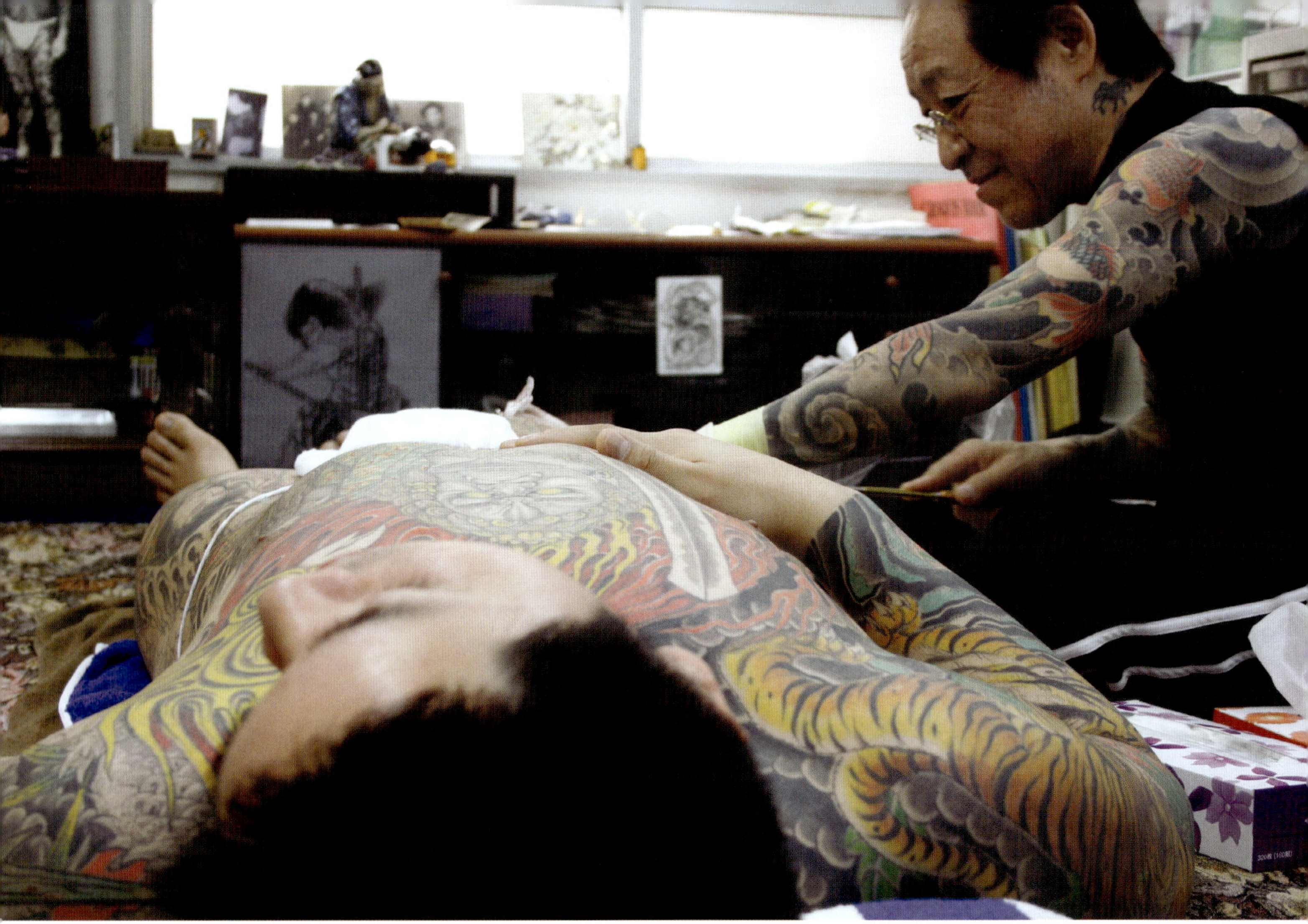

Every time I take a trip to Japan I feel that my understanding of *reigi* grows. Some of the practices can feel limiting and it is easy for Westerners to feel like the bull in the china shop of polite Japan. Not everything is entirely foreign to me, for instance, waiting on elders before eating is considered polite and quite normal by Western standards. The notion of humbling oneself before those of higher rank or age seniority is familiar in my upbringing. Helping my parents carry heavy bags or never walking in front of my grandmother are also unconscious signs of respect. I was also taught to be ever mindful of my surroundings and to act accordingly. When you walk into a tattoo shop and music is blaring and people are hanging out, socializing, there is a certain lax attitude that is conveyed. On the other hand, the example of the somber tone in Horiyoshi III's presence suggests a very different ambience. I have attended Jewish religious services my whole life and there is a practice of covering the head with a yarmulke or lace, depending on the wearer's gender. This is a symbolic gesture acknowledging a higher power by literally covering your head and thereby putting somebody above you. This tradition also prepares you to enter the temple, not in appearance but in demeanor. A temple is a place of respect and I found it easy to practice quiet observation in the studios, shrines and temples I visited in Japan. *Reigi* is a constant awareness of your place and the necessary respect, patience, and restraint that follows.

[1]Gerhart, Karen M. *Copying the Master and Stealing His Secrets.* Edited by Brenda G. Jordan and Victoria Weston, University of Hawai'i Press, 2003,11.

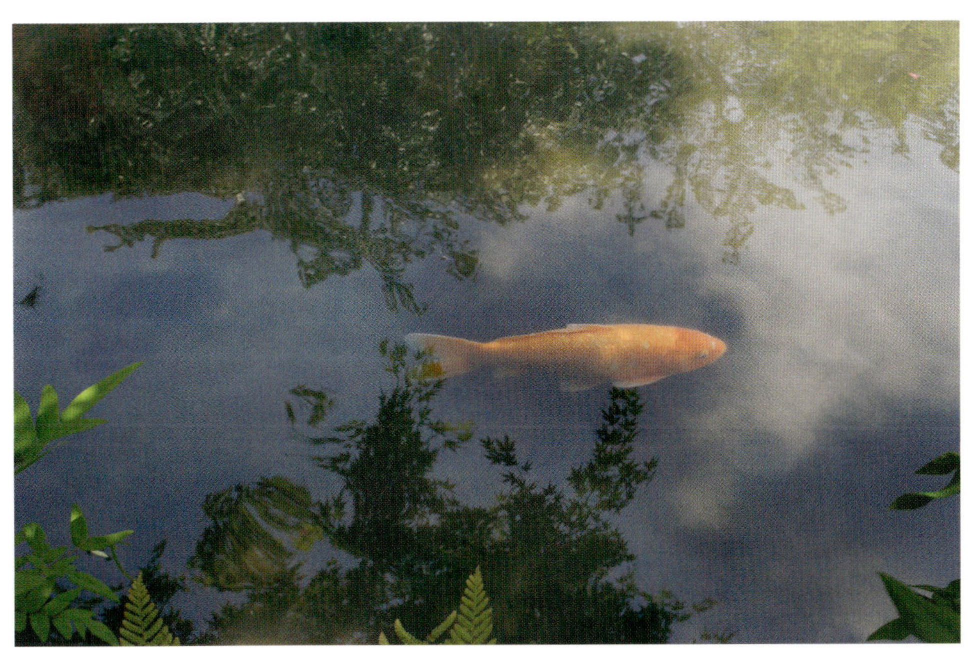

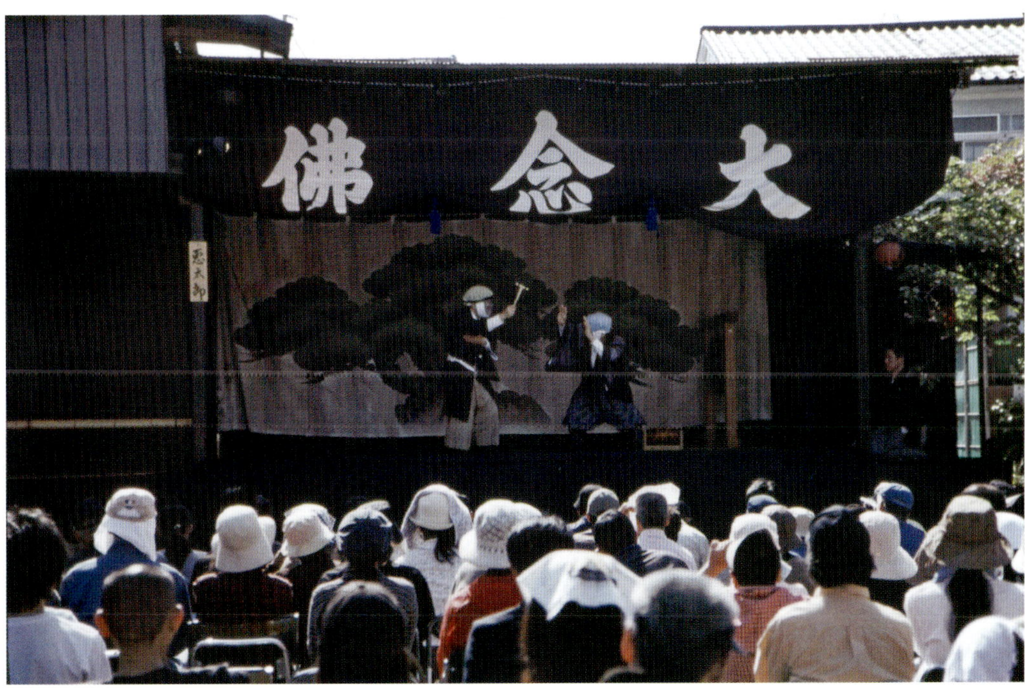

A comedic *kyogen* performance entertains the crowd.

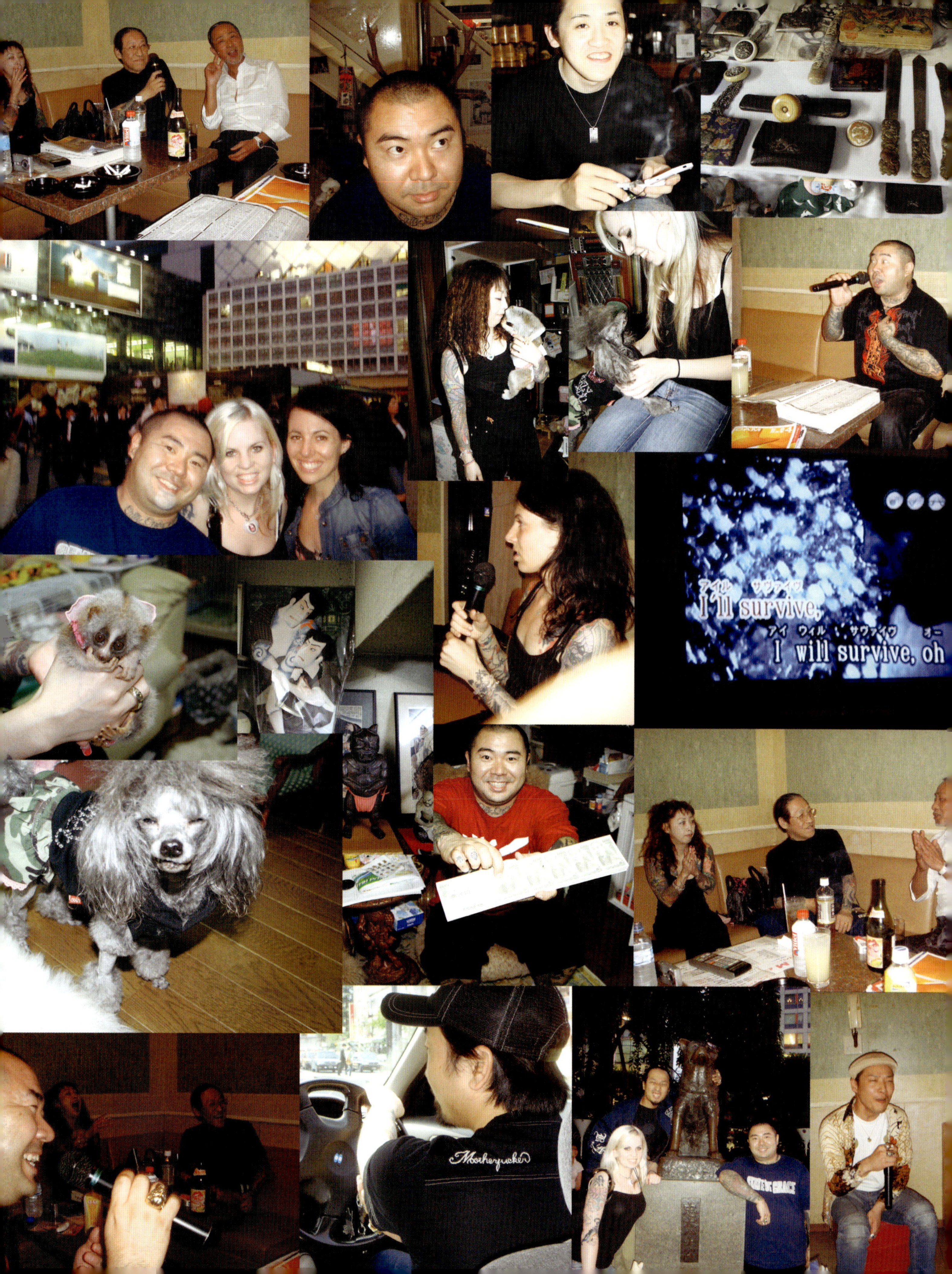
アイル サヴァイヴ
I'll survive,
アイ ウィル サヴァイヴ オー
I will survive, oh
Motherfucker

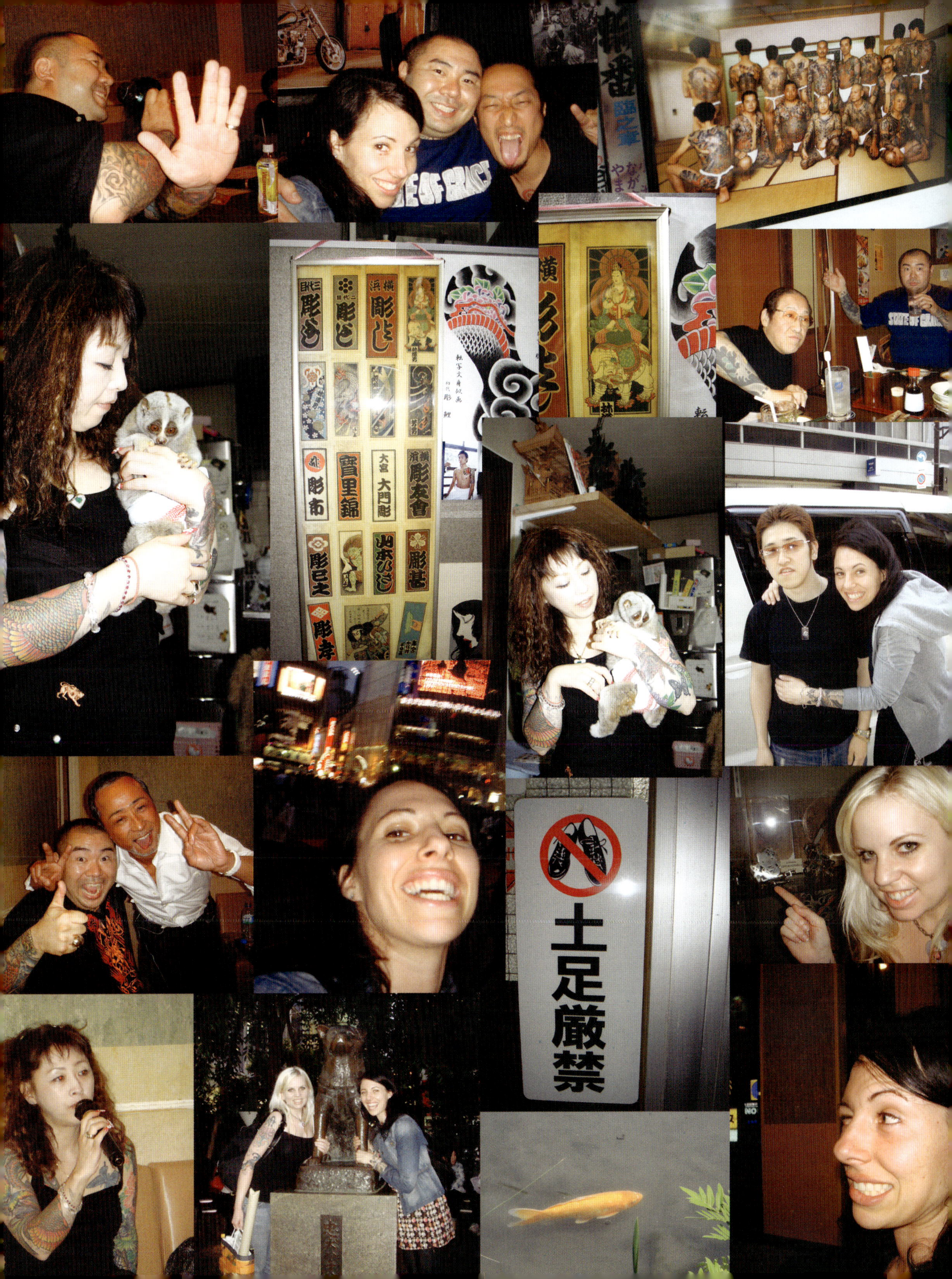
土足厳禁

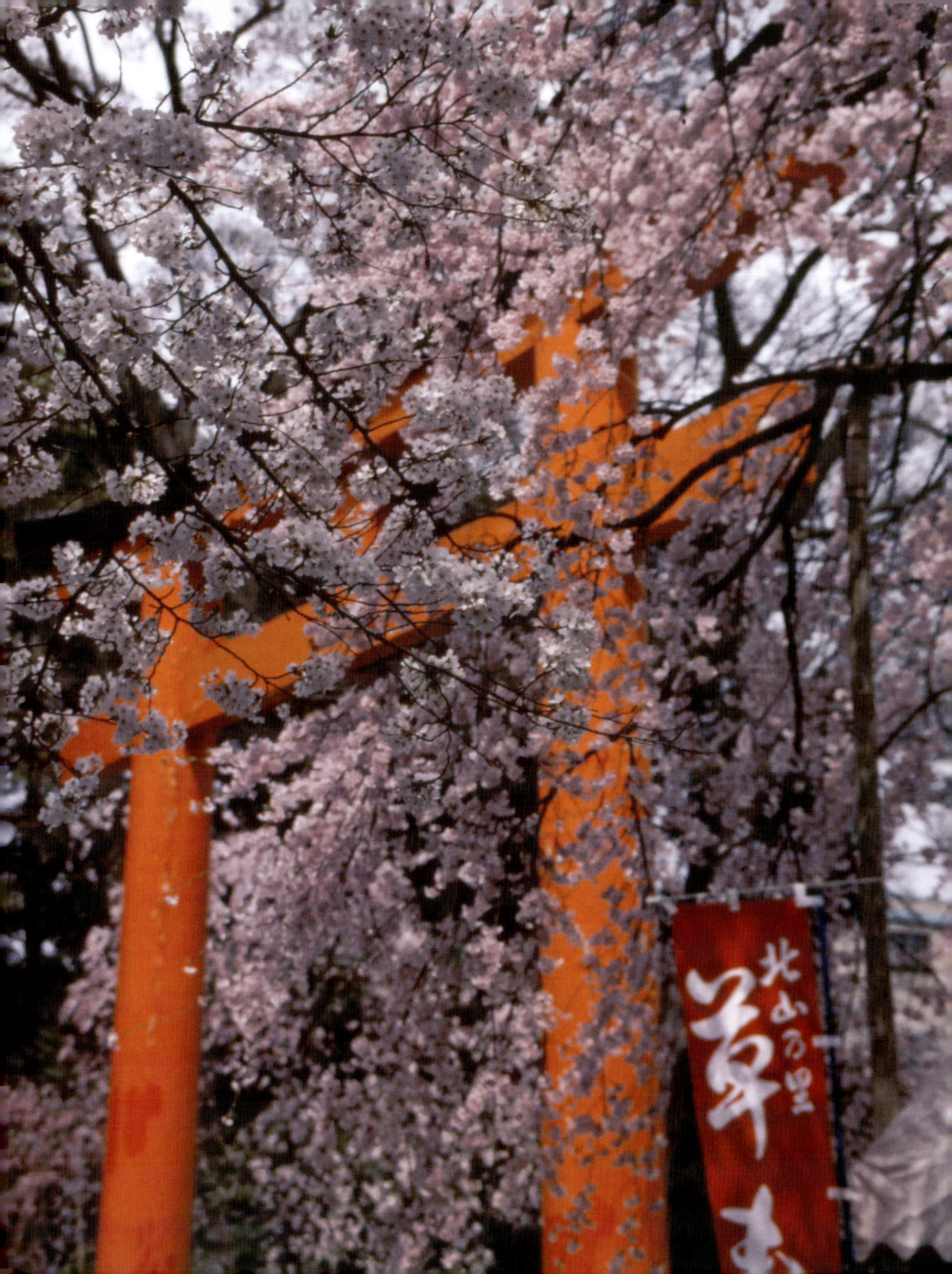
北山の里
草

Chapter 5
Shrines and Temples

My regular visits to Japan have always been focused on my study of Japanese tattooing. Part of this time is spent in the tattoo studio, directly immersed in the tattoo arts but this alone has never been enough. Horiyoshi III has always encouraged me, and all interested in the Japanese tattoo, to visit shrines and temples because they embody the culture and spirit of Japan. And I think he would definitely agree that one cannot separate culture and spirit from *irezumi*.

The wellspring of Japanese tattoo iconography includes nature, folklore, religion, history and mythology. In my pursuit of the origins of tattoo iconography, there are real places and things to see. An important facet of this study is an awareness of the flora of Japan. Japan's climate is one of well-defined seasons, and the flowers and plants of each season play a critical role in Japanese art by denoting the time of the year. There is a significant fascination with the dynamic turning of seasons and these changes are well celebrated in art and craft. Floral themes connote more than just beauty, many flowers hold much deeper meaning. For example, the *sakura*, or cherry blossom is not only the beloved national flower of Japan but also captures the essence of the warrior spirit. *Sakura* fall off of the tree while still alive, blooming in a short but brilliant show of vitality. Poetically, this is interpreted as representing the glorious but short life of a warrior, ever willing to sacrifice his life in battle. Thus, the tattooing of *sakura* can really enhance a tattoo design in multiple ways, aesthetically as well as with the coded cultural communication. Describing season in art helps set the mood and lends many visual elements to the allegory.

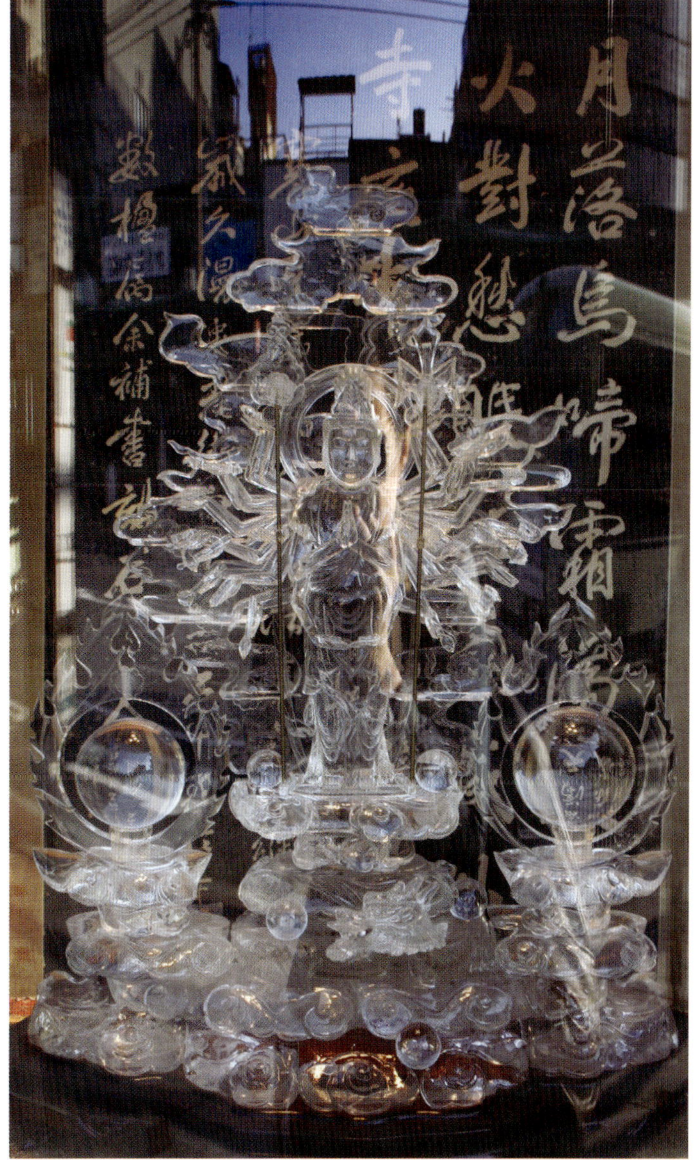

Senju (thousand arm) Kannon statue for sale in a store window, Kyoto.

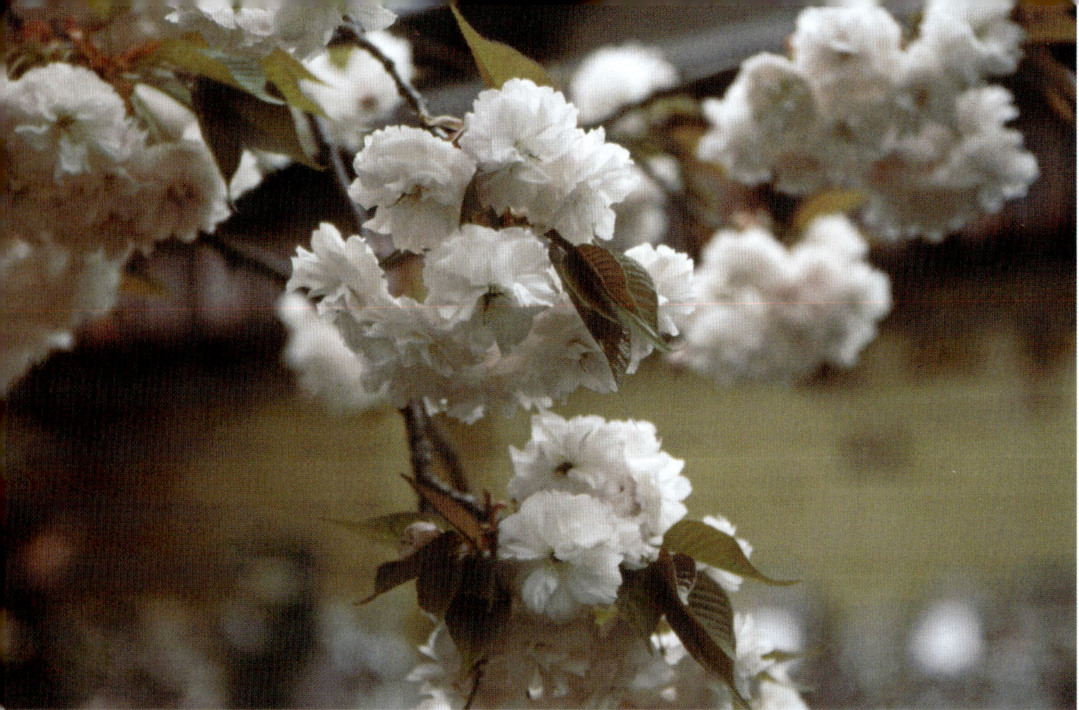

Left:
This specific strain of *sakura* falls off the tree in a clump, not petal by petal. Samurai considered this flower to be a bad omen due to the similarities between it and one's severed head.

Right:
An elaborate *kurikaraken temizu ya.*

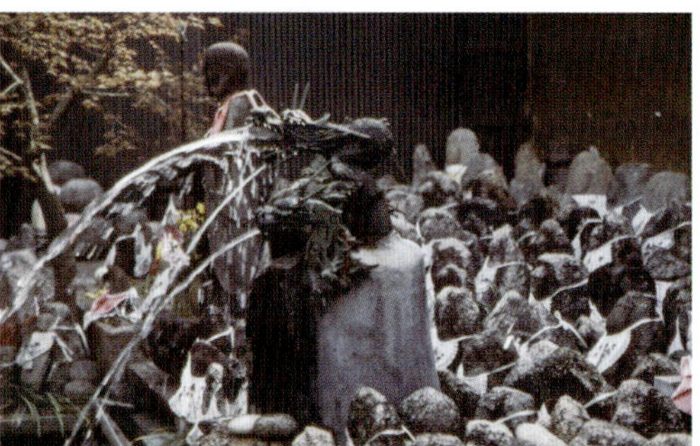

Japanese spirituality is rooted in nature and it is believed that the spirit is present in natural surroundings such as rocks and trees. Nature is conserved and honored in shrines and temples and these places may also act as a nature preserve for people to enjoy. Many shrines are built into mountains or have been carefully worked into urban sprawl, acting as an escape from the densely packed Japanese cities. Horiyoshi III commented that the air in the shrines was cleaner. At one shrine we walked around, there was a physical barrier of bamboo that covered an entire city block buffering it from the bustling street. The air within the walls of this shrine was fresh and the noise levels were noticeably lower than in the surrounding area. It was an incredible contrast to the sensory overload of city life in Japan. In comparison to the small standard of domiciles, shrines can be expansive and feature large fields of open space. It is the one place in Japan where space management is ignored. Even real estate developers cannot go against the gods here.

It has always been important for me to visit as many shrines and temples as possible when I am in Japan. Shrines, or *jinja*, are sacred to the Shinto religion while temples, or *otera*, are Buddhist houses of worship. Although I am not a Buddhist, I am a Japanese art enthusiast and I am familiar with famous shrines and temples from reading books about Japanese art. It is safe to say that many of these shrines and temples not only house great works of art, they are great works of art.

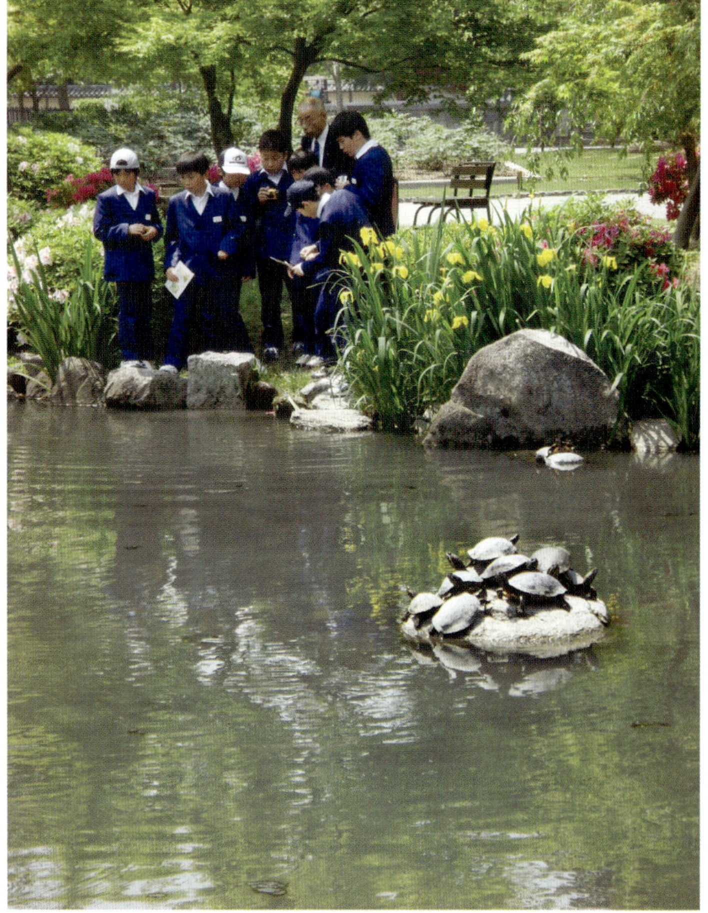

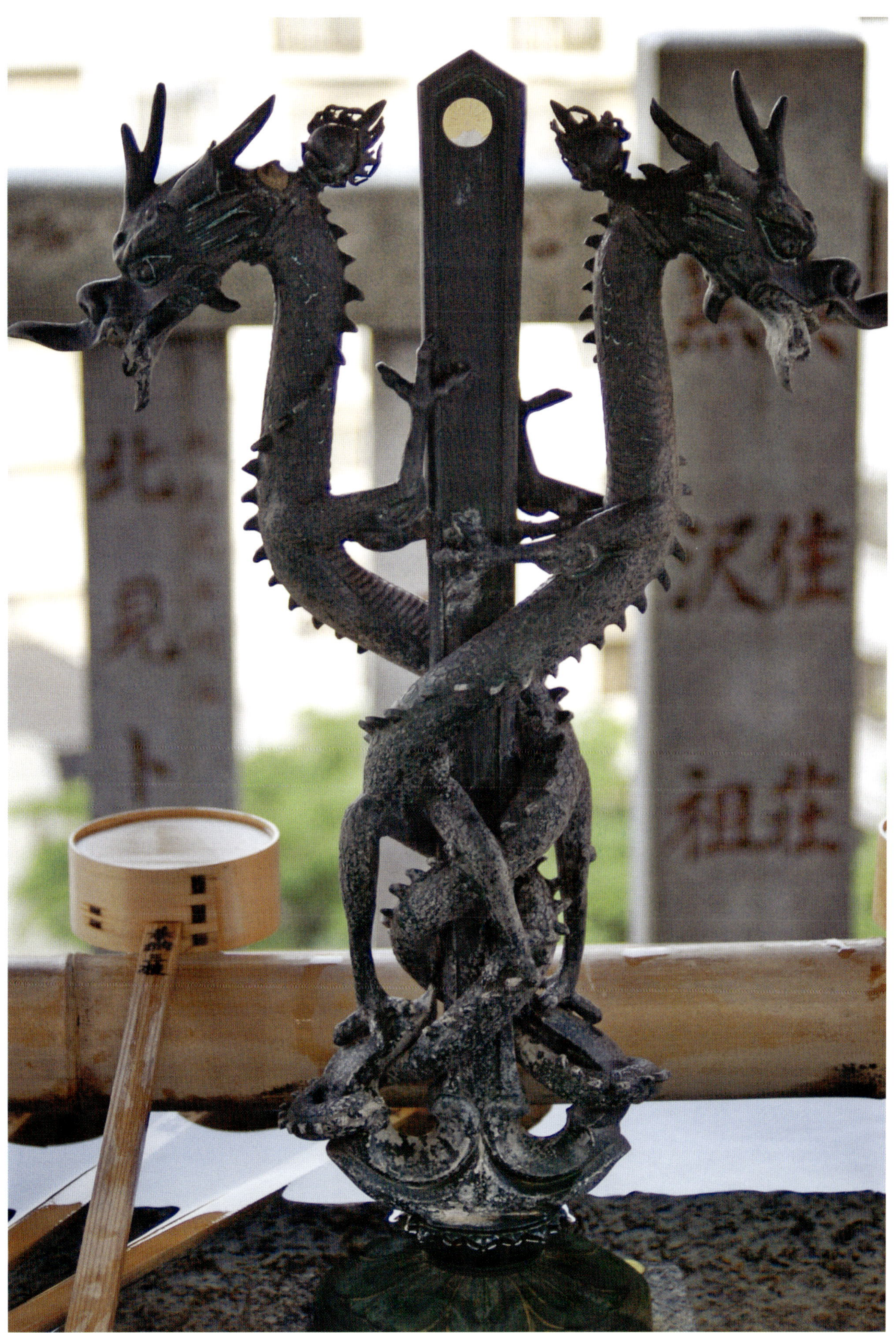

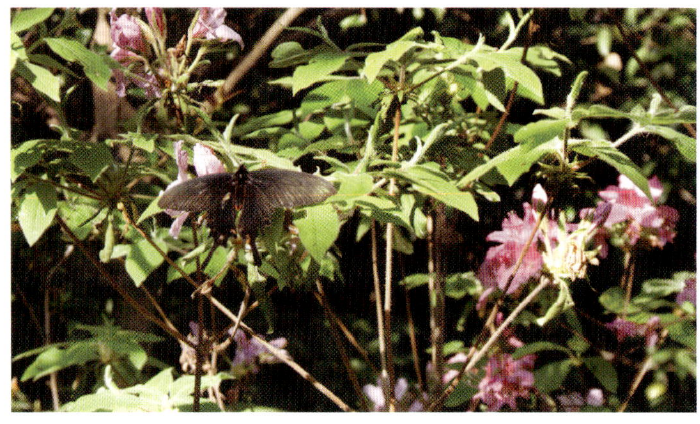

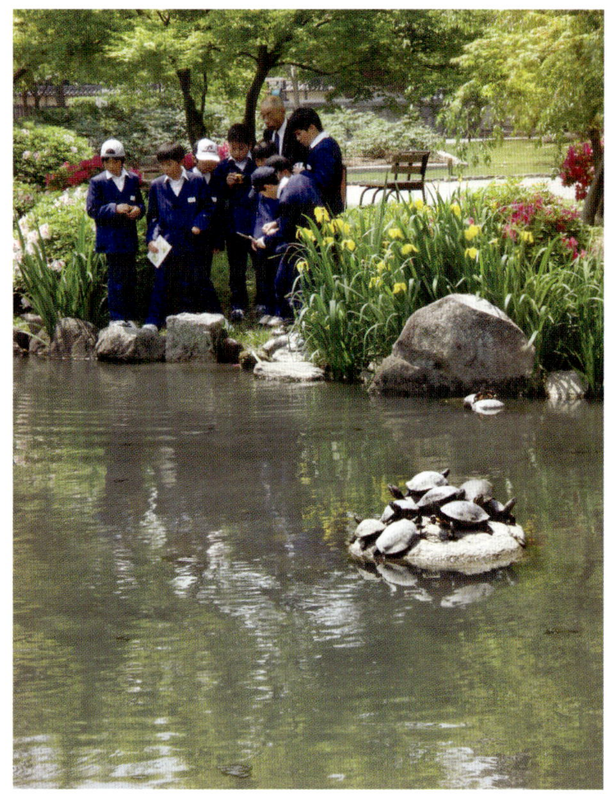

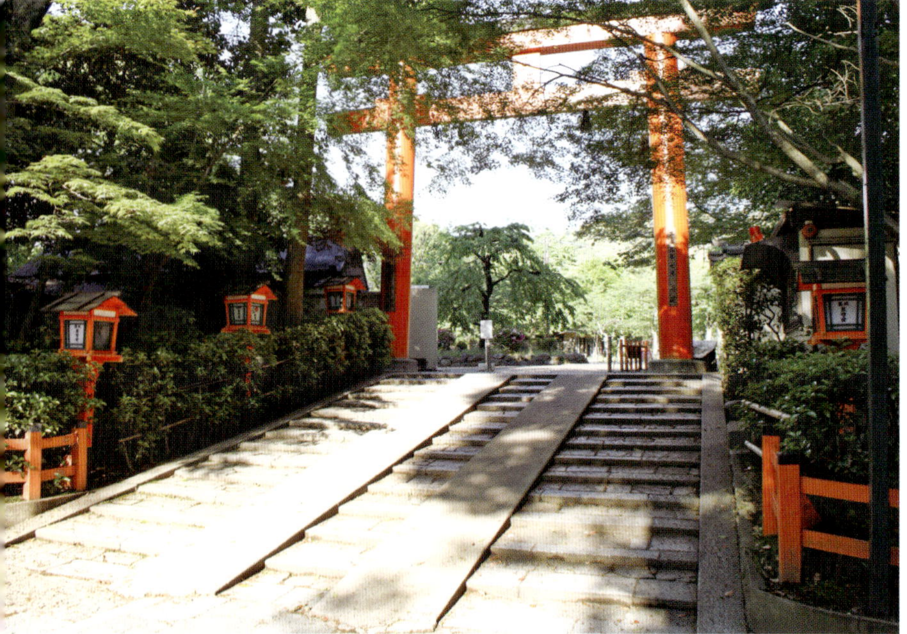

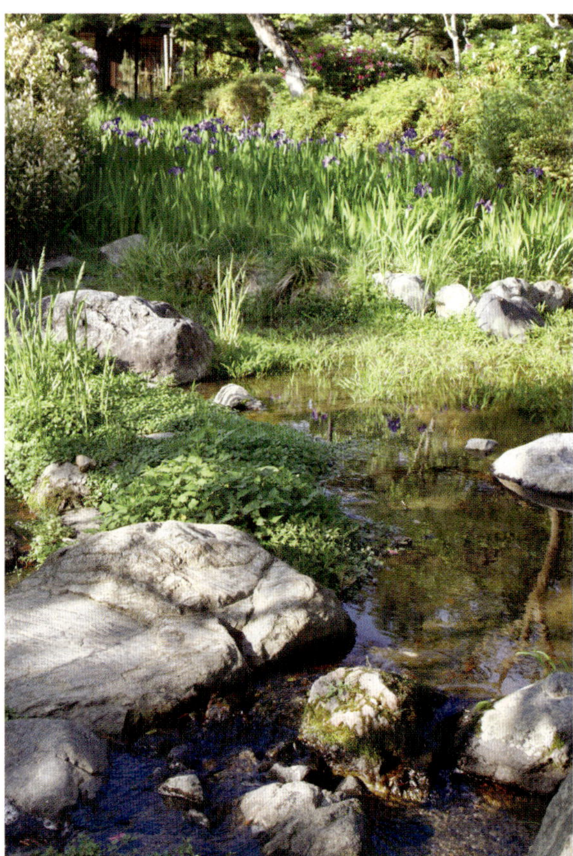

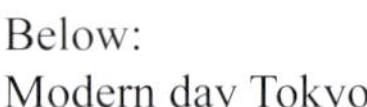

Below:
Modern day Tokyo

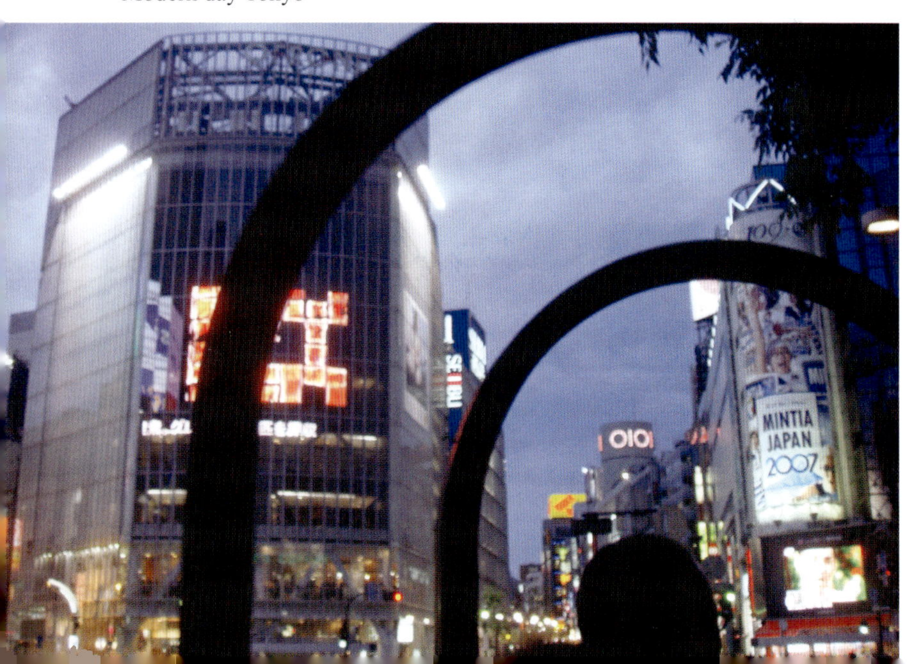

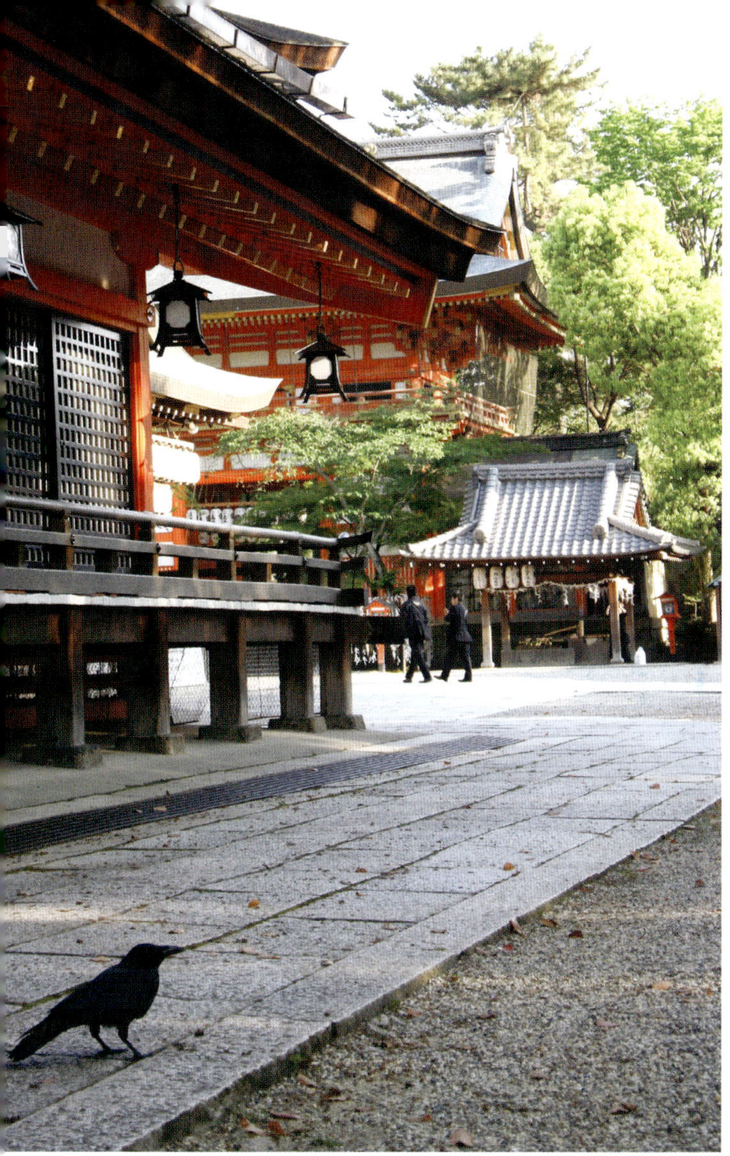

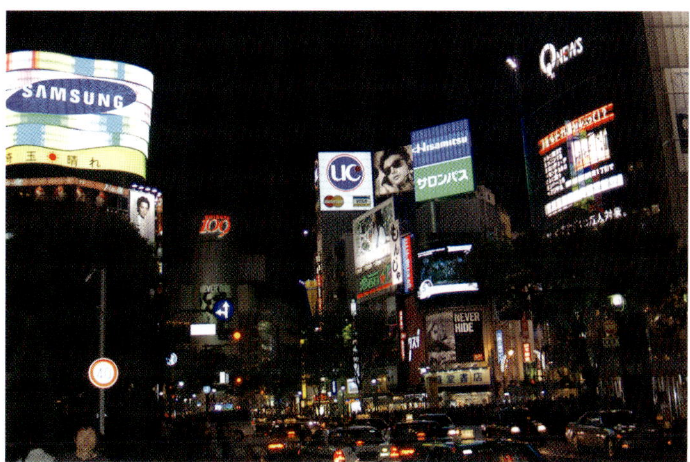

Above:
Bustling city life.

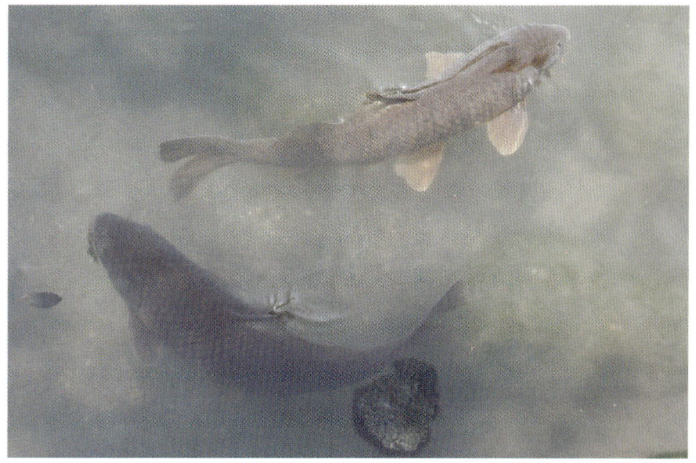

Right:
Old meets new on a sunny day in this shrine in Kyoto.

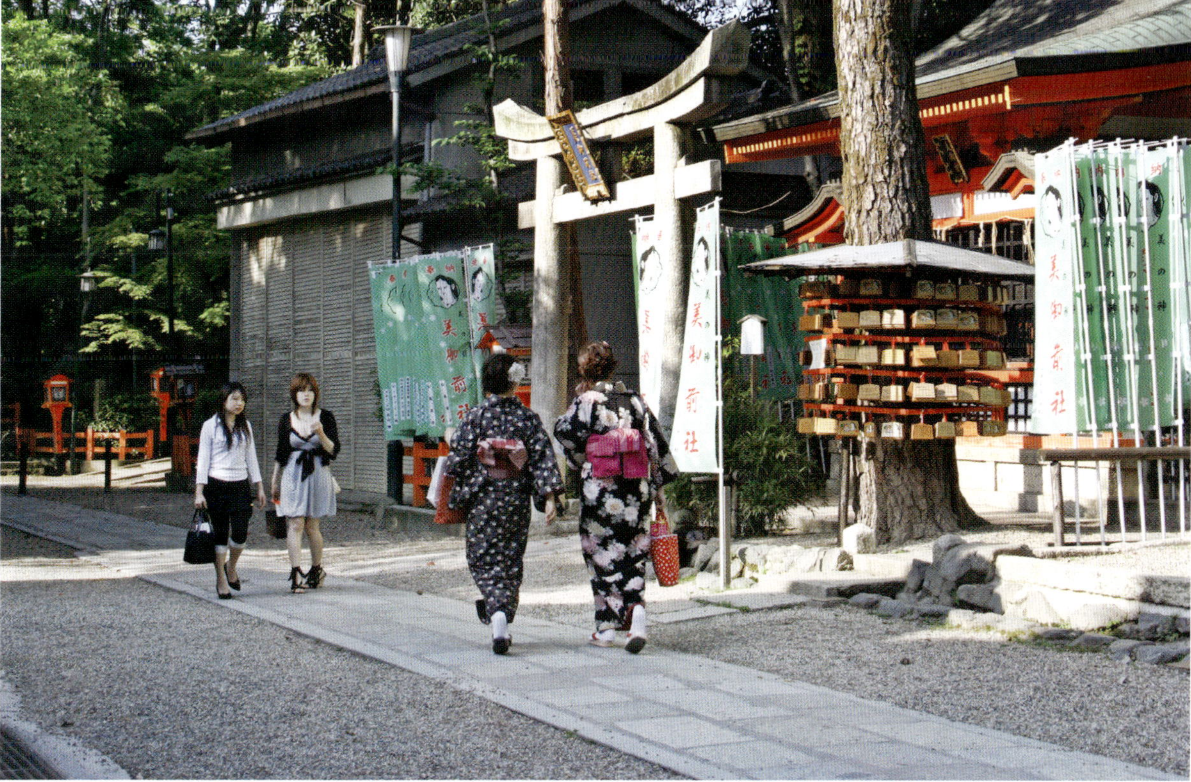

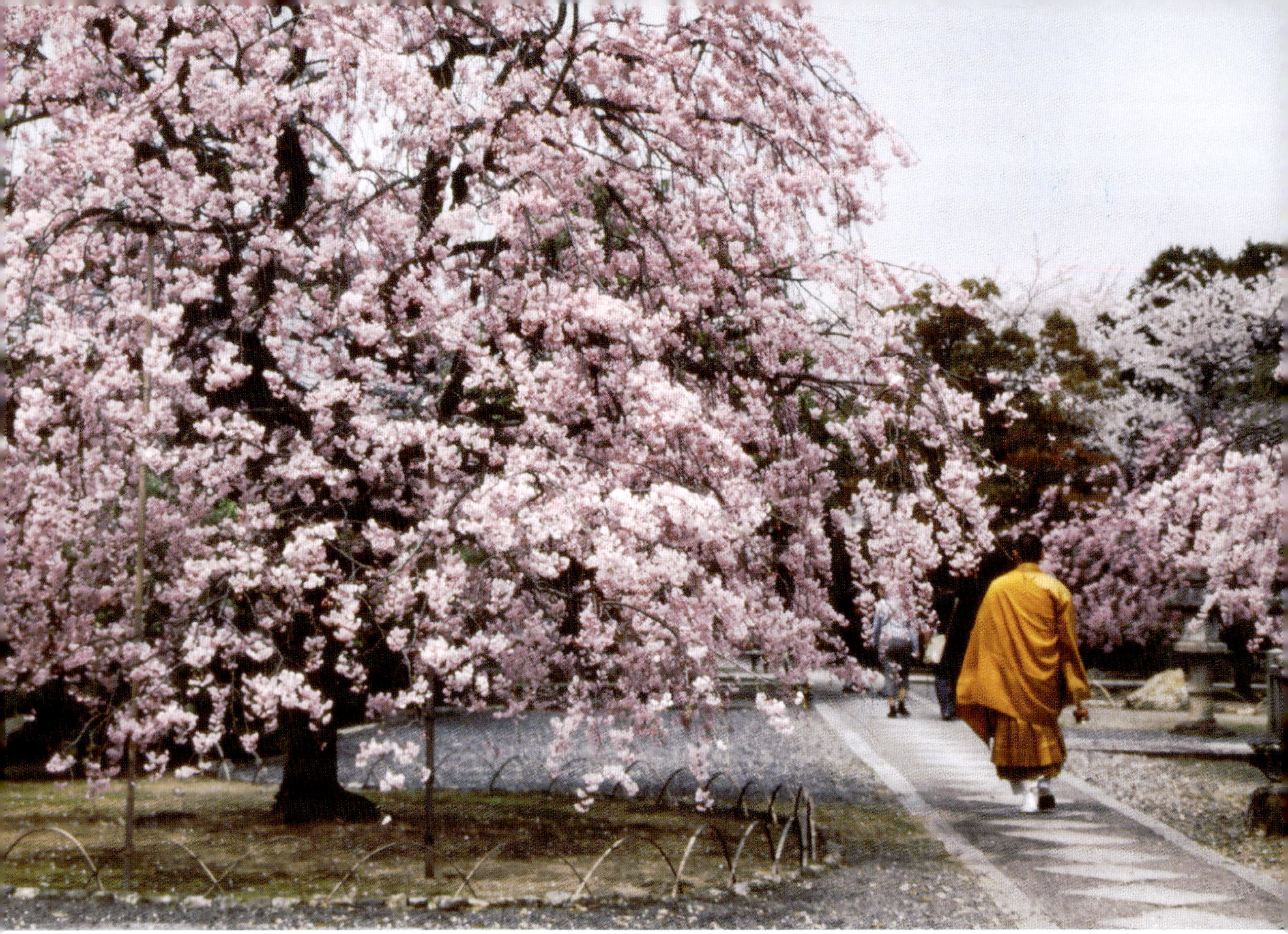

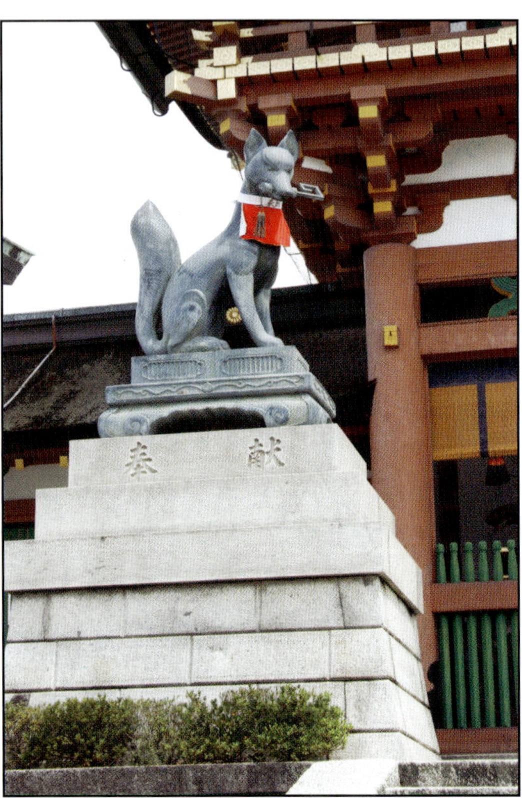

One city that I have had the pleasure of visiting numerous times is Kyoto. Kyoto was once the nation's capital and is considered historically to be a center of art and culture. There are almost one thousand shrines and temples in Kyoto that have survived for centuries, and the US government intentionally left Kyoto out of its firebombing campaigns during World War II. Even with regular trips, I have only experienced a fraction of them. The visceral experience of seeing these places in person far surpasses looking at pictures in books; it is like seeing your favorite paintings in person. There are many famous paintings and statues that I am familiar with from books that I have seen referenced in tattoo design. I have always sought inspiration here for my own work. Like the experience at the antique fair, I am overwhelmed at these sacred places and find new ideas everywhere I look. Unlike seeing art in a conventional museum gallery, the entire space is considered from the landscaping of the grounds to the fine details on the buildings themselves; even the structure is often an art object. It is nice to see that many of the artisans and monks involved in the construction and decoration of these monuments have not been forgotten over time and are oftentimes formally credited.

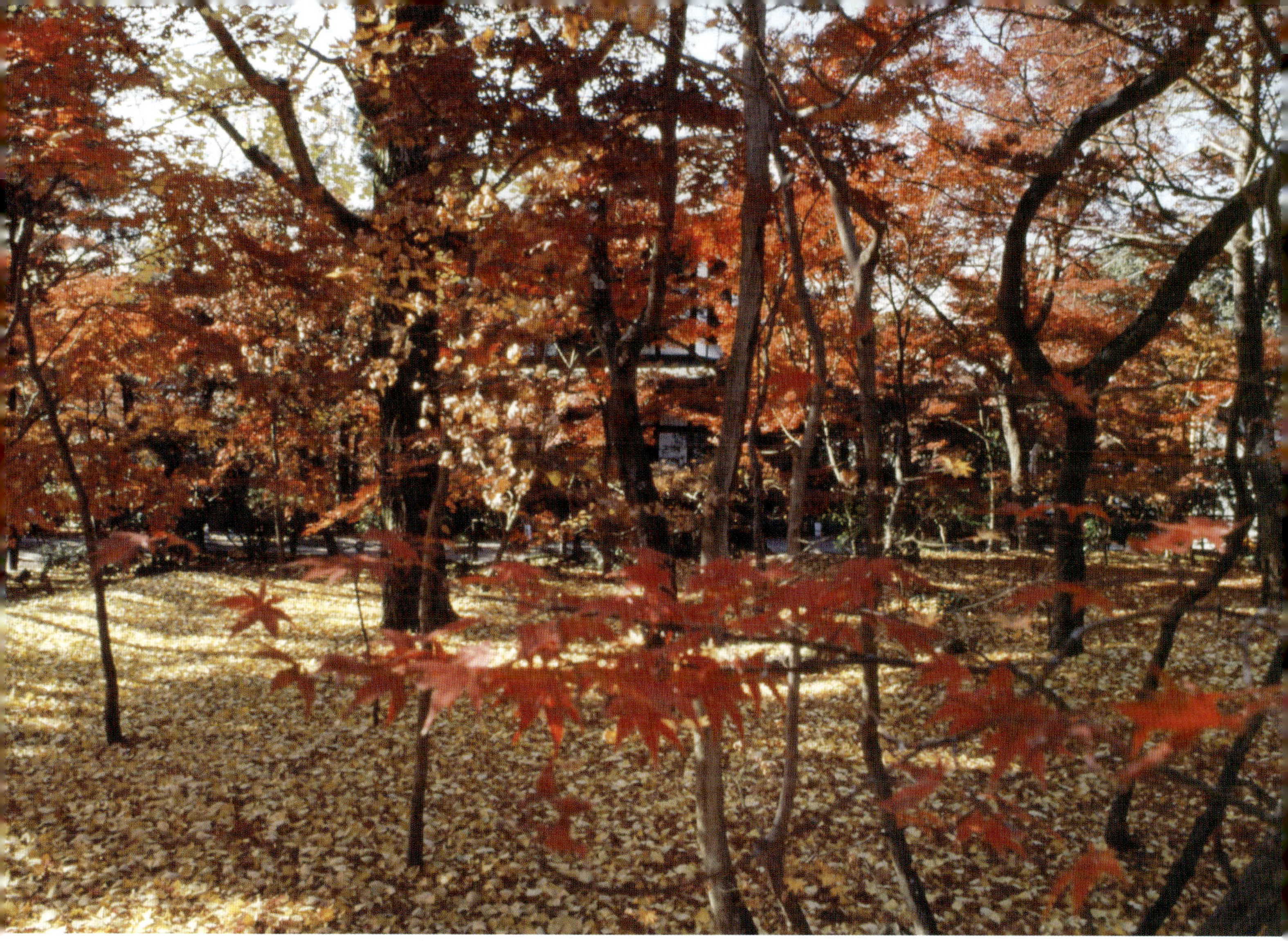

Once you take in the bigger picture, you start to focus on the details. The religious artifacts and interior spaces are rich with mythology and convey deep religious significance as well as beauty and craftsmanship. One often sees images of mythological creatures such as dragons and phoenix in the carvings above entrances. Many gates of shrines are flanked with a pair of *koma-inu* statues, a mythological creature similar in appearance to a *karajishi* or Chinese lions, *koma-inu* are considered to be messengers of the gods of the shrine in which they reside. Oftentimes, one will be depicted with an open mouth and the other will have a closed mouth. I also saw pairs of foxes at the Inari shrine in Kyoto, standing guard in place of the *koma-inu*.

Nature is integral to the design and feel of a shrine or temple. There may be natural or man-made bodies of water accommodating animals, such as koi and turtles. One shrine we visited had a pond with thousands of irises in bloom. It was very

Opposite page upper:
A monk strolls through *sakura* trees in full bloom.

Opposite page lower:
A *Kitsune,* fox, sits guard at the Inari Shrine in Kyoto.

Above:
Momoji, maple leaves. The dynamic hues of fall are expressed on an autumn day.

Below:
Shobu, irises.

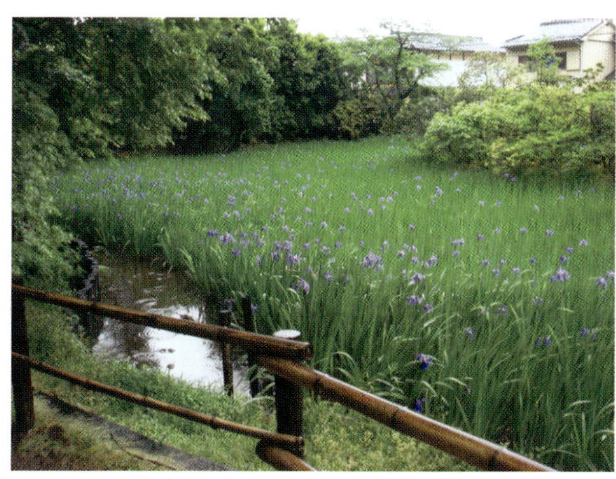

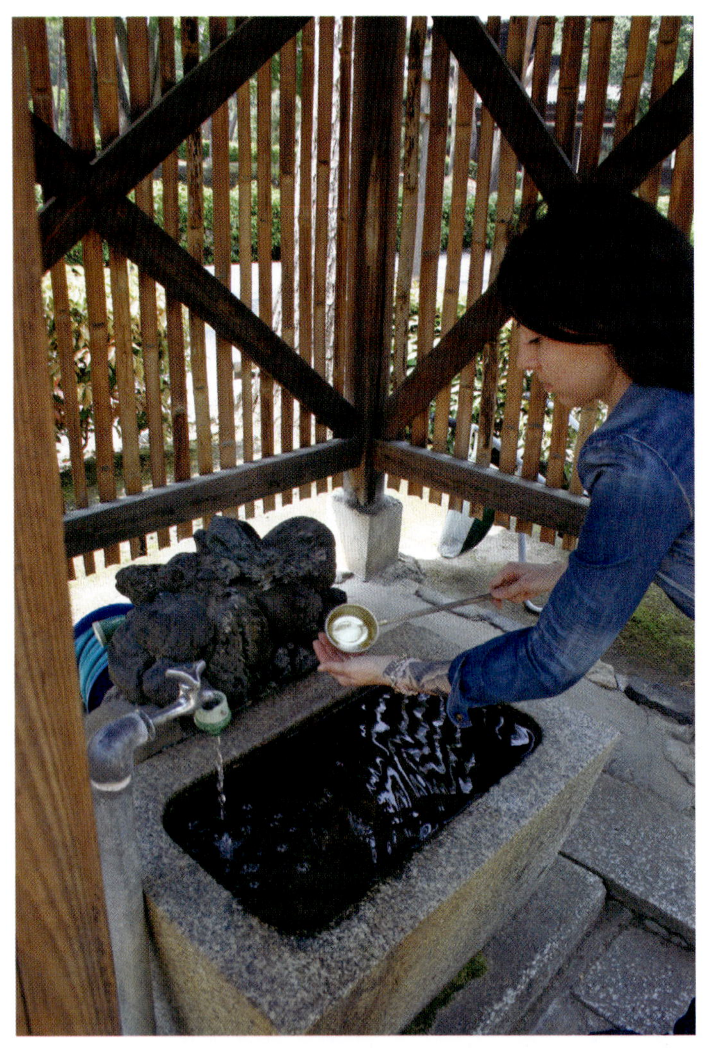

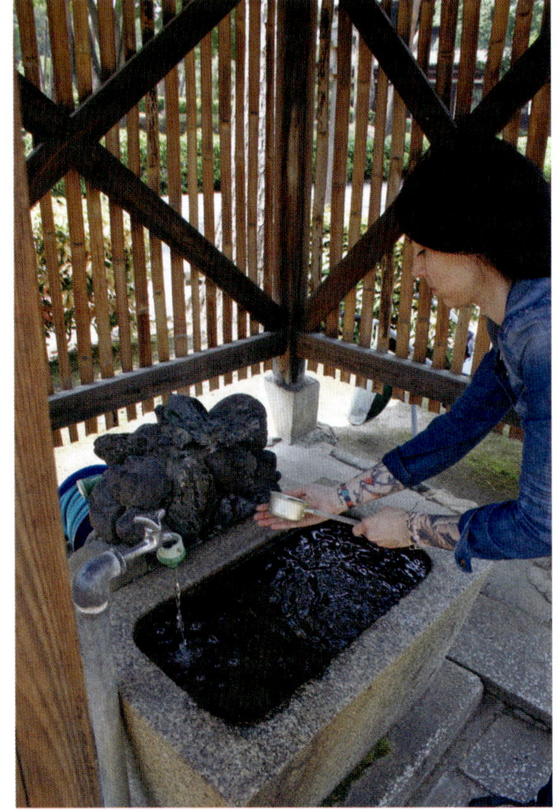

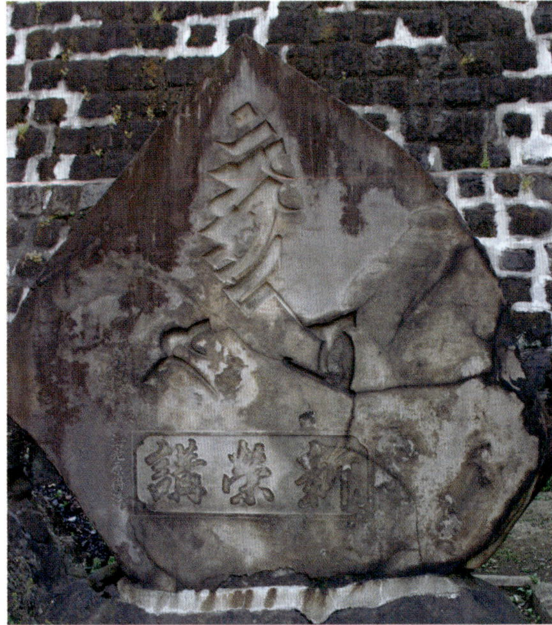

Bonji for Fudōmyō-ō, Seitaka and Kongara.

small and tucked away in a suburban neighborhood. These places combine culture with a visual expression of aesthetic taste. Horitaka's mother pointed out the bright orange paint to me on the facade of one shrine. She noted that this orange color was from China and looked slightly out of place to the Japanese eye. She continued that it was more favorable to the Japanese taste when the paint aged into a muted rust color and there was evidence of the elements chipping away at it. This stood out to me as another example of connecting the shrines to nature, creating a unified landscape merging man made objects with the environment.

People visit shrines as part of their religious and cultural traditions; to pray, wish, and think. There are certain practices that are customary when visiting a shrine. Hand washing is the first step in this routine. A designated area called the *temizu-ya* where water flows into a basin is used. Fresh water is ladled onto each hand and then into the mouth. The remaining water runs to the drain. This custom is a ritual cleansing. At the altars of the individual gods, money is offered in a *saisen bako* or money box. Its visitors practice a ritual that includes placing the palms together, bowing, clapping twice and ringing a large bell. This is the meditative gesture that sets the tone to ask for something or make a wish. These prayers are personal; it is the physical movement that is necessary, words are not spoken nor are hymns sung. I relate this practice, although very different, to my own religious background. Attending a Jewish temple and praying are crucial parts of Jewish spiritual practice. The movement

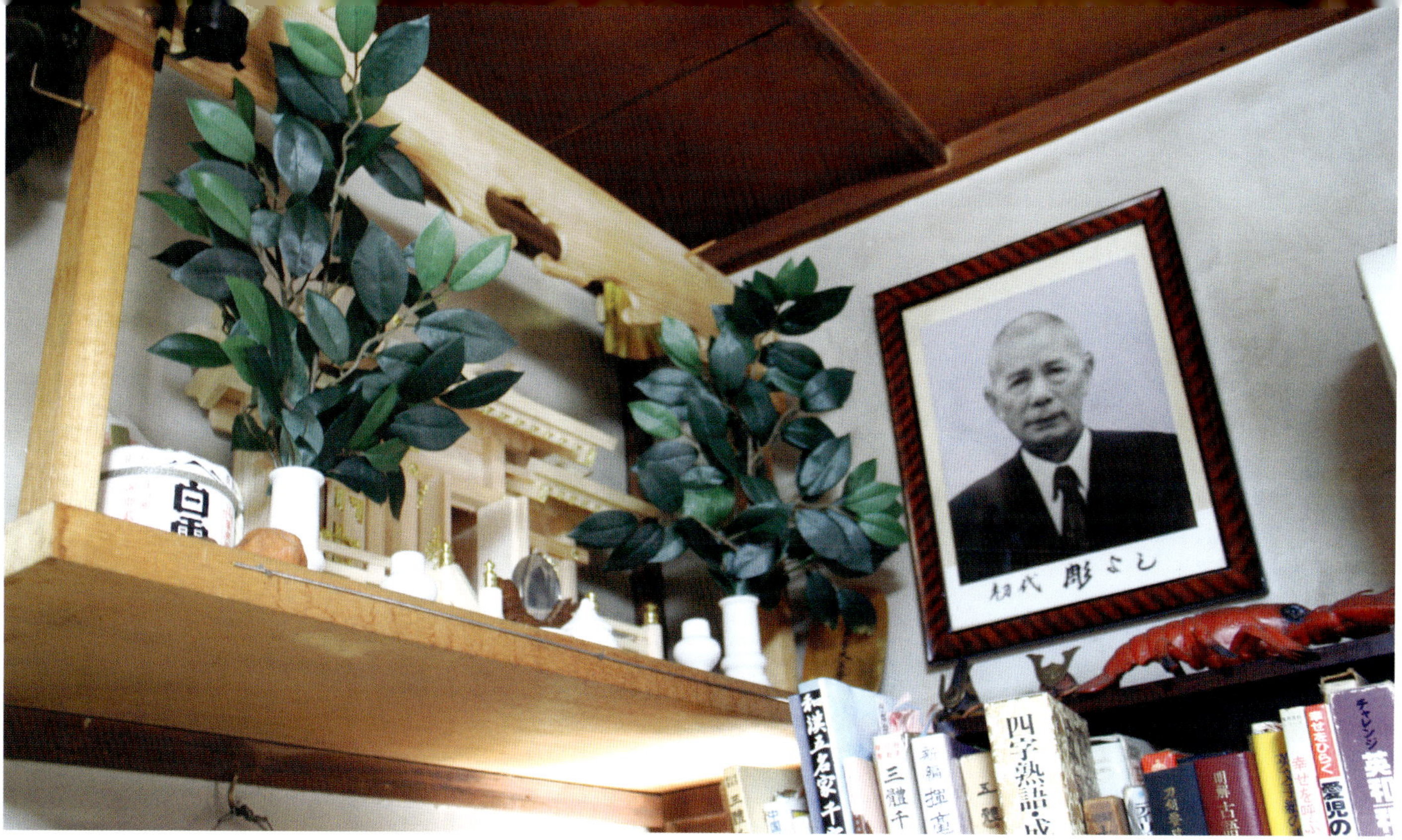

Above:
Butsudan, at Ise-Cho.

Below:
Kitamura family *butsudan* in Kyoto.

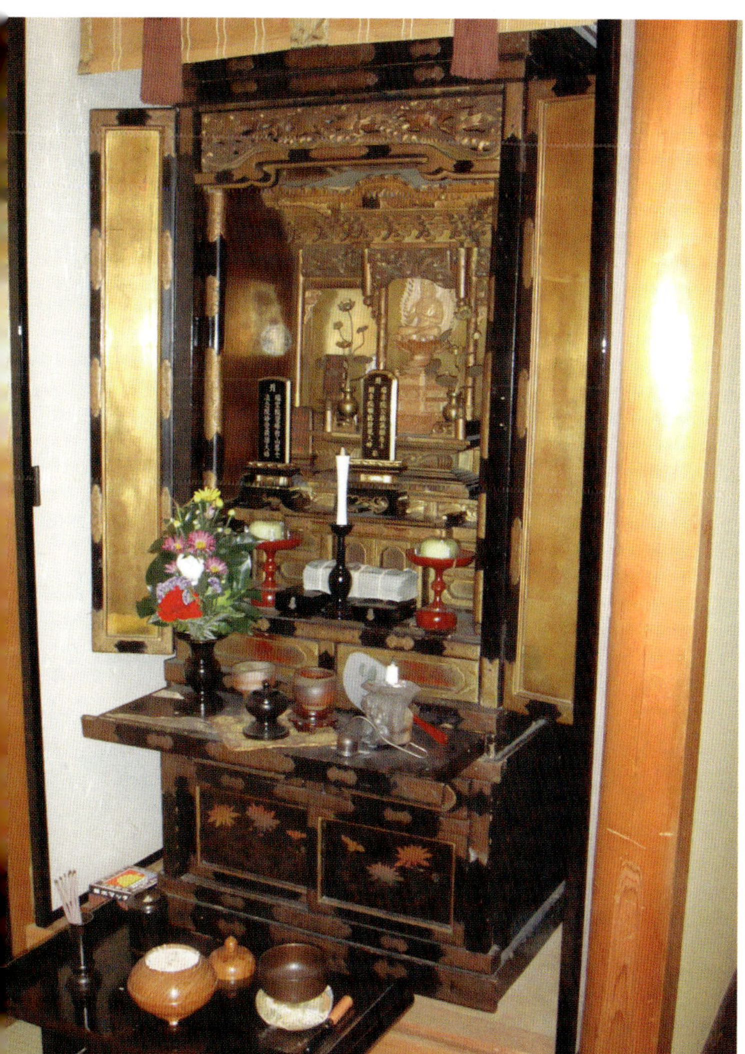

of bowing is vital to Japanese *reigi* and prayers. It is a universal action that has the same connotation in the West as in the East. The spiritual tension that is present at shrines and temples, even if the visitor does not act out the prayer, is powerful. This cultural practice and display is easy and all visitors are welcome to participate, I even saw signs in English explaining the bowing, clapping order to foreign visitors. Visiting the shrines and temples is essential to the Japanese spiritual practice.

Spiritual practice also carries into the home. The most obvious manifestation is a familial altar called a *butsudan*. This is an altar honoring ancestors. Offerings such as tea, rice and other food are made at these private altars and many families engage in a daily ritual of prayer. Before the prayer, incense is lit and a bell is rung. The Kitamura *butsudan* displays a shelf with all the books written by the family; from Horitaka, his sister and his father. Effigies of gods, Buddhist prayer tools and fresh fruit and flowers are some of the general objects found on them. I have noticed *butsudan* in Horiyoshi III's home as well as small personal altars at his studios. Mayumi even has a teacup and offers tea each morning to not only each of the past ancestors, but to the family's deceased pets. At Ise-cho, a framed photo of Shodai Horiyoshi is displayed on the altar.

In Japan, the concept of nationalism permeates all aspects of culture including religion. The dominant religion in Japan is both Buddhism and Shinto. Shinto is indigenous to Japan and this is the

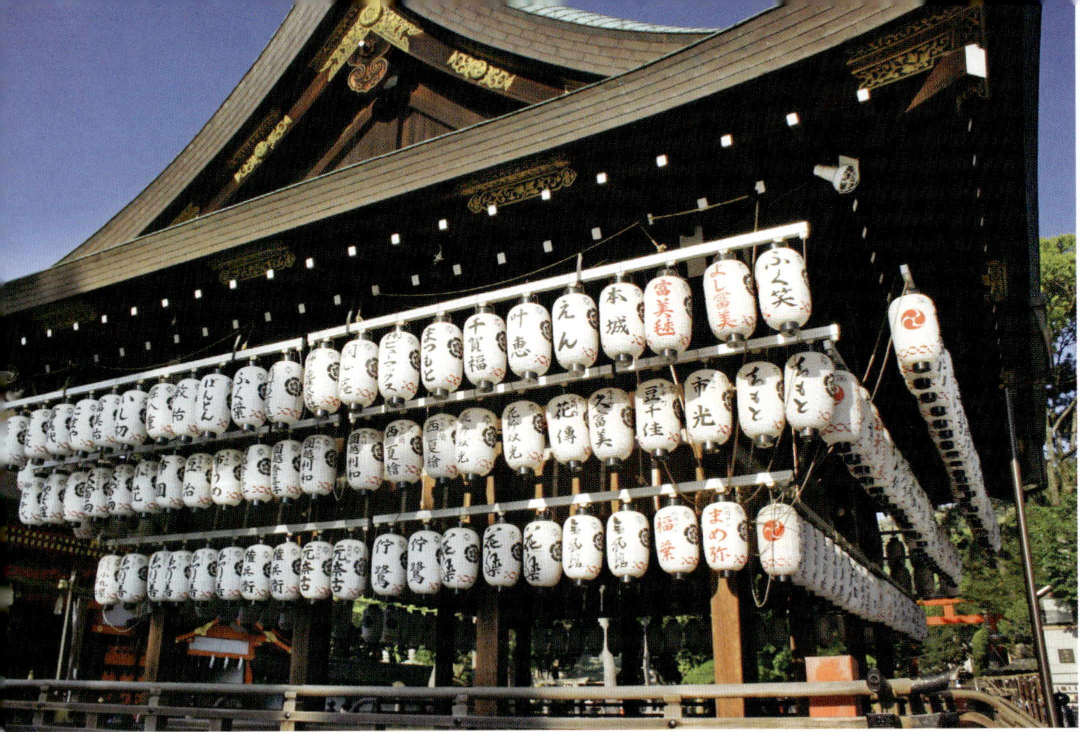

only place it is practiced. Buddhism came later and is originally of Indian origin. Japanese patriotism and spirituality coalesce, thus creating an environment where the concept of organized religion is blurred by notions of national loyalty. However, it seems that both coexist and create a uniquely Japanese religion and national ideology.

When I asked Horiyoshi III about the difference between shrines and temples, he explained simply that one was Shinto and one was Buddhist. He told me that historically the Shogunate was Buddhist and the Emperor was Shinto. Thus you will find shrines inside temples and vice versa. Sometimes the time line of these transitions and separations follow shifts in the political and religious power dynamics of the Edo period. Mr. Kitamura, Horitaka's father, joked that he associated shrines with birth and temples with death. The funerals were Buddhist and the weddings and births were Shinto. Children ritually visit shrines at the ages of three, five, and seven and New Years celebrations take place there. The shrine is a unifying force within the neighborhood with local families belonging and contributing. Each family or home is a member of a temple of their choice. Shinto differs from Buddhism also because it does not have written scripture; the focus is more on the community and nature. Buddhism is a more rigid practice with ancient texts and customs. They are both polytheistic and their practices and rhetoric compliment each other. It is hard for foreigners to conceive that two different religions could cohabitate and that the people would accept both. In America we are of a melting pot mentality and religious persuasion is a key factor in our individual identity. Japanese religious identity is not separate from Japanese identity and it feels like the religion there blends seamlessly with and is a part of the culture.

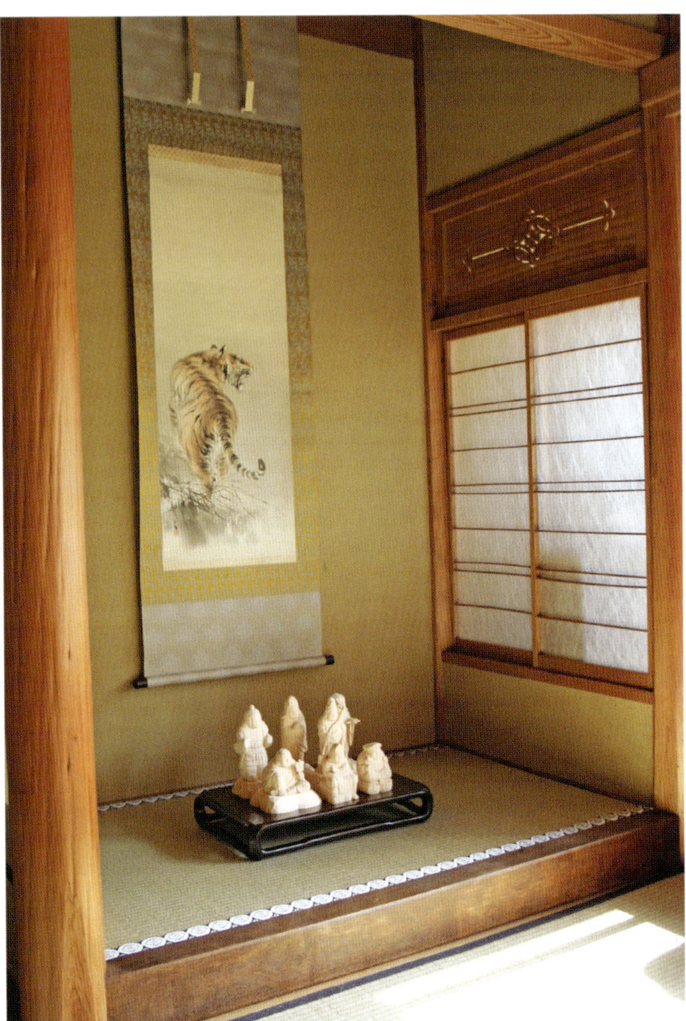

Wooden statues of the Shichifukujin (Seven Gods of Good Fortune) in the Kitamura home, Kyoto. These were carved by Mrs. Kitamura.

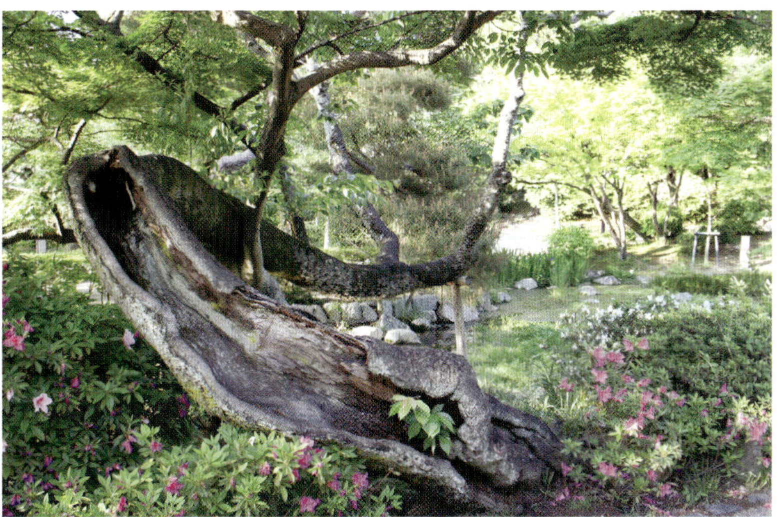

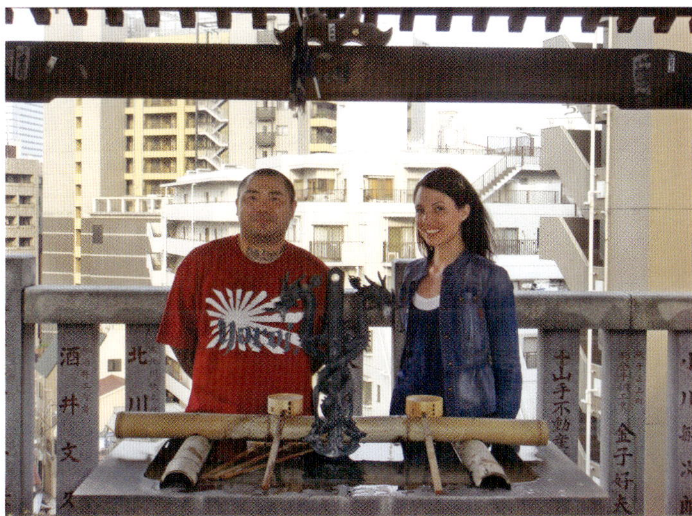

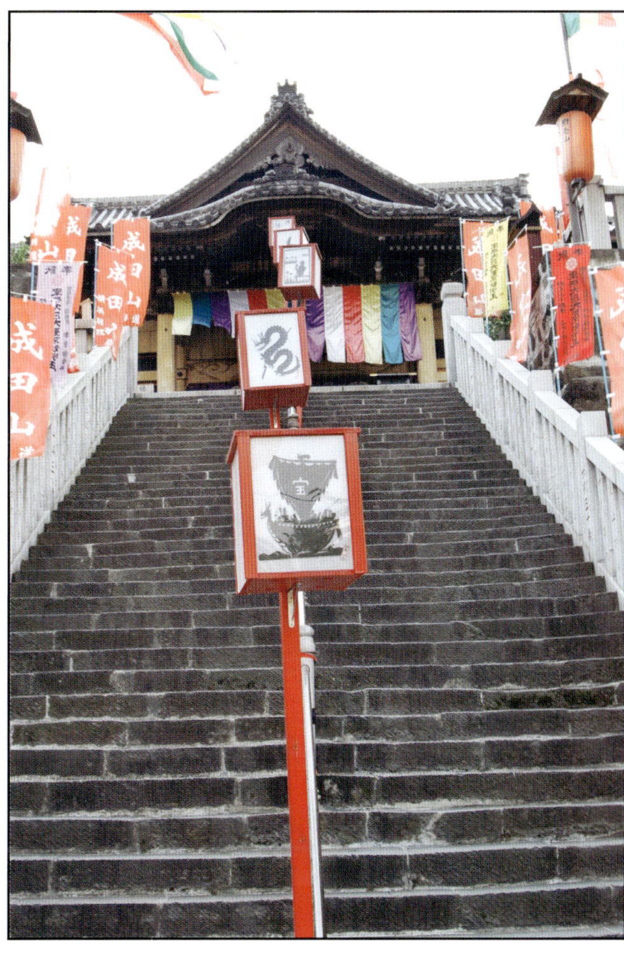

Below:
Man-made and natural elements coexist in the morning at this mountain shrine.

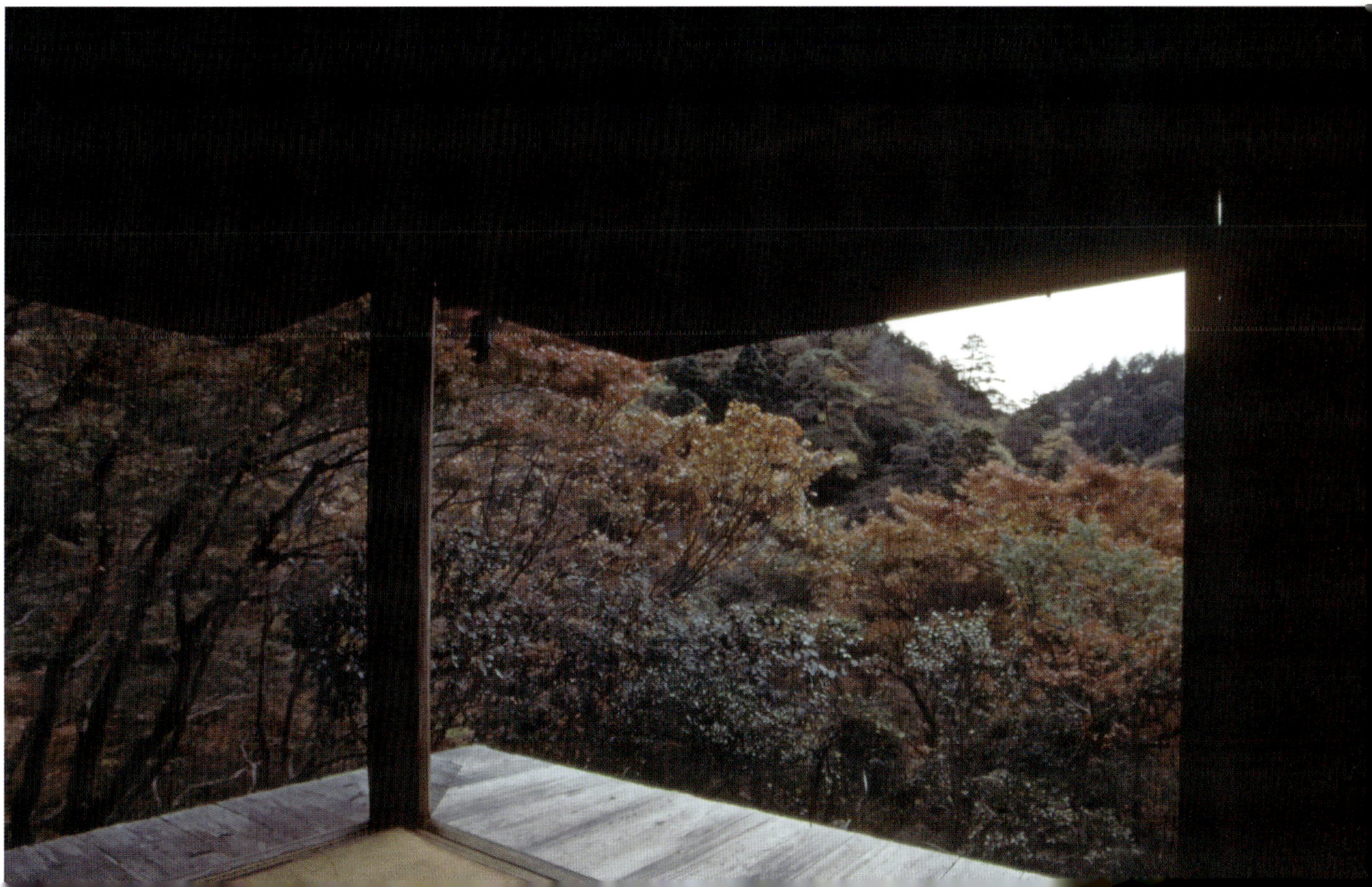

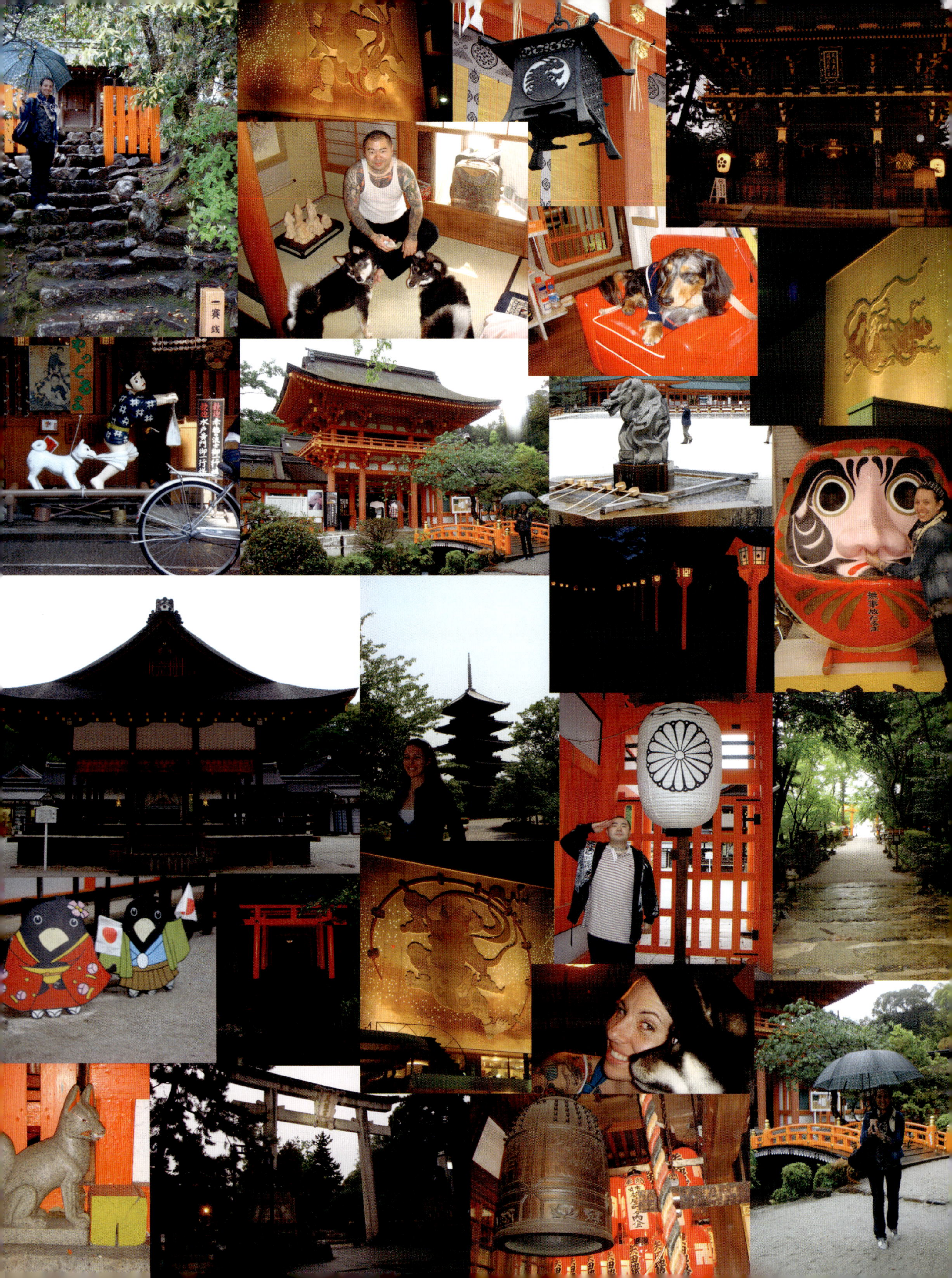

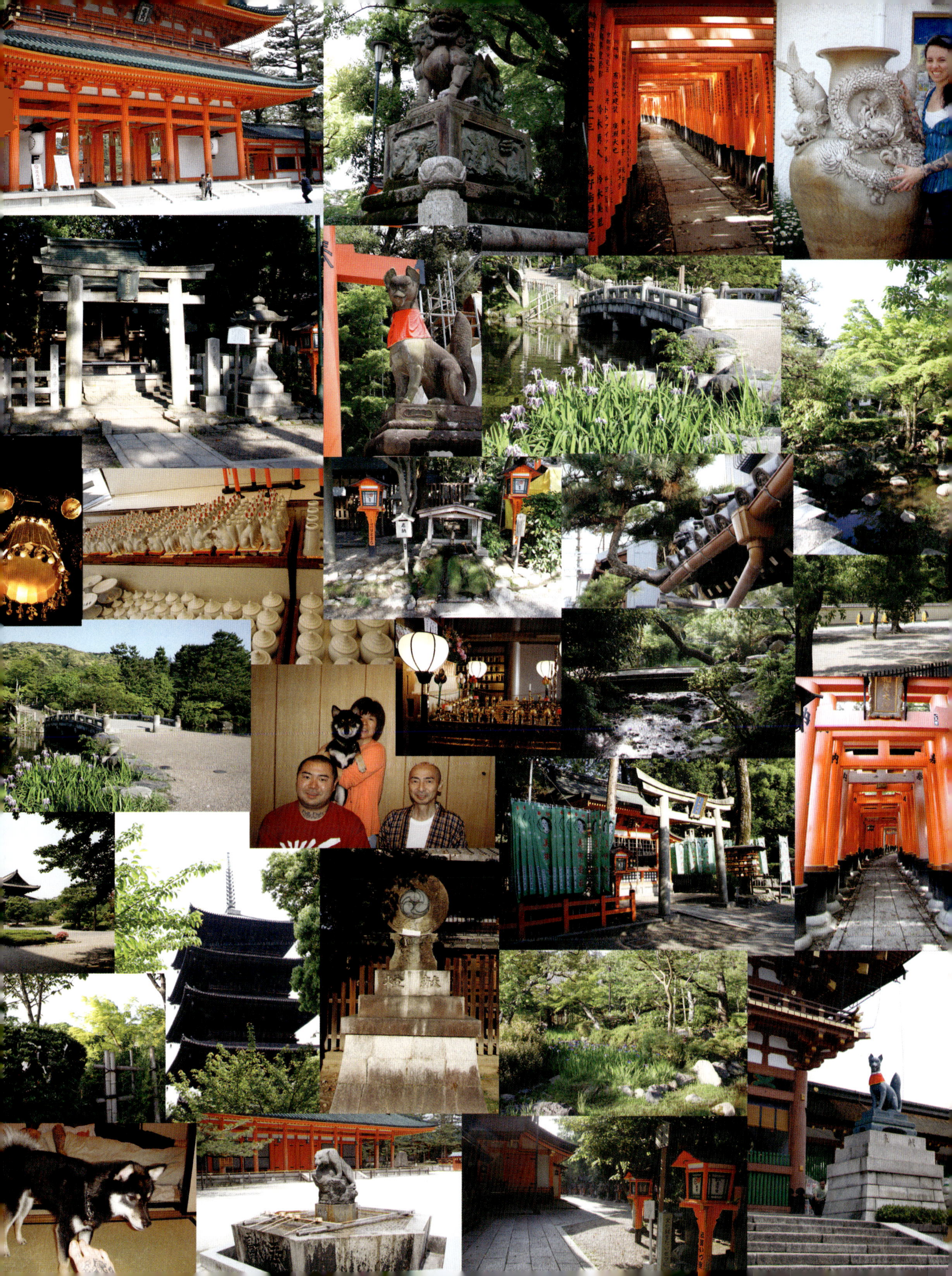

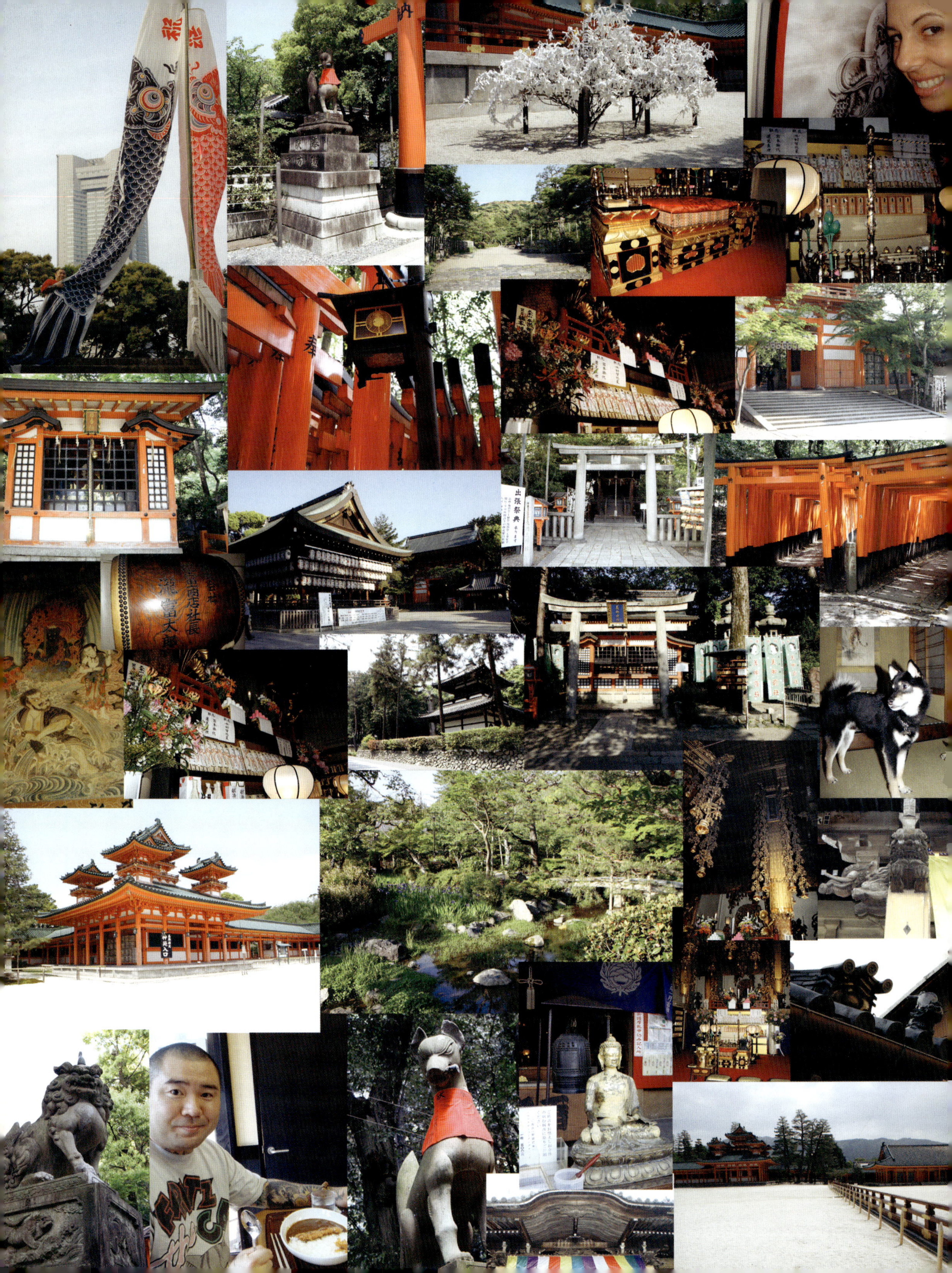

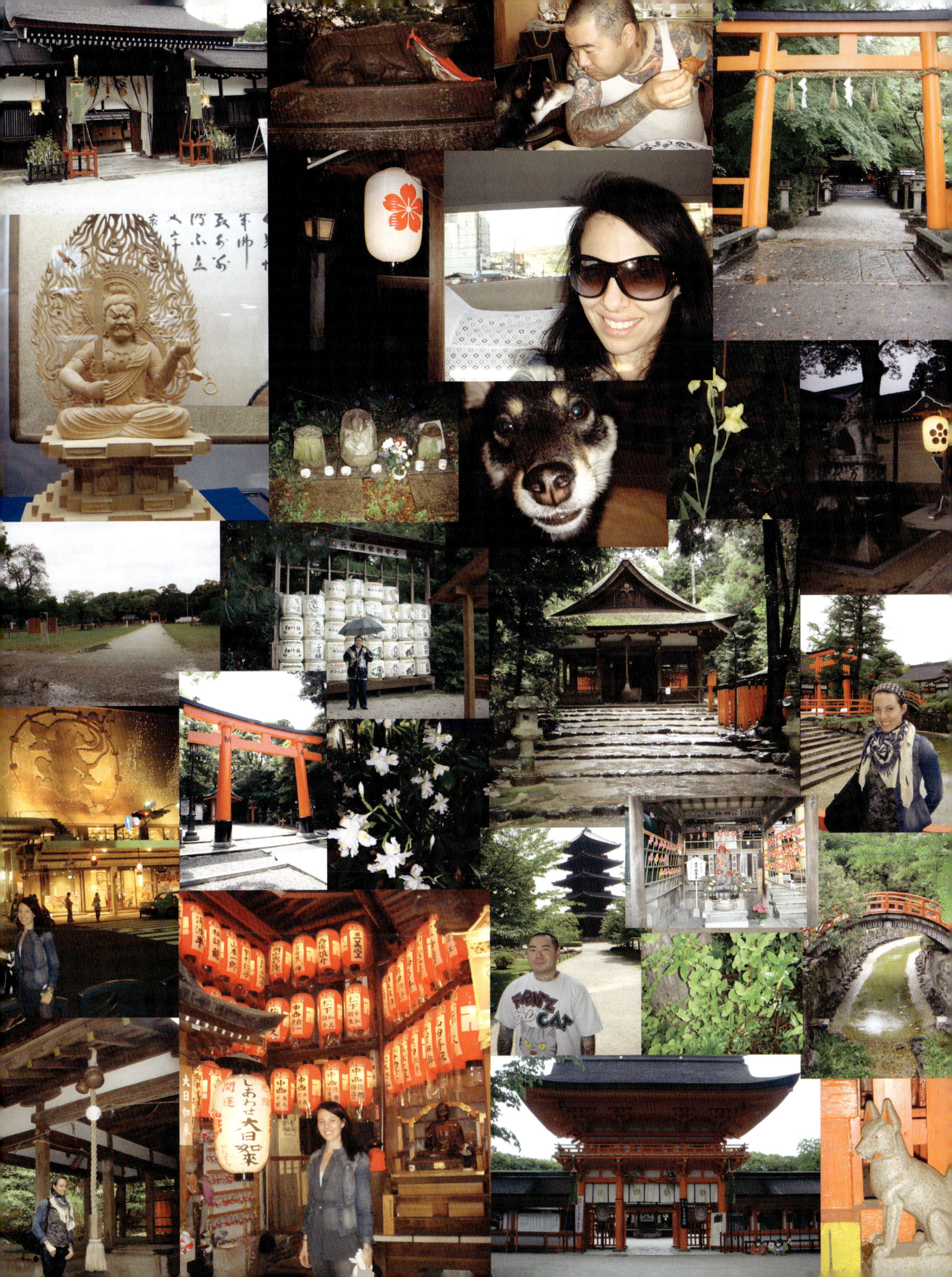
開運
しあわせ大日如来
大日如来

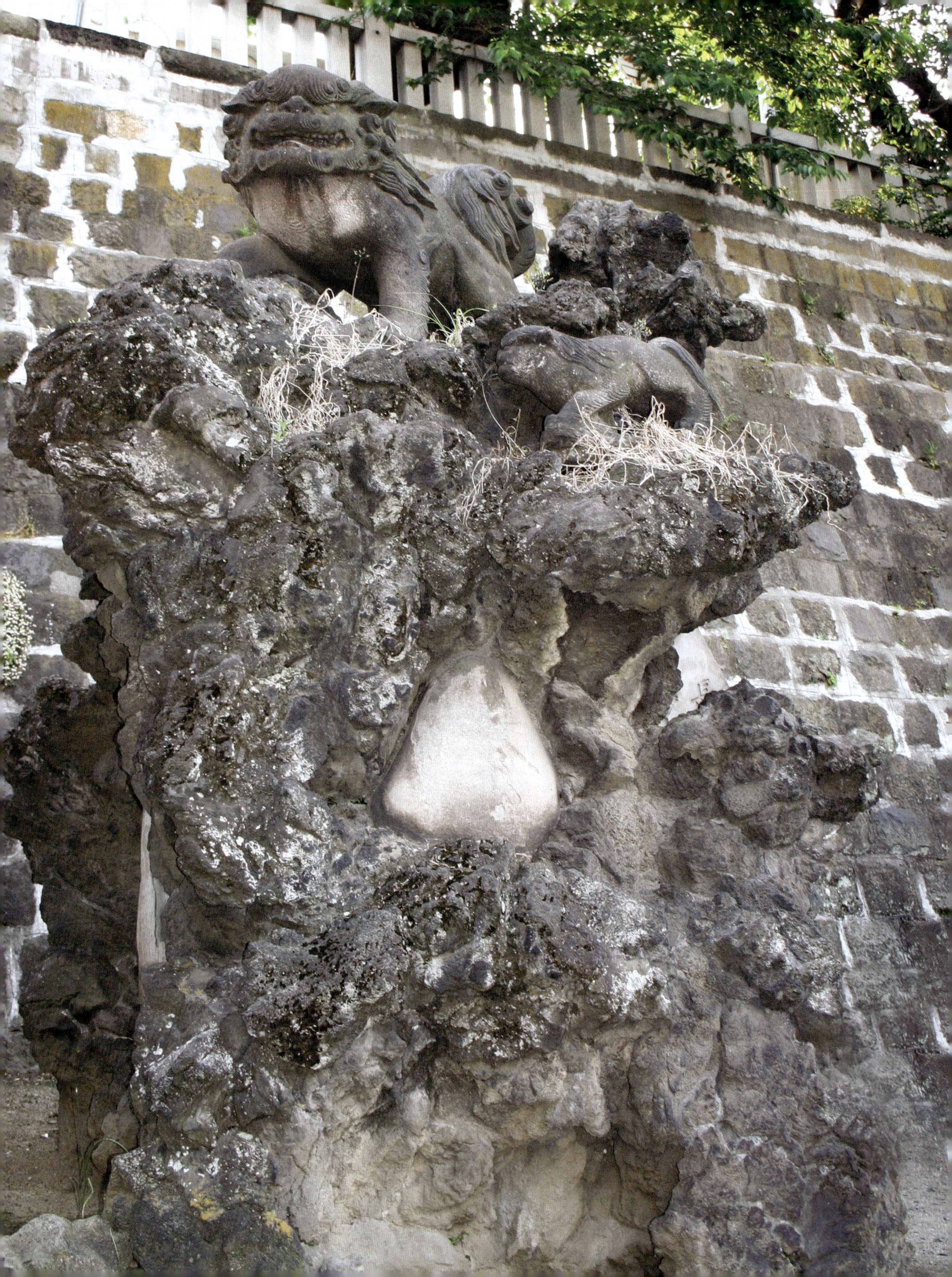

CLOSING

Japanese culture can, at times, appear to be self-contained, and this observation can be extended to Japanese tattooing. It is a craft characterized by a limited pool of icons and their formulaic transfer of image to skin. It is uniquely Japanese visually; citing history, aesthetic, spirituality and taste and the tradition surrounding it, a tradition passed from master to deserving apprentices. The mores associated with tattooing are the result of centuries of interactions between art and a gangster sub-culture. The product of these dissimilar influences, Japanese tattooing is more than a pedagogy of design techniques, but a lifestyle that requires conscientious manners and etiquette. The tattoo world in Japan, is one founded on respect: giving it and earning it. Horiyoshi III is a prime example of an individual who embodies all of these things. There are few artisans of any discipline that can truly be seen as innovators or prodigious in their field. Horiyoshi III is an artist that has not only achieved mastery in a learned tradition, but understands the code of ethics that comes along with it. He has never forgotten these roots personally or artistically. Another important aspect of his personality is the curiosity that has motivated him to re-evaluate the entire tattoo process from image to application: rethinking it with a new vision. Hungry for change and evolution he has pushed the craft to the far reaches of its potential. Integrating the tattoo machine (an American invention) into his hand-tattooing practice in 1985 forever changed the course of Japanese tattooing. This decision had an immeasurable impact on his work and completely redefined the look of modern Japanese tattooing. The feeling of the Japanese style is maintained while the potential for rendering detail has been completely revolutionized. In the last fifteen years, Japan has become a vastly different social climate. Tattooing has seen its emergence out of the underground; in the mid-nineties there were already street shops. These competing influences of the modern era have served to distill that which is uniquely Japanese. Horiyoshi III's role as a teacher coexists with his perspective as a student. Always evolving, he has as much to share as he is eager to learn. Life experience is his teacher and the scope of his work is always expanding and morphing. As onlookers we can absorb his attitude of humility and follow his example of translating inspiration to final product. He is a bridge between the old ways and new energy.

Secure in his own work Horiyoshi III publishes every part of his process from his sketches, to tattoo designs, to finished photos of his work and even hand tattooing kits of his own invention are sold in his museum. His work and the descriptions he makes available educate the public on specifics of Japanese tattooing. He enjoys sharing these things with the public and his style has become virtually synonymous with Western notions of Japanese tattooing itself. In my study of Horiyoshi III's teachings, it is more than the art that I can model my own practices after, but a wide array of experience ranging from behavior and conduct to culture and knowledge. Artists of all disciplines can learn from his example. A perpetual student, his evolution is constant, always revising and integrating new ideas into his practice. I feel like an embryo watching his growth and development and as far as I think I have come, in his shadow, I realize how much more there is to learn and develop. It is the common mistake to claim a complete understanding in any art or craft. Horiyoshi III shows us by example the humility in keeping tattooing new, cool and fun. From our drawing lesson, seeing his personal sketches and listening to lectures on composition I have firsthand tutelage from the master. I am acquiring the tools to improve my own tattoo practices. I am constantly learning through these various conduits. The door has been opened and I have crossed the threshold. I humbly accept this challenge with the hope that he will one day be proud of my accomplishments.

While on my travels in Japan I met an event coordinator who shared an anecdote with me about Horiyoshi III. Because of his health and busy schedule Horiyoshi III was declining the invitation to his event. Horiyoshi III remarked, "Don't mind me, soon I will be gone, soon I will be just the air." The man respectfully replied, "We cannot breathe without air."

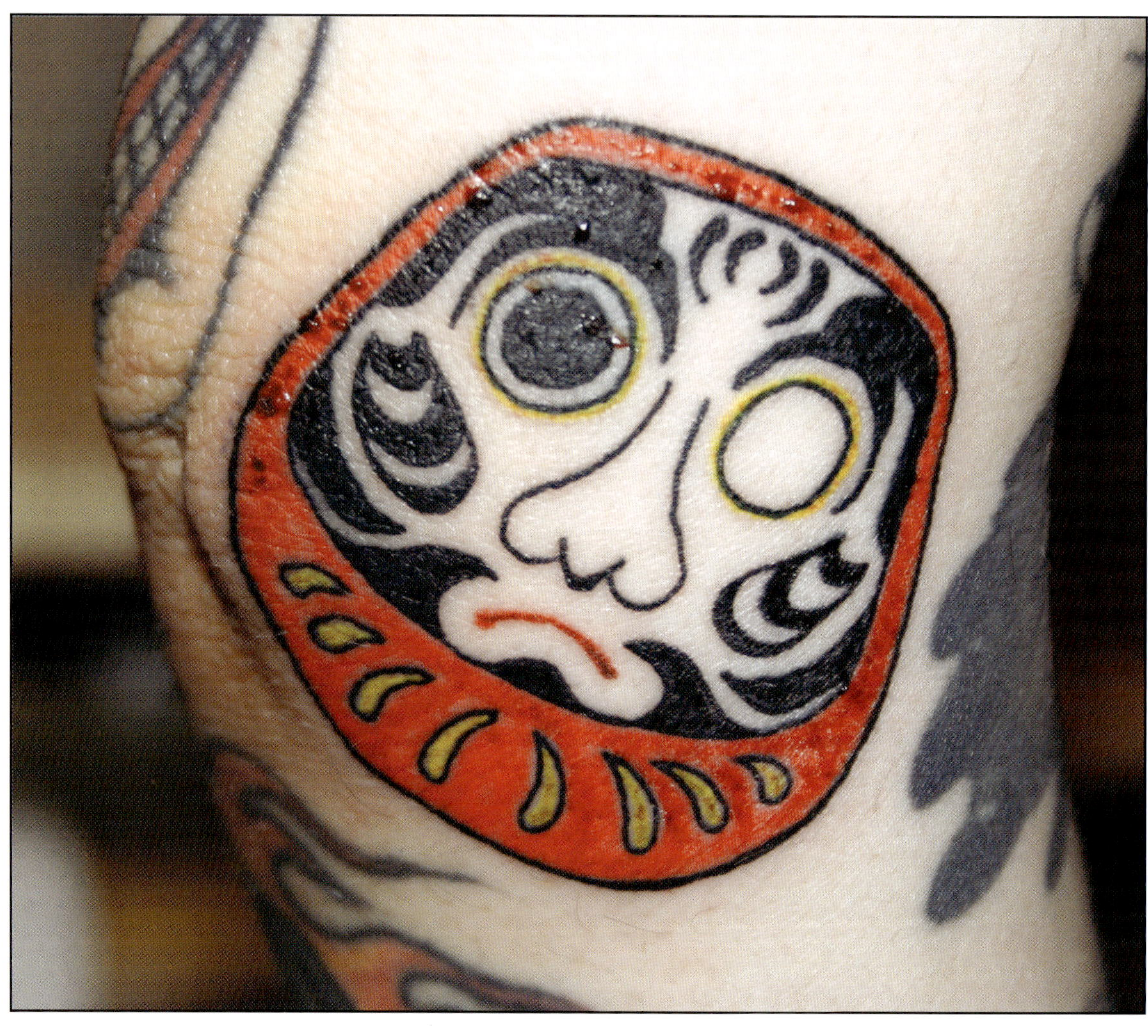

Tattoo on Horiyuki by Horitaka. It is customary, in Japan, to fill in one eye of a small Daruma statue at the launch of a project and when it is completed the other eye is painted in.

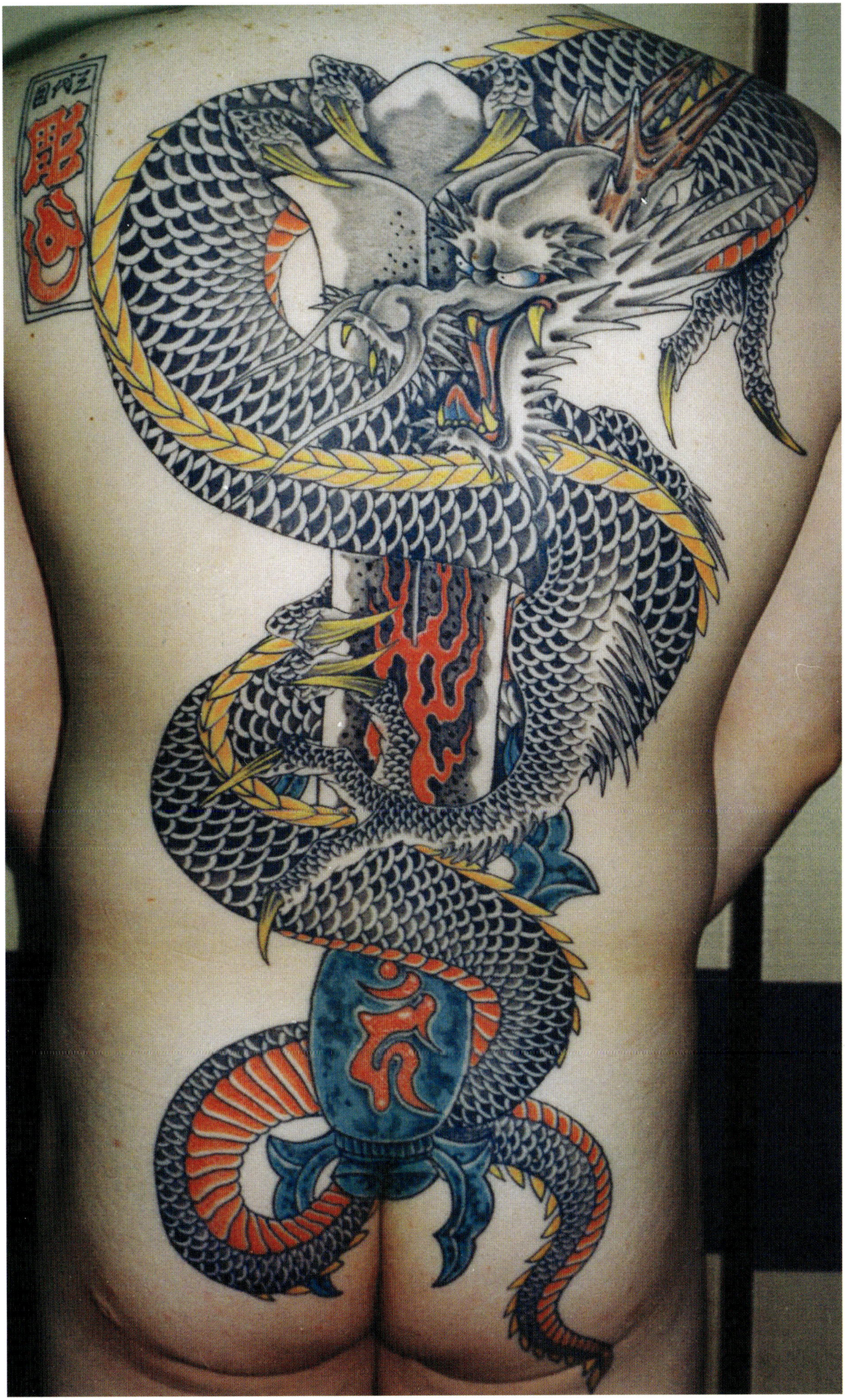

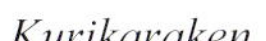

Kurikaraken.

Suggested Readings

Frederic, Louis. *Japan Encyclopedia*. Cambridge and London: The Belknap Press of Harvard University Press, 2002.

Grime and Horitaka. *Horiyoshi III*. San Jose: Grimmelbein Kitamura Editions, 2006.

Gulik, Willem R. van. *Irezumi, the pattern of dermatography in Japan*. Leiden: Mededelingen van het Rijks-museum voor Volkenkunde and E.J. Brill, 1982.

Hardy, D.E. (ed.) *Tattootime Number 1: New Tribalism*. Honolulu: Hardy Marks Publications, 1988.

Hardy, D.E. (ed.) *Tattootime Number 2: Tattoo Magic*. Honolulu: HardyMarks Publications, 1988.

Hardy, D.E. (ed.) *Tattootime Number 3: Music and Sea Tattoos*. Honolulu: HardyMarks Publications, 1988.

Hardy, D.E. (ed.) *Tattootime Number 4: Life and Death Tattoos*. Honolulu: HardyMarks Publications, 1988.

Hardy, D.E. (ed.) *Tattootime Number 5: Art From the Heart*. Honolulu: HardyMarks Publications, 1991.

Hardy, D.E. (ed.) *Sailor Jerry Collins: American Tattoo Master*. Honolulu: HardyMarks Publications, 1994.

Hardy, D.E. (ed.) *Pierced Hearts and True Love*. Honolulu: HardyMarks Publications, 1995.

Hardy, D.E. (ed.) *Tatttooing the Invisible Man*. San Francisco and Santa Monica: HardyMarks Publications and Smart Art Publications, 1999.

Jordan, Brenda G. and Victoria Weston. *Copying the Master and Stealing His Secrets*. Honolulu: University of Hawai'i Press, 2003.

Keyes, Roger. *The Male Journey in Japanese Prints*. Berkeley and Los Angeles: University of California Press, 1989.

Kitamura, Takahiro and Katie M. *Bushido, Legacies of the Japanese Tattoo*. Atglen: Schiffer Publishing, 2001.

Kitamura, Takahiro. *Tattoos of the Floating World, Ukiyo-e Motifs in the Japanese Tattoo*. Leiden: Hotei Publishing, 2003.

Kitamura, Takahiro. *Tattooing From Japan to the West*. Atglen: Schiffer Publishing, 2004.

Klompmakers, Inge. *Of Brigands and Bravery, Kuniyoshi's Heroes of the Suikoden*. Leiden: Hotei Publishing, 1998.

Mo, Johanna and Onita Wass (ed.) *Horiyoshi III The Art of the Japanese Tattoo*. Stockholm: Koala Press, 2005.

Nakano, Yoshihito. *The History of Techniques of Tattooing in Japan, in Ozuma, Kaname*. Woman in Tattoo. Tokyo: Tatsuma Publishing, 1995.

Nakano, Yoshihito. *Hyakki zu. 100 Demons of Horiyoshi III*. Tokyo: Nippon Shupansha, 1998.

Nakano, Yoshihito. *Suikoden retsuden zufu. 108 Heroes of the Suikoden by Horiyoshi III*. Tokyo: Nippon Shupansha, 2000.

Nakano, Yoshihito. *Namakubi by Horiyoshi III*. Tokyo: Nippon Shupansha, 1998.

Nakano, Yoshihito. *36 Ghosts of Horiyoshi III*. Tokyo: Nippon Shupansha, 2007.

Puente, Juan. *Legacy: The Horiyoshi III Tradition*. Fullerton: JM Publications, 2006.

Richie, Donald. *The Japanese Tattoo*. New York and Tokyo: Weatherhill, 1980.

Schaap, Robert. *Heroes and Ghosts, Japanese Prints by Kuniyoshi (1797-1861)*. Leiden: Hotei Publishing, 1998.

Shaver, Cynthia, Noriko Miyamoto and Sachio Yoshioka. *Sumi Collection: Hanten and Happi, Traditional Japanese Work Coats: Bold Designs and Colorful Images. Trans. Ai Shimoyama and Monica Benthe*. Kyoto: Shikosha Publishing Co. Ltd., 1998.

Contact Information

Horiyoshi III
3-123 Ise Cho
Nishi Ku
Yokohama, Japan
Tel: +045-231-3187
www.ne.jp/asahi/tattoo/horiyoshi3/

Yokohama Tattoo Museum
Imai Building 1-11-7
Hiranuma Nishi-ku
Yokohama-shi
Kanagawa 222-0023 Japan
Tel: +045-323-1073

State of Grace Tattoo
11561 Berryessa Rd.
San Jose, CA 95133
Tel: 408-441-7770
www.stateofgracetattoo.com
www.horiyukitattoo.com